Danielle
Greenwood

# SUSTAINABLE
# COMMERCIAL INTERIORS

**Penny Bonda**, FASID
**Katie Sosnowchik**

John Wiley & Sons, Inc.

**Front Cover** *(clockwise from top left)*

Project: The Gordon & Betty Moore Foundation
Interior Design: Gensler
Photography: Richard Greenhouse

Project: Toyota
Interior Design: Gensler
Photograph: Paul Warchol

Project: REI Portland
Interior Design: Mithun
Photography: Peter Eckert, Eckert and Eckert

Project: Nusta Spa
Interior Design: Envision Design
Photography: Eric Laignel

Project: Boulder Associates
Interior Design: Boulder Associates
Photography: LaCasse Photography

**Back Cover**

Project: The Future Links pattern, Lee's Visio Collection
Designs: Ken Wilson and Colleen Waguespack, Envision Design
Photography: Envision Design

100%
TOTAL RECYCLED PAPER
100% POSTCONSUMER PAPER

This book is printed on acid-free paper. ∞

Published by John Wiley & Sons, Inc., Hoboken, New Jersey
Published simultaneously in Canada

No part of this publication may be reproduced, stored in a retrieval system, or transmitted in any form or by any means, electronic, mechanical, photocopying, recording, scanning, or otherwise, except as permitted under Section 107 or 108 of the 1976 United States Copyright Act, without either the prior written permission of the Publisher, or authorization through payment of the appropriate per-copy fee to the Copyright Clearance Center, 222 Rosewood Drive, Danvers, MA 01923, (978) 750-8400, fax (978) 750-4400, or on the web at www.copyright.com. Requests to the Publisher for permission should be addressed to the Permissions Department, John Wiley & Sons, Inc., 111 River Street, Hoboken, NJ 07030, (201) 748-6011, fax (201) 748-6008, or online at www.wiley.com/go/permissions.

Limit of Liability/Disclaimer of Warranty: While the publisher and the author have used their best efforts in preparing this book, they make no representations or warranties with respect to the accuracy or completeness of the contents of this book and specifically disclaim any implied warranties of merchantability or fitness for a particular purpose. No warranty may be created or extended by sales representatives or written sales materials. The advice and strategies contained herein may not be suitable for your situation. You should consult with a professional where appropriate. Neither the publisher nor the author shall be liable for any loss of profit or any other commercial damages, including but not limited to special, incidental, consequential, or other damages.

For general information about our other products and services, please contact our Customer Care Department within the United States at (800) 762-2974, outside the United States at (317) 572-3993 or fax (317) 572-4002.

Wiley also publishes its books in a variety of electronic formats. Some content that appears in print may not be available in electronic books. For more information about Wiley products, visit our web site at www.wiley.com.

*Library of Congress Cataloging-in-Publication Data:*

Bonda, Penny.
  Sustainable commercial interiors / Penny Bonda, Katie Sosnowchik.
      p. cm.
  Includes bibliographical references and index.
  ISBN-13: 978-0-471-74917-2 (cloth)
  ISBN-10: 0-471-74917-6 (cloth)
  1.  Sustainable buildings—Design and construction. 2.  Interior architecture—United States. 3.  Office buildings—United States. 4.  Commercial buildings—Design and construction. 5.  Sustainable engineering—United States. I. Sosnowchik, Katie. II. Title.
  TH880.B66 2007
  725'.23047—dc22

                                                        2006026647

Printed in the United States of America

10  9  8  7  6  5  4  3  2  1

# CONTENTS

# PREFACE

Ours is a story like many others in the sustainable design field, a story of two individuals traveling along divergent paths who suddenly and irrevocably found themselves united by a singular passion. Two women who, at the time, discovered that their talents complemented each other: an interior designer with the knowledge and devotion to help halt the devastating ecological consequences of the built environment, and a journalist with the desire and ability to use the printed word to help motivate others to do the same.

We first met during the early days of what is often described as the beginning of the "green building revolution," and not long after the architect William McDonough, FAIA, gave an eloquent, impassioned sermon entitled "Design, Ecology, Ethics and the Making of Things" in celebration of the 100th anniversary of the Cathedral of St. John the Divine in New York. Nearly ten years later, his words from that day still resonate, reigniting time and time again why we believe in design as a powerful instrument for change. It is with Bill's blessing that we share here two especially poignant passages from his centennial sermon that strike deep into the heart of our convictions.

> Our culture has adopted a design stratagem that essentially says that if brute force or massive amounts of energy don't work, you're not using enough of it. We made glass buildings that are more about buildings than they are about people. We've used the glass ironically. The hope that glass would connect us to the outdoors was completely stultified by making the buildings sealed. We have created stress in people because we are meant to be connected with the outdoors, but instead we are trapped. Indoor air quality issues are now becoming very serious. People are sensing how horrifying it

can be to be trapped indoors, especially with the thousands upon thousands of chemicals that are being used to make things today.

> Le Corbusier said in the early part of this century that a house is a machine for living in. He glorified the steamship, the airplane, the grain elevator. Think about it: a house is a machine for living in. An office is a machine for working in. A cathedral is a machine for praying in. This has become a terrifying prospect, because what has happened is that designers are now designing for the machine and not for people. People talk about solar heating a building, even about solar heating a cathedral. But it isn't the cathedral that is asking to be heated, it is the people. To solar-heat a cathedral, one should heat people's feet, not the air 120 feet above them. We need to listen to biologist John Todd's idea that we need to work with living machines, not machines for living in. The focus should be on people's needs, and we need clean water, safe materials, and durability. And we need to work from current solar income.

> •

> We must face the fact that what we are seeing across the world today is war, a war against life itself. Our present systems of design have created a world that grows far beyond the capacity of the environment to sustain life into the future. The industrial idiom of design, failing to honor the principles of nature, can only violate them, producing waste and harm, regardless of purported intention. If we destroy more forests, burn more garbage, drift-net more fish, burn more coal, bleach more paper, destroy more topsoil, poison more insects, build over more habitats, dam more rivers, produce more toxic and radioactive waste, we are creating a vast

industrial machine, not for living in, but for dying in. It is a war, to be sure, a war that only a few more generations can surely survive.

When I was in Jordan, I worked for King Hussein on the master plan for the Jordan Valley. I was walking through a village that had been flattened by tanks and I saw a child's skeleton squashed into the adobe block and was horrified. My Arab host turned to me and said, "Don't you know what war is?" And I said, "I guess I don't." And he said, "War is when they kill your children." So I believe we're at war. But we must stop. To do this, we have to stop designing everyday things for killing, and we have to stop designing killing machines.

We have to recognize that every event and manifestation of nature is "design," that to live within the laws of nature means to express our human intention as an interdependent species, aware and grateful that we are at the mercy of sacred forces larger than ourselves, and that we obey these laws in order to honor the sacred in each other and in all things. We must come to peace with and accept our place in the natural world.

—© William A. McDonough

Bill gave his stirring, disconcerting discourse on a cold February day nearly six years after he began working with the chemist Michael Braungart on the design of what they call the Next Industrial Revolution. This seemingly unconventional pairing of architect and chemist parallels other such unlikely alliances in the green building movement—a biologist and a carpet mogul, a physicist and an entrepreneur, a Native American tribal leader and an economist, to name a few—all who have used their unique perspective of the world to teach us, first, to imagine a future filled with hopeful progress, and second, to dig deep to find our inner tenacity to achieve all which we imagined. What they taught us foremost, however, was that each individual has a contribution to make, each person provides a unique set of lenses through which we can collectively envision a condition that respects the natural world and our place in it.

And so it was with that tenet in mind that we decided to write this book. From the first word written to the last edit made, our intention has been to honor the members of a design team who often toil long hours with less recognition than some of their colleagues, whose expertise is often called upon late in the design process, and yet whose contributions are essential to prevent the creation of what Bill described as "machines for dying." Millions of people in the U.S. workforce rely on interior designers to create an environment that makes them happy and productive and that keeps them healthy. Yet their efforts are oftentimes mistakenly dismissed as less significant. What this book sets out to prove is that it is only with knowledgeable interior design that the manifestation of all that green buildings represent can truly be accomplished. The most ecologically intelligent building in the world will fail if the interiors are not an integral part of a more holistic approach that seeks to alter ingrained paradigms.

Our final message to all who read this book—whether novice or veteran—is threefold: Never waver in your efforts. Never doubt in the lasting impact your decisions will have. And always keep in mind this apt analogy from The Body Shop's Anita Roddick, who said, "If you think you're too small to have an impact, try going to bed with a mosquito."

Enjoy what you do, be proud of who you are, celebrate what you are able to accomplish and, above all, continue to imagine the fierce commotion that you—like the mosquito—can create.

PENNY BONDA
KATIE SOSNOWCHIK
November 2006

# ACKNOWLEDGMENTS

It would not be possible to write a book such as this without the contributions of many people to whom we are overwhelmingly appreciative for their willingness to share their wisdom and talents.

For technical input and peer review: David Nelson, Marilyn Black, Beth Brummitt, Hernando Miranda, Greg Kats, Sally Wilson, John Koeller, Paul O'Brien, Dave Linamen, Bill Walsh, Glen Fasman, Steven Bliss, John Irvine, Marc Cohen, Kirsten Ritchie, Holley Henderson, Kirsten Childs, Keith Winn, Bob Berkebile, and Kath Williams.

For assistance in assembling the case study information: Ken Wilson (Envision Design), Sara Graham and MaryAnn Lazarus (HOK), Robin Guenther and Iva Kravitz (Guenther5), Jill Goebel, Barbara McCarthy, and Kate Kirkpatrick (Gensler); J. D. McKibben (Perkins + Will/Eva Maddox Branded Environments); Gary Gardner (DGGP); Brad Franta (Mithun); Rand Ekman and Pat Rosenzweig (OWPP); Erica Meylan (Boulder Associates); Joe Connell and Sarah Busch (The Environments Group).

For sharing their knowledge through insightful essays written especially for the readers of this book: Gina Baker, Marilyn Black, Bill Browning, Nancy Clanton, Jay Enck, Judy Heerwagen, Scot Horst, Stephen Kellert, Nadav Malin, Bill Reed, Marcus Sheffer, Ross Spiegel, and Ken Wilson.

For their willingness to share resources and intellectual property: Alex Wilson and Nadav Malin of BuildingGreen.

For his willingness to let us share our previous written works: Robert Nieminen of *Interiors & Sources*.

For administrative and graphic assistance: Hamlet Paoletti, Kim Barbrie, and Sarah Raposa.

For their patience and forgiveness for our absence while writing this book: our professional colleagues at *Interior Design*, USGBC and ASID's Sustainable Design Council, and especially our families.

For ongoing inspiration: the visionaries, the leaders, and the down-in-the-trenches folks who are proving every day that progress toward an enviable future is possible.

# INTRODUCTION

*Perhaps it was the influence of Hale-Bopp visible in the crystal clear night sky. Perhaps it was the surprisingly strong desert winds blowing in on opening night. Perhaps it was the confluence of 100 or so curious and committed minds gathered together in Phoenix, Arizona, for three days to explore and debate some of the most important environmental issues of the day.*

This description of the first EnvironDesign conference, which the two of us attended in 1996, one of us a conference originator, the other a speaker, provided the nexus for this book, although we certainly couldn't have known it at the time. That conference and all those that followed recognized that green design is not practiced in a vacuum, that it is, like the comet, a beacon—fast-moving, larger than anticipated, and endlessly fascinating.

EnvironDesign was conceived to bring together superstars and students, practitioners and manufacturers—anyone with an abiding interest in exploring the emerging science of green design. The attendees, all of them, regarded each other as resources, someone from whom each can learn and to whom each can give—and it is through this constant sharing of knowledge that green design has evolved.

In planning the EnvironDesign conferences, we deliberately selected a diverse group of speakers that represented the amazingly broad reach of the movement itself. Not content to limit themselves to the predictable, attendees gathered to hear Native American leaders, government policy wonks, NGO activists, researchers, and polar explorers deliver their take on sustainability, proving year after year that design professionals are eager to expand beyond their own niche.

> *"It is amazing for me to see a gathering of people drawn together not by narrow occupational categories, but by the implications and possibilities of a thematic approach to change in all its diversity."*
>
> —Bruce Babbitt, former secretary of the interior
> EnvironDesign8, Minneapolis, MN

## Why We Wrote This Book

We wrote this book to continue the mission of EnvironDesign—to bring the issues of sustainability to a greater understanding and relevance. Green design isn't just one thing. It touches all of the aspects of what we have traditionally included in the design vocabulary—function, aesthetics, and costs—and layers on new concerns. It isn't enough to plan a great space if the location of that space infringes on the habitats of critters. It isn't worth our energy to design a spacious interior if the energy that it uses is at the expense of the seventh generation coming. Beautiful materials quickly lose their appeal if they cause wheezing and sneezing. Stunning woods become less rich when mountaintops in Oregon are clear-cut as a result. Newly constructed schools become harmful when children are forced to breathe the "new school" smell.

> *"We must raise leaders of vision who think and make decisions in the long term. We must redirect and correct our course in life to ensure health and a good life for the seventh generation coming. Think positive, be courageous, be generous, share your wealth. Divest for the future."*
>
> —Chief Oren Lyons, Native American leader
> EnvironDesign2, Monterey, CA

This book seeks to offer an introduction and exploration into the vast field of sustainable design as it specifically relates to commercial spaces. It will provide those designers who are still searching for more meaning in what they do a glimpse into the possibilities ahead. It is based on the premise that designers, with their power to create, have responsibilities beyond others, and it will offer them both the philosophical and technical knowledge important to their success.

Our concept evolved from our desire to present holistic thinking to the practitioners of green design. We address commercial interiors, and though we offer practical guidance, we begin with a review of the broad global issues, for without context, the implementation of the design strategies becomes little more than busywork. Green design is a discipline to be learned, just like any other, and it includes many, many facets.

> "The Earth gave rise to both the hummingbird on my pond and to the humans in this room and I'm hoping that one can learn from the other and that both can be here for a very long time."
>
> —Janine Benyus, biomimicry writer
> EnvironDesign5, Atlanta, GA

## What You'll Find

Chapter 1 will define the issues. To the novice this section will begin to lay the foundation of understanding for the more explicit information to follow. The more experienced green designer will find it useful for defining context as well as establishing the vocabulary to be used throughout the book. By examining unfamiliar processes such as the design charrette and commissioning early on, the reader will begin to understand the significant differences between standard interior design practice and designing for sustainability.

In Chapter 2 it will become apparent that the core of the book is organized in a way that is similar to the LEED Green Building Rating System (LEED) by sorting the design process into five categories: sustainable sites, water efficiency, energy issues, materials, and indoor environmental quality. This is deliberate because of LEED's recognition by the building design and construction industry as the commonly accepted standard. We believe that by choosing this organizational model, the book will be more valuable to the practitioner. The chapter will look at the five categories through the filter of "why" followed by the "how" in Chapters 3, 4, and 5. By fostering an understanding of the scope of the issues and the consequences of ignoring them, the designer is more likely to be open to new strategies. We believe this to be an important point. Interior design is often product-oriented, and successful green design requires a more wide-ranging approach that seeks to alter ingrained paradigms.

One further note about LEED. At the end of Chapters 3, 4, and 5 are sidebars entitled "What's LEED Got to Do with It," in which we present a truncated version of the LEED for Commercial Interiors credits and requirements. These are included for convenience only and should not be considered a substitute for the actual rating system or the reference guide. Both are information-rich documents with far too many details to be included here. Clients and designers wishing to use LEED-CI—and we hope you will—must use the original documents provided by the U.S. Green Building Council.

> "We—all of humankind—are guilty of intergenerational remote tyranny in that we are making decisions of enormous impact for future generations over which they are powerless. Considered in this context, it is not enough to be eco-efficient. We must become eco-effective, accepting nothing less than 100% sustainability."
>
> —Bill McDonough and Michael Braungart,
> architect and chemist
> EnvironDesign4, Denver, CO

Chapter 3 combines site, water, and energy issues, acknowledging the limited impact that the interiors project has traditionally had in these areas and then introducing new, outside-the-boundaries thinking. The narrative will focus on tenancy issues and will highlight the commercial interiors project's opportunities to affect change. Most interior designers are neither educated nor experienced in these subjects, and this chapter will attempt to provide them with the knowledge they need to work effectively with the architects and engineers on their project teams.

Chapter 4 will focus on materials, with a strong emphasis on life cycle thinking. The LCA discipline will be described in detail, followed by product comparisons using life cycle techniques. Other product attributes such as toxicity and "natural versus synthetic" will be discussed. The remainder of the chapter offers our admittedly selective choices of products we believe to be representative of the green innovations in the marketplace.

> *"Industrialism has a metabolic problem: it eats too much and it eats the wrong things."*
> —Paul Hawken, environmental activist
> EnvironDesign1, Phoenix, AZ

Indoor environmental quality will be examined in Chapter 5, covering the very broad issue of indoor air quality as well as other factors that contribute to the health and well-being of building occupants: acoustics, thermal comfort, daylighting, and views.

Chapter 6 will list and explain some of the green design tools available to the practitioner, such as standards, certification programs, specifications, green libraries, and other product resources. Making the business case for green design is becoming increasingly important to design firms, and Chapter 7 will address the oft-asked economic questions "How much does it cost?" and "How can I justify and diminish the expenses of building green?"

> *"Stand up for what we know is true and use your personal creativity in the journey toward a regenerative world."*
> —Michael Ray, Stanford School of Business
> EnvironDesign5, Atlanta, GA

Chapter 8 brings it all together by highlighting twelve case studies of projects that, in our opinion, exemplify the best of the sustainable commercial interior. Each has incorporated the issues presented throughout our book with exceptional insights, care, and beauty. Finally, a glossary and a listing of important books, publications, and Web sites are included in the back of the book.

A unique and important feature of the book is the contributing authors whose work we present as essays. Each is a recognized expert in his or her field, and their submissions are a powerful addition to the body of knowledge the book seeks to embody. We are immensely grateful to Gina Baker, Marilyn Black, Bill Browning, Nancy Clanton, Jay Enck, Judy Heerwagen, Scot Horst, Stephen Kellert, Nadav Malin, Bill Reed, Marcus Sheffer, Ross Spiegel, and Ken Wilson for sharing their amazing intellects with us and with our readers.

> *"When we destroy nature we diminish and impoverish our communities, our children and our lives. Our children need to know that they are part of a continuum."*
> —Robert Kennedy, Jr., environmental advocate
> EnvironDesign6, Seattle, WA

## Our Hopes for the Future

Buildings are the physical embodiment of shelter, and as we enter them we are grateful for the protections they offer. Yet they are more than simply roof and walls; in the context of day-to-day comfort, the interiors matter, perhaps more than the building itself. A worker in a landmark office building in Chicago said, "What good does it do me to work in a Mies van der Rohe building if I can't open my file cabinet and close my office door at the same time?" Integrating the additional attributes of sustainable thinking, which focuses on the people inside those buildings, with the traditional standards of good design will save other employees from similar frustrations.

> *"When horrific things happen we tend to look to assess blame, rather than to ask what's wrong with the way society has designed itself. The concept of natural selection suggests that if something doesn't work we should do something else."*
> —Daniel Quinn, author, *Ishmael*
> EnvironDesign3, Baltimore, MD

Thoughtful consideration of the indoor environment coupled with a protective commitment to the world beyond the walls is what we have brought to this book. However, no matter how strong our convictions, a reality check tells us that it isn't possible to accomplish all that we would like or even all that we are able, but we must try. Janine Benyus said at EnvironDesign8, "The priority is life and the continuation of life. We're doing nothing less than reimagining the world here. We're reweaving it. It's important if you're reimagining the world to have something big and beautiful to dream of."

> "The global conservation movement will form the spearheads that governments will follow to save the integrity of this magnificent planet and the life it harbors because, darn it, it's the right thing to do!"
>
> —E. O. Wilson, entomologist
> EnvironDesign7, Washington, DC

# 1
# SUSTAINABLE DESIGN: PAST, PRESENT, AND FUTURE

**Help Wanted**

Seeking commercial interior designer with a desire to eradicate the causes of sick buildings, nurture the health and well-being of the occupants of interior spaces as well as increase the retention and productivity of said occupants (thus improving a client's return on the building investment), and assist in halting the rapid depletion of precious natural resources. Candidate must possess the innate talent to interpret sometimes complex and complicated standards, as well as the knack to separate fact from fiction. Only those interested in constant learning and able to demonstrate a willingness to challenge conventional thinking need apply.

Chances are you probably won't find this classified ad posted on Monster.com anytime soon, yet it represents some of the big-picture responsibilities facing an interior designer who chooses to pursue a practice that is grounded in the tenets of sustainable design. It is a career that can be as challenging as it is satisfying, filled with unlimited possibilities largely because, as many sustainable design pundits predict, the day will come when the delineation between green design and great design no longer exists—all great design will be green design. When that happens, environmental design solutions will be de rigueur. Codes will be in place to guide design professionals toward the right decisions. Accepted standards will provide benchmarks against which to measure new products and procedures. Those with experience—the veterans who have participated in the development of this new approach to design—will be ahead of the curve and well positioned to capitalize on its potential.

For now, however, interior designers and architects are on their own, striving to understand the issues and learning to separate valid information from phony claims. Current efforts focus on translating the outcomes of early anecdotal success stories and initial research studies while undertaking further investigation to help solidify the case for green building from ecological, economical, and sociological standpoints.

Interpreting data, though, can be frustrating and difficult and often comes down to understanding the significant elements involved with ecology and sustainability. It also requires an understanding of developing—and diverse—mind-sets in order to best extrapolate these principles and practices into mainstream thinking.

# Sustainability Defined and Refined

The word *sustain* comes from the Latin word *sustinere,* which means "to hold up from below" (*sus-,* "from below," and *tenere,* "to hold"). Throughout the centuries, the use of the word has evolved, and today it is cloaked in many subtle variations: to give support or relief; to provide nourishment or the necessities of life; to buoy up; to make something continue to exist; to maintain through time. The term first appeared in the environmental vernacular a few hundred years ago when the Germans invented a new form of forestry practice that was designed to ensure that their forests were not run down—it was called in the English-speaking world "sustainable-yield forestry."[1] One of the term's first appearances in the business arena occurred in an article entitled "The Blueprint for Survival," appearing in *The Ecologist* magazine in January 1972, in which the authors wrote of the need for "sustainable development" and for "ecological and economic stability that is sustainable far into the future."[2]

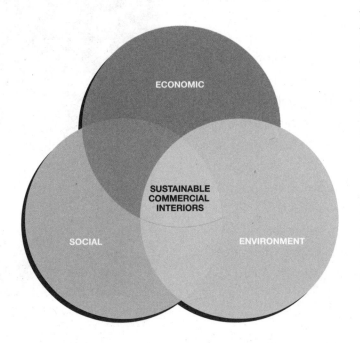

Anecdotal evidence and early research studies demonstrate that sustainable design practices can positively impact business from three distinct yet overlapping perspectives: economic, environmental, and social. The task at hand is to strengthen the case with a wealth of solid empirical data.

*"Our vision is of a life-sustaining Earth. We are committed to the achievement of a dignified, peaceful, and equitable existence. A sustainable United States will have a growing economy that provides equitable opportunities for satisfying livelihoods and a safe, healthy, high quality of life for current and future generations. Our nation will protect its environment, its natural resource base, and the functions and viability of natural systems on which all life depends."*

—The President's Council on Sustainable Development, "Towards a Sustainable America," May 1999

Also in 1972, the relationship between economic development and environmental degradation earned global attention at the United Nations (UN) Conference on the Human Environment, held in Stockholm, Sweden. Not long after, the United Nations Environment Programme (UNEP) was formed to "act as a global catalyst for action to protect the environment." Despite UNEP's efforts, however, environmental degradation continued at an accelerating rate, so much so that in 1983 the UN established the World Commission on Environment and Development, which served to "emphasize that environmental degradation, long seen as a side effect of industrial wealth with only a limited impact, was in fact a matter of survival for developing nations." Led by Gro Harlem Brundtland of Norway, the commission put forward the concept of sustainable development as "a necessary alternative approach versus one simply based on economic growth." The Brundtland Commission, as it came to be known, defined sustainability as that "which meets the needs of the present without compromising the ability of future generations to meet their own needs." A critical factor in achieving this objective, notes the report, is the ability to "overcome environmental degradation without forgoing the needs of economic development as well as social equity and justice." Sustainability, then, requires that human activity, at a minimum, uses nature's resources only to the point where they can be replenished naturally so that they can continue to sustain—in other words, support, nourish, and maintain—human populations.

It wasn't until nearly a decade later, however, at the UN's Earth Summit in Rio de Janeiro, Brazil, that widespread international support for UNEP's efforts was fully realized. The summit, which was attended by representatives of 112 countries and more than 2,400 nongovernmental organizations (NGOs), was organized by the United Nations in an effort to "help governments rethink economic development and find ways to halt the destruction of irreplaceable natural resources and pollution of the planet." As the UN describes, "Hundreds of thousands of people from all walks of life were drawn into the Rio process. They persuaded their leaders to go to Rio and join other nations in making the difficult decisions needed to ensure a healthy planet for generations to come."[3]

At the end of the summit, participating nations adopted a set of twenty-seven principles, the Rio Declaration on Environment and Development, to guide future sustainable development. Included in these principles was the precept that "human beings are at the center of concerns for sustainable development" and are "entitled to a healthy and productive life in harmony with nature." The declaration also acknowledged that "in order to achieve sustainable development, environmental protection must constitute an integral part of the development process and cannot be considered in isolation from it" and that "the right to development must be fulfilled so as to equitably meet developmental and environmental needs of present and future generations." Finally, the declaration noted that to "achieve sustainable development and a higher quality of life for all people, states should reduce and eliminate unsustainable patterns of production and consumption and promote appropriate demographic policies."

Fast-forward through the subsequent ten-plus years and today you can stumble across as many definitions and interpretations of "sustainability" or "sustainable development" as there are experts willing to offer one. What becomes obvious from this analysis is that each definition is characterized by the perspective from which it is being viewed. The report "Integrating Economic and Environmental Policies: The Case of Pacific Island Countries," produced by the UN Economic and Social Commission for Asia and the Pacific, listed dozens of definitions of sustainability from varying perspectives, a handful of which are described here.[4]

- "Traditional neoclassical economics supposes that economic growth is maximized when all opportunities to increase the efficiency of resource use have been exhausted," which ultimately equates sustainable development with sustainable economic growth.
- "From the ecological perspective, the quality of life depends on environmental quality. Therefore, retaining ecological integrity and the assimilative capacity of the natural environment is crucial for the functioning of the economic system."
- Sociologists, on the other hand, propose that "human beings' patterns of organization are important for developing viable solutions to sustainable development. From this perspective, failure to devote attention to social factors in the development process will seriously hamper the progress of programs and policies aimed at achieving sustainable development."
- The intergenerational equity perspective suggests that "the rate at which natural resources are being exploited is too fast and works against the interests of the unborn." Thus, the definition of sustainable development must address "the maintenance of non-declining per capita income over the indefinite future (the neoclassical definition) and maintenance of the stock of renewable resources (ecological definition) with the added proviso that the net value of the stock of nonrenewable resources must also be non-declining."
- The anthropocentric approach put forth by the World Conservation Union defines sustainable development as "the maintenance of essential ecological processes and life support systems, the preservation of genetic diversity, and the sustainable utilization of species and ecosystems." This approach places emphasis on "achieving a quality of life (or standard of living) that can be maintained for many generations. Sustainability is described in terms of fulfilling people's cultural, material, and spiritual needs in equitable ways."

Clearly, arriving at a general consensus of what sustainability means is a daunting and perhaps unachievable task, as stakeholders emphasize their own particular interests. And while one may be dismayed by such conflicting viewpoints, it is not necessarily detrimental; not only has it expanded the base of parties advocating for sustainability, but each has also assumed ownership of the concept in some way—an essential condition to the continued advancement of any emerging policy or practice.

In fact, Sandra Mendler, the leader of HOK's sustainable design initiatives, suggests that the reason today's sustainable design movement is more successful than the energy efficiency movement of the 1970s is because the underlying goals and purpose are larger, and the constituencies that are attracted to the cause are broader and more diverse. "Under a single umbrella of sustainability are the individual causes of energy efficiency, recycling, indoor air quality and building health, waste management, healthy buildings, native plants, backyard habitat, dark sky initiatives, etc. Each of these has passionate advocates, and many people are motivated to action because they see the synergies. By endorsing sustainable design, one can accomplish *all* of this," she notes.[5]

> "Environmentalism is much more than a hodge-podge of pleas and campaigns to save the Everglades, the tundra, or the snowy egret. Mountains, forests, streams, clear skies, and wildlife are parts of environmentalism because they are essential parts of man's well being. But environmentalism is also a vital element in dealing with problems of health, economic prosperity, social development, education, justice—indeed, with the full range of human aspirations. It is the basic undertaking if we are to attain the objectives this country subscribed to 200 years ago: life, liberty, and the pursuit of happiness."
>
> —William D. Ruckelshaus, first administrator, U.S. Environmental Protection Agency, 1973

# Defining "Green"

During the decades that the concept of sustainability was being debated on an international platform, environmental problems at the local level weren't going unnoticed. The 1962 release of Rachel Carson's book *Silent Spring* brought overwhelming attention to the impact of pesticides on human and environmental health; people were horrified to learn how DDT and other chemicals being used to enhance agricultural productivity were actually poisoning our lakes, rivers, oceans, and ourselves. Eight years later, the first Earth Day was instigated by Wisconsin senator Gaylord Nelson and patterned after the teach-ins staged at many U.S. university campuses protesting civil rights violations and the Vietnam War. Nelson hoped that by holding the first nationwide environmental protest, it would "shake up the political establishment and force the environmental issue onto the national agenda."[6]

That first Earth Day saw 20 million Americans take to the streets, parks, and auditoriums in what an October 1993 article in *American Heritage* magazine called "one of the most remarkable happenings in the history of democracy." Some credit the environmental consciousness raised by Earth Day as the impetus behind the passage of the Clean Air, Clean Water, and Endangered Species Acts. It provided a mobilizing force, a formal way for ordinary citizens to protest against the medical waste washing up on shorelines, the increasing numbers of toxic waste dumps dotting the landscape, and oil spills that were despoiling the beauty of our country's coasts and threatening the sea life that inhabited them. That same year, the U.S. Environmental Protection Agency (EPA) was formed, and the Natural Resources Defense Council (NRDC) also was established. In 1990 Earth Day went global, mobilizing 200 million people in 141 countries and lifting the status of environmental issues onto the world stage. As the millennium approached, Earth Day began focusing on global warming and a push for clean energy. By the time April 22, 2000, rolled around, the Internet had helped bring five thousand environmental groups worldwide on board, reaching out to hundreds of millions of people. Earth Day is now celebrated in 174 countries by over half a billion people, making it the most celebrated secular holiday in the world.

After that first Earth Day, a generation of committed citizens emerged, a group who recognized the importance of environmental health and its related causes. And while most chose to concentrate their activities on local initiatives conducted with little publicity, the more radical activists took on the biggest environmental offenders, chaining themselves to smokestacks, living in trees, or even commandeering oil tankers.

The first Earth Day in 1970 provided ordinary citizens with the opportunity to formally protest the environmental degradation occurring in their own backyards, from toxic wastes washing up on shorelines to rivers filled with industrial scum to oil spills threatening the sea life of our nation's coasts. © *Photographer: James Jurica*

Much of that radical element no longer exists today (baby boomers have, after all, gotten considerably older and tamer); instead we have reached a juncture where much of the global debate on sustainability has merged with industry-specific efforts. Some in the electronics industry, for example, have made sweeping product design changes and instituted take-back programs to keep their products out of landfills, where they can leach dangerous chemicals into the groundwater. In fact, it seems the tenor of the agenda has changed: where before our voices cried out against the wrongdoers, we now understand the value of rallying for those who are cleaning up their act and doing things right. We celebrate the fact that the Cuyahoga River in Cleveland, Ohio, no longer burns, and the Hudson

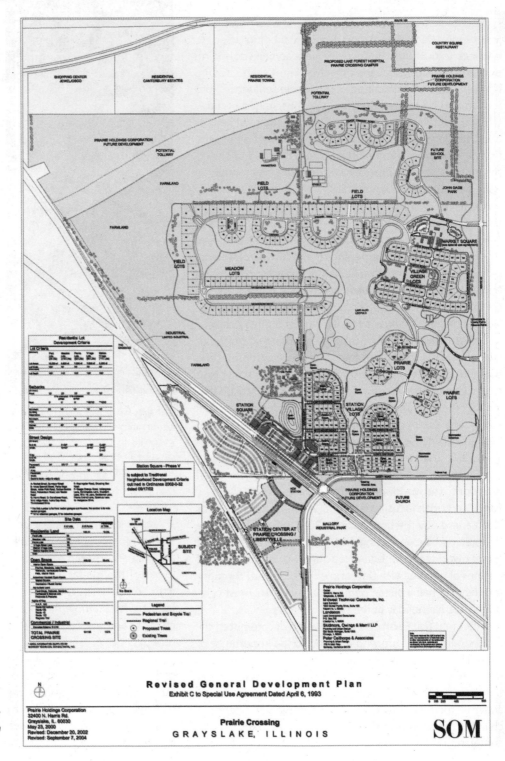

Conservation communities, such as Prairie Crossing in Illinois, provide a way of life that respects the environment and enables residents to experience a strong connection between community and the land. *Source: Site plan courtesy of Prairie Crossing*

River, known thirty years ago as the "Dead River" filled with industrial scum, today supports fish, harbor seals, and porpoise populations as well as many recreational areas.

Today, our consciousness is raised and our access to information is unparalleled. So why, then, do we still wonder what's green and what's not?

Like the debate on sustainability, the determination of whether something is green or not green usually depends on who's asking and in what context. (It's ironic that the word *green* represents the holy grail of sorts for two often contentious interests, economics and environment, leaving one to wonder if perhaps this might be symbolic that the two can in fact be mutually beneficial.) For example, a subdivision developer might think being green is as simple as leaving as many trees as possible around the new homes he builds, or may take a more sophisticated view and plan an entire community with a number of ecofriendly amenities. Consider the Prairie Crossing conservation community located about one hour northwest of Chicago. It features more than 10 miles of trails (which lead to two colleges, the local high school, train station, and local stores and restaurants), a stable, a large lake, and three community buildings: a historic barn, a schoolhouse, and a farmhouse, the last of which supplies fresh organic vegetables, flowers, and fruits to the community. Rail service runs to both Chicago and O'Hare Airport, and a wind turbine provides power to the farm.

A home builder, on the other hand, takes a different approach and markets "green" as above-standard insulation, highly efficient windows, or a money-saving heating and cooling system. The more environmentally astute builder will throw in passive solar energy and cisterns to collect rainwater. A typical home owner probably believes she's green because she separates out glass, plastic, and metals before throwing them in the trash. More enlightened consumers shop for energy-efficient appliances and have retrofitted their lamps and fixtures with compact fluorescent light bulbs. A business office goes green when it

Some consumers take heart in separating out glass, plastic, and metals for curbside recycling pickup. Though considered a small green action on the part of an individual, as a collective effort these recycling programs diverted an estimated 30 percent of waste from landfills in 2001. © *Photographer: James Jurica*

begins separating its white paper from the rest and installs motion detectors to control lighting usage and cut utility bills. Small efforts such as reusing the backside of paper for notepads, using washable ceramic coffee cups instead of Styrofoam, and recycling toner and ink cartridges also may qualify.

Politicians who propose a "green" agenda usually translate their efforts into environmental regulation. The Clean Water Act and the Clean Air Act are examples of government actions that worked. Many hope that official legislative action on global warming will be enacted in the not-too-distant-future, encouraged by the bipartisan support and passage of the 2005 Sense of the Senate on Climate Change resolution, where the U.S. Senate went on record for the first time in calling for a mandatory limit on our nation's global-warming pollution.

The EPA cites green goals such as ridding our cities of smog so that everyone can breathe clean air. Ecologists today think green globally and act to protect our earth and its most precious attribute, biodiversity. They worry that nature's fragile balance is in constant peril and that every ecosystem is in an accelerating and perhaps irreversible decline. Ecologists can cite hundreds of frightening examples of species extinction and rain forest endangerment: at least 20 percent of all freshwater species globally are

# Conspicuous Conservation

Well-informed consumers are emerging as a new force in the global struggle to create an environmentally sustainable world, reports a 2002 study by the Worldwatch Institute entitled "Vital Signs" and produced with the support of the UNEP and the W. Alton Jones Foundation. Aided by labeling programs, standards, and an expanding group of social and environmental certification organizations, Worldwatch notes that "the world's consumers are voting with their wallets for products and services that promote sustainable development."

Michael Renner, Worldwatch senior researcher and project director for Vital Signs, argues in the report against the notion proposed by some free market advocates who claim that the market automatically gives people all the choices and information they want. "What consumers are demonstrating is that they want more environmentally acceptable choices than the market has been delivering, and more trustworthy information about the social and environmental impact of the products they might buy," he says.

One significant aspect of this movement is being fueled by those consumers who want to be seen being environmentally friendly. Called "conspicuous conservation," this concept is similar to the better-known spectacle of conspicuous consumption and espouses the same belief that "you are what you own." However, it exalts virtue over tawdry materialism. The idea really isn't new, says Edwin Stafford, marketing professor at Utah State University/Logan. "A counterculture lifestyle without cars, refrigerators, or electricity from the grid has been around since the 1960s. It's been conspicuous, but hardly alluring. Today's new conspicuous conservation, however, carries a smarter, high-tech appeal," he explains.

Wordspy.com defines "conspicuous conservation" as "using technology to live more frugally and to conserve resources," and it reflects the increasing popularity of state-of-the-art wares and technologies designed elegantly to protect the planet. Energy Star appliances, compact fluorescent lights, photovoltaic solar panels, high-performance homes, and wind turbines atop skyscrapers (as initially planned for New York City's Freedom Tower) all embody smart frugality with superior performance and style. In the wake of 9/11, the Iraq war, and soaring oil prices, environmentalists' advocacy for energy conservation has taken on added resonance. High-tech prudence simply makes sense.

As the SUV fades as the icon of the good life, Toyota's hybrid, the Prius, now symbolizes the socially better life.

"The rising zeal for hybrids and chic frugality could spread, encouraging companies to give other products much-needed efficiency makeovers, such as high-speed computers and air conditioners," Stafford notes. "Ideally, the trend could spark innovation and create jobs while reducing society's energy gluttony. Clearly, businesses can take advantage of conspicuous conservation—and perhaps profitably encourage its proliferation—with the right product features and promotional messages."

*Sources:* "Choosing A Better Future: Consumers Pressure Business to Go Green," Worldwatch Institute, www.worldwatch.org; and "Conspicuous Conservation," by Edwin Stafford, *green@work* magazine, Winter 2004, www.greenatworkmag.com.

Canadian architect Peter Busby drives a hybrid Prius, which serves as a tangible symbol of his personal and professional advocacy of sustainable design principles, subtly communicating to clients and colleagues a commitment to environmental stewardship. *Photography by Jim Robinette* © Interiors & Sources

extinct or at risk, a figure that is twice as high in North America; deforestation has quadrupled in the Brazilian Pantanal, which means that 17 percent of the region's original vegetation has been lost and that its wetlands may vanish in fewer than forty-five years if conservation actions don't begin immediately. The fact that Fresh Kills, the Staten Island landfill, is larger than the Great Wall of China speaks volumes about the harm that humans are inflicting on the earth. Ecologists also speak of the devastating consequences that come from natural disasters, which were greater in the 1990s than in the previous four decades combined. Their dire warnings hit home and hit hard in the form of Hurricanes Katrina and Rita in 2005. Poor development choices, from deforestation and river engineering to poor siting of cities and buildings, have made us more vulnerable to disaster than ever.

In the design fields, architects and designers are increasingly introducing the concept of green building into their projects through techniques such as daylighting, light shelves, and light sensors. They also know that the antithesis of green is called a "sick building" and work hard to develop innovative strategies for heating and cooling air and keeping it clean. Separate exhausts for print/copy rooms, monitors for noxious chemicals, and operable windows help to keep a building—and its occupants— healthy. So do safe building materials such as paints, adhesives, and floor coverings that emit few or no VOCs. Some of the most forward-thinking product developers and manufacturers conceive of being green as an opportunity to differentiate themselves from the competition. Some producers of modular carpet tiles recognize that their product doesn't wear out, it "uglies out," and they've developed a process of renewal and reuse, keeping the carpet out of landfills and saving their customers money in the process.

Furniture manufacturers are going green by placing a greater emphasis on the three R's: reduce, reuse, and recycle. Chairs are now being designed with fewer materials, and their components are clearly identified for easier separation and recycling. One progressive manufacturer even prints the recycling instructions on the bottom of its chair in several languages, thus increasing the odds for its desired disposal and reuse.

What all these examples illustrate is that there are varying shades of green, from pale green to dark green—but

From species extinction to widespread rain forest endangerment, ecologists warn of the devastating consequences to global ecosystems as a result of human activity. © *Photographer: Lim Seang Kar*

the fact is, some green is better than none. Of course, there's always the practice of greenwashing to cloud the issue. Best described as "the deliberate dissemination of misleading information or the implementation of token ecofriendly initiatives in an effort to conceal a larger abuse of the environment and present a positive public image," *greenwashing* takes its roots from the term *whitewash*, thus emphasizing the cover-up part of the equation. Some argue that greenwashing plays a big role in the public's confusion about green versus not-so-green by introducing a third choice: not green at all but convincingly faking it. For example, consumers were especially taken with Madison Avenue's wholesome images that promote cotton as "the fabric of our lives." Yet the commercial cotton industry accounts for 10 percent of the world's annual pesticide consumption. In addition, the bleaching, dyeing, and finishing of cotton fabric use industrial chemicals such as chlorine, chromium, and formaldehyde that the EPA has identified as hazardous substances. Hotels will advertise that they're green simply because they offer guests the opportunity to reuse towels and bedding instead of having these items changed out each day—yet energy-guzzling and heat-producing fixtures light and warm empty rooms for hours on end, unhealthy chemicals are used for cleaning, hundreds of pounds of disposable cups, plates, and silverware are thrown away each day, and a guest can't find an operable window anywhere in the building.

> *"When the final scorecard is tallied, shame on us if it's not a field of green."*
>
> —Clay Johnson III, deputy director for management, U.S. Office of Management and Budget

## ■ What Is Green Design?

So what's a designer to do? If it's difficult to determine what's green and what's not, how does a designer even begin to start unfolding the complicated layers surrounding the core principles of sustainable design?

Working within the constraints of available technology and processes, today's green design and building professionals concentrate on achieving practical environmental solutions to the most practical extent possible. Practically speaking, the ideal totally green facility would have no negative impact on the environment, would use only sustainable or renewable resources, and all material components would be returnable to their manufacturer after the end of their useful life to be used as food for another material. In addition, this facility would be nurturing and restorative, aid productivity, and produce a sense of well-being for its occupants. Sound impossible? Actually, describes architect William A. McDonough, FAIA, one of the very first sustainable design gurus, this facility does exist: it's called a

The Bedouin tent is an example of a perfect green building, suggested William McDonough, in that it produces no negative impact on the environment, it uses only sustainable or renewable resources, and all material components can be returned to the manufacturer at the end of their useful life to be used as food for another material. In addition, it is nurturing, restorative, and produces a sense of well-being for its occupants. © *Photographer: Steven Tilston*

Bedouin tent, and it's used by nomads wandering the desert, where temperatures often exceed 120 degrees and there's virtually no shade and no air movement. To survive in this hostile environment, the nomad relies on a black tent that produces a deep shade that brings the temperature down to 95 degrees. Its coarse weave creates an interior beautifully illuminated with millions of specks of light beneath which air rises and is drawn through the membrane, creating a breeze and dropping the temperature even lower. Even rain, when it occurs, isn't a problem, as the moisture causes the fibers to swell and create a tight enclosure. Finally, the Bedouin tent is completely portable.[7]

For most climates and cultures, however, the Bedouin tent won't do. Do modern building types exist that meet our totally green criteria? Are we able to produce interior spaces well suited to our lifestyle needs without negative environmental impacts? Can we buy or specify products capable of complying with evolving protocols? The answer is yes . . . and no. Nature provides us with everything we need to be sustainable and healthy with minimum impact on the environment: natural materials that if used correctly can be returned to the earth to be used again, an unlimited supply of energy from the sun, and the biodiversity necessary for our complex human requirements. Couple all this with the best of intentions and designing green should be attainable.

How, then, do we do it?

In *The Hannover Principles: Design for Sustainability*, McDonough sought to provide "a platform upon which designers can consider how to adapt their work toward sustainable ends (designers being *all* who change the environment with the inspiration of human creativity)."

Designing for sustainability, he said, "requires awareness of the full short- and long-term consequences of any transformation of the environment."[8]

If we must be aware of the consequences of our design decisions, as McDonough suggests, we necessarily need to explore all the issues and elements that those decisions have the potential to impact. The discussion below categorizes the issues according to three primary areas of concern—economics, environment, and social—as well as identifies those issues where more than one factor comes into play. A brief explanation follows of the relationship between sustainable design principles and each impact area.

## ECONOMIC

- **Productivity.** Increased control of ventilation, temperature, and lighting along with exposure to increased daylighting produces higher yields per worker.
- **Capital Costs.** Green buildings deliver increased operating efficiencies and a quicker return on investment, offsetting any higher first costs.
- **Operating Costs.** Operating efficiencies associated with green building strategies include lower energy and water costs as well as reduced cleaning and maintenance requirements.
- **Liability/Mitigation Costs.** Increased indoor environmental quality reduces exposure to litigation stemming from related illnesses and eliminates the expenses associated with mitigation.
- **Property Values.** Reductions in operations and maintenance expenses can enhance a building's profitability and appraised value.
- **Lease-outs and Occupancy Rates.** The superior performance aspects of green buildings stimulate increased interest from tenants.
- **Asking Rents.** Higher demand for green buildings can translate into higher rental income.
- **Tax Incentives.** Implementing green design strategies can earn tax subsidies at federal, state, and/or local levels.
- **Shareholder Value.** Reduced operating costs and higher productivity improve the bottom line and attract increased interest from investors
- **Retail Sales Levels.** A nurturing environment, the addition of daylighting, and a welcoming atmosphere stimulate increased sales.

## ENVIRONMENTAL

- **Emissions.** Building systems that consume less energy reduce a building's greenhouse gas emissions.
- **Ozone Depletion.** Lower greenhouse gas emissions reduce the subsequent impact on the ozone.
- **Quantity of Waste.** The reuse of existing building stock reduces waste volume.

- **Materials Usage.** Materials from local sources have lower levels of embodied energy associated with their transportation.
- **Natural Resources Consumption.** Green materials and products reduce the consumption of scarce or nonrenewable natural resources.
- **Toxic Substances.** Eliminating the use of known or questionable chemicals reduces human exposure to noxious materials.
- **Off-gassing/VOCs.** Choosing materials with low to zero VOCs prevents the off-gassing of fumes that make occupants sick.
- **Material Life Cycles.** Products are evaluated from raw material extraction through to disposal (or renewal) at the end of their useful life.

## SOCIETAL

- **Perception.** A sustainably designed building serves as a visible symbol of corporate responsibility.
- **Public Relations/Marketing Opportunities.** Green design benefits often receive positive publicity, which in turn can attract new customers.
- **Relationships with Private/Public Community Stakeholders.** Sustainable buildings provide evidence of being a good corporate neighbor.
- **Customer Loyalty.** Green buildings demonstrate a concern for customer's health and well-being.
- **Personal Satisfaction.** Employees at all levels gain satisfaction from a corporation's commitment to positive social change.
- **Aesthetics.** Green buildings provide aesthetic harmony between a structure and the surrounding natural area.

## ECONOMIC/ENVIRONMENTAL

- **Heating, Ventilation, and Air-conditioning (HVAC) Costs.** Energy-efficient heating and cooling systems may translate into substantial utility savings.
- **Water Consumption.** Efficient plumbing fixtures conserve potable water, a resource facing global shortages.
- **Electricity Costs.** Energy-efficient lighting combined with individual control systems may dramatically lower electricity usage.

- **Landfill/Tipping Fees.** Less construction waste or its redirection decreases the costs associated with landfilling.
- **Churn Rates.** Designing for flexibility and future use lowers expenses related to space reconfiguration.
- **Mitigation Hazards.** Improved indoor air quality (IAQ) eliminates the potential exposure and expenses related to remediation.

## ENVIRONMENTAL/SOCIAL

- **Employee Health and Well-being.** Green design increases the amenities that improve occupants' physical and psychological condition.
- **Quality of Learning Environments.** Green design increases the factors that directly impact a student's ability to learn.
- **Occupant Comfort.** Green design addresses the need for occupants to control their own lighting and temperature requirements.
- **Indoor Air Quality.** Specifying materials with low or zero VOCs, along with superior ventilation systems, improves indoor air quality.

## SOCIAL/ECONOMIC

- **Absenteeism.** Improvements in levels of employee health and well-being contribute to reductions in absentee rates.
- **Health Care Costs.** Improvements in indoor environments may reduce health care costs and someday may lead to lower insurance premiums.
- **Turnover Rates.** Healthy, happy employees are less likely to look for greener pastures.
- **Recruitment/Retention Costs.** As turnover decreases, so too do the expenses related to attracting and training new workers.
- **Approval Times.** Many local municipalities offer streamlined review and approval processes for green buildings.
- **Marketing Differential.** A green building stands out in the crowd of available real estate.

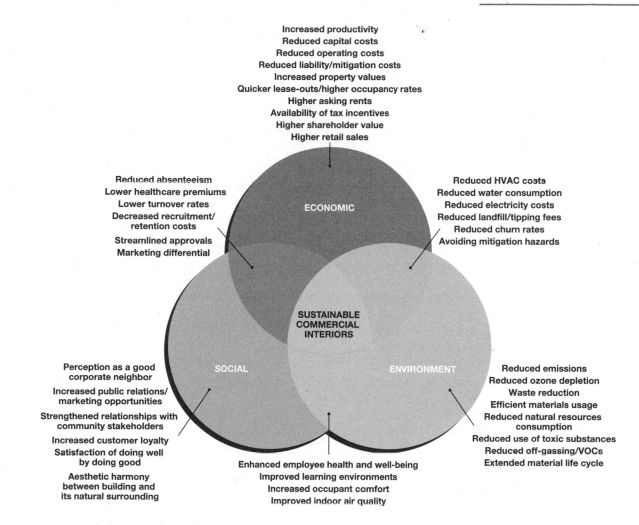

Increased productivity
Reduced capital costs
Reduced operating costs
Reduced liability/mitigation costs
Increased property values
Quicker lease-outs/higher occupancy rates
Higher asking rents
Availability of tax incentives
Higher shareholder value
Higher retail sales

Reduced absenteeism
Lower healthcare premiums
Lower turnover rates
Decreased recruitment/
retention costs
Streamlined approvals
Marketing differential

Reduced HVAC costs
Reduced water consumption
Reduced electricity costs
Reduced landfill/tipping fees
Reduced churn rates
Avoiding mitigation hazards

ECONOMIC

SUSTAINABLE
COMMERCIAL
INTERIORS

SOCIAL

ENVIRONMENT

Perception as a good
corporate neighbor
Increased public relations/
marketing opportunities
Strengthened relationships with
community stakeholders
Increased customer loyalty
Satisfaction of doing well
by doing good
Aesthetic harmony
between building and
its natural surrounding

Reduced emissions
Reduced ozone depletion
Waste reduction
Efficient materials usage
Reduced natural resources
consumption
Reduced use of toxic substances
Reduced off-gassing/VOCs
Extended material life cycle

Enhanced employee health and well-being
Improved learning environments
Increased occupant comfort
Improved indoor air quality

The three primary areas of concern—economic, environmental, and social—and the results/reductions/improvements resulting from their integration.

Clearly, the consequences of sustainable design strategies are intertwined into many vital aspects of a company's operations and its culture. While subsequent chapters address all of these issues (and their related green design strategies) in depth, even the briefest of examinations illustrates how the sustainable design process—from conception to completion—provides vast opportunities to support, nourish, and maintain all segments of corporate America.

As our knowledge of and experience with sustainable design expands, most likely the issue parameters will change accordingly. As an emerging discipline, sustainability will not remain static.

HOK's Mendler, an architect who has devoted much of her career to the pursuit of sustainable design, proposes in the August 15, 2002 issue of *Design Intelligence* that a fundamental shift in the discourse on sustainability is pending, one that society is ready for. "By shifting to a vision of humanistic sustainability, the synergies become more expansive and more powerful. The tools and technologies that support environmental sustainability are the same as those that support humanistic sustainability. The motiva-

## The Hannover Principles

1. Insist on rights of humanity and nature to co-exist in a healthy, supportive, diverse and sustainable condition.
2. Recognize interdependence. The elements of human design interact with and depend upon the natural world, with broad and diverse implications at every scale. Expand design considerations to recognizing even distant effects.
3. Respect relationships between spirit and matter. Consider all aspects of human settlement including community, dwelling, industry and trade in terms of existing and evolving connections between spiritual and material consciousness.
4. Accept responsibility for the consequences of design decisions upon human well-being, the viability of natural systems and their right to co-exist.
5. Create safe objects of long-term value. Do not burden future generations with requirements for maintenance or vigilant administration of potential danger due to the careless creation of products, processes or standards.
6. Eliminate the concept of waste. Evaluate and optimize the full life cycle of products and processes, to approach the state of natural systems, in which there is no waste.
7. Rely on natural energy flows. Human designs should, like the living world, derive their creative forces from perpetual solar income. Incorporate this energy efficiently and safely for responsible use.
8. Understand the limitations of design. No human creation lasts forever and design does not solve all problems. Those who create and plan should practice humility in the face of nature. Treat nature as a model and mentor, not as an inconvenience to be evaded or controlled.
9. Seek constant improvement by the sharing of knowledge. Encourage direct and open communication between colleagues, patrons, manufacturers and users to link long-term sustainable considerations with ethical responsibility, and re-establish the integral relationship between natural processes and human activity.

The Hannover Principles should be seen as a living document committed to the transformation and growth in the understanding of our interdependence with nature, so that they may adapt as our knowledge of the world evolves.

*© 1992, William McDonough Architects. Reprinted with permission.*

tions, however, are more explicit within the framework of humanistic sustainability.

"Humanistic sustainability focuses on people as an integral part of the natural environment," she continues. " When people are of primary concern: community matters, health and wellness matters, safety and security matters, and connecting with personal values matters. What has been traditionally referred to as sustainable design, with its focus on health, resource conservation, and ecosystem protection, follows as a logical consequence."

As a result of this thinking, Mendler says, HOK is very deliberately overlaying traditional sustainable design strategies with design strategies that foster community and connectivity, two issues that can potentially impact projects at a strategic level and on a number of scales— from the workplace to the city. "Technology, space planning and design, building configuration, master planning and transportation are all affected," she notes. "These solutions influence behavior, and behavior impacts sustainability."[9]

# Historic Buildings: A "Nonrenewable" Resource

Perhaps the most responsible form of green design is the kind that occurs in the renovation of our existing building stock. Currently, more than 90 percent of construction projects today involve existing buildings, providing tremendous opportunities for realizing the potential that sustainable design principles can bring to such projects. Reusing our aging buildings preserves the energy and materials imbedded within their walls, and it also reduces the need to employ additional resources toward the construction of something new. Land consumption, ecosystem modification, increased infrastructure, and other new development are minimized when older buildings receive a new life. So too are many energy-related expenses. For example, in "Preservation = Green Building?" by Dwayne Meadows, which appeared in the August 2004 issue of *Preservation Seattle*, Carl Elefante of Quinn Architects reported that the green renovation of the University of Michigan's S. T. Dana Building resulted in a savings of 135 tanker trucks of gasoline.

> *"Cultural resource preservation intrinsically is a form of sustainable conservation. The built environment represents the embodied energy of past civilizations."*
>
> —National Park Service, "Guiding Principles of Sustainable Design"

The renovation of historic buildings is of special significance to the sustainable design paradigm because it contributes to the preservation of an intangible symbol of our culture, contributes to a sense of place, and forms a physical connection to our heritage that can never be replaced once gone. The National Park Services (NPS), in its "Guiding Principles of Sustainable Design," refers to historically significant buildings as "a non-renewable resource" that should be "protected, conserved, interpreted and left unimpaired for future generations."

According to the U.S. Department of Energy's database of standing buildings, the historic building segment is increasing by 10 million buildings a year. The U.S. General Services Administration (GSA), the nation's biggest real estate player—owning, leasing, and managing nearly 350 million square feet—reports that nearly one-fourth of the space in its owned inventory is in historic buildings.

When applying sustainable design principles to historic projects, NPS requires that "all site and facility designs incorporate methods for protecting and preserving significant cultural resources over the long term." The architectural style, landscape design, and construction materials of new developments should also "reflect the cultural heritage of the locality or region." Additionally, whenever possible, cultural resources should be "interpreted to include lessons about the environmental exploitations or sustainable environmental successes of the past."

Designers who work with historic structures often find that these projects are especially ideal to sustainable design parameters: they often involve urban redevelopment, are in close proximity to mass transit, have operable windows, and are filled with old-growth timber and locally quarried stone—elements that more often than not could never be replaced. That's not to say that greening historic buildings is not without obstacles: designers may uncover toxic materials, such as lead-based paint and asbestos, which must be removed

*(continued)*

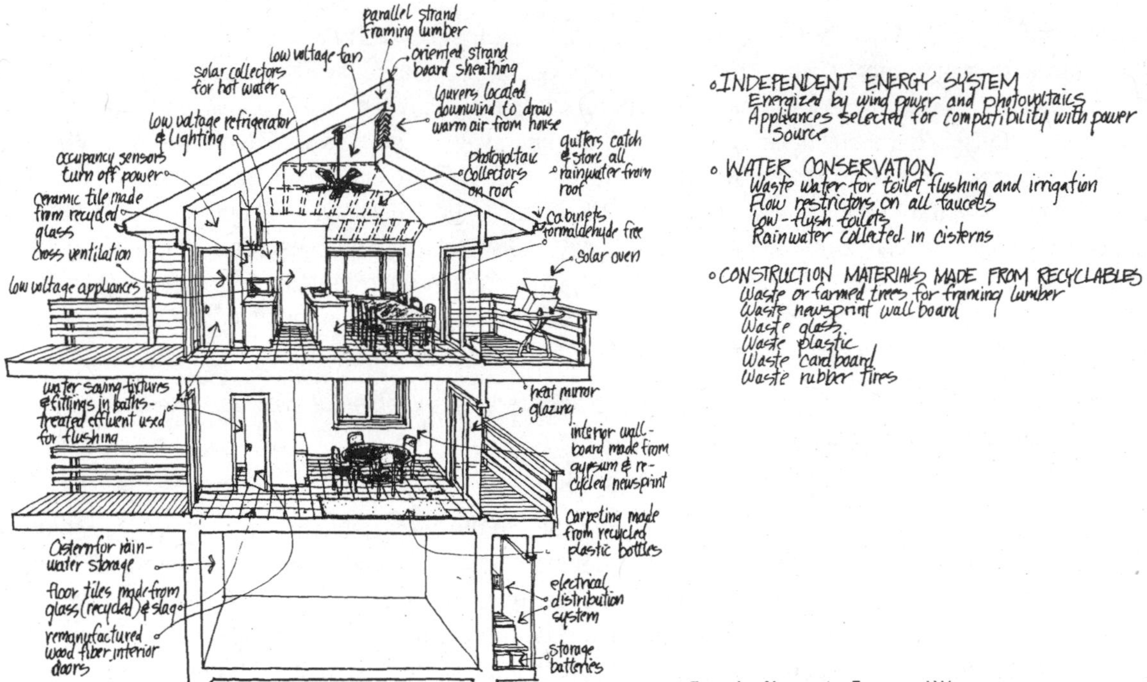
parallel strand framing lumber
low voltage fan
oriented strand board sheathing
solar collectors for hot water
louvers located downwind to draw warm air from house
low voltage refrigerator & lighting
occupancy sensors turn off power
photovoltaic collectors on roof
gutters catch & store all rainwater from roof
ceramic tile made from recycled glass
cross ventilation
cabinets formaldehyde free
solar oven
low voltage appliances
water saving fixtures & fittings in baths - treated effluent used for flushing
heat mirror glazing
interior wall-board made from gypsum & recycled newsprint
carpeting made from recycled plastic bottles
cistern for rain-water storage
floor tiles made from glass (recycled) & slag
remanufactured wood fiber interior doors
electrical distribution system
storage batteries
INDEPENDENT ENERGY SYSTEM
Energized by wind power and photovoltaics
Appliances selected for compatibility with power source
WATER CONSERVATION
Waste water for toilet flushing and irrigation
Flow restrictors on all faucets
Low-flush toilets
Rainwater collected in cisterns
CONSTRUCTION MATERIALS MADE FROM RECYCLABLES
Waste or farmed trees for framing lumber
Waste newsprint wall board
Waste glass
Waste plastic
Waste cardboard
Waste rubber tires

Example of Integrating Energy and Water Conservation with Environmentally Responsible Building Materials

The National Park Service provides this conservation and building materials diagram to illustrate ways of integrating water and energy conservation with environmentally responsible building materials. *Source: National Park Service*

and properly disposed of; systems often must be brought up to code; close proximity to neighboring buildings may make daylighting strategies difficult to achieve; and older, ill-fitting windows, doors, and other exterior architectural details may impact energy-saving strategies.

When Farr Associates decided to design a 3,000-square-foot green build-out for its own architecture and urban design firm in the landmark Monadnock Building in Chicago, mediating between historic rehabilitation practices (with original materials and methods) and sustainable building principles presented a tremendous challenge. In the end, though, the firm incorporated a number of green features: Energy Star equipment, air quality monitoring, green power, daylight-responsive lighting, energy-efficient lighting, natural daylight and ventilation, energy-saving glazing strategies, linoleum work surfaces and flooring, recycled-content materials, locally manufactured materials, milk-based and low-VOC paints, formaldehyde-free wood products, and salvaged and reused materials.

Farr Associates successfully applied green design strategies to the renovation of its own offices in Chicago's historic Monadnock Building. © *Farr Associates Architecture/Planning/Preservation, Chicago, Illinois*

# Overcoming the Obstacles to Sustainability

The exploration of any new and uncharted territory is always a little intimidating; the decision to embrace and actively champion sustainable design strategies can be especially fraught with daily challenges as designers attempt to win over as yet unconvinced clients. But perhaps some of the biggest obstacles that designers need to conquer come from within.

## Ignorance

"What we don't know can't hurt us." This mind-set is dangerous when it pertains to all matters relating to sustainability. As humans continue to wreak havoc on the planet's natural resources, whether through overconsumption or degradation, the call for education and information

becomes increasingly urgent. Rain forests the size of New York City are being destroyed every day. The world's oceans have warmed substantially during the past forty years due to global warming. Human health is being jeopardized by the VOC emissions from common paints, coatings, and adhesives. An hour a week visiting the Web sites of organizations such as the NRDC, the Worldwatch Institute, Conservation International, and the World Resources Institute will deliver a much-needed wake-up call. The antidote to ignorance is knowledge with a caveat: when ignorance ends, negligence begins.

## Inconvenience

Time is a precious commodity, and so sometimes it's easy to convince ourselves to take the quicker route: dumping all of our trash into one big can, instead of separating it for recycling; tossing discontinued carpet folders, instead of returning them or donating them to schools; sending dam-

## Studying Sustainable Design in School

In January 2006, the new professional standards set forth by the Council for Interior Design Accreditation (formerly FIDER) went into effect. These standards undergo extensive scrutiny and constant monitoring to ensure that interior design education—and the graduates it produces—are fully prepared for what lies ahead in the profession. Of special note in the 2006 revisions is the enhancement and inclusion of specific sustainable design criteria, a change that reflects the increasing impact of green design on professional practice, both today and in the future. According to Kayem Dunn, executive director of the Council, a recent survey of accredited programs identified the Council's standards as being the most influential factor on interior design curricula, ranked higher than faculty composition, discipline base, and geographic location. "This suggests that the strengthening of sustainability in Council Standards will produce results and, ultimately, ensure that graduates . . . are well prepared to practice sustainable design," she says. "Furthermore, the revisions poise the Council and interior design education to move forward as sustainable design gains momentum in the profession."

*Source:* "25 Environmental Champions for 2005," *EnvironDesign Journal,* a supplement to *Interiors & Sources,* Fall 2005.

## Lack of Education and Experience

Green design has only recently begun to be taught in design schools, and most design professionals have either a skimpy education in sustainability or none at all. Those who are just beginning to acquaint themselves with its principles are often intimidated by its vastness and complexity. Interior designers accurately note that some of the more technical energy issues and those involving the mechanical systems of buildings are the purview of engineers and beyond the scope of their knowledge base. However, one of the basic tenets of successful green design insists on the integration of all project participants from the beginning. It is essential, therefore, that designers acquire a fundamental understanding of the principles of sustainability and then a thorough knowledge of the science and technology necessary to provide their clients with valid services and advice. Also, the aspiring green designer must realize that this field requires constant continuing education, for there is always something new to learn. Designers should take advantage of any professional learning opportunity possible, as well as subscribe to one—or all—of the environmental news services (such as Environmental News Network, Green@Work Today, Green Biz, Green Buzz, and GreenClips, or set up a "green buildings" Google alert) to get a big-picture view of current environmental events and happenings. Those who do so will reap market advantage benefits.

## Reluctance to Change

Humans tend to prefer the comfort associated with familiarity, and so often we find it difficult to deviate from our established practices, especially if there's risk involved. It is safer to write specifications from the boilerplate models we've used for years than it is to experiment with newer ones. We are less anxious about specifying tried and true products and technologies versus testing those that are newer and more ecologically responsible. Reluctance to change is rampant among a number of professionals and in a variety of fields. For example, designers have oftentimes seen their specifications disregarded by contractors who, through fear or ignorance, refuse to consider the greener process or product.

aged furnishings to the landfill, rather than to refinishers; discarding used inkjet and toner cartridges, rather than returning them to the manufacturer or bringing them to a recycler to be refilled. Yet each of these seemingly small actions can, when considered collectively, have significant ecological repercussions.

## Special Interests

The mission of a trade association is to protect and promote the industry it represents. For the most part, trade associations can be useful resources for design practitioners looking for technical data. However, some trade associations' primary role is that of lobbyist, pressuring legislators to act in ways that are self-serving to the industry, yet perhaps contrary to ethical practice. As a result, regulations are written that are too lax or compliance measures are softened in order to boost the sales of trade association members. For those individuals who are uneducated about the many facets and issues impacting a particular industry, it's often difficult to distinguish fact from fiction.

## Lack of Standards, Guidelines, and Consensus

During many of the earliest years of the green building movement, design practitioners operated somewhat blindly, learning what worked and what didn't as they experimented with various strategies and practices. This problem has subsided somewhat since the U.S. Green Building Council released LEED (Leadership in Energy and Environmental Design), its green building rating system, in 2000. However, LEED is a continuously evolving program, and even its developers admit that a significant number of unresolved issues exist. Two controversial topics include the measurement of emissions from furniture and the debate over the toxicity of polyvinyl chloride (PVC). Experts are also wrestling with ways to best incorporate life cycle analysis (LCA) into materials selection. While there is widespread agreement that LCA is an essential tool in evaluating the ecology of a product, reaching consensus on how to frame the protocol has proved difficult. (See Chapters 4 and 6 for more information on this topic.)

> "Regardless of how efficiently we use resources, if design doesn't inspire people, it will not last. If we get it right, sustainable design promises to bring art and science together."
>
> —Lance Hosey, co-chair, Architecture of Sustainability conference

## Aesthetics

Remember the days when "green design" meant "homegrown and dull"? Green designers everywhere are celebrating the fact that this obstacle to sustainability from years past has largely disappeared. It would be difficult to find more beautiful projects than the ones featured in this book's case study section. Recognizing the growing interest in creating green interiors that delight and inspire, manufacturers have climbed aboard the sustainable product development train, providing designers with a plethora of stunning choices in furnishings and finishes. (See Chapter 4 for a review of some interesting choices currently available.)

## Budget and Time Constraints

The argument that "green design costs too much and takes too long" has been made so often that it's almost become a mantra. While it does contain kernels of truth (green design is a discipline to be learned), once it is mastered it becomes second nature, and with use it develops into an exciting and immensely valuable skill. Though intimidating at the beginning, the process of researching a product's environmental properties, of learning the fundamentals of energy-efficient technologies and querying manufacturers about their environmental performance are truly rewarding intellectual pursuits.

Some clients also balk at the costs associated with certifying their buildings according to the LEED Green Building Rating System. Experienced firms have found successful ways to deal with the cost arguments. TVS Interiors, for example, charges one fee for design and a separate fee for the LEED certification process to cover the costs associated with coordinating meetings, tracking, documentation, and third-party certification. TVS clients can also choose from one of three levels of professional green guidance:

- The Design Level is standard on each project, ensuring that project designers are educated in sustainable design practices, and providing a program of project quality assurance in design, technology, and business.
- The Reach Level incorporates higher sustainable design initiatives that are appropriate to the basic project parameters, including project cost. Projects may be

# Experience Makes a Difference

A 2004 survey of construction executives by Turner Construction indicates that the more experience an organization has with green buildings, the more effective and cost-efficient they become, according to Rod Wille, senior vice president, manager of sustainable construction, Turner Construction Co. For example, Turner Construction reports that roughly three-quarters of executives at organizations involved with green buildings said that these buildings generated a higher return on investment (ROI) than other buildings, while only 47 percent of executives lacking direct experience with green buildings believed that green buildings generate increased ROI.

Another gap reported by Turner existed among executives at organizations involved with green buildings: 65 percent of executives involved with six or more green buildings said the residents or occupants of green buildings enjoy much greater health and well-being, compared to 49 percent of executives involved with three to five green buildings and 39 percent of executives involved with only one or two green buildings.

"With many decision-makers, a near-term cost bias often overshadows the reduced long-term operating expenses due to energy efficiency, labor productivity, occupant wellness and the resulting decrease in liability that are apparent in a lifecycle cost analysis for a green building project," Wille said.

According to the survey findings, "executives at firms involved with more green buildings were far more likely to report that ongoing costs of green buildings were much lower than those of nongreen buildings. Thirty-six percent of executives at organizations with six or more green buildings said that

green buildings have much lower operating costs, compared to 19 percent of those at organizations involved with only one or two green buildings. Of those executives most actively involved with green buildings, 37 percent said that ten-year costs are much lower, compared to 18 percent of organizations involved with only one or two green buildings."

"The survey uncovers a misperception about the initial costs of green buildings on behalf of the inexperienced," said Wille. "Executives who have little or no experience working with green buildings believe up-front costs are higher, ROI is farther into the future, and energy and natural resource savings are lower. Beyond these measures, many underestimate the human reactions to these projects—that is, productivity enhancements, higher occupancy rates and asking rents, and increased retail sales."

Turner Construction also reported that a comparison of the perceptions among executives with experience in green buildings versus those who have not worked with green buildings shows that while many benefits are understood, the extent to which they affect the bottom line is not. "Although a February 2003 USGBC white paper says that LEED certification can be achieved with as little as 2 percent premium, executives involved in green buildings on average estimated green construction costs to be 14 percent higher, while executives not involved with green buildings estimated construction costs at 20 percent higher," noted the survey results, adding, "still, 80 percent or more of each group believed that green buildings repay these perceived higher construction costs through lower operating costs and other benefits."

*Source:* Turner Green Building Survey, September 15, 2004. Turner Construction, www.turnerconstruction.com.

guided by a specific LEED certification level, although formal LEED certification does not have to be pursued. (Some clients choose to spend the funds related to LEED certification on project-related improvements instead.) Every project contracted under this level is reviewed by members of the TVS Sustainable Design Committee.

■ The LEED Level ensures the project will reach a predetermined level of LEED certification. Projects designed according to this level require greater design integration and carry some first-cost impacts, including additional design services.

## Functional Limitations

Some materials perform beautifully but are so dangerous they should never be used. One of the most well-known examples is asbestos. Another is PVC, which is especially problematic in the interior furnishings field because designers, accustomed to specifying vinyl flooring, furnishings, and window treatments, struggle to find practicable alternatives. It can be done, however, as many progressive practitioners have succeeded in installing PVC-free projects without compromising either quality or performance. (The analysis of life cycle assessments in Chapter 4 provides background information on methods for investigating alternative product choices.)

## Apathy and Denial

Despite a growing public awareness of some of the most pressing global environmental concerns (the world is getting warmer, potable water is becoming scarce, species are being lost at an alarming rate, and resources are being depleted), some people steadfastly refuse to believe what documented science is reporting. Equally troubling are those who recognize that our planet is in trouble but refuse to take ownership of the problem, preferring instead to assign blame to someone else. Unfortunately, for every designer who is careful to specify only certified wood, many others continue to use endangered tropical hardwoods for furniture and flooring in order to satisfy their self-centered personal gratification.

# ■ The Integrated Profession

So . . . you've made the personal decision to pursue the path of green design. In a perfect world, getting the rest of your firm's colleagues on board would be an easy task. However, communicating the personal convictions that led you to this decision might easily sway one or two others, but most likely not all. What's needed is a commitment from firm management. Small firms might hesitate to take a chance on pursuing green design, reluctant to commit the time and financial resources necessary to bring staff up to speed on the topic. Larger firms, though better able to devote the resources necessary to pursue green design opportunities, might be hindered by top management reluctance or bureaucracy to make inroads into this field. Ken Wilson founded his architectural and interiors firm along with his partner, Diana Horvath, to include environmental accountability as part of its core mission. In the following essay, he offers a number of insights into how best to green your design firm.

### Integrating Sustainability into Your Design Practice

By Kendall P. Wilson

*The sustainable design movement has arguably had a greater effect on the design community than any other trend in our lifetime. It has caused us to question the effects of our work on both humanity and our natural environment. Evidence of our negative impact on the ecosystem is indisputable, and slowly the world is recognizing that we have the ability to change our course. We are learning that there is a better way to live and do business—and there is a better way to design.*

*Design firms are making a shift toward integrated sustainable approaches for numerous reasons—many because they are looking to differentiate their services or are trying to keep pace with current trends, and some because they know it is the right thing to do. Enlightened clients are asking for green design, and* many are even seeking LEED certification—especially institutional clients. Design firms need to be able to respond if they are going to keep pace with the times.

In order to successfully integrate sustainable thinking into a design practice, change must start with a commitment from the top people in an organization. Sustainability should never be viewed as an add-on service, but rather should be integrated into the firm's overall design philosophy in order to be successful. Consider the idea of designing some projects that are handicapped-accessible and some projects that are not—it just doesn't make sense. Neither does designing some projects that are ecofriendly and some that are harmful to people and our ecosystem. As designers of the built environment, we have an obligation to design for the health and well-being of people; this notion needs to extend to our effect on the natural environment as well.

Although young designers seem to exude universal enthusiasm for sustainable design, they cannot be relied upon to lead the change toward sustainable practices within a firm. Successful integration of sustainable design must start with an honest commitment from the firm's leadership. Firm leaders, in turn, must understand and appreciate the benefits in order to promote a real shift in thinking.

In the design profession, learning comes from doing. One of the best ways to promote a change toward sustainable design within your firm is to find a client who wants to build a green project. This isn't as hard as it sounds—and the best opportunities may come from a repeat client. A repeat client already has your trust and knows you have their best interests in mind. I ask clients, "If I could show you a way to design a space that is filled with natural light, doesn't off-gas harmful chemicals, provides improved indoor air quality, reduces energy costs, aids in the recruitment of new staff, and increases your productivity, would you be willing to consider it?" The answer should be a no-brainer—and I didn't even mention the word Sustainability.

Firm personnel responsible for marketing need to understand sustainable design and be able to explain it to their clients. Bringing in the recently LEED-accredited intern to do the job will not instill much confidence. Clients want to know that firm principals think sustainability is a good idea and that they are committed to delivering a successfully integrated design.

As with the learning curve required in taking on any unfamiliar project type, additional time and effort needs to be accounted for in getting up to speed on green design. Think of it as an investment in a whole new area of market differentiation for your firm. Whereas individual efforts to learn green practices should be recognized and applauded, design firms seeking substantive change need to make a firm-wide commitment. If not, the self-taught brain trust of environmental expertise may end up walking out the door in favor of a firm with an honest commitment. Making a financial commitment to office-wide professional development programs about sustainable design will be necessary.

Project managers and specification writers must learn to change old procedures and processes with the understanding that it is principal-driven. Attendance at one of the many green design conferences now offered is a good first step, especially the Greenbuild conference held annually in November. Regional USGBC chapters are also a great source for events and learning opportunities that are close to home.

Promoting LEED accreditation is also an excellent way to get your staff up to speed. Passing the LEED exam requires a basic understanding of green building practices as well as knowledge about the LEED rating system. Your staff will need a copy of the appropriate LEED Reference Guide as a study tool, and attendance at a USGBC-sponsored LEED seminar will be beneficial. Consider covering the cost of the LEED exam as both a firm benefit and a way to encourage professional development. Creating an incentive is also helpful. One suggestion is to send staff to Greenbuild or some other green building conference as a reward for achieving LEED accreditation.

Although it is tempting to give the next sustainable project to the same group that just finished

## TEN WAYS TO INTEGRATE SUSTAINABLE PRACTICES INTO YOUR DESIGN FIRM

1. Don't consider sustainable design as an add-on service. Incorporate equal- or low-cost sustainable design strategies in all projects. Sell other sustainable design strategies based on value or a return on investment over time.

2. Promote green professional development through membership and participation in organizations that promote green building, such as the American Institute of Architects (AIA), the International Interior Design Association (IIDA), the American Society of Interior Designers (ASID), and the USGBC. Encourage staff participation in events and on committees.

3. Commit to sustainable design practices from the top down. Agree that the principals should be the first to achieve LEED accreditation, thereby setting an example for the rest of the staff.

4. Promote LEED accreditation to the staff by paying for the LEED exam, and reward staff members who achieve LEED accreditation by sending them to green building conferences.

5. Seek out a green project or convince an established client to incorporate green strategies into a new project.

6. Commit to additional time researching green products and designate a file cabinet or shelf to green materials in your library.

7. Invite manufacturers of green products to give lunchtime presentations. Encourage staff to challenge questionable environmental claims.

8. Select consultants that have demonstrated a commitment to sustainable design and integrate them into the design process early.

9. Subscribe to magazines or newsletters that focus on green design.

10. Think about how you run your own life and what you can do personally to change bad habits and be more environmentally friendly. You may not live in an area that has easy access to public transportation, but you could consider buying a fuel-efficient hybrid when the lease runs out on your Chevy Tahoe.

your first one, try very hard to pass these projects around to other staff members. It is important for staff to understand that everyone needs experience in this area and that no one can avoid changing bad habits out of convenience. It is especially important to rotate projects seeking LEED certification. More-experienced staff can certainly coach the novice staff and help them with lessons learned on previous projects. Whether you are LEED accredited or feel you are very familiar with the LEED rating system, there is no substitute for actually going through the process.

Once you have, you will never think the same way about another project. The goal is to have all your staff thinking this way.

Firm leadership needs to work at keeping sustainable design in the forefront of the firm's mind-set and culture in order to maintain momentum and prevent slipping back into the old ways of thinking. New products need to be evaluated based on their environmental impact as well as their functionality and cost. Regular in-house professional development meetings are a good way to share knowledge. These meetings *can be focused on a particular project or can be a general review of new green products coming on the market. Staff members should be encouraged to ask tough questions of manufacturers and filter out any "greenwash."*

*Design can be considered the combination of beauty and functionality, and the measure of functionality can be defined as how well programmatic requirements are met. In addition to operational efficiency, durability, image, and value; programmatic requirements also need to include consideration for environmental impact and human well-being as well. For a project to be considered good design, it still needs to be beautiful. The saying "Easy things have the greatest chance of being mediocre and hard things have the greatest chance of excellence" is a way of describing that the greater the challenge, the better the results.*

*Ultimately, practicing sustainable design is about leadership. It is about taking the high road and doing what is right for the community and the natural environment instead of acquiescing to the old way of designing. It is about educating clients to alternative strategies that provide return on investment for their companies and organizations. And it is about designing in ways that improve human well-being. Isn't that the way we all want to run our firms?*

Ken Wilson is a founding principal of Envision Design, an award-winning Washington, D.C.–based multidisciplinary design firm with a focus on sustainable design.

Nearly every major design firm in the United States is now actively seeking to develop green capabilities, reports the May 2004 issue of *Environmental Building News,* especially in market sectors such as science and education, where demand from clients is the greatest.[10] Transforming firms that think conventionally into big-picture thinkers, however, requires that "change has to take place within a firm both from the bottom up and from the top down," the article notes. As a result, firms are employing a range of actions (some project-specific, others more general in nature) to gain green design capabilities (see Table 1-1).

All, however, are intended to accomplish one or more of four things to promote the implementation of green design:

- Inspire and motivate designers
- Disseminate the information designers must know
- Provide the skills designers must have
- Change processes to improve support for integrated design

What the action plans indicate, notes the article's authors, is that there's no single right way to green a design firm: "Different actions are appropriate for different settings, and at different stages in each company's evolution."

*"As much as a tenth of the global economy is dedicated to buildings: to construction, operating, and equipping our built environment."*

—Worldwatch Institute

It has been estimated by the EPA that 80 percent of all buildings that will be standing worldwide thirty years from now have not yet been built. Whether or not this projection is true, the implications are clear: buildings of all types need to begin to address resource use and depletion, human health implications, and global consequences. Home builders, home owners, and the developers, managers, and tenants of commercial buildings will turn to the design professional for guidance and expertise. More and more architects, engineers, and interior designers are realizing the business advantages of marketing green design strategies.

Traditionally projects have operated on a linear model, with the architectural/engineering and interior design work occurring sequentially rather than as a fully integrated team approach in which all those involved understand, at least in concept, each other's contributions to the design and construction process. Mechanical engineers will continue to retain the primary responsibility for heating and cooling, for example, but if interior designers are going to retain their relevance as green buildings proliferate, they are going to have to become familiar with the impact of their decisions upon the "greenness" of the project, and vice versa. To do otherwise results in a lack of coordination,

## TABLE 1-1: Survey Results: Actions for Greening a Design Firm

| Action | % of Firms for Which a Focus[1] | Self-Reported Value[2] | Cost in Time (hrs/month[3]) | Cost in Dollars ($/year[3]) | Comments |
|---|---|---|---|---|---|
| **GREEN TEAM** | | | | | |
| Organize a green team | 65% | very high | 35 | $6,238 | Very common, especially at firms with many offices, as a way of sharing resources and approaches |
| Publish in-house newsletter | 35% | high | 4 | – | Common at largest firms but too time-consuming for others |
| Offer internal consulting to projects | 65% | moderate | 40 | – | Most useful when an element of training is explicitly included |
| **TRAINING AND EDUCATION** | | | | | |
| Provide regular education sessions in the office | 88% | very high | 32 | $7,475 | Often provided at no cost by consultants who are working with the firm on a project |
| Host regular presentations by green vendors | 59% | moderate | 32 | – | Vendors typically provide lunch, and those that bring the best food get the best attendance! |
| Support and encourage training | 59% | very high | 30 | $6,190 | Everyone recognizes that training is essential, but it's expensive. The best support is in firms with strong buy-in from management. |
| Support conference attendance | 82% | very high | 12 | $5,257 | High value for promoting motivation and knowledge, but expensive. Clever green teams are investing in their future by sending their bosses to conferences. |
| Pursue research funded by outside entities | 29% | very high | 30 | – | A huge opportunity to gain knowledge and skills at little cost (even at a profit!). Funding sources vary by state and region. |
| **INFORMATION MANAGEMENT** | | | | | |
| Hire a green-focused librarian | 47% | moderate | – | – | Seems to happen more by chance and personal inclination than by design |
| Maintain a library of in-house research | 29% | very high | 19 | – | – – – |
| Make a firm-wide effort to green in-house specs | 59% | high | 20 | – | Nearly all firms with a strong in-house specification system are working on greening that spec. Others are relying on outside spec-writers or on ARCOM's greening efforts with MasterSpec™. |
| **TOOLS FOR GREENING** | | | | | |
| Provide information and modeling tools | 47% | moderate | – | $2,200 | Providing tools company-wide helps develop a shared set of language, concepts, and metrics. |
| Use information and modeling tools widely | 29% | very high | – | – | Getting busy designers to use new tools is a challenge. |
| **EXPERTISE FROM THE OUTSIDE** | | | | | |
| Give green champion input on new hires | 24% | high | 3 | – | Green team members rarely have the opportunity to influence hiring on the basis of their green interests. |
| Cultivate relationships with capable consultants | 47% | very high | 3 | – | Consultants' attitudes and abilities can make or break a project. Those who are strong in sustainable design can help bring a less-advanced in-house team along as well. |
| **GREEN PROJECT GOALS** | | | | | |
| Use LEED as a goal-setting tool with clients | 71% | high | 2 | – | More and more firms are introducing LEED as a goal-setting tool, even when clients don't ask for it. |
| Conduct an internal LEED review of all projects | 35% | high | – | – | LEED self-assessments can be overly optimistic. |
| Start with a green intent for all projects | 35% | very high | 10 | – | A green intent that diverges from LEED can be useful to focus a team. |

Notes: 1. Indicates percent of firms for which this is a focused effort, not just something that happens casually (based on data set of 20).
2. Self-reported value among firms that focus on this action.
3. Amount spent in time (labor hours per month) and direct expense (dollars per year) by firms that focus on this action, based on data from those firms that were able to provide an estimate, normalized to a hypothetical 100-person firm.

Source: Nadav Malin and Jim Newman, "Greening Your Firm: Building Sustainable Design Capabilities," *Environmental Building News*, May 2004.

duplication of efforts, and cost overruns, and jeopardizes the environmental integrity of project.

Just how critical is the concept of an integrated design team to the sustainable design process? According to veteran green building consultant Bill Reed, it is absolutely essential.

## Integrated Design

### By Bill Reed

*In case you hadn't heard, the age of specialization is dead. Or more accurately, the age of disconnected specialization is dead. After 150 years, the pattern of isolated thought processes and activities that have typified the industrial era have reached a wall of unavoidable consequence—no natural system or human activity can be considered apart from any other. Everything is connected; everything and everyone are in some kind of relationship with everything else. The growing awareness of these interrelationships has led to a different way of designing buildings and the spaces within, seeing them as systems and subsystems embedded in larger systems. This has led to a much more integrated design process. Hence the term: Integrated Design.*

*The industrial age has been an era in which humankind has generated so much information that no one person can hold it all, even in a specific area of expertise. Certainly we can't fully understand the consequences of the interactions between, for instance, resource extraction, energy production, manufacturing, agricultural systems, transportation, land development, social systems, economic systems, and, ultimately, the impact of all these on our life support system: nature.*

*In all of society, and specifically at all levels of the building industry, we find ourselves attempting to address these complex interrelationships with inadequate knowledge and fragmented management approaches—holdovers from an era when we assumed that a simple cause and effect existed for every activity in which we were engaged.*

*We can look to what we presume to be a simpler past to understand the kind of connected thinking we need to embrace as we move into a more complex future. Before the industrial revolution our buildings and communities were built through a different process. Local resources, both natural and human, were the basis for what was designed and built. Master builders were primarily responsible for the built environment. They designed and built based on their understanding of local issues. Their intimate knowledge of local materials, workforce skills, economy, culture, and traditions, as well as conditions such as microclimates and soil conditions, enabled them to produce buildings and communities that were truly integrated with their environment. These are buildings that lived and breathed and became a timeless part of their place; buildings and communities that we often envy today and even use as inspiration to build theme parks in order to capture some hint of that life and quality.*

*The industrial age resulted in the loss of the "management structure" of the master builder. Things became too complex and too dynamic. Resources could come from anywhere as new materials and technologies were rapidly and continuously introduced. Specialists were needed to resolve and implement the complex aspects of electricity, lighting, ergonomics, municipal waste systems, automatic climate control, "smart" buildings, et cetera. Where once we had one mind internalizing and integrating local building issues, now we have anywhere from dozens to several hundred companies/organizations or individuals involved in designing and making decisions on issues ranging from zoning policy to stormwater management, building product design, energy efficiency, construction methods, ergonomics, and so on. We have moved from a time of common sense integration to a century of it's-not-my-job disintegration.*

*How do we shift to a process that will result in better integrative and sustainable design? To realize any movement toward a sustainable condition requires change—change from the conventional*

## THE BASIC ELEMENTS OF INTEGRATED DESIGN

The following is a list of the essential aspects of an effective integrative design process.

1. Client (main decision maker) involvement in the design decision process

2. Selection of the right design team (attitude is critical—i.e., teachable)

3. Alignment of expectations and purposes between the stakeholders and design team

4. Setting the targeted environmental goals (if you can't measure it, you can't manage it)

5. Identify champions or a core team (to hold these goals through the project)

6. Optimization of the design of systems (using evaluation tools and an iterative process in predesign and schematic design—after this it can get expensive to add green technologies to a project that wasn't designed with these in mind from the beginning)

7. Follow-through in the construction process

8. Commissioning of the project (making sure it performs the way it was designed to perform—just because it's built doesn't mean it works)

9. Maintenance and monitoring (entropy happens—feedback is essential to maintain performance)

way of thinking and doing things. As Albert Einstein said, "Problems cannot be solved at the same level of awareness that created them."

Moving toward sustainability means that we need to move toward more complex system awareness. This way of approaching problems helps us address and make use of many more issues and systems than we typically address when working within a conventional framework.

For example, a conventional design process will have the interior designer create a space to meet typical functional and aesthetic requirements. The interior designer then sends the design to the mechanical and electrical engineer to make it comfortable and provide adequate light. Just as often, the designed space will be sent to the interior designers, who are expected to conform to what the architects/mechanical, electrical, plumbing engineers (MEPs) already have in place. In a systems design process—an integrative design process—the engineers, interior designer, and client are programming and designing the spaces in a joint manner from the very beginning. Instead of simply adding more efficient lighting and

comfort equipment to the space or building (which alone can be costly), the engineer may alert the designer that a more appropriate functional layout of the offices or activities in the space relative to daylighting opportunities may save more energy than any level of equipment efficiency. Integrated decisions usually decrease the cost of the building while increasing its environmental performance.

We might go even deeper than the immediate technical issues of space design. We can make more informed choices by understanding upstream and downstream system ramifications resulting from what we specify. To get a general impression of a particular practice or product—whether its use is more or less sustainable than some alternative—we need to lift our heads out of our immediate sphere of action. This requires that we follow the implications of the practice or product logically. What was needed to produce this product? What happens to it after you're done using it? For example, consider where water comes from: rain. Can you drink the rain? If the answer is yes, then why aren't you drinking it from your roof? If you can't drink the rain, from *where do you get water? A well? Where does the well get its water? The rain. If you can't drink the rain, what makes it clean in the well? The earth. What kind of earth is required to clean the water? Healthy earth. What makes the earth healthy? Habitat does: microbes, animals, plants in healthy diversity. So it seems we need habitat to create fresh water. Not many of us think of this when we have readily available tap water, but this is a critical relationship that we ignore at the expense of fresh water for our future. How do our material choices and transport methods impact fresh water? How does the manufacturer address habitat health in the sourcing of materials and through reducing its manufacturing footprint?*

*While most designers and engineers believe they are "systems designers" by the nature of their work in delivering complex program solutions, they usually are not. Sustainable design requires a different mindset or mental model. This model is able to look at systems in a more complex way. Instead of looking at just the physical elements of the building and the furniture, furnishings, and equipment, the invisible connections between the elements need to be understood. These invisible connections and patterns, for example, may be manifest in the downstream impact of toxins in building materials, the multiple efficiency and cost relationships between the many variables in an HVAC system, daylighting and the building envelope, or the impact on social systems due to logging practices or other raw material extraction. This level of analysis requires a rigorous level of enthusiastic and early engagement from the participants and an understanding of tools used to make these evaluations. Since no one has all of this knowledge themselves, the role of the team takes on great importance; the role of questioning assumptions takes on an equal importance in order to elicit answers beyond the conventional.*

*For teams to embrace this process a different mind-set is required, one that has the desire to change the way things are done. A mental model that is open and willing drives the successful integration of green design.*

*A systems approach requires a collaborative approach. Yet the very strength of the integrative approach has in it a potential weakness, for it depends on collaboration from the key players— client, architect, engineers, interior designers, landscape architects. Fostering and working within a collaborative framework is hard because we have been trained to be "experts." The client expects it, and the design team members feel they need to exhibit it.*

*It is necessary to move from being "experts" to being co-learners. The basis of a systems approach is the establishment of a network of mutual learning. Sustainability expert and architect John Boecker has observed that no one person can know all the issues that need to be addressed; collective knowledge is far greater than individual knowledge. As Carol Franklin of the ecological landscape design firm Andropogon says, "To design ecosystems we need to deal with ego-systems."*

*By far, most successful green projects (i.e., projects that achieved the high environmental goals they originally set out to achieve, within budget) have done so not because of adding technology and products to the building, but because the design team members had the willingness to focus on the environmental issues— the invisible and critical connections—as essential to the success of the design. They had the willingness to ask many questions about the potential beneficial relationships between all the systems in the building, interiors, site, and region and explore the many different ways to reach toward better ecological integration. The environmental concerns were not secondary, nor were they dominant—they were just an integral part of the design. The usual "right" answers were never assumed and they were always questioned.*

*It is the role of the client, should they wish to reach toward cost-effective sustainable building solutions, to select design teams (or green building experts) with expertise in integrative design and the design process to optimize systems in a cost effective manner. Even more important than green expertise, however, is the willingness or attitude of the design team to learn new ways of looking at systems and the willingness to change their design process.*

*The process to incorporate sustainable thinking in any project is really not that difficult. The difficulty is accepting that the older conventional practices need to be reconsidered. Change is hard for humans. It is the process of changing that is actually the most exciting aspect of reaching toward sustainability. The technologies will always be improving in sometimes subtle and sometimes significant leaps. When we build in a sustainable manner it is the change of perspective, the change of heart, and a fundamental reawakening of an awareness of our relationships to the systems of life that makes all this worthwhile.*

An internationally recognized specialist in issues related to green design, Reed is the principal of the Integrative Design Collaborative and an ally of the strategic environmental planning firm Natural Logic and the regenerative planning firm Regenesis.

# ■ The Design Charrette

The process for beginning a design project has become somewhat standardized, proceeding rather predictably from programming and data collection to the design and construction phases. Goal setting, if included, is often perfunctory. What's missing from this traditional process is the opportunity for true creativity and innovation on a level that can yield extraordinary results such as those achieved by the Chesapeake Bay Foundation headquarters in Annapolis, Maryland, and the Interface Carpet showroom in Atlanta—both LEED Platinum certified projects.

In the fledgling green design arena, standard practices are likely to preclude the types of relationships and synergies necessary for incorporating sustainable thinking. As Bill Reed states in his essay, incorporating sustainable thinking on a project is not difficult. The difficulty is in accepting that older, conventional practices need to be reconsidered. One of the surest ways to step away from traditional thinking and achieve green design excellence is to begin the process with a charrette—an intensive planning session where the design team collaborates on a vision for the project.

> *"The term 'charrette' is adopted from the storied practice of Ecole des Beaux Arts architectural students in nineteenth century Paris who reputedly could be seen still drawing their projects until the last minute as they were carried on the 'cart' or en charrette on the way to the design jury."*
>
> —AIA Committee on the Environment (COTE)

A good way to describe a charrette is as a fast-paced work session for group brainstorming. Its value lies in the charrette's ability to compress the amount of time needed to arrive at consensus by bringing together disjointed information. It reduces redundancies and the probability of unforeseen results, increasing the likelihood of the project's success. The role of the team is critical, as is listening to each team member to establish trust and to more easily reach agreement. The charrette's success is based on the ability of the team to work together toward goals determined by all participants.

The exercise can be used for any type of project; when the focus is on sustainability, the term *eco-charrette* may be applied. All disciplines should be represented, although they do not necessarily have to be on the team that will eventually design the project. Depending on the type of project, charrette participants may include the client, broker, community representative, building owner, architect, facility manager, contractor, interior designer, MEP engineers, lighting consultant, product suppliers, code officials, commissioning agent, and landscape architect—in other words, anyone who may contribute unique and valuable knowledge to inform the outcome of the exercise.

Although it is essential to involve as many disciplines as possible, it is equally important to make sure that the participants have the necessary knowledge and experience to contribute positively to the outcome. Charrettes can be intellectually demanding and physically exhausting exercises under the best of circumstances; the importance of selecting the right team cannot be overemphasized.

David Nelson, an architect and lighting designer and a participant in many charrettes, differentiates between the

The Philip Merrill Environmental Center, headquarters of the Chesapeake Bay Foundation, was the first project to receive a LEED-NC Platinum certification. © 2005, Loretta C. Jergensen, Chesapeake Bay Foundation

The Interface Carpet Showroom in Atlanta was the first project to receive a LEED-CI Platinum certification. *Photography courtesy of Brian Gassel, TVS*

*design charrette,* a one-day intensive exercise to discuss broad issues and concepts, and a longer *building design charrette,* which is more detailed and in-depth. The first exercise may identify some opportunities for a client that will be further fleshed out during the subsequent meeting. The value of this two-stage process is to allow ideas to be digested before any substantial investment is made in design time or fees.

Charrettes may evolve in different ways, but Nelson provides some common strategies that have proven successful.

■ Convene team-building opportunities, prior to the actual meeting, to establish relationships and understandings, perhaps via e-mail "conferences" or at a social gathering the evening before.

- Begin the charrette with a show-and-tell introducing some of the sustainable concepts that may be considered.
- Form focus groups of individuals with complementary skills to work on developing goals and strategies. Encourage cross-pollination and movement between the groups.
- Reconvene to share ideas and develop integrated strategies.

Nelson advises to be wary of some common pitfalls such as forming quick opinions and cherry-picking the easy and obvious solutions (although they may be what the client wants to hear). Ultimately, better results will be obtained by pushing the concepts further. Buildings or interior spaces will not be completely designed in the course of one charrette, but a road map may be created that will guide the project through to completion.[11]

# Taking the Mystery Out of Commissioning

Commissioning is the least understood yet potentially most valuable green building strategy to be added to the design and construction process. It ensures that the building mechanical, electrical, and plumbing systems are installed and operate as the designers intended. The commissioning agent inspects and tests during the design and construction phases, which makes it far easier and less expensive to find and correct errors than it would by waiting until the project is completed.

Commissioning agents charge for their services—costs will vary depending on the size of the project and what systems are included—but commissioning *always* results in energy and/or construction savings and may help avoid liability exposure. Consider, for example, a situation where a contractor incorrectly installs a damper that obstructs air passage through a duct. A commissioning agent doing field testing prior to drywall installation will catch the error when corrective measures are inexpensive. Had the walls been closed in, the mistake might not have been discovered until the occupants started complaining of being too

## An Actual Charrette Case Study

Here is an example of the factors at play in an actual project and of how the presence of key players in one room at one time in a charrette fostered rapid communication and decision making.

- The *client* wanted to optimize use of natural light in the new office building and contain costs.
- The *architect* proposed high-performance glazing for the windows to maximize light coming into the building and control heat loss.
- The *electrical engineer* suggested using fluorescent lamps with light sensors to modulate the electric light in proportion to available natural light, and then proceeded to calculate the annual savings.
- The *contractor* surmised that the glazing and the lights with sensors would substantially increase the project budget.
- The *mechanical engineer* suggested smaller mechanical units because the building would be in a cooling mode most of the year and the electric light fixtures would be a source of heat.
- Quickly calculating the cost of the smaller mechanical units, the *contractor* determined that this integrated solution would reduce the total project cost.
- The *electrical utility representative* offered substantial rebates for the high-performance glass, energy-efficient light fixtures, and daylight sensors.
- The *owner* was delighted with this collaborative problem solving.

The result was a high-performance building at a lower cost, annual energy savings, and naturally lighted interior spaces for the building occupants.

*Source:* Contributed by Nathan Good, AIA, IIDA, Architect PC, Salem, Oregon. From "Eco-Charrettes Save Resources, Build Teams," January 2003, www.aia.org.

hot or cold. The investigation into the problem and the repair would then be far more costly, to say nothing of the loss of productivity from uncomfortable workers.

Commissioning agents are valuable additions to the integrated design team and should have a place at the charrette table to help develop and clarify system goals. Many recommend that the process begin as early in the project as possible. Karl Stum of Portland Energy Conservation, Inc. is quoted in an *Environmental Building News* article as saying, "Owners considering commissioning for the first time have more of a show-me attitude. Any owner who has done commissioning at some point during the construction phase will say, 'Next time we want to start sooner.'"[12]

Originally commissioning involved only HVAC systems, but it has expanded to include other building components such as water delivery, lighting, shell, structure, and even finishes. For that reason, commissioning has been placed here at the front of the book to put it into the context of whole-building thinking. Jay Enck, an experienced commissioning agent, presents in his essay a comprehensive look at the not-so-mysterious commissioning process.

## Commissioning the Interiors Project

### By Jay Enck

*Integrating sustainable development principles, including commissioning, can significantly improve the quality of life of building occupants. In the work environment quality of life is affected by our surroundings, including lighting, heating and air conditioning, ventilation, indoor air quality, thermal comfort, availability of daylight, views to the outside, and the aesthetics of the space. Compromises in these comfort parameters that define our indoor environment affect our productivity, feeling of well-being, enjoyment of our surroundings, and desire to return to that indoor environment day after day.*

*Designers focus on the nuts and bolts needed to create buildings. They listen to the owner's needs, define square footages and adjacencies of tasks within a building, select construction materials, and devel-*

*op construction documents that communicate the scope of the work to the contractor. The contractor then focuses on execution of the construction documents, obtaining the building materials, hiring the labor to construct the project, and focusing on schedule and budget. Unfortunately, this traditional method of developing a project has often resulted in failing to meet the owner's requirements and constructing long-term problems into buildings that result in poor energy efficiency and low indoor air quality. If occupants are uncomfortable, the results can be poor work performance, increased absenteeism, increased maintenance requests, and higher than normal tenant turnover. These problems lead to the need for commissioning.*

*Commissioning, a term coined by the U.S. Navy to describe a process that verified the performance of ships during sea trials, is now used to describe a process for verifying systems and assembly performance of the built environment. Commissioning was first applied to HVAC systems to improve performance and occupant comfort and has evolved to include most systems in the built environment, including but not limited to building envelope, electrical (including voice and data systems), security, fire protection, and so on.*

*The commissioning process as defined by the American Society of Heating, Refrigeration and Air Conditioning Engineers (ASHRAE) in Guideline 0 provides an outline of each of the elements that define the process and provides guidance for implementation. The commissioning process can provide significant benefit to project teams and owners wishing to integrate sustainable development principles and practices into their projects by helping avoid one of the main pitfalls of project teams: not defining the owner's project requirements early in the development process.*

*The success or failure of applying sustainable development principles to a project often hinges on good assessment of which sustainable development principles to apply. This requires documenting the owner's project requirements and the specific sustainable goals of the project. Failure to start out with a* clear vision for the project and its associated criteria typically results in redesign efforts, increased cost, lost opportunity, and marginal results. Project teams that do not start with a clear vision and experienced leadership in applying the sustainable development principles contained in LEED will have considerably increased difficulty and higher costs meeting the goals of a better work environment and LEED certification.

If the commissioning process is implemented in the predesign phase, it can significantly improve both the delivery process and reduce project cost. Developing the owner's project requirements (OPR) during the predesign phase of a project provides decision criteria for the sustainable development features being considered, establishes the project budget, defines the owner's needs and functional requirements, and forms a benchmark that the commissioning authority and owner can use to communicate to the design and construction team, thus avoiding wasted effort and spiraling costs.

Many sustainable development principles have economic returns and owners may elect to implement them based on both the cost and environmental benefits. LEED for Commercial Interiors (LEED-CI) provides strategies that owners and their teams should consider when building out an interior space. An example of this is water and sewer savings, which can be realized by implementing low-water-consumption toilets, waterless urinals, and low-flow lavatory faucets in lieu of standard plumbing fixtures. In a recent project in Atlanta, the owner is saving 4.4 million gallons and $53,781 per year by implementing water-efficient plumbing fixtures. Collecting rainwater to displace potable water used for flushing toilets on this project saved an additional 1.8 million gallons and $14,072 per year, resulting in an annual total savings of $67,853 with a 1.6-year simple return on investment.

Projects implementing sustainable development principles should compare financial savings and environmental benefits when defining OPR. Many project teams become focused on the credits and miss the intent of sustainable development and the LEED rating system. This misunderstanding results in projects "buying" credits in lieu of integrating good sustainable design—a practice that prevents owners from reducing the total cost of ownership and can result in owners and their project teams becoming disenchanted with the concept of sustainable development. Investing in higher efficiency or other sustainable principles such as underfloor air distribution without verification of performance can lead to higher costs and lower returns.

LEED certification is easy enough to attain with a small investment, typically from 0.7 to 1.5 percent of the construction cost, including hard and soft expenditures such as the sustainable development consultant, commissioning, and LEED documentation, and most improvements evolving from integrating sustainable development principles. The selection of commissioning providers who are also experienced sustainability consultants provides a synergy that can lower costs. This strategy during construction also helps the contractor because the commissioning provider can identify problems relative to implementing sustainable development principles such as construction IAQ and construction waste management.

Commissioning a performance verification process focuses on verifying the owner's project requirements, the design team's basis of design and design intent, the contractor's interpretation of the contract documents, the building operator's understanding of the systems, and the performance of commissioned systems. Commissioning supplements the design team's efforts to understand the owner's requirements and needs and the contractor's quality assurance practices, which in turn results in better quality, fewer problems, improved quality of life for the occupants, lower operating costs, and increased financial return. Commissioning can lower project risk, reduce misunderstandings between team members, improve project efficiency, and identify problems early while the team is fully engaged.

Design phase commissioning (Dx) provides the project a second pair of eyes to identify problems when they are easiest to fix. Dx also helps with coordination between disciplines and delivers better con-

*struction documents that provide more concise instructions to the contractor and result in tighter bids. Using the OPR, the commissioning provider can compare the needs, requirements, and sustainable goals to the design team's documents and help identify disconnects or misinterpretations so that the team as a whole can address these issues and implement course correction if necessary.*

*Construction phase commissioning can identify installation, serviceability, and operational problems early in the construction process and bring these problems to the team for a timely resolution. Teams can efficiently develop solutions to issues the commissioning process identifies while they are still engaged and all materials and equipment are on site, improving the development and subsequent operation and maintenance efficiency of the facility. The commissioning process can also identify compromises in construction practices and installation schedules that would impact current and future building occupants. Areas of occupied buildings under construction can and often do affect the occupied areas. Implementing a construction indoor air quality plan monitored by the contractor and commissioning*

*authority can significantly reduce the impact on adjacent occupied spaces or, for new construction, the building as a whole.*

*Most commercial and institutional projects significantly benefit from commissioning by reducing or eliminating disturbances to the occupants as well as the tenant's administrative time typically associated with leftover construction problems, nonperformance of systems, and uncomfortable conditions. These typical problems affect occupant comfort and productivity, the perception of well-being, indoor environmental quality, and energy consumption. Occupants who are uncomfortable in their indoor environment will spend time blocking supply air registers and installing and adjusting electric heaters, fans, and filtration systems, and they will avoid being in their work areas. Commissioning helps to ensure that the money invested provides the desired results both financially and environmentally to benefit the business owner and occupants. It is money well spent.*

Jay Enck, the principal of Commissioning and Green Building Services (CxGBS), has conducted commissioning processes for over $1 billion in construction.

# 2

# GLOBAL ISSUES: AN OVERVIEW

I t is tempting to think about interior spaces separate and apart from the buildings that house them and the land that they sit on and the planet they inhabit. Interior designers have traditionally divorced themselves from the issues of land use and water and energy consumption. Even the use of materials and the interplay of conditions that define the indoor environment have been confined within the walls. As we learned in the preceding chapter, though, green interior design doesn't stop at the walls. The new paradigm requires that we think holistically as a member of not only a larger team, but of a larger world.

Context is important when grappling with global issues. The approaching—but largely ignored—worldwide water shortages and increasingly apparent climate changes will significantly impact our lives and the lives of our children. Collectively, as designers, our influence over these issues—how materials, land, water, and energy are used—is not insignificant. The green movement grows, it seems, not by huge leaps but by tiny steps taken by governments, corporations, and individuals. However, we cannot change what we do not know. A quick review of our global environment will reveal, in surprising ways, how the decisions we make in our personal and professional lives impact our global conditions.

# As the Earth Warms

In 1979, the National Academy of Sciences, at the request of then-president Jimmy Carter, convened a panel to study global warming. The conclusions of the Ad Hoc Study Group on Carbon Dioxide and Climate (which has since become known as the Charney panel, after its head, distinguished Massachusetts Institute of Technology meteorologist Jule Charney) were detailed in a comprehensive examination of climate change in a series of articles in the *New Yorker* in May 2005.[1] "If carbon dioxide continues to increase, the study group finds no reason to doubt that climate changes will result and no reason to believe that these changes will be negligible," the report concluded, and warned that it may be decades before evidence of warming is certain. Waiting, however, is risky, the panel noted. "We may not be given a warning until the $CO_2$ loading is such that an appreciable climate change is inevitable."

It has been twenty-five years since the Charney panel report, and thus far its predictions have proven true. Carbon dioxide ($CO_2$) emissions, the most significant of the greenhouse gases, have continued to increase, and the earth's temperature has steadily risen. From the *New Yorker* article: "Year 1990 was the warmest year on record until 1991, which was equally hot. Almost every subsequent year has been warmer still. The year 1998 ranks as the hottest year since the instrumental temperature record began, but it is closely followed by 2002 and 2003, which are tied for second; 2001, which is third; and 2004, which is fourth."[2]

Although there are some who attribute these temperature increases to natural fluctuations, the scientific evidence of global warming is unambiguous. Indicators such as a shrinking Arctic ice cap and unusually high ocean temperatures in the Gulf of Mexico clearly support the findings. "The American Geophysical Union, one of the nation's largest and most respected scientific organizations, decided in 2003 that the matter had been settled. At the group's

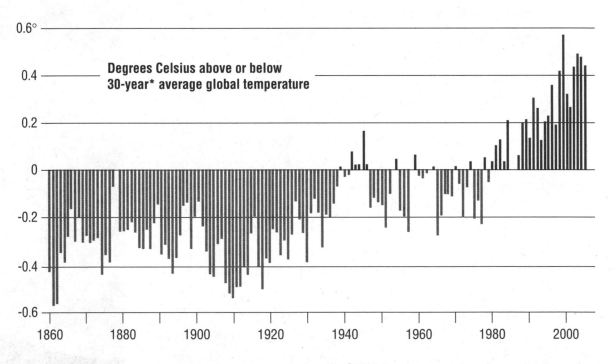

The planet has been experiencing a warming trend in recent decades. ©2005, The Washington Post. *Reprinted with permission*

annual meeting that year, it issued a consensus statement declaring, 'Natural influences cannot explain the rapid increase in global near-surface temperatures.' As best as can be determined, the world is now warmer than it has been at any point in the last two millennia, and, if current trends continue, by the end of the century it will likely be hotter than at any point in the last two million years."[3]

Scientists can only speculate on the consequences of a hotter earth. The devastating hurricanes that hit Florida and the Gulf Coast in 2004 and 2005 cannot be directly attributed to global warming; however, hurricanes are fueled by warm ocean waters. As a September 2005 editorial in the *New York Times* stated, it's time to connect the dots. "Ocean temperatures have been rising over the last 100 years, along with atmospheric temperatures. Hurricanes have therefore become bigger and more destructive and are likely to grow even more violent in the future."[4] The editorial goes on to warn, "Global warming will have other undesirable consequences, including a significant rise in sea level. In the last century, sea level rose four to eight inches around the world, and most scientists expect a further rise of two to three feet in this century. According to one government study, a 20-inch rise in sea level by 2100 could put 3,500 square miles of the southern coast of the United States underwater. A large-scale breakup of the polar ice sheets would, of course, make matters much worse. Dikes could protect some regions, like Manhattan and The Netherlands, but most coastlines would be inundated."

*"Whether we like it or not, global warming is shaping up as one of the most important challenges of the 21st century. It is going to drive far-reaching changes in how we live and work, how we power our homes, schools, factories and office buildings, how we get from one place to another, how we manufacture and transport goods, and even how we farm and manage forests. It touches every aspect of our economy and our lives, and to ignore it is to live in a fantasy land where nothing ever has to change—and where we never have to accept what the science tells us about what is happening to our world."[5]*

—Eileen Claussen, president, Pew Center for Global Climate Change

Climatologists have attributed the rising temperatures to the excessive burning of fossil fuels, which releases greenhouse gases such as $CO_2$ into the atmosphere. The greenhouse effect, which occurs naturally, in fact protects the earth from being too cold by trapping heat. However, when disproportionate concentrations of greenhouse gases accumulate, the average temperature rises and climate patterns are disrupted. Scientists predict that some areas will become wetter, others drier, altering water supplies, agriculture, pests, and diseases. It's difficult to know how different areas will be affected, but avoiding the most dire outcomes depends on a coordinated effort by all the nations of the world to reduce the emissions of greenhouse gases.

High concentrations of $CO_2$ in the atmosphere are due to human activity, whether it be large-scale deforestation, thereby robbing the earth of its ability to absorb excess carbon, or the burning of fossil fuels, such as coal, natural gas, and petroleum. The United States, representing less than 6 percent of the world's population, is by far the planet's worst polluter, producing more than 25 percent of greenhouse gases. While its citizens recognize the problem, many are unwilling to make sacrifices to combat the problem.

The key to reducing $CO_2$ emissions is to use less energy, especially in the industrial and transportation sectors, the largest emitters by far. Some of the strategies to lessen $CO_2$ emissions include alternative energy, such as wind and solar power, and conservation measures including greater use of mass transit and driving smaller, more fuel-efficient cars. However, buildings also use enormous amounts of energy. In the United States, commercial, institutional, and residential buildings account for more than 36 percent of primary energy use, over 65 percent of total electricity consumption, and 30 percent of greenhouse gas emissions. Energy strategies for interiors projects will be fully explored in Chapter 3, but an emissions reduction plan should also be considered.

The World Resources Institute (WRI) has published a comprehensive guide to assist businesses measure and reduce $CO_2$ emissions. *Working 9 to 5 on Climate Change: An Office Guide* is available online and offers a step-by-step plan.[6]

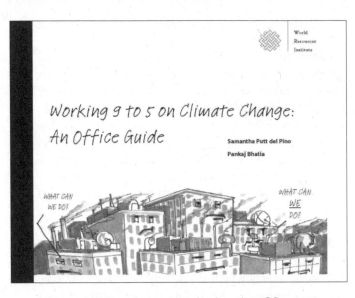

Businesses seeking to measure and reduce their $CO_2$ emissions will find a step-by-step plan in *Working 9 to 5 on Climate Change: An Office Guide*, produced by the World Resources Institute.

Suggestions are offered for securing organizational support, planning a $CO_2$ inventory, gathering data, calculating emissions, establishing reduction targets, identifying opportunities for reductions and sharing your results with your stakeholders. The guide also includes tips, scattered throughout the publication, as well as instructions on calculating emissions to help offices achieve their goals and track progress.

Staffers at WRI conceived of this plan after moving to new "green" office space in 1999 in order to publicly commit the organization to taking action on climate change by reducing its $CO_2$ emissions. Employees were briefed on actions that could be taken and the potential benefit of each. Some directly affected the employees, such as encouraging staff to use mass transit; others, such as turning off equipment when not in use, would potentially save WRI money; and some would cost money, such as purchasing green power.

Three years after embracing this plan, WRI had reduced its emissions by 12.7 percent and had realized other benefits as well. Using less energy means paying for less energy, which will improve the bottom line. Health benefits accrue from improved air quality, and employee morale increases through awareness and advocacy efforts. (More detailed explanations of these benefits and others are in Chapter 7.)

# Living Lightly on the Land

Whether we like it or not, rapid growth is a fact of life in many parts of the United States, but it need not always assault our senses with its ugliness, infringe on our countryside with its sprawl, or deprecate our environment with its carelessness. Sad to say, many of the current land use problems in the United States were inadvertently put in place by local government officials. The common planning tools that have governed suburban development in this country since the end of World War II, such as zoning laws and master planning, have contributed to this mess. Practices that strictly separate residential land use from commercial and industrial sites have created an automobile-dependent society. Author James Kunstler put it bluntly in an article in the *Atlantic Monthly*:

> What zoning produces is suburban sprawl, which must be understood as the product of a particular set of instructions. Its chief characteristics are the strict separation of human activities, mandatory driving to get from one activity to another, and huge supplies of free parking. After all, the basic idea of zoning is that every activity demands a separate zone of its own. For people to live around shopping would be harmful and indecent. . . . The pattern it represents is also economically catastrophic, an environmental calamity, socially devastating, and spiritually degrading.[7]

In every area of this country, greenfields are still being plowed under to make way for more suburban sprawl, which is likely contributing to a far greater number of problems than simply increased automobile use. Dr. Richard Jackson, an adjunct professor at the University of California, Berkeley, in the Division of Environmental Health Sciences in the School of Public Health, has extensively studied the built environment's effect on human health. While serving as a senior advisor to the director of the Centers for Disease Control and Prevention, in Atlanta, he documented the alarming rise in incidence of asthma, diabetes, heart disease, and obesity, all of which he attributes to lifestyle choices forced on us by the design of our built environment.

Sprawl is poorly planned growth that fails to consider community implications, contributes to the disappearance of farmland and natural woodlands, segregates land uses into isolated categories, and mandates the dominance of the automobile as the primary means of transportation.

## Wanted: A Systems Approach to Curing Our Ills

Blame, Richard Jackson asserts, must be shared by urban planners, designers, city administrators, and health-care providers. "We're on the threshold of just horrific health problems. We actually don't know why we're looking at an asthma epidemic. There are schools now where a third of the kids have inhalers. It probably has something to do with the design of our homes. We spend 90 percent or plus of our time indoors so it's got to be in some way related to indoor air quality. For example, we're covering most of our floors with wall-to-wall carpet and the allergen load in a carpet is far greater than it is on a bare floor. We've done studies of the health effects of mold, radon and volatile organic chemicals and the fix for all of these is the same. If a house is badly designed, badly ventilated, you're going to see these problems.

"It only costs one or two percent more to build a home that is well ventilated, well insulated, keeps moisture and pests out and all the rest, as long as it's done upfront. Trying to retrofit is often very, very difficult and very expensive, and that's where a lot of the opposition comes from. Consumers need to demand these smart homes and contractors will build them . . . We in healthcare have really not paid enough attention to the design of the environment. . . . Western science has been brilliant in terms of breaking apart problems to grapple with the challenges that we face. Over time, we have become so reductionist that urban planners aren't talking to

*(continued)*

5

the architects, who aren't talking to the health officials, who aren't talking to the bankers, etc. The problem is that many of the problems with the 21st century are systems problems. They are not isolated, and pure reductionism impedes our ability to deal with them."

> *"We're creating the first generation that will live less long than its parents by overfeeding ourselves and removing physical activity from our environments."*

—Dr. Richard Jackson

Jackson says that we've "engineered physical activity out of our environment. For example, only 7 percent of our kids walk to school at this point versus 50 percent when I was a child. . . . I think good physical environments probably could reduce our obesity rates by 5 or 10 percent. . . . I do think that providing your children a place where they can walk and bicycle and be connected to their community resonates. When you talk to people that have moved into smart growth developments, they always say that they don't know how they ever lived anywhere else.

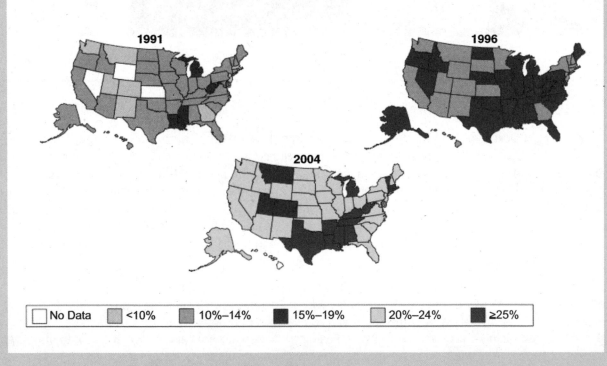

## Obesity Trends Among U.S. Adults

1991    1996    2004

No Data    <10%    10%–14%    15%–19%    20%–24%    ≥25%

Rising obesity rates in the United States between 1991 and 2004.

Public health officials attribute part of the responsibility for the growing rate of obesity in the United States to poor urban and suburban design. Cul-de-sacs designed without sidewalks and fences separating yards force children into cars in order to visit with their friends.

"Lousy density is what we all hate—the types of places where you can hear your neighbors through the wall, where you don't feel safe and the schools are dreadful. That's why most people move out of cities. There's nothing wrong with density, but it has to be accompanied by smart growth. Sooner or later, people are going to decide they don't want to spend 58 hours a year stopped in traffic. These folks are commuting an hour and a half each way to a 10-hour-a-day job and they're wondering why they don't know who their kids are. I'm an advocate of communities that allow people to exercise, that allow them to connect with each other and that use minimal amounts of environmental resources, including land."

Jackson notes, "I'm oftentimes accused, by homebuilders for example, of junk science when we argue that sprawl is a health issue. I am not saying that how we build our environments causes obesity and other health problems, but even if it contributes only a small percentage it represents a huge number of overweight people. My point is, we need a systems approach to this rather than an individual medical approach. . . . [T]here are multiple issues at work here. One is financing. At many banks there is a specialist for retail, another for residential and a specialist for commercial, etc. Smart growth really requires that the financing community finds a home for multi-use development."

*Source:* "Curing Our Ills," interview with Richard Jackson, *EnvironDesign Journal,* a supplement to *Interiors & Sources,* March 2004.

A sense of place in
Bethesda, Maryland.
© 2006 Interface
Multimedia, Inc.

Combating sprawl and designing communities, not just neighborhoods, are two of the goals of the New Urbanism, a decade-long movement pioneered by architect Peter Calthorpe. The concept has been further developed by town planners Andres Duany and Elizabeth Plater-Zyberk, whose projects include Seaside, Florida, and The Kentlands in Maryland, and who have gathered much acclaim for restoring the concept of the community to suburbia.

The purpose of good community planning is to create neighborhoods that promote physical and mental well-being. The first step is to better understand the elements that comprise healthy environments. According to newurbanism.org, the New Urbanism movement is "the revival of our lost art of place-making, and is essentially a re-ordering of the built environment into the form of complete cities, towns, villages, and neighborhoods—the way communities have been built for centuries around the world. New Urbanism involves fixing and infilling cities, as well as the creation of compact new towns and villages."[8]

The methodology to achieve these goals has been well defined by the proponents of the movement, specifically the Congress for the New Urbanism (CNU), a Chicago-based nonprofit founded in the early 1990s. Its purpose is to make available to designers, planners, and developers the best-practices principles outlined in their charter and presented at annual conferences, known as Congresses. "We stand for the restoration of existing urban centers and towns within coherent metropolitan regions, the reconfiguration of sprawling suburbs into communities of real neighborhoods and diverse districts, the conservation of natural environments, and the preservation of our built legacy."[9]

The concepts of New Urbanism are beginning to resonate with people who have grown weary of long commutes and otherwise spend too many hours in their cars simply to get through the normal chores of everyday living. Spending less time in automobiles not only reduces emissions and lessens air pollution but also relieves the stress of traffic congestion and contributes to a better quality of life. How buildings of all kinds—homes, offices, schools, hospitals, shopping centers—are integrated into their communities will, to a large extent, determine the design of transportation systems. The most pedestrian-friendly cities, towns, and suburbs have evolved because of networks of high-quality and convenient subways, light-rail trains, and bus routes that encourage walking and bicycling within a diverse mix of building types.

Arlington County, Virginia, just across the river from Washington, D.C., is an excellent example of the smart growth promoted by New Urbanism. Described more as a collection of urban villages than a suburb, the county has a diverse population that lives and works in compact residential neighborhoods supported by mixed-use urban centers. Joan Kelsch, Arlington County's environmental planner, credits early planners in the 1960s with the foresight to design dense urban development around the Metro stations then under construction and at the same time preserve well-established residential neighborhoods.

The Arlington model is referred to as transect planning, with the highest densities at town centers and progressively less dense toward the edges. Hard boundaries between land use types disappear, and the best characteristics of each are preserved.

Business owners, office tenants, and individuals have the ability to influence land development policies by choosing to locate in smart-growth communities. In November 2005, the Sierra Club recognized outstanding land planning efforts in its first-ever *Guide to America's Best New Development,* which names a dozen cutting-edge projects that have positively transformed neighborhoods. Ranging from massive projects such as Atlantic Station in Atlanta, which encompasses 138 acres and includes 12 million square feet of retail, office, residential, and hotel space, to smaller-scale projects such as 66 residential homes and an industrial building in Hopkins, Minnesota, the guide demonstrates how healthy and livable communities can be built.

"The single most important factor in all of these projects is that neighborhood residents actually had a say in how they were built," explained Carl Pope, the Sierra Club's executive director. "And when you ask people what they want, they ask for ways to get to and from work without sitting in traffic, and they want walkable neighborhoods, clean water, and green space."

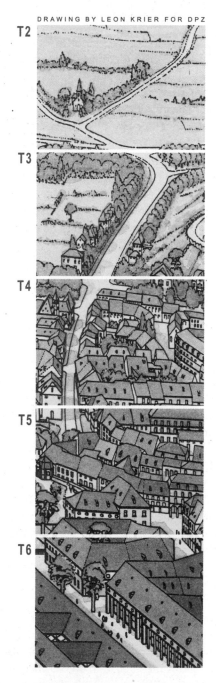

DRAWING BY LEON KRIER FOR DPZ

T2
T3
T4
T5
T6

The transect planning system preserves natural space by maintaining appropriate land uses for each urban to rural sector. © *Leon Krier*

The criteria for inclusion in the Sierra Club's top development honors include:

- A range of transportation choices, including walking, biking, and public transportation
- Redevelopment of existing areas, rather than development of natural areas, working farmland, or wetlands
- Location of homes, retail shops, and offices close to each other
- Preservation of existing community assets by reusing older buildings and protecting rivers, woodlands, and farms
- Minimization of stormwater pollution and handling of runoff in an environmentally responsible manner
- Meaningful input by local citizens and inclusion of a broad set of local values

Outstanding examples of best development practices can be found in these recognized projects:

- Downtown Tacoma, Washington, has been revitalized by the University of Washington's decision to locate its new campus in the warehouse district of the city rather than a suburban location. Retail shops, cultural attractions, restaurants, and housing projects have been constructed, attracted by the lively activity surrounding the campus and the light rail line that opened in 2003. This development is an example of how visionary leadership by local leaders and the community at large can transform a city.
- The Town Green Village Project in Windsor, California, was guided by the concepts of smart growth and New Urbanism. The plan is based on traditional neighborhoods and town centers with residential, commercial, and retail buildings clustered around a town green. In an article in the local newspaper, the *North Bay Bohemian,* developer Orrin Thiessen said, "I can build on 10 acres what would probably require 50 acres if you developed it using a traditional sprawl model."[10]
- Atlantic Station is being constructed on 138 urban acres in Atlanta and is the largest urban brownfield redevelopment project in the United States. Jacoby Development is leading the effort to transform what was once the site of the Atlantic Steel Company mill into an environmentally sustainable mixed-use community.

The heart of the project is a public transit transportation plan that reconnects the east and west parts of midtown Atlanta, runs a fleet of electric shuttles to the city's subway system, and limits parking for private vehicles. This "live-work-play community" is setting a precedent that will influence the future of Atlanta and other cities.

# ▮ Wet Gold

For most of us, clean water right out of the tap is something we take for granted. However, many experts are predicting shortages of fresh water, more acute and widespread than energy shortages, by midcentury. In fact, adequate supplies of water are likely to become so critical that some have begun referring to potable water as "wet gold." The late Paul Simon, senator from Illinois, described the approaching crisis in his book *Tapped Out: The Coming World Crisis in Water and What We Can Do About It* as a confluence of dwindling supply, increased pollution, and political disputes. "It is no exaggeration to say that the conflict between humanity's growing thirst and the projected supply of usable, potable water will result in the most devastating natural disaster since history has been accurately recorded, unless something happens to stop it."[11] Some experts are predicting that by 2025, at least sixty-five nations will experience serious water shortages.

Unlike the residents of the United States and Europe, about 1.2 billion people globally cannot take for granted that when they turn on their faucets fresh water will come out. The comparison is so stark, the authors of a *Washington Post* op-ed piece state, "that just one flush of a toilet in the West uses more water than most Africans have to perform an entire day's washing, cleaning, cooking and drinking." More than simply a supply problem, water scarcity is a health problem, as demonstrated during the aftermath of Hurricane Katrina in 2005. Notes the op-ed article, "Unsafe water and sanitation is now the single largest cause of illness worldwide."[12] Water-related diseases are so severe that they could claim the lives of 135 million people by the year 2020.

The western United States serves as an example of global water problems. Access to the still-abundant resources of

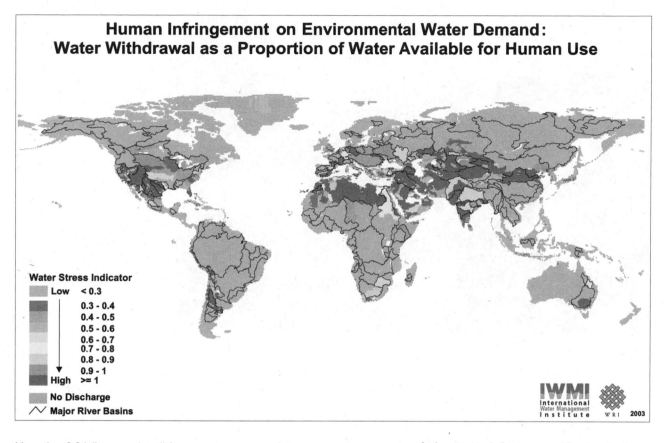

## Human Infringement on Environmental Water Demand:
## Water Withdrawal as a Proportion of Water Available for Human Use

**Water Stress Indicator**

| | |
|---|---|
| Low | < 0.3 |
| | 0.3 - 0.4 |
| | 0.4 - 0.5 |
| | 0.5 - 0.6 |
| | 0.6 - 0.7 |
| | 0.7 - 0.8 |
| | 0.8 - 0.9 |
| | 0.9 - 1 |
| High | >= 1 |

No Discharge
Major River Basins

More than 2.8 billion people will face water stress or scarcity conditions by 2025, with most occurring in West Asia, North Africa, or Sub-Saharan Africa. *World Resources Institute*, Earth Trends: The Environmental Information Portal, *Washington, DC, 2006*

the Colorado River is regulated through an agreement between seven states that was signed in 1922. Since that time, however, much has changed—think of the exploding populations of Phoenix and Las Vegas—and political bickering over future water rights is becoming testy.

The problem stems from a continually growing world population—projected to increase from 6.4 billion to 8.4 billion by 2025—and reductions in water supply reliability. In his book, Simon quoted a 1994 World Bank study that indicated per capita renewable water supplies will have fallen dramatically over the course of one lifetime (1960 to 2025). Industrial and agricultural contamination are partly responsible, as is the salination of soil and groundwater aquifers, which is occurring because they are overused. In

some parts of the United States, aquifer levels have dropped to alarmingly low levels in recent decades.

Despite reductions in U.S. water usage due largely to industrial reuse strategies, the nation is running at an annual water deficit of 3.7 trillion gallons. The water supply becomes stressed when the amount of water withdrawn from available sources is inadequate to meet human and ecosystem requirements. The United Nations, the World Bank, the G8 nations, and others are researching solutions. Simon, however, a proponent of desalinization (the process of converting salt water to fresh water), admitted frustration that more is not being done with available desalting technology. What makes it so appealing, Simon wrote, "is that most of the nations and areas with water shortages border the sea. And almost 70 percent of the world's population lives within 50 miles of the ocean. If we spent 5 percent as much each year on desalination research as we spend on weapons research, in a short time we could

Wastewater enters the Living Machine solarium and flows through three open aerobic reactors. Tropical, subtropical, and native plants such as papyrus, calla lilies, and willows root into the planted aerobic reactors and assist in the treatment process. © *Oberlin College*

enrich the lives of all humanity far beyond anything anyone has conceived."

At the end of his book Simon advocated other strategies, both simple and complex, that can and should be implemented to address the water crisis and to raise awareness of its seriousness.

- Charging consumers the actual cost of water delivery
- Repairing leaky pipes, irrigation canals, and wasteful ditches
- Reusing water, known as graywater, for nonpotable purposes, even though it is "aesthetically unpleasing"
- Monitoring aquifers and guarding them carefully
- Initiating aggressive conservation plans
- Preventing water pollution and treating it where it exists

Buildings consume 80 percent of the nation's drinking water, and the potential exists for significant water use reductions through some of the inventive strategies that are beginning to be implemented. The Natural Resource Defense Council's Redford Building in Santa Monica, California, for example, collects and filters both rainwater and water from sinks to be used on-site for flushing toilets and landscaping, resulting in a 60 percent water use savings. Another cutting-edge technology, known as the Living Machine, purifies wastewater by using a system of engineered ecologies that include microbes, plants, snails, and insects. One such system installed at Oberlin College in Ohio is designed to treat up to 2,000 gallons of the building's wastewater daily in a beautiful, garden-like atmosphere.

Though not yet mainstream, innovations such as these are beginning to decrease the stress on the world's fresh water supply. Strategies for water use reduction in buildings are outlined in Chapter 3.

## ▌ Want Not, Waste a Lot

It is irrefutable that one of the most significant long-term consequences of the twentieth century's industrial revolution—and the mass quantity of goods it has produced—is that we now live in a highly disposable society. In our constant quest for the next best thing, we throw away thirty-two truckloads of waste in this country for every truckload of goods produced. In fact, 90 percent of things made in America end up in a landfill within one year. Consider these statistics from the Clean Air Council regarding a handful of common goods we produce, use, and then squander:

■ An average child will use between 8,000 and 10,000 disposable diapers ($2,000 worth) before being potty-trained. Each year, parents and babysitters dispose of about 18 billion of these items—that's 570 diapers per second, or 49 million diapers per day.

■ Americans throw away 2.5 million plastic bottles every hour.

■ Americans toss out enough paper and plastic cups, forks, and spoons every year to circle the equator 300 times.

■ The average American office worker goes through nearly 500 disposable cups every year.

■ In the United States, an additional 5 million tons of waste is generated during the holidays. Four million tons of this is wrapping paper and shopping bags.[13]

It's not just seemingly small and insignificant items we throw away, either. Americans discard about 270 million tires every year and get rid of 20,000 cars and 4,000 trucks and buses each day. Additionally, approximately 315 million computers in the United States are predicted to become obsolete, and thus useless, by 2006.

This staggering waste generation is taking a significant toll on our natural resources and global life support systems. Many NGOs, such as the Product Policy Institute, con-vincingly argue that life cycle impacts during extraction, processing, use, and disposal of toxic and nontoxic materials are linked to most major environmental problems, from habitat destruction and loss of biodiversity to global warming. One example that highlights this continuing devastation: deforestation has claimed nearly 50 percent of the world's original forests, yet demand for wood will increase 50 percent in a decade.

The Clean Air Council estimates that the average American, in one lifetime, uses 18 tons of paper, 23 tons of wood, 16 tons of metal, and 32 tons of organic chemicals. It would be wonderful if every human being on Earth enjoyed the same standard of living as do those of us in the United States, but if that were so, it would take *four planets* to sustain life. The United States represents slightly more than 5 percent of the world's population, yet we consume one-third of the earth's timber and paper, making paper, at 37.5 percent, the largest part of the total waste stream. That's in addition to the fact that we also consume 25 percent of the world's energy and drive 32 percent of its automobiles. In terms of resources, a single American uses the same amount of goods as three Germans, six Mexicans, fourteen Chinese, or thirty-eight Indians.

These statistics drive home the imperative need for an emphasis on material and product stewardship along the entire product life cycle, notes the Pacific Northwest Pollution Prevention Resource Center (PPRC).[14] The responsibility for reducing that footprint, the organization argues, lies with all participants in the product life cycle,

U.S. consumption of resources and materials, adapted worldwide, would overwhelm the carrying capacity of the earth. Four planets would become necessary to sustain life. © *Photographer: Antonio Petrone*

including designers, manufacturers, suppliers, distributors, retailers, consumers, and finally recyclers and disposers. Each participant in some way has the potential to influence how a product impacts the environment.

> *"A product is like a river: a chain of causes and effects from the headwaters to the mouth. Product stewardship is reducing the product's environmental footprint at each step up and down the stream."*
>
> —Pacific Northwest Pollution Prevention Resource Center

One concept rapidly gaining momentum is extended producer responsibility (EPR), a common-sense strategy that encompasses many aspects of material and/or product stewardship. According to a 1998 article in *Pollution Prevention Review* entitled "EPR: What Does It Mean? Where Is It Headed?" by Bette K. Fishbein, the term was coined early in the 1990s by Thomas Lindhqvist to describe a policy then emerging in Europe and now sweeping the industrialized world. Lindhqvist, a Swedish professor of environmental economics, defined EPR as the extension of the responsibility of producers for the environmental impacts of their products to the entire product life cycle, and especially for their take-back, recycling, and disposal.

In practice, Fishbein reflects, the term most commonly describes postconsumer products, those that have been discarded by end users at the end of the product's useful life, thereby shifting the responsibility for discarded materials from local governments directly to private industry. The costs of product disposal or recycling are factored into the product price. EPR policies originated in Germany in 1991 and have spread to other nations, where they can be controversial. The reason for the debate? Some governments call for legislative mandates, forcing industry to be responsible for the management of the waste associated with its products. Others argue that this practice should be a strictly voluntary one on the part of industry—that industry should police itself, so to speak.

EPR exists in the United States, Fishbein writes, but with some marked differences. "In 1996, the President's Council on Sustainable Development recommended an EPR policy of 'extended *product* responsibility,' which it defined much more broadly as the shared responsibility of government, consumers, and all industry actors in the product chain for all the environmental impacts of a product over its life cycle."[15] This recommendation removes the producer's unique responsibilities for postconsumer products.

Some groups, though, such as the Product Policy Group, argue instead that the onus for product stewardship necessarily rests on the brand owner because, as the product designer, it is in the best position to select safe materials, minimize toxic waste throughout the product's life cycle, increase the useful life of the product, and facilitate disassembly and reuse of the product at the end of its life. Rather than seeking remedies following a product's useful life, the group emphasizes that effective EPR calls instead for the *design* and *development* of products that are safe and sustainable throughout their entire life cycle—thus preventing pollution and waste rather than just controlling it.[16] Additionally, proponents of a "polluter pays" concept argue that internalizing end-of-life management costs of a particular product into the price of that product serves as an economic stimulus to reduce toxicity and promote resource conservation. The bottom line, they say, is that when environmental costs are reflected in a product's price, minimizing those costs makes the product more competitive in the marketplace.[17]

How can EPR best be accomplished? The Northwest Product Stewardship Council (NWPSC) has identified five general practices that support its long-term success:

*Materials management.* Producers can reduce environmental impacts by using materials that result in the least environmental impacts. Examples include:

- Use of renewable materials that are replenished rapidly through solar energy
- Use of biodegradable materials that break down into soil without any harmful chemicals or materials entering the ecosystem
- Use of recycled and/or recyclable materials
- Use of low or no toxicity materials that emit, contain, or produce low levels (or zero levels) of chemicals that are hazardous to human health
- Use of sustainable harvesting methods so that the long-term viability of the resource is not jeopardized

# The Benefits of Extended Producer Responsibility

According to the Product Policy Institute, EPR has a number of beneficial objectives, which are described on its web site and listed here in detail:

## Engage Producers in Eradicating Social Injustice

Many products used today are either disposed in landfills and incinerators that tend to reside in or near low-income communities and communities of color, or they are exported to developing countries with inadequate health and labor standards. As a result, people in developed and developing countries are exposed to toxic materials that cause cancer, reproductive problems, and other irreversible diseases. EPR can reverse this trend by ensuring that producers make safe products, take them back, and recycle them responsibly.

## Help Moderate Resource Consumption

Consumer products are typically designed for one-time use, to be thrown out by consumers at the end of life and disposed of in landfills and incinerators. This has led to unsustainable consumption patterns that are depleting the world's stock of raw materials at a rate faster than nature can sustain. EPR encourages producers to create products that last longer and manage materials so they are continually reused and recycled in a closed loop system.

## Achieve Better Product Design

Many of the materials used in products are harmful to human health. As a result, harmful pollutants are dispersed from products during production, use, and disposal. Society as a whole pays for the added costs of these impacts, whether it be in higher health care bills or increased waste management expenses. When producers pay for managing product waste at end of life, they have an incentive to design products that are less toxic, less over-packaged, longer-lasting, and designed for reuse and recycling.

## Achieve a More Vibrant Economy

EPR will lead to product innovation, cost savings, reduced environmental liabilities, and increased customer satisfaction. It will also increase competitiveness in a global marketplace where European and Japanese companies are already adapting to legally binding EPR requirements.

## Create Safer Workplaces and More Jobs

EPR sets a standard for cleaner raw materials that are safer to handle in workplace facilities. Up the supply chain, brand owners hold their suppliers to a higher standard of environmental performance and workplace safety. EPR also creates new, meaningful jobs in redesign, repair, reuse and recycling, while recognizing the need for a just transition toward clean production. Workers must not bear the costs of a transition toward clean production.

*Product as service (product leasing).* In many cases, consumers are not interested in owning a product, but need the product because it enables them to get a service. For example, consumers usually don't want to own the plastics, glass and chemicals in a television set, rather they want the service—viewing of TV programs—that the television set provides. Manufacturers that lease their products to consumers have a better incentive to design durable, upgradeable products.

*Dematerialization.* Dematerialization means taking materials out of products, but still getting the same, or better, performance. Companies dematerialize by substituting intelligence and creativity for materials, by restructuring their products, or resizing the product.

*Resource conservation.* Companies can save money as well as the environment by adopting practices that reduce waste, prevent pollution, preserve the climate and conserve habitat.

*Product take-back.* Some manufacturers are taking their old products back when consumers are finished with them. By taking products back, manufacturers can acquire low cost feedstock for manufacturing, or remanufacture parts for reuse.[18]

Many of the practices proposed by the NWPSC are becoming more common. For example, some carpet manufacturers are experimenting with the concept of leasing carpet rather than selling it, which allows end users to exchange it for new carpet at the end of its use. The concept of product take-back is increasingly prevalent in the electronic industry, and is also being implemented in the carpet industry through such programs as the Carpet America Recovery Effort (CARE).

In the end, using fewer materials, using materials with less environmental impact, and intelligently managing waste are the goals when considering material use. Most people think of recycling as the defining environmental characteristic of a product or material. However, the Waste Pyramid shown above illustrates several other strategies for keeping materials away from the incinerator or out of landfills.

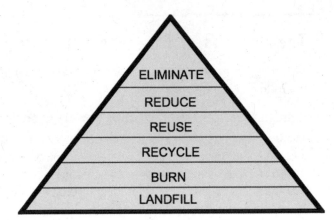

The waste pyramid.

## Eliminate and Reduce

The elimination of waste, as well as source reduction, means consuming and throwing away less. It is the best approach to managing solid waste because it avoids creating the waste in the first place. Source reduction helps reduce waste disposal and handling costs because it avoids the costs of recycling, municipal composting, landfilling, and combustion. Source reduction also conserves resources and reduces pollution, including greenhouse gases that contribute to global warming. The U.S. Environmental Protection Agency (EPA) recommends the following reduction strategies: purchasing durable, long-lasting goods; seeking products and packaging that are as free of toxins as possible; and redesigning products to use less raw materials in production, have a longer life, or be reusable. For example, the weight of a two-liter plastic soft drink bottle has been reduced from 65 grams to 51 grams during the past eight years, which has kept 250 million pounds of plastic out of the waste stream each year.

## Reuse

This is the next most preferable waste management strategy in that it calls for the reuse of items by repairing them, donating them to community groups, or selling them. It is a more effective strategy than recycling because the item doesn't need to be reprocessed before it can be used again. Unfortunately, many goods, including packaging, that can be reused end up in the landfill anyway; the EPA cites local studies in Berkeley, California, and Leverett, Massachusetts, that indicate between 2 and 5 percent of the waste stream is potentially reusable. Consider that if 236 million tons of municipal solid waste were generated in 2003, the 2 to 5 percent that was reusable represents a significant amount of material that really isn't waste.

## Recycle

This strategy turns materials that would otherwise become waste into valuable resources. It is fourth on the list of most preferable strategies because the process of recycling results in some of the same detrimental environmental impacts found in many manufacturing practices. (These impacts, however, are significantly less: recycling an aluminum can, for example, saves 96 percent of the energy used to make a can from ore and produces 95 percent less air pollution and 97 percent less water pollution. Producing recycled white paper creates 74 percent less air pollutants and 35 percent less water pollutants and requires 75 percent less energy than producing paper from virgin fibers.) The good news is that recycling is on the rise; the EPA estimates that recycling diverted 72 million tons of material away from landfills and incinerators in 2003, up from 34 million tons in 1990—doubling in just ten years. Curbside programs, along with drop-off and buy-back centers, resulted in a diversion of about 30 percent of the nation's solid waste in 2001.

For the recycling strategy to continue to work, however, consumers must buy products with recycled content. Doing so creates an economic incentive for recyclable materials to be collected, manufactured, and marketed.

## Recovery

This strategy calls for the collection or reclamation of material input that has been diverted from the solid waste stream so that it can replace the use of new primary material for a recycling or manufacturing process. It is not unlikely that someday in the future, industry will be forced to mine landfills for raw materials such as paper, plastics, metals and glass. As resources become scarce, it may be financially beneficial to reclaim these materials. There also

## Environmental Marketing Claims

The Federal Trade Commission provides guidance about the use of environmental marketing claims included in advertising, labeling, promotional materials and all other forms of marketing, whether asserted directly or by implication through words, symbols, logos, depictions, product brand names, or any other means.

- *Degradable/biodegradable/photodegradable.* The product or package will completely break down into elements found in nature within a reasonably short period of time after disposal.
- *Compostable.* The product or package will break down into usable compost.
- *Recyclable.* The product or package can be collected separately or recovered from the solid waste stream and turned into raw materials used in new items.
- *Recycled content.* The product or package contains materials that have been diverted or recovered from the solid waste stream either during the manufacturing process (preconsumer) or after consumer use (postconsumer).
- *Source reduction.* The product or package is lower in weight, volume, or toxicity than comparable or previous products.
- *Refillable.* The product or package can be collected and returned for refilling, or refilled by consumers with material sold in other packaging.
- *Ozone-safe and ozone-friendly.* The product or package does not contain any ozone-depleting substance.

# Waste in the Construction and Building Industries

In addition to the estimated 236 million tons of municipal solid waste generated by Americans annually, there's also the 136 million tons of building-related construction and demolition debris to consider (and that's based on 1998 figures). The majority of this waste comes from building demolition and renovation, notes the EPA, while roughly equal percentages of building-related waste are estimated to come from the residential and commercial building sectors.

What's getting thrown away at the construction site? According to the EPA, the composition of the debris varies from project to project. Older buildings, for example, tend to generate more plaster and lead piping waste. New construction waste usually contains significant amounts of drywall, laminates, and plastics. For building debris, Table 2-1 illustrates EPA estimates of overall percentages for specific materials.

What products can be recovered? There are many specialty items found in construction debris that may offer significant return through their recovery and subsequent resale. And while salvaging generates additional costs, proceeds from the sale or reuse of salvaged materials can be used to offset those dollars. Table 2-2 shows a sampling of typical material components that offer high recovery potential.

| TABLE 2-1: Building Construction Waste | |
|---|---|
| Concrete and mixed rubble | 40–50% |
| Wood | 20–30% |
| Drywall | 5–15% |
| Asphalt roofing | 1–10% |
| Metals | 1–5% |
| Bricks | 1–5% |
| Plastics | 1–5% |

Source: EPA

| TABLE 2-2: Typical Components/Materials with a High Recovery Potential | | | | |
|---|---|---|---|---|
| Appliances | Bathroom fixtures | Bricks | Cabinets | Carpeting |
| Dimensional lumber | Doors | Ductwork | Flooring | Insulation |
| Light fixtures | Marble | Metal framing | Paneling | Pipes |
| Plywood | Shelving | Siding | Soil | Stairs |
| Tile | Trim | Windows | Wood beams | |

Source: U.S. Army Corps of Engineers, Public Works Technical Bulletin No. 42049-32, 2001

are studies under way to examine material flows between industries, as the by-products of one industry may be a useful commodity to another.

The term *recover* is also sometimes used to address the practice of recovering energy from wastes that cannot be used for something else. Landfill sites account for a significant portion of the total methane emissions in the United States. Currently, efforts are under way to harness these releases of methane, which is estimated to be about twenty times more potent a greenhouse gas than $CO_2$.

While waste management strategies generally focus on specific materials and components, these same principles can also be applied to a bigger picture: the building as a whole. According to a 1995 report issued by the

Worldwatch Institute, the modern buildings we live and work in rival such well-known polluters as cars and manufacturing as sources of harm to the environment, adding greatly to deforestation, the risk of global warming, overuse of water, and acid rain. For example, 55 percent of the wood cut for nonfuel uses is for construction, while 40 percent of the world's materials and energy is used by buildings.[19] The U.S. Department of Energy estimates that buildings represent a whopping 70 percent of all U.S. energy consumption. Statistics from the U.S. Geological Service indicate that buildings use 12.2 percent of all potable water globally (that's 15 trillion gallons per year).

Because the way buildings are designed can impact resource use as much as the materials that go into making them, a strategy called Design for Adaptability is garnering increasing attention. This approach refers to the capacity of buildings to accommodate substantial change, thus making them less vulnerable to becoming poorly utilized, prematurely obsolete, and unable to accommodate new and more efficient technologies. In their report "Assessing the Adaptability of Buildings," a white paper published by Annex 31, a working group of the International Energy Agency's Agreement on Energy Conservation in Buildings and Community Systems, authors Sebastian Moffatt and Peter Russell explain that change is inevitable during a building's lifetime because the needs and expectations of its occupants change. Consequently, they argue, "a building that is more adaptable will be utilized more efficiently and stay in service longer, because it can respond to changes at a lower cost. A longer and more efficient service life for the building may, in turn, translate into improved environmental performance over the life cycle." Moffatt and Russell break down the concept of adaptability into three simple strategies that are familiar to most designers: flexibility, or enabling minor shifts in space planning; convertability, or allowing for changes in use within the building; and expandability (alternatively shrinkability), or facilitating additions to the quantity of space in a building.[20]

Another building strategy targeting waste minimization is design for deconstruction. This practice focuses on the ease of disassembling elements and components for reuse and recycling when a building is wholly or partially deconstructed or demolished. By carefully disassembling a building, components and equipment may be able to be reused in a closed-loop materials cycle rather than entering the waste stream.

## Healthy Buildings, Healthy People

Want to capture the attention of corporate CEOs in the United States—or any other country, for that matter? Just tell them that a new worker-related policy has been identified that can significantly reduce the estimated $70 billion in total annual costs related to employee sick days, restricted activity, or healthcare costs.[21] On top of these savings, make sure they know that this new policy would also create an estimated $20 billion to $160 billion in added productivity from direct improvements in worker performance. These eye-opening projections underscore why the issue of indoor environmental quality (IEQ) is gaining prominence not only in corporate America but also among this country's—and the world's—leading public health officials. The fact is, Americans spend 80 percent to 90 percent of their time indoors, oftentimes in built environments that are literally making them sick. The EPA estimates that the concentration of pollutants (such as volatile organic compounds, or VOCs) inside a building may be two to five times higher than outside levels, contributing to higher instances of building-related illness (BRI), a term used to describe symptoms of diagnosable illness that are identified and can be attributed directly to airborne building contaminants. Indoor air pollution, for example, has been cited by the EPA as a leading cause of cancer and the likely cause of 3,500 to 6,000 deaths per year.

Certainly, as a nation we are experiencing unprecedented levels of communicable respiratory diseases, allergies, and asthma symptoms, as noted earlier in this chapter by Richard Jackson. A 2000 study by W. J. Fisk of the Lawrence Berkeley National Laboratory (the results of which are reported in Table 2-3) indicates that 56 million Americans, or 20 percent of the U.S. population, suffer from allergies, while 20 million, or 7 percent, suffer from asthma.[22] Escalating numbers of workers are also suffering from symptoms associated with sick building syndrome (SBS), a term used to describe situations in which building occupants experience acute health and comfort effects that appear to be linked to time spent in a building, yet no specific illness or cause can be identified. Fisk estimates that 16 million people—23 percent of office workers—suffer from SBS on a frequent basis.[23]

These dismal public health trends make improvements to IEQ all the more essential. What does beneficial IEQ entail? In general, five primary elements are considered when evaluating indoor environmental quality: lighting, sound, thermal conditions, air pollutants, and pollutants on surfaces.

The best IEQ, notes the Oakland Sustainable Design Guide, embodies the following goals: "provide an environment for occupants that is physiologically and psychologically healthy; minimize production and transmission of air pollution; provide the full range of support sensory conditions (olfactory, thermal, vibroacoustic, tactual, and visual) for occupants; provide needed operational control of systems to occupants; and produce environments that enhance human comfort, well-being, performance and productivity." [24]

It is unfortunate that for too many years, costs were almost always the predominant consideration when making facility decisions. Although that precept still exists today, designers now have at their disposal evidence that clearly demonstrates that cheaper is not better when it comes to designing commercial interiors—and actually may be far more costly in the long term in regard to employee recruitment and retention, increased liability, and a building's return on investment. The chart below, created by Fisk, illustrates exactly how IEQ stimulates economic benefits.

This link between employee productivity and business profitability is a convincing argument that is slowly gaining momentum in the sustainable design field. More and more case studies are documenting how IEQ can positively impact the bottom line. One widely quoted example occurred at West Bend Mutual Insurance. In the early 1990s, the company's new 150,000-square-foot headquarters building became the subject of one of the most carefully documented studies of productivity increases due to facility design. West Bend Mutual was able to verify a minimum 2.8 percent gain in productivity by tracking the number of claims processed per week in the old building and in the new one. With an annual payroll of $13 million at the

| TABLE 2-3: Productivity Gains and Synergies | | |
|---|---|---|
| Source of Productivity Gain | Potential Annual Health Benefits | Potential U.S. Annual Savings or Producitivity Gain (1996 $ U.S.) |
| Reduced respiratory illness | 16–37 million avoided cases of common cold or influenza | $6–14 billion |
| Reduced allergies and asthma | 18–25% decrease in symptoms for 53 million allergy sufferers and 16 million asthmatics | $1–4 billion |
| Reduced sick building syndrome symptoms | 20–50% reduction in sick building syndrome health symptoms experienced frequently at work by approximately 15 million workers | $10–30 billion |
| Improved worker performance from changes in thermal environment and lighting | Not applicable | $20–160 billion |

Source: "Health and Productivity Gains from Better Indoor Environments and Their Relationship with Building Energy Efficiency," by William J. Fisk, *Annual Review of Energy and the Environment*, Vol. 25:537–566 (2000).

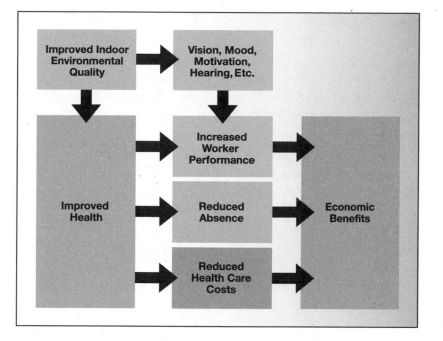

Improvements to indoor environmental quality positively impact the health of workers, as well as lead to improved vision, mood, and comfort factors, thus increasing performance and reducing absence and healthcare costs. The bottom line is significant economic benefits for the company. *Adapted from information provided by W. J. Fisk, Lawrence Berkeley National Laboratory*

time of the study, the increase is worth $364,000 each year. The gains were realized by giving workers direct control over their immediate environment. All employees, whether in private offices or open workstations, are able to control temperature, airflow, task lighting, and white noise. Personal control not only makes workers happier but also affects performance by reducing the amount of time and effort needed to achieve comfort. Strategies to implement IEQ design features are detailed in Chapter 5.

One element of IEQ that is perhaps more intangible than some of the others is the ability of a work space to inspire and invigorate its occupants—spaces that the Rocky Mountain Institute's Amory Lovins says create "delight when entered, pleasure when occupied, and regret when departed."[25] And while such things as effective lighting and thermal comfort certainly contribute to this feeling, designers are also finding that spaces that provide some kind of a connection to the natural environment receive the highest marks from the people who inhabit them. This "spiritual" connection can be provided via increased daylighting, views to the outside, and operable windows, but also through the use of patterns and textures that deliver sensory cues. Explains John Connell, principal

of Yestermorrow Design/Build School, "The thing about natural materials, and not just the woods but also stone, fabrics and fibers—things that have been around since the dawn of time—is that we have an association with them that is probably more profound than we realize."[26]

In fact, this association has a name: biophilia, which is defined by E. O. Wilson, the Harvard biologist who coined the term, as "the connections that human beings subconsciously seek with the rest of life." Increasing studies on this subject, examined in the Heerwagen and Kellert essay that follows, are helping to better explain this phenomenon, as well as document ways in which it operates not just in the workplace but also in healthcare facilities, where it can help reduce recuperation times and decrease mortality rates, and in our schools, where it can help students of all ages learn more effectively. The interior furnishings industry has been quick to jump on the bandwagon: a plethora of nature-inspired floor coverings, wall coverings, window treatments, surface materials, and fabrics can be seen during a walk down the aisles of any interior design exposition these days. This trend is destined to continue for years to come, for as we learn from Heerwagen and Kellert, people innately seek a connection with the natural world.

## Growing Sensitivities

Along with increases in allergies and asthma, public health officials have also noted a rise in the number of people who report physical sensitivity or intolerance to common materials and chemicals, such as those found in some building products, floor coverings, cleaning products, and fragrances. These individuals may experience a range of incapacitating physical symptoms, such as fatigue, irritability, depression, chest pain, dizziness, headache, and nausea.

One such condition, multiple chemical sensitivity (MCS), describes an acute reaction to various types of chemicals. The range and severity of reactions are as varied as the potential triggering agents. In addition, other people report reactions from exposures to electrical devices and frequencies, a condition referred to as electromagnetic sensitivity (EMS). Office equipment and other sources can produce electromagnetic fields and may be problematic for those with EMS. Noise and vibration can adversely affect some people with MCS or EMS and may even set off seizures in susceptible individuals.

Ironically, a study conducted by the National Institute of Building Sciences, with funding from the Architectural and Transportation Barriers Compliance Board, found that some elements of green design, though initially designed to increase occupant health and well-being, may actually be contributing to the rise in these illnesses. For example, the study reports that some measures recommended to promote energy and water conservation—such as reducing the supply of outdoor air, reducing the amount of time HVAC systems are used, employing motion sensors that can create electromagnetic fields, using waterless urinals that need continuous chemical treatment, recommending cold water for cleaning, and promoting the use of alcohol-containing hand sanitizers instead of hand washing—can cause or increase indoor pollution and create less healthful environments. In addition, green cleaning products often contain citrus- and/or pine-based substances, which the report says can react with even low levels of oxidants such as ozone to produce hazardous by-products. Cleaning and other products that contain synthetic or natural fragrances are also problematic for chemically sensitive individuals. Other common green building recommendations, such as building on brownfields, using tuck-under parking, and putting heliports on roofs, can also lower indoor air quality and negatively affect people with chemical sensitivities.

*Source:* National Institute of Building Sciences, "IEQ: Indoor Environmental Quality," http://ieq.nibs.org/om/bi_intro.php.

## *Biophilic Design*

By Judith H. Heerwagen and Stephen R. Kellert

*The human mind evolved in a sensory-rich natural environment. Light, sounds, odors, wind, vegetation, water, and animals provided the context for learning and, ultimately, created the capacity for humans to modify nature and build their own habitats, often at the expense of the natural world.*

*Despite our presumed ability to dominate nature, there still lives within the human psyche an evolved propensity to affiliate with living organisms and natural systems. We still feel the tug of nature, whether in backyard gardens, street trees, bird feeders, flowers, or the changing patterns of light indoors as the sun makes its pathway across the sky. E.O. Wilson calls this fascination with nature "biophilia." In his 1984 book Biophilia, he writes: "To explore and affiliate with life is a deep and complicated process in mental* development. To an extent still undervalued in philosophy and religion, our existence depends on this propensity, our spirit is woven from it, hope rises on its currents." [27]

Understanding the deep-seated interdependence with nature and its consequences for the environment and for human well-being is the focus of a new project under way at Yale University. The project has three primary goals:

- To identify critical biophilic features and attributes of buildings and landscapes

- To document the emotional, social, cognitive, health, and spiritual benefits of living and working in biophilic buildings and spaces

- To develop a design methodology/system that integrates biophilic experience with sustainable building design and landscape practice

As noted in the third goal, biophilic design is intended to work in harmony with sustainability. However, as currently practiced, the benefits from sustainable design come primarily from risk reduction associated with improved indoor environmental quality, including energy and resource efficiency and minimization of waste and pollution. Biophilic design, while embracing risk reduction strategies, emphasizes how buildings and surrounding landscapes positively influence health, well-being, performance, emotional functioning, and sense of place.

Although the Yale project is in its beginning phases, we have begun to identify key features and attributes of biophilic design. These are shown in Table 2-4 and in the photographic examples. Biophilic components, as noted in the table, are both literal (trees, water, vegetation) and symbolic (use of ornamentation, décor, and materials with natural themes). The symbolic representation of nature in buildings, which has been largely neglected in modern architecture, may prove to be a powerful means to achieve biophilic benefits in urban settings.

The most biophilic buildings are likely to incorporate multiple features that are revealed in the building façade, lobby, interior design, and surrounding landscape. For instance, the marble used in the façade of the Beinecke Rare Book and Manuscript Library at Yale University is both a natural building element and a feature that provides sensory variability and novelty due to its translucency. As the sunlight changes outdoors, the lighting patterns vary dramatically inside the building.

Another example of a cross-category design feature is illustrated in the Stata Center at the Massachusetts Institute of Technology, designed by Frank Gehry. The building has Gehry's signature organic shapes and forms, but the unique biophilic

| TABLE 2-4: Biophilic Design Components | |
| --- | --- |
| Component | Examples |
| Natural elements | Trees, flowers, grasses, water, rocks, daylight, natural ventilation, natural building materials (wood, stone); naturalistic ornamentation (such as flowers or animals) and patterns used for surface treatments. |
| Natural attributes | Sensory variability in sounds, light, color, temperature, and air movement; patterned complexity ("rhyming"); growth and development of features over time; organic forms; color splashes; some degree of spatial and element novelty; information richness that encourages exploration and discovery; shiny or glimmering surfaces that symbolize water; changing color or intensity of light to mimic sunlight. |
| Spatial relationships | Distant views and view corridors; sense of enclosure and sensory retreat using overhead canopies and vertical screening; irregular clustering of elements; curvilinear surfaces that gradually open information to view. |

The marble used in the façade of the Beinecke Rare Book and Manuscript Library has a translucency to it that alters daylight entering the interior; lighting patterns vary as the sunlight changes outdoors. *Courtesy of Yale University*

feature is the way in which the forms and materials reflect varying patterns of light as the sun shifts in the sky. A third example focuses on the building interior and how light, nature elements, and spatial attributes are integrated. The Seattle Public Library, designed by Rem Koolhaas, has a large public space with a sloped, canopy-like ceiling, distant views, nature elements, and carpeting with a naturalistic pattern. Furnishings and architectural elements featured in the living-room-like space on the main entrance level of the Seattle Public Library take many of their cues from nature-based elements. Interestingly, all three building examples use natural light in unique ways to create a sense of surprise and delight. Further, each design also shows that the essence of biophilia can be captured through symbolic representation.

### Biophilic Experience

*In his book* Building for Life: Designing and Understanding the Human-Nature Connection, *author S. R. Kellert has identified three categories of biophilic experience. Direct experience involves contact with self-sustaining features of the natural world such as the woods, a natural wetland, or a mountain forest. Indirect experience is contact with nature that requires human input and control, such as trees in building atria, an outdoor water feature, or a fish tank. Symbolic experience involves contact not with* real nature but with materials, ornaments, and décor that represent nature. Indirect and symbolic experience are likely to be more common approaches in high-density urban areas, while direct biophilic experience is more easily supported in suburban and rural environments or in urban areas close to green spaces and parks.[28]

For example, the Philip Merrill Environmental Center in Annapolis, Maryland, which houses the Chesapeake Bay Foundation (CBF), uses both direct and indirect experience of nature. The building is situated on the edge of Chesapeake Bay adjacent to a wildlife refuge and wetland. The CBF's mission, to restore the bay, is reinforced through the restoration of the oyster beds and natural beach grasses on the site. Research on the occupants' experience shows very high levels of satisfaction and well-being associated with daylight, views, natural ventilation, and engagement with the outdoor landscape and wildlife.[29] For instance, an outdoor video camera captured daily events at a nearby osprey nest and conveyed to personal computers images of the young birds.

Symbolic experience of nature is highly varied and can include exterior ornamentation or the use of murals, surface treatments, or design features that contain nature elements or patterns, as shown in the photographs on the upper and lower right on the facing page.

The offices at the Philip Merrill Environmental Center are filled with sunlight and a view of Chesapeake Bay. © 2005, Loretta C. Jergensen, Chesapeake Bay Foundation

The symbolic presentation of a sky is apparent in this building on the Yale University campus. *Photography courtesy of Judith Heerwagen*

Organic and naturalistic shapes are shown in the entry to this San Francisco gallery designed by Frank Lloyd Wright. *Photography courtesy of Judith Heerwagen*

### Benefits of Biophilic Experience

Research in a variety of fields provides compelling evidence of benefits from contact with nature. For instance, studies summarized in Kellert's Building for Life and an article by J. Heerwagen and G. Orians entitled "Humans, Habitats and Aesthetics"[30] show that:

- Living in or near green spaces, especially spaces with large trees, enhances human health and mental well-being relative to locations with reduced green space.

- Contact with nature through window views reduces stress at work and improves recovery from illness in hospital settings.

- Moderate amounts of indoor sun improve mood in work settings and reduce depression in mental health settings.

- Daylight, natural ventilation, and good access to window views improve overall satisfaction and comfort at work, and may also influence cognitive effectiveness.

- Urban housing developments with green spaces and large trees are more likely to attract people and build community ties than housing developments lacking outdoor sitting areas with trees.

At this time, the majority of research focuses on direct and indirect experience of nature. Little is known about the impact of symbolic experiences of nature beyond their aesthetic appeal. Does symbolic representation promote well-being, cognitive functioning, or stress reduction? Do buildings with symbolic biophilic representation create a stronger sense of place and community ownership than buildings lacking such features?

Although there is much to learn, especially about the symbolic representation of nature in buildings, the existing research provides sufficient evidence that biophilia can provide a blueprint for a new approach to building design, one that incorporates both sustainable practices and human potential.

Judith Heerwagen, Ph.D., is a psychologist whose research and consulting focus on design human factors—the interrelationships among behavior, psychosocial context, and physical space. Stephen R. Kellert, a social ecologist at Yale and E. O. Wilson's collaborator, is recognized as the world's foremost authority on human relationships to animals.

# 3

# SITES, WATER, AND ENERGY

SUITE
110

The vast majority of people who go to work have little to say about the architecture, major systems, operations, and ongoing maintenance of the buildings in which they spend their days. However, they or their employers can and should make intelligent, informed location decisions based on environmental and quality-of-life attributes. The overriding considerations in deciding where to locate involve the big-picture issues of land planning, the protection of green space, and the restoration and revitalization of urban areas. Equally important are choices based on lifestyle enhancements such as alleviating the stress of commuting and traffic congestion. In her essay, architect and land planning advocate Gina Baker writes about the importance of site selection for tenants and offers advice to design teams and their clients on implementing this key ingredient in a successful green interior.

## Site Sustainability Matters

### By Gina Baker

When it comes to sustainable commercial interiors, site may not seem like a topic of importance. However, concerns for sustainability do not stop just at the door of a commercial interiors project. Selecting the right building and the right location has a significant impact on the environment. Since the interiors construction market accounts for almost thirty times the square footage of new building construction, the issues that relate to the outdoor environment are just as relevant, if not more.

### Finding the Right Building

The first step in developing a sustainable commercial interiors project is finding the right building in which to construct it. Buildings account for 30 percent of our annual energy use in the United States, including 60 percent of annual electricity consumption. Finding a space with the right square footage for a client is always a top priority for most brokers. Why shouldn't finding a high-performance building be a priority, too? The real estate industry is slowly becoming tuned in to the green building market, but it's still far behind designers and builders in promoting sustainability.

Emergency preparedness continues to be a topic of major importance for the Building Owners and Managers Association International (BOMA) in the wake of the September 11 tragedy.[1] Though the organization instituted an award for green buildings in 2003, called the Earth Award, only 10 of the 100 points in the evaluation are for performance in energy and water conservation combined. Occupant health and indoor air quality are most heavily weighted, at 25 of 100 points, but site issues are not even considered. Sustainability has almost no mention on the organization's Web site. The National Association of Realtors (NAR) is slightly ahead of BOMA; the organization recently constructed its new green headquarters in Washington, D.C.[2] NAR's Web site provides a library of resources about green building for the education of its members, which include residential and commercial real estate brokers. Educating brokers about the features of high-performance buildings is an important step for sustainability in the commercial real estate market.

Although some environmentally savvy organizations might be looking for green buildings when they begin to seek out available commercial real estate, most clients are unaware of how green features can impact their bottom line. Because designers often aren't yet involved when a client begins the search for a location, brokers should be looking for buildings with a host of green features as they evaluate potential space for a commercial interiors tenant. Locating in a LEED-rated building is one easy way of reaching that goal, but there are not many LEED-rated buildings. This is why a clearinghouse on green building information is so important. Brokers need to know how to evaluate a building for energy performance, water conservation, indoor environmental quality, and its impact on site sustainability. Understanding such features will help sustainable commercial interiors projects further reduce their impact on the environment.

### Finding the Right Location

One thing real estate brokers truly understand is location, location, location, and this factor has an undeniable impact on sustainability. When trying to find a new location, one should be looking for a site that follows the principles promoted by the Smart Growth Network.

First, priority should be given to areas that are of mixed use. According to the Urban Land Institute, mixed-use centers and mixed-use downtowns outperform suburban real estate products when comparing office and retail leases, property values, and retail sales.[3] People want to live and work near amenities such as shops and restaurants. Brokers should help clients look for places in existing urban areas. This may go against a trend in the market. According to the Brookings Institute, the suburban share of office space grew from 26 to 42 percent between 1979 and 1999.[4] Suburban locations often come with lower leasing costs, making them attractive. But locating in such dispersed and placeless areas has numerous social and environmental costs.

Second, locate in an area that provides transportation options. Based on the 2000 U.S. Census, 80 percent of Americans live in metropolitan areas. Maintaining critical mass and keeping city centers dense is the best way to support public transportation and preserve transportation options. It is when growth and development are allowed to sprawl that light rail and bus systems begin to fail. Just as important as mass transit options is providing viable opportunities for car sharing, carpooling, biking, and walking. Commercial interiors projects can promote these options by not leasing unnecessary parking, creating incentive programs, providing showers, and locating near areas that provide a variety of housing options.

### Why Does It Matter?

The benefits of choosing the right location and a high-performance building are threefold. Lessening the time employees and customers lose to commuting can reduce social costs. Locating near amenities such as shopping builds community and adds to quality of life. Economic impacts include a reduction in absenteeism when employees can take care of personal errands close to their workplace, in addition to the performance impacts that are attributed to healthy workplaces. Employee retention is also influenced by the features of a healthy workplace located in a mixed-use area. And the environmental benefits of selecting a more sustainable location contribute to reductions in pollution and energy expenditures. Tenants will be much better served if the issues of sustainability are considered when they are selecting a new building and location.

---

Gina Baker, the director of sustainable services for Burt Hill, is an architect with an intense dedication to green development.

# ■ Matters of Site

In the past little attention has been paid to the environmental benefits of informed site selection for interiors projects. Clients, their brokers, and design teams evaluate buildings on the customary criteria prior to signing a lease: location, suitability to meet the organization's space, mechanical and electrical needs, rents and other lease arrangements, build-out costs, amenities, and aesthetics. These are still important, of course, but other factors—green qualities—have been added for tenant consideration. Also, in order for innovative development strategies to succeed, prospective tenants must become educated about the value of green building characteristics previously overlooked and seek out properties with these features.

## Building Selection

The first step in green building selection is often going to be identifying the right broker. The real estate industry is just starting to "get it," and for the enlightened client, finding a knowledgeable agent may prove difficult. However, as an encouraging sign, the U.S. Green Building Council lists more than 150 firms in its real estate service providers membership category, from small, localized firms to some of the nation's largest organizations—Hines, Staubach, Cushman and Wakefield, Trammell Crow, and CB Richard Ellis (CBRE).

Sally Wilson, the director of advisory services for CBRE, believes the developer community is beginning to get on the bandwagon and is starting to see that green is a good investment. "In some ways there's a little bit of a tipping point going on," Wilson states. "With energy and healthcare costs rising, people are starting to pay more attention to real estate costs. Our clients are looking not just at rent—anyone can find cheap space, but it might not be the best investment for your business or your business strategy. There are a lot of hidden real estate costs outside of rent—vacancy, churn, turnover, loss of productivity, absenteeism. We try and find the right balance between the property strategy and the business strategy. I'm sure we're unique in that because when we put out an RFQ [request for quote] to landlords requesting environmental qualifications of buildings, their response is 'What's this?' "

Wilson should know. As part of a team from CBRE that assisted Toyota Motor Sales (TMS) USA in locating space for its Government Affairs office in Washington, D.C., she created a list of twelve environmental impact qualifications lifted from the LEED-CI rating system, and asked the landlords of each potential location to address them in their proposals (see sidebar).

Based upon the responses to the questionnaire and other selection criteria, five buildings were chosen for the short list, and the CBRE team toured and analyzed each of them according to their potential to achieve LEED-CI points.[5] A spreadsheet was created that scored all the buildings in order to determine who had what. The way to control and mitigate costs and to ensure the highest LEED rating is to start early, according to Wilson. "Most people will start after hiring the architect, but we believe you should start with the lease. That was what we sold to Toyota and what we did by putting the twelve environmental points in the RFP [request for proposal]. Once we selected the Homer Building and began lease negotiations, we held them to their commitments. For example, they committed to the bicycle racks, but didn't realize until after documentation what it really meant."

Wilson and her team compiled a notebook for the client, tabbed for each of the five buildings, that included transportation and density maps plus calculations for the LEED-

## Twelve Environmental Impact Qualifications

Toyota Motor Sales is recognized as a leader in sustainability. TMS is seeking a location that provides the opportunity to certify high-performance, healthy, durable, affordable and environmentally sound workplaces. Please provide a detailed description in your proposal of which, if any, of the following green building strategies your building employs:

1. Building has been awarded or is currently registered for LEED certification.
2. Building has zero use of hydrochlorofluorocarbon (HCFC) and chlorofluorocarbon (CFC) based refrigerants and halon fire suppression systems in the entire building.
3. Building has adopted a five-year phase-out plan for current system of HCFC- or CFC-based refrigerants and halon fire suppression systems.
4. Building meets at least 5 percent of the total energy load with usable energy converted from the sun, wind, or biomass.
5. Building has operable windows in at least 75 percent of regularly occupied spaces on the perimeter.
6. Building has an Energy Star–compliant roof with a minimum emissivity of .9 for at least 75 percent of the roof area of the building.
7. Building provides secure bicycle storage with convenient changing and shower facilities for at least 5 percent of occupants.
8. Building provides an easily accessible dedicated area for the collection and storage of material for recycling including (at a minimum) paper, corrugated cardboard, glass, plastic, and metals.
9. Building provides submetering equipment to measure and record energy uses within individual tenant spaces.
10. Building allows energy costs to be paid for by the tenant and not included in the base rent.
11. Building meets the minimum requirements of voluntary consensus standard ASHRAE 62-2001, Ventilation for Acceptable Indoor Air Quality, and approved published addenda using the Ventilation Rate Procedure.
12. Building provides for zero exposure of nonsmokers to environmental tobacco smoke (ETS) by locating any exterior designated smoking area away from entries and operable windows.

CI site selection credits that simplified the building analysis process. The client was fully supportive of this approach. In fact, Toyota hired CBRE because of Wilson's green credentials—she's a LEED Accredited Professional—and, with two LEED-certified facilities already in their portfolio, the auto company was fully committed to going after a LEED-CI certification for their new offices. "We have the highest green standards," said Earl Quist, a Toyota director, "but what we do has to make business sense."

**Table 3-1: Density Development And Density Radius Calculations for Selected Buildings in Washington, D.C.**

| Project Building | Building Space (sf) | Site Area (acres) | Development Density (sf/acre) | Density Radius (lf) |
|---|---|---|---|---|
| 1300 Eye St. NW | 465,356 | 1.03 | 451,802 | 635 |
| 1350 Eye St. NW | 342,014 | 0.81 | 422,240 | 564 |
| 1625 Eye St. NW | 384,218 | 0.91 | 422,218 | 597 |
| 701 13th St. NW | 416,014 | 0.80 | 520,018 | 560 |
| 601 13th St. NW | 448,426 | 0.99 | 452,956 | 623 |

*Source:* CBRE

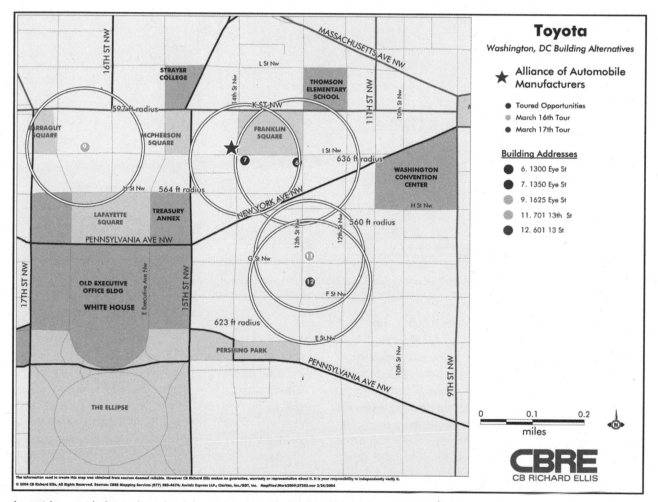

An aerial map with density boundaries for each potential building location assists with LEED credit compliance.

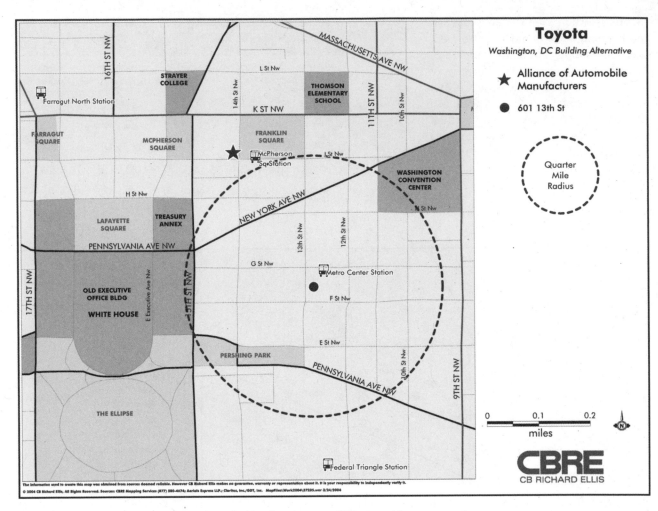

The quarter-mile radius is mapped to indicate building location accessibility to public transportation.

The Toyota project is a good example of the impact that LEED-CI has had on site selection by highlighting how a building's attributes can add value to the lease negotiation. Another aspect, typically not on the design team's radar but an important financial and environmental consideration, is the length of the lease itself. Tenants with long leases are more likely to stay put than those with shorter terms. The environmental impact kicks in because moving and the renovations associated with it use resources and create waste. When an organization vacates a space, it leaves behind the build-out—such as floors, walls, ceilings—that it

then re-creates in its new space. The tenant moving into the vacated space often rips out what it finds there and installs new materials—and so on, much like a domino effect. Signing a longer lease will at least delay this process.

Transportation is an issue to be addressed during lease negotiations. Many buildings provide parking as an amenity or because zoning regulations require them to do so. Should the latter be true, the employer can designate its allotted spaces for car- or vanpools, thereby discouraging single-occupancy vehicle use. Subsidized public transportation as an alternative to parking availability is another strat-

## Toyota Green Lease Initiatives (with LEED-CI Prerequisites and Points Achieved)

1. Select building with heat island reduction. (0.5 points)
2. Select building meeting development density requirements. (1 point)
3. Select building meeting alternative transportation requirements. (1 point)
4. Landlord to provide bicycle racks accommodating 5 percent of the occupants of the building, six showers, and changing facilities for both men and women. (1 point)
5. Select building meeting minimum energy performance and CFC reduction in HVAC&R equipment. (Energy and atmosphere prerequisite)
6. Tenant shall have the right to separately meter electricity for all the premises and use its preferred power company of tenant's choice. (3 points)
7. Landlord shall collect recyclables (including paper, corrugated cardboard, glass, plastics, and metals) and deposit in a dedicated area of the building. (Materials and resources prerequisite)
8. Ten-year commitment. (1 point)
9. Select building meeting minimum indoor air quality performance. (IAQ prerequisite)
10. Landlord prohibits smoking by all occupants and users within the common areas of the building. Any exterior designated smoking area will be at least 25 feet away from entries, outdoor air intakes, and operable windows. (IAQ prerequisite)
11. Innovation credit: in the event landlord contemplates any upgrades to the building structure or systems that are reasonably anticipated to cost $150,000 or more, the landlord agrees to perform a commercially reasonable analysis to determine if a more environmentally friendly way to complete such upgrade is available, and will choose such an environmentally friendly upgrade if its cost is less than or equal to the cost of performing the landlord preferred upgrade and provides the same or higher quality. (1 point)
12. All cleaning products used shall be environmentally friendly. (1 point)
13. LEED Accredited Professional. (1 point)

egy to remove as many cars as possible from jam-packed highways.

LEED has been criticized for including a credit for bicycle racks and changing showers. Many felt it frivolous when there are so many more serious issues to be tackled. However, decreasing the number of cars on our streets and reducing the congestion and pollution they bring is critical to the development of livable communities. Additionally, as discussed in Chapter 2, encouraging employees to bicycle or walk to work will help abate the growing obesity problem and all of the attendant health consequences.

Landlords should be encouraged to provide convenient and secure bicycle storage for at least a portion of the building occupants. Showers and changing areas are equally important, either within the tenant space itself, elsewhere in the building, or at nearby fitness facilities.

Commitments made by a landlord during lease discussions can be a terrific boon to a project going after LEED-CI certification. The Toyota green lease initiatives (above) negotiated by CBRE literally handed the client five prerequisites, seven credits, and two innovation points before the design process had even begun.

# Reducing Water Use

Despite the acute global water shortages and the critical need to conserve the use of potable water described in Chapter 2, there are, admittedly, few ways in which to limit water use in the commercial interiors project. Tenants cannot normally alter the plumbing systems in office buildings, nor do tenants usually have control over the common floor restrooms. Within tenant spaces, especially the smaller ones, water use is often limited to pantry sinks and perhaps a dishwasher, each of which uses minuscule amounts of water compared to toilets and showers.

Many of the water reduction strategies available to the designers and occupants of whole buildings are also unattainable to tenants, such as capturing rainwater or establishing graywater systems to use in toilets or to irrigate landscaping. It is troubling that in the developed world, and certainly in North America, almost all of the water used for flushing toilets is potable at the same time that clean and drinkable water is so scarce in other parts of the world. However, the best that is currently achievable by commercial interiors projects is to reduce the amounts of potable water used as much as possible. As previously noted, larger tenants, or those deemed highly desirable by landlords, may be able to effect change within their buildings or, at least, with the restrooms adjacent to their spaces.

Consider the following scenario. A potential tenant is negotiating a lease for five floors of an eight-story building and is willing to sign a longer-than-usual lease if the landlord renovates the relevant restrooms to the tenant's specifications. Depending on the landlord's situation, this may be a reasonable request, giving the tenant—and landlord—an opportunity to achieve significant water use reduction. Persuasion strategies should include predicted cost savings from lowered utility bills, which may convince the building owner to retrofit all of the restrooms throughout the building.

The tenant's goal is to achieve as large a water use reduction as doable within the project's limits. If an ultraefficient dishwasher is all that's possible, up to 8 gallons per load can be saved over some of the water-hogging models, which adds up over time. *Consumer Reports* currently gives the Asko D3000 Series model excellent ratings, not only for low water use but also for energy savings and performance.

## A Lesson Learned

Interface Americas Inc., a leading carpet manufacturer and a pioneer of sustainable business and design initiatives, chose the ground floor of an urban mixed-use building for the location of its Atlanta showroom. The restrooms were outside the tenant's space, yet the project captured both of the water efficiency credits in LEED-CI (on its way to a Platinum rating) because the design team was able to persuade the landlord to retrofit the plumbing fixtures.

"We had a rare landlord, one with a background in indoor air quality, and he 'got' what we were trying to do. It didn't take a lot of convincing," said Holley Henderson, the LEED Accredited Professional (AP) on the project.

In the showroom's pantry, everything—the dishwasher, refrigerator, icemaker, and sink—was specified to be as water- and energy-efficient as possible. The sink faucet, however, provided some challenges. Due to the large number of events and the need to constantly clean bulky items such as platters, the faucet's motion sensor did not function well, and although the installer made every effort to adjust the settings, it could not be made to work for the user. The sink was retrofitted with an extremely efficient low-flow fixture. "The lesson learned here," stated Henderson, "is that if it doesn't function, it isn't sustainable."

Designers at TVSA implemented water use reduction strategies at the Interface Carpet showroom in Atlanta, Georgia, which contributed to the project's LEED-CI Platinum certification. *Photography courtesy of Brian Gassel, TVS*

Similarly, it may be that a pantry sink faucet represents an office's only opportunity for water savings. Installing a flow restrictor is an easy and inexpensive modification to standard faucets. By adding air to the water stream, these aerators reduce water flow from 3.5 gallons per minute (gpm) to 1.5 gpm, which at an estimated thirty minutes of use per day saves nearly 22,000 gallons of water annually.

The above numbers for dishwashers and faucets are impressive when multiplied by the total number of users worldwide but by themselves won't earn commercial interiors projects any points in LEED-CI. There simply isn't enough volume created by one or two sinks to meet the rating system's requirements. The goal of the single water efficiency credit is the reduction of potable water use in buildings,

Kitchen faucet aerator with swivel and full flow and the easy-touch flow restrictor. © *Niagara Conservation Corp.*

thereby also reducing the amount of water withdrawn by municipal utilities from lakes, rivers, aquifers, and other fresh water sources. To achieve the two available points, projects must use 20 to 30 percent less water than the baseline case established by the Energy Policy Act of 1992 (EPAct).

With this act the U.S. government set water conservation standards for toilets, urinals, showerheads, and faucets in order to minimize the nation's water consumption. For example, prior to its implementation, older toilets used 4 to 8 gallons of water per flush (gpf), while the newer models, mandated under the law, must have a maximum flush volume of 1.6 gpf. Compliance with EPAct has become the law of the land and does not earn any LEED points; it simply sets the baseline that must be exceeded.

Water volume is measured in one of two ways: gallons per flush for toilets and urinals, or gallons per minute for flow-type fixtures such as lavatories, sinks, and showers. (Metered faucets that have controlled flow rates for pre-set time periods are measured in gallons per cubic yard.) Table 3-2 lists the EPAct fixture requirements.

Baseline calculations are computed by determining the number and gender of the users. As a default, LEED will let you assume that females use toilets three times per day while males use the toilet one time per day and the urinal two times in a typical day. All will use the bathroom faucets three times each day and the kitchen sink once for 15 seconds each. Assuming an office of fifty people, thirty females and twenty males, a baseline calculation would look something like the spreadsheet in Table 3-3.

Replacing the fixtures used in the above scenario with high-efficiency models, as shown in Table 3-4, will result in water use reductions topping 30 percent and, for a LEED-CI project, earn 2 points.

### Table 3-2: EPAct Fixture Requirements

| Fixture Type | Maximum Flow Requirement |
|---|---|
| Toilets | 1.6 gpf |
| Urinals | 1.0 gpf |
| Showerheads | 2.5 gpm |
| Faucets | 2.2 gpm |
| Replacement aerators | 2.2 gpm |
| Metering faucets | 0.25 gcy |

### Table 3-3: Water Use, Baseline Calculation

| Daily Uses | Fixture Type | Duration | Flow Rate | Water Use (gallons) |
|---|---|---|---|---|
| 20 | Toilets—male | 1 flush | 1.6 gpf | 32 |
| 90 | Toilets—female | 1 flush | 1.6 gpf | 144 |
| 40 | Urinals | 1 flush | 1.0 gpf | 40 |
| 200 | Lav and kitchen faucets | .25 minutes | 2.2 gpm | 110 |
| Daily total | | | | 326 |
| Annual work days | | | | 260 |
| Total annual volume (gallons) | | | | 84,760 |

### Table 3-4: Water Use, High-Efficiency Calculation

| Daily Uses | Fixture Type | Duration | Flow Rate | Water Use (gallons) |
|---|---|---|---|---|
| 20 | Toilets—male | 1 flush | 0.8 gpf | 16 |
| 90 | Toilets—female | 1 flush | 0.8 gpf | 72 |
| 40 | Urinals—non-water | 1 flush | 0.0 gpf | 0 |
| 200 | Lav and kitchen faucets | .25 minutes | 0.5 gpm | 20 |
| Daily total | | | | 108 |
| Annual work days | | | | 260 |
| Total annual volume (gallons) | | | | 28,080 |

Interestingly, if the gender ratio was reversed, with thirty males and twenty females, the total water use reduction would have narrowly missed the 30 percent threshold, calling into question a methodology that relies, at least in part, on demographics. However, LEED aside, the mission is to use less potable water in buildings, and the above example demonstrates the positive results that can be achieved with little effort beyond product research.

David Linamen, the principal for engineering at Burt Hill, is regarded as an expert in environmental solutions and has taken a special interest in searching out water-conserving plumbing products—work for him that has yielded very gratifying results. When the owners of a recent hotel project expressed interest in claiming Maryland's green building tax credits, Linamen set out to find the lowest-flow fixtures on the market that would also meet the client's strict performance standards. While he wasn't able to find a low-flow showerhead to meet the hotel's exacting specifications, he did find a toilet that passed every test: the Gerber Plumbing Fixtures Ultra Flush 1.1 gpf model, one of the new generation of high-efficiency toilets (HETs) being introduced by a number of plumbing manufacturers.

Hotel guests, according to Linamen's client, will flush or try to flush (either on purpose or accidentally) an amazing array of objects, including bars of soap, those little shampoo bottles, hairbrushes, and other items most toilets, even those using large amounts of water, just can't handle. Linamen, however, traveled to Gerber's test labs and witnessed the Ultra Flush successfully pass every challenge by flushing double the amount of the hotel's minimum waste standard.

More than eighty models of HETs are now available in the North American marketplace from sixteen different manufacturers. Each of these products flushes at less than 1.3 gallons, some as low as 1 gallon. Tenants who have the opportunity to either retrofit existing restrooms or specify the fixtures for new installations will find many options on the market. The following section will examine available products in some detail.

## Toilets

In January 2004 *Environmental Building News* published an extensive article on toilets and their fascinating history

### The Giblin?

"In a history of toilets, it is important to point out that Thomas Crapper did not invent the flush toilet. Crapper had an active career in the English plumbing industry from 1861 to 1904, and he patented some minor improvements in drains, pipe joints, and water closets. But the "Silent Valveless Water Waste Preventer" (a siphon-discharge toilet) that he is often credited with inventing was actually developed by Albert Giblin. Crapper marketed this device under his name, however, and World War I soldiers passing through England came to identify the "Crapper" with water closets—a term that has certainly stuck (in some circles)."

*Source:* Alex Wilson, "All About Toilets," *Environmental Building News,* January 2004.

beginning more than four thousand years ago.[6] Of current concern, however, are the 1.6 gpf toilets that have been the law of the land since 1994, when the Energy Policy Act went into effect. Many of the early models performed badly, spawning a bit of a black market in the older toilets. Manufacturers have since improved the performance of the 1.6 gpf products, so they are no longer shunned.

Some, however, are significantly better than others, and the specifier should consult performance standards and reports prior to making product decisions. According to the *Environmental Building News* article, though, many of the usually reliable resources such as ASME/ANSI and *Consumer Reports* are seriously flawed when it comes to toilet performance, with inconsistent results and recommendations of products that will fail to meet consumer expectations.

The most recent series of performance studies, originally sponsored by a consortium of Canadian and U.S. municipalities and utility companies, re-created real-life toilet usage by developing a soy-based material designed to replicate human waste. More than 200 different fixture models have so far been subjected to the Maximum Performance (MaP) Test, all adjusted to flush at a volume of

**Table 3-5: Top-Performing High-Efficiency Toilets (HETs)**

| Brand | Model Series | Flush Technology | Range of Waste Removal Performance (grams)* |
|---|---|---|---|
| American Standard | FloWise (single flush) | Gravity-flush | 500–600 |
| Caroma | Caravelle, Royale, Reflections (dual flush) | Gravity-flush | 500–900 |
| Toto | Aquia (dual flush) | Gravity-flush | 800 |
| Vitra | Dual-Flush | Gravity-flush | 800 |
| Gerber | Ultra-Flush 1.1 (single flush) | Pressure-assist | 800–1,000 |
| Gerber | Ultra Dual-Flush | Pressure-assist | 1,000 and better |
| Mansfield | QuantumOne (single flush) | Pressure-assist | 500–1,000 |
| Mansfield | EcoQuantum Dual-Flush | Pressure-assist | 800–1,000 |
| Zurn | EcoVantage (single flush) | Pressure-assist | 800–1,000 |
| Zurn | EcoVantage (dual flush) | Pressure-assist | 800–1,000 |

\* Minimum performance threshold for satisfactory performance: 250 grams

*Source:* Created by John Koeller, P.E.; adapted from Maximum Performance (MaP), Sixth Edition; www.cuwcc.org/MaPtesting.lasso

1.6 gallons with a minimum level of acceptable performance identified as 250 grams of waste removal. The top performers, those clearing more than 500 grams per flush, are shown in Table 3-5. The MaP report is updated on a four-month cycle, with additional test results added as they become available. The full report (as well as a condensed version focused only on the essential results), available at the California Urban Water Conservation Council Web site, contains complete information on the MaP test criteria and procedures.[7]

Toilets use one of several technologies. The most common, especially in residential and light commercial installations, is gravity flush, named because the tank is positioned above the bowl and the flush is powered by gravity. The hydraulics have been improved over the last few decades to perform better with less water. One of the most significant advances was pioneered by Toto, a Japanese manufacturer that introduced a larger (3-inch versus 2-inch) flush valve that increased the flow rate and reduced clogging. Now, all manufacturers are transitioning their gravity-flush products to the larger flush valve technology.

A second type of tank toilet, pressure-assisted, houses a pressure vessel inside the ceramic outer tank. That vessel captures water under pressure from the building plumbing

Sloan Valve Co.'s Flushmate IV. *Photography courtesy of Sloan Valve Co.*

system when it refills, compressing the air within the tank, then uses that pressure to force the water into the bowl when flushed. While often producing a brief whooshing sound, the refill rate is very fast on these types of fixtures. The Sloan Valve Co. recently introduced its Flushmate IV pressure assist system, which uses just 1.0 gpf; WDI Plumbing has developed an equivalent system based upon the same technology. Numerous toilet manufacturers use the Sloan and WDI products within their tanks.

Larger commercial projects do not use tank-type toilets but rather a technology referred to as flushometer bowl type. Designed for heavier usage, these flushometer toilets use either a wall- or floor-mounted flushometer bowl together with a flushometer valve that relies on line pressure from the municipal water system. While they're somewhat noisy, they also have a rapid recovery and are available in the 1.6 gpf configuration. Flushometer toilets are used in all types of heavy and light use applications; however, many designers think of them as low-end and confine their use to airports and other high-volume installations.

Though these are the most commonly used toilets, there are others that may bear looking into: vacuum-assist, pump-assist, and air pressure toilets all show promise as good performers and water savers, although few manufacturers have introduced them into their lines. However, a technology that is becoming increasingly popular is the dual-flush toilet, which offers two volumes—1.6 gpf for solid waste and 0.8 to 1.1 gpf for liquids and paper. Most use the gravity flush method and have different mechanisms for users to select the appropriate flush, from graphically designated buttons to handles that can be lifted for one type of flush and pushed down for the other. The dual-flush technology is being well received, with most of the criticism centered on the difficulties of educating consumers so that the right button is pressed. This is particularly true in the nonresidential sector, where dual-flush toilets are as yet uncommon and public restroom users are likely to be unfamiliar with the technology. Because of this, many believe that such toilets are not considered to be viable for public restrooms at this time.

Electronic motion sensors on toilets and urinals to initiate flushing, although popular, have a distinct disadvantage. Despite their hygienic advantages, they often flush repeatedly or unnecessarily and contribute to excessive water usage.

One additional toilet type—composting toilets—bears mentioning, although its feasibility for interiors projects is limited and logistically difficult. However, because they use no water, they are a great solution for certain types of

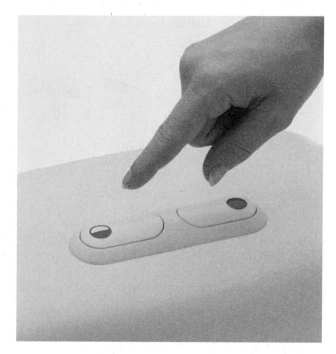

Dual-flush toilets are good water savers if users can be taught to operate them correctly. *Photography courtesy of Caroma USA Inc.*

buildings, specifically low-rise projects and those relying upon septic systems. Popular in remote parks, rest centers, golf courses, and homes, composting toilets carry waste directly to a composting system below, where it can break down into useful nutrients.

## Urinals

Urinals are available at several flow rates—1.0 gpf (as allowed by law), 0.5 gpf, or no water use at all. This last type, non-water urinals, operates under a different technology than the flush types and may be the primary water use reduction strategy in selected applications.

The design is simple, as demonstrated by the illustration on page 74. A non-water urinal consists of a porcelain or acrylic fixture and, in the case of the Falcon Waterfree Technologies unit in the figure, a replaceable cartridge. Urine flows into the cartridge and passes through a liquid sealant to the drainpipe below. The sealant liquid in the cartridge is lighter than water and creates an airtight seal, so the urine passes through and becomes trapped

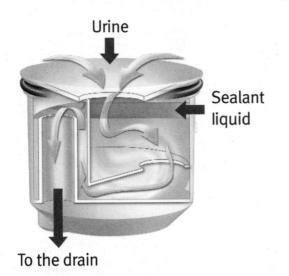

Urine

Sealant liquid

To the drain

A replaceable cartridge eliminates the use of water in a waterless urinal. *Illustration courtesy of Falcon Waterfree Technologies*

beneath it. At least four manufacturers (Falcon, Waterless, Zurn, and Zero-Flush) currently sell non-water urinals in the North American marketplace, each with a slightly different approach to the technology.

Without flushing mechanisms and water supply lines, non-water urinals are sometimes less expensive to purchase and install. Because they don't use water, utility bills are lower. The maintenance required is routine cleaning of the fixture and a change of the cartridge approximately three to four times per year depending upon frequency of urinal usage. The environmental benefits are obvious— Falcon Waterfree estimates that each urinal saves 40,000 gallons of fresh water per year, although other estimates are significantly less than that amount—and the complaints of odor can be eliminated by following the manufacturer-prescribed maintenance procedures. Most users feel that the lack of a flush handle creates a more hygienic restroom by eliminating a source of bacteria transfer.

Despite all of these advantages, some problems have prevented widespread acceptance. First, some local building officials will not permit the installation of non-water urinals. In many cases, however, it's simply a matter of old code restrictions that haven't kept up with technology; requests for special approvals have been readily granted.

Another obstacle is change reluctance. Some construction companies and custodial staffs have resisted modifying their familiar and comfortable ways. A push from the designers plus the helpful videos the fixture manufacturers will readily provide should ease the transition.

The most significant concerns over non-water urinals, however, are focused in two important areas: life cycle economics and drain line buildup of crystallized urine salts. Maintenance requirements, including the frequent replacement of fluids and cartridges, may outweigh the economic benefits over the lifetime of the fixture. In addition, reports of the buildup of hardened salts in the drain lines behind non-water urinals have concerned some facilities managers. Independent field studies of non-water urinal installations (and their drain lines) have not yet been completed that would substantiate or deny the veracity of these reports.

Because of the demand for more water-efficient urinals and the issues associated with the non-water type, several manufacturers are introducing high-efficiency urinals (HEUs) that operate with significantly reduced flush volumes. Urinals that use 1 pint to 1 quart per flush are entering the marketplace and will become more and more common. As such, the new competing flushing technologies are expected to seriously affect the demand for the non-water fixtures.

## Faucets

In addition to the aerated flow restrictors discussed earlier in this section, another water-saving strategy to be considered in restrooms is sinks with touchless controls. Studies have shown reduced water use following installation. Infrared sensors detect the motion of the user's hands and turn the water on and off. They limit water flow as well as promote hygiene. The most popular are battery-powered, making installation quick and easy.

As with other plumbing fixture types, manufacturers are introducing new products with many innovative improvements. Sloan Valve's new Solis EAF-275 is the first solar-powered electronic faucet and can translate light from any source into electrical energy. Other advantages include 0.5 gpm water flow, electronic sensors, and integral temperature control. The Toto EcoPower faucet, on the other hand, uses the energy within the flowing water to

Sloan Valve Co.'s Solis solar-powered electronic faucet. *Photography courtesy of Sloan Valve Co.*

keep its own battery charged, eliminating the need to hardwire a faucet installation and the need to continually replace sensor batteries.

## Showerheads

> *"The interior designer for a luxury hotel project specified dual showerheads in the guest bathrooms. Using them would have lost the opportunity to take advantage of a Maryland tax credit. Single showerheads were installed. This is a good example of how tax incentives achieve good environmental results."*
>
> —David Linamen, principal for engineering, Burt Hill

Possibly one of the worst innovations in shower design is the dual showerhead used in some upscale hotel bathrooms. While each showerhead may meet EPAct's maximum flow rate of 2.5 gpm, when combined they represent significant waste. Also, hotel guests demanding good water pressure recognize that adding another head will not improve poor pressure or spray patterns.

Ultra-low-flow showerheads do exist, according to Linamen, but have not been well received by the lodging industry. Others, however, cite their installation in a number of hotels in Las Vegas as evidence of their growing popular-

ity. Fixtures with a flow rate of 1.5 gpm will deliver good performance and meaningful water use reduction. One ten-minute shower per day at 1.5 gpm will use approximately 5,000 gallons of water per year versus 9,000 gallons for a 2.5 gpm model. For businesses that offer shower facilities to their employees or customers, the savings can be significant. Older showerheads that predate the current standard can use 5 to 8 gpm, and early replacement of these showerheads can lead to even greater water savings.

## What's LEED Got to Do with It?

The Water Efficiency section of LEED for Commercial Interiors offers 1 credit and up to 2 points.

*WEc1: Water Use Reduction.* Reduce the amount of potable water used by tenants. The credit is additive and has two parts:

*1.1: 20 percent reduction.* Use 20 percent less water than the baseline after meeting Energy Policy Act of 1992 fixture performance requirements. (1 point)

*1.2: 30 percent reduction.* Use 30 percent less water than the baseline after meeting Energy Policy Act of 1992 fixture performance requirements. (1 point)

Adapted from the LEED Green Building Rating System for Commercial Interiors, Version 2.0. Visit ugsbc.org to access the complete rating system.

## ◼ Optimizing Energy Use

*Energy.* Both the word and the concept are central to truly sustainable interiors. For the designers of whole buildings, the opportunities to reduce energy use—and the combustion of fossil fuels such as oil and coal—are numerous and are increasing as technologies advance. Placement of the building on its site and modifications to the envelope and major systems are generally out of the scope of interiors projects. However, the urgency of optimizing energy use is no less great, and many strategies are available to do so.

Consider the use of energy modeling, an exercise that establishes a benchmark of energy use based on project characteristics such as floor plan, solar exposure, and occupancy plus standard assumptions for the mechanical system, connected load, and plug load. The designed energy plan, when compared to the baseline case, will show the success the team has had in reducing energy use—and costs. Hiring an energy modeler is recommended; however, if one cannot be found, then use an Energy Star benchmark or contact the local utility for help.

Submetering proved to be an effective strategy for the Toyota Motor Sales offices in Washington, D.C. Located on the ninth floor of a full-service building, the suite is metered separately from the other tenants so that Toyota can track the savings from its aggressive energy use reduction. CBRE broker Sally Wilson said that the idea of being able to negotiate and do submetering is very important, especially in Washington, because many buildings house law firms that operate from 7 a.m. to 11 p.m. Toyota's 9 a.m. to 5 p.m. schedule meant that with a triple net pro rata lease, they essentially would be paying for a portion of the overtime HVAC energy used by the law firms. "When it's all hidden in rent, it's a fixed cost," says Wilson. "Operating costs escalate on an annual basis, but typically the escalation is fixed and usually more than covers the cost for the landlord, so there's no incentive to save. Submetering enables tenants to see exactly what they pay and to become more efficient. It's one of the best things to get into a lease."

Toyota has also purchased green power credits for 100 percent of its energy needs. Green power is a voluntary program to encourage the development and use of renewable energy such as solar, wind, geothermal, biomass and low-impact hydro. Interiors projects will be limited in their ability to connect directly to renewable energy sources, and the green power credits provide an opportunity to encourage others to get off the grid. Green-e certificates can be purchased from independent marketers or accredited utility programs. The Green-e Web site, www.green-e.org, details the programs.

Marcus Sheffer, an energy and environmental consultant with more than twenty years of experience, believes that "significant improvements in energy efficiency are not generated by a 'black box' solution implemented at one time. It is the result of many, mostly small, measures taken over time. . . . How the facility is operated is equally as important (if not more so) as the system's efficiencies. Reductions of greater than 50 percent of energy use are possible with the right equipment and the right attitude." In the following essay Sheffer addresses the issues and provides an overview of the design opportunities that will be explored in detail throughout this chapter.

## Energy Efficiency in an Interiors Project

### By Marcus Sheffer

*Recent events continue to underscore the importance of energy efficiency. Rising prices, fossil fuel emissions (including mercury contamination and climate change gases), dwindling oil supplies, and an increase in resource-driven conflicts all point to the need to develop a transition to alternative, cleaner, more local, and equitably distributed sources of energy. Many energy prognosticators have predicted that the world has already or will shortly hit peak oil production, resulting in less supply than demand and rapidly escalating prices.*

*Energy efficiency can soften the inevitable blow to our economy, our environment, and our security. It lessens demand, which can reduce costs and emissions while extending supplies and allowing renewable energy sources to be developed. For many construction projects energy efficiency provides the economic incentive, which enables the green building project to provide a positive return on investment. Unfortunately, in many tenant situations a disincentive to producing energy savings exists. The tenant has no incentive to upgrade a property owned by another, especially if the tenant does not pay the utility bills. The building owner often sees utility costs as a fixed expense, and as long as the tenant is not using considerably more energy than projected, it is an overlooked opportunity.*

*The adage "You can't manage what you don't measure" applies well to energy usage. Submetering* of tenant spaces enables energy management and can provide the incentive to reduce usage. A net lease where the tenant pays the utility bills can encourage greater energy efficiency since the tenant is the direct beneficiary of the savings. Tenant spaces with a gross lease that includes utilities have no such incentive. In this case the building owner has the incentive to reduce operating expenses through energy savings.

Innovative leasing and financing arrangements can be implemented so that tenants and owners can share the cost and benefits of energy efficiency projects. Owners can increase net operating income and the value of the asset. Every dollar saved is worth a $10 increase in asset value. Tenants can lower operating costs and in many cases can use energy-saving projects to finance major system upgrades and other tenant improvements.

Numerous opportunities exist to reduce operating costs, increase income and asset value, and improve cash flow. Many of these opportunities are outlined below.

## Commissioning

Building design and construction as currently practiced makes a very unusual "industry." Compared to the manufacture of almost any other product, the building industry lacks investment in research and development, feedback loops, definitive accountability, vertical integration, and in most cases no one is solely responsible for quality control. This last issue is where the commissioning authority comes in. Commissioning provides a bridge between design and construction to ensure that the systems are installed and operate as the designers intended.

The building systems are inspected and tested in the commissioning process to ensure proper sequence of operation in the lighting and control systems. Too often fit-outs are completed but the systems do not function properly. A direct result in most projects that are commissioned is energy savings. (Refer to the detailed discussion of commissioning in Chapter 1.)

## Lighting

The greatest energy efficiency opportunity for most tenant spaces will be in the area of lighting design. Lighting accounts for approximately 25 to 40 percent of total energy use in most commercial spaces. Lighting power density (LPD) is a measure of the total connected wattage divided by the square footage of the space. Best-practice lighting design typically involves a task-ambient approach. Supplemental task lighting is provided where it is needed for the performance of a particular task such as reading. Ambient lighting levels are provided primarily for circulation rather than to accommodate all possible tasks in a space. A well-designed lighting system will reduce first costs compared to standard practice since fewer fixtures are typically needed.

Lighting controls can also be used to reduce lighting energy use and lower LPD values. Occupancy sensors, daylight dimming, and zone controls should be used where appropriate. Occupancy sensors are particularly useful in intermittently occupied spaces with more than four light fixtures. Restrooms, offices, conference rooms, and stack aisles are all prime candidates. Studies show that most cubicles are vacant approximately 30 percent of the day. An occupancy sensor can be used to turn off task lighting, computer monitors, and other nonessential items when the space is unoccupied. Daylight sensors are effective in perimeter zones and in areas with skylights or other overhead daylighting strategies. Zone controls should be used in large spaces to ensure that the lights are turned off at night and on the weekends.

## Equipment

When purchasing equipment and appliances, consider the future operating costs; in many cases this cost will exceed the purchase price over time. The U.S. EPA's Energy Star program evaluates and rates the energy use of more than forty different types of products. Equipment with the lowest energy use earns an Energy Star rating. Major categories include appliances, electronics, lighting, commercial food service, and office equipment.

*Office equipment, in particular, can be a significant energy user in many leased facilities. LCD screens, laptops, and ink jet printers all consume considerably less energy than CRT screens, desktop computers, and laser printers. Power management features in computers and copiers reduce energy use by putting the equipment to "sleep" when not in use.*

### HVAC

*Although often not under the control of a tenant, the heating and cooling equipment will likely use the greatest amount of energy in most leased spaces. The effective utilization of building controls can often yield the greatest savings.*

*Zoning, especially in relatively large spaces, can be an effective measure to ensure that areas are not being overheated or overcooled. Perimeter spaces with differing solar orientations as well as interior spaces should be separately zoned. Each of these spaces may have vastly different thermal properties relative to direct sunlight, wind, envelope performance, internal gains, and occupancy densities.*

*Controls such as occupancy and $CO_2$ sensors can offer effective energy-saving strategies. Occupancy sensors tied to HVAC system components, such as variable air volume (VAV) units, reduce airflow when a space is unoccupied. Demand-controlled ventilation (DCV) is an effective strategy in spaces with highly variable occupancy such as training rooms. DCV systems use $CO_2$ concentrations to determine the optimal amount of outside air to bring into a large-volume space.*

*Displacement ventilation systems, such as underfloor air, can provide significant performance benefits in terms of indoor air quality and improved thermal comfort and can generate energy savings. These systems tend to operate at lower pressures that require less fan energy. In addition, delivered air temperatures can be 5 to 7°F higher to further reduce energy costs.*

---

Marcus Sheffer of Energy Opportunities provides technical consulting services on projects relating to energy management, efficiency, and conservation; renewable energy systems; and the environmental impacts of human enterprises.

# ▌Lighting

## Turning Off the Lights

The best way to save energy is to turn things off, and there's no better way to do that than by eliminating, or at least reducing, unnecessary lighting. Few things are more exasperating than rooms flooded with daylight *and* electric lights, or an empty suite of offices all lit up throughout the night. Many interiors projects featured in magazines articles that claim to be green will limit the list of sustainable attributes to the materials used and yet ignore the substantial environmental benefits of good lighting design.

There are three components to proper lighting: the source, the distribution, and the controls. When these are integrated into a well-designed plan, not only is the experience of the building's occupants maximized but energy use is optimized.

Light comes from two primary sources, the sun and electric lighting. Our solar source is, of course, perpetual; our challenge is to learn how to effectively capture and use this free and abundant resource that generates no waste and creates no pollution. Daylight is also the most pleasing illumination available to humans, and the producers of electric lighting constantly strive to replicate its color spectrum and color-rendering properties. Unfortunately, the products that do this best can be the biggest energy hogs, which further strengthen the case for good daylighting design. When properly implemented, daylighting not only lessens the need for electric lighting but also offers energy savings by reducing the heat gain generated by electric lamps. Daylighting is a complicated issue that must be integrated into the project design as early as possible. It also has many other benefits tied to productivity and well-being. These as well as the design issues will be fully discussed in Chapter 5.

## Turning On the Lights

There are times, of course, when daylighting isn't available or isn't sufficient and must be augmented by electric lights. How this is done is enormously important since lighting and the cooling associated with it can account for up to 40 percent of a building's energy use. A commonly accepted

## Table 3-6: Lighting Power Density Targets

| LPD (watts/ft²) | ASHRAE 90.1-1999 | ASHRAE 90.1-2004 | Best Practice |
|---|---|---|---|
| Offices | 1.3 | 1.1 | 0.6 |
| Retail | 1.9 | 1.7 | 0.9 |
| Dining | 1.5–1.8 | 0.9–1.4 | 0.8 |
| Warehouse | 1.2 | 0.9 | 0.5 |

Source: Marcus Sheffer

## Table 3-7: A Lighting Glossary

| Light Levels | |
|---|---|
| Lumens | The light output from a lamp. |
| Luminance | The amount of light that reaches a surface. |
| Footcandles (FC) | The measurement of the amount of light or luminance falling on a surface. One footcandle is equal to one lumen per square foot. Lumens per square meter are called lux. |
| **Light Quality** | |
| Color rendering index (CRI) | The measurement of how realistically a light source represents color, on a scale of 0–100. Daylight and incandescent light sources have a CRI of 100. |
| Color temperature | The measurement of the color of the light output, expressed in Kelvins. Generally, sources below 3200K are considered "warm," while those above 4000K are considered "cool." |
| **Light Sources** | |
| Lamp | An electric light source, sometimes referred to as a bulb. |
| Luminaire | A complete lighting unit consisting of one or more lamps, reflector housing, and power source connection, also referred to as a fixture; can be portable or permanently mounted. |
| **Light Energy** | |
| Watt | A measure of the electric power used by a lamp to produce light. |
| Lighting power density (LPD) | The maximum allowable lighting power permitted by the code. It is expressed in watts per square foot for a given occupancy/space type. |

Source: Adapted from Environmental Building News, June 2002

rule of thumb is that every watt saved in lighting saves an additional ¼ watt in avoided HVAC energy.

Many interior spaces are overlit, and right-sizing the lighting plan not only saves energy but also adds considerably to occupant comfort.

In the not-too-distant past it was common for lighting plan designs to provide maximum lighting levels throughout a space rather than be tailored to specific ambient, task, and accent requirements, often resulting in a uniform and irritating wash of light. Fortunately, this practice is transitioning to customized levels specific to different uses. In his essay, Marcus Sheffer discusses the importance of lighting power density (LPD) as a measurement tool, and in Table 3-6 he provides recommended LPD targets for typical tenant spaces. Achieving the best-practice levels noted in the table requires a careful balance of many elements: lamp choices, energy-efficient fixtures, placement, and controls.

Another concept important to good lighting design is efficacy, which compares light output to energy consumption and is measured in lumens per watt (lm/W). For example, if a 100-watt source produces 9,000 lumens, then the efficacy is 90 lm/W. Higher numbers are better because energy not converted to light is released as heat, causing occupant discomfort that must be removed by the cooling system, thereby using more energy. According to a June 2002 article in *Environmental Building News*, a typical incandescent lamp converts about 10 percent of the electric current (electrons) into visible light; the rest—about 90 percent—is released as heat.[8] Efficacy's relevance will become clearer as we look at a variety of light sources.

## Lamps and Luminaires

Optimal lighting depends upon the pairing of the right lamp and luminaire. For example, in a garage a bare fluorescent strip light would be appropriate and highly efficient, whereas in an office it would create too much glare and be distracting. Mounting the light strip in a direct/indirect luminaire is a far better choice. Fixtures, unless they are distinctive decorative elements, should be unobtrusive. Oftentimes they are integrated into the architecture—in coves, for example. Luminaires will have different parts (housings, reflectors, ballasts, diffusers, etc.) depending on the application and lamp.

*Incandescent lamps* have been lighting's workhorse for some time, and for good reason—low initial cost, pleasing color (measured by a lamp's color rendering index, or CRI), easy dimming, and the ability to precisely focus the beam. Unlike other lamps, they contain no mercury, which is a good environmental benefit. However, they have a relatively short life and generate a lot of heat. A standard 100-watt bulb has an efficacy of about 17 lm/W, although recent advances can boost the number.

*Halogen lamps,* a variation of the incandescent bulb, give off a bright white light. This quality plus the ease of directing the light with reflectors makes their use particularly appealing for retail, gallery, and museum applications, especially low-voltage MR-16s. However, they are often used as multiples at high wattages in order to achieve the desired effect and can become extremely hot.

Although *fluorescent lighting* has been around since the 1940s and has been used almost exclusively in commercial offices and retail applications such as supermarkets for many decades, it carried a stigma, and rightly so. Row upon row of evenly spaced, ceiling mounted luminaries fitted with fat fluorescent tubes and magnetic ballasts that hummed and flickered, low CRI numbers, and high ("cool") color temperatures resulted in very unpleasant visual experiences. However, many improvements have been made, and today's fluorescent lighting approaches the attractiveness of incandescent sources while providing excellent efficacy and long life, as shown in Table 3-8.

Light quality and color rendering of fluorescent lamps have improved through the development of new phosphor coatings, and CRI ratings approaching 95 have been achieved. Mercury levels have been reduced, so they are no longer considered hazardous waste in most jurisdictions. However, the most significant development in fluorescent lamps has been their size and shape, with the two basic types being tubular and compact fluorescent lamps.

Fluorescent tubes are defined by their diameters. T-12 lamps were for many years the industry standard. However, they are being replaced by smaller and more energy-efficient T-8s and T-5s. The numbers refer to the tube diameter in eighths of an inch, and the smaller lamps are better, with superior efficacy and control. T-8 lamps are currently the most commonly used partly because they are so easily retrofitted into the older T-12 luminaires. Although manufacturers continue to introduce advanced T-8s that deliver increasingly good energy savings (Philips Alto TR825W, for example), T-5s are the next generation of lamp technology and, in many ways, a better environmental and stylis-

### Table 3-8: Lamp Characteristics by Type

| Lamp Type | Efficacy (lm/W) | CRI | Color Temp (K) | Life (hours) | Life Cycle Cost |
|---|---|---|---|---|---|
| Incandescent | 8–20 | 100 | 2700 | 800–3,000 | High |
| Halogen | 12–24 | 100 | 2800–3100 | 2,000–5,000 | High |
| Fluorescent tubes | 49–89 | 49–90 | 2700–6500 | 7,500–24,000 | Low |
| CFL | 40–87 | 85 | 2700–5400 | 8,000–10,000 | Low |
| LED | 1–40 | 60 | n/a | 10,000–80,000 | Low |

*Source:* Information adapted from *Environmental Building News,* June 2002

### Table 3-9: Performance Comparison of Linear Fluorescent Lamps

| Lamp Type | Length (inches) | Rated Watts | Rated Lumens | Rated Life (hours) | Efficacy (lm/W) | Luminance (cd/sf) |
|-----------|-----------------|-------------|--------------|--------------------|-----------------|-------------------|
| T-12 | 48 | 40 | 3,300 | 20,000 | 74.3 | 800 |
| T-8 | 48 | 32 | 2,950 | 24,000 | 87.5 | 1,200 |
| T-5 | 45.8 | 28 | 2,900 | 20,000 | 98.4 | 2,000 |
| T-5 HO | 45.8 | 54 | 5,000 | 20,000 | 92.6 | 3,400 |

*Source:* Adapted from *Advanced Lighting Guidelines,* 2003 edition, New Building Institute

tic choice. Table 3-9 compares the performance of the most commonly used T-12, T-8, and T-5 lamps and demonstrates the benefits of the newer lamps over their older predecessors.

Since 1995, when T-5s first entered the market, they have become popular for a number of reasons.

- Smaller and more stylish luminaries can be used.
- The smaller size of the lamps allows more optical control.
- A wide variety of ballast options is available.
- High-output (HO) T-5s, though sized the same, are available with higher wattages, making it possible to achieve the same light output with a two-lamp luminaire using T-5 HO lamps than a three-lamp luminaire using T-8 lamps, reducing the number of fixtures per project.
- The smaller size of T-5s makes them suitable for use in narrow spaces such as coves, cabinets, and displays, replacing the less efficacious halogen lamps that have been commonly used in such applications.

Many manufacturers offer luminaires, both decorative and functional and often with minimal structure, to house T-5s and control glare. Available with parabolic louvers and acrylic and metal mesh panels to shield the lamps from direct view, they are often used as direct/indirect light sources, which will be discussed in greater detail below. New advances, such as Lithonia's RT5, use refractor systems and precisely extruded prisms to efficiently and evenly diffuse light.

The environmental benefits of T-5 lamps mainly accrue from their reduced size. Compared to T-8s, less material, including mercury and phosphor, is used and packaging

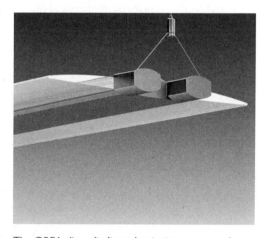

The OREA direct/indirect luminaire accommodates T-5 or T-5 HO lamps and delivers optimal low-glare lighting. © *Zumtobel Staff 2006*

RT5, a recessed fluorescent lighting fixture, uses up to 33 percent less energy than the industry standard for office lighting, which is an 18-cell, 3-lamp T8 parabolic fixture. *Photography courtesy of Lithonia Lighting*

and transportation costs are reduced. However, T-5 lamps cannot be used to replace T-8s because they are a different size and require different ballasts. Retrofits require replacement of the system, which may or may not make sense depending on the situation. T-8 lamps with electronic ballasts will be a big improvement and yield significant energy savings over T-12s with magnetic ballasts. Although retrofitting a twenty-year-old luminaire with a replacement reflector kit and lamp will cost half as much as a new system, design opportunities have been lost. Installing a new direct/indirect T-5 system that can be programmed to do almost anything is much more expensive than a simple retrofit but yields better energy use reduction, and the overall result will be so much more elegant and attractive.

An excellent publication on T-5 lighting systems and the source for much of this information is available through Rensselaer Polytechnic Institute and its National Lighting Product Information Program (NLPIP).[9]

*Compact fluorescent lamps (CFLs)* were introduced into the market in the early 1980s and have had a big impact. The U.S. Department of Energy states that if every household in the U.S. replaced one light bulb with an Energy Star-qualified CFL, it would prevent enough pollution to equal removing one million cars from the road. A Green Seal report lists the following stats, which further emphasize the many cost and energy advantages of CFLs:

- By switching from incandescent lighting to compact fluorescent lighting, the average consumer can save 50 to 80 percent in energy costs without any loss in lighting quality.
- The average compact fluorescent bulb lasts eight to ten times longer than any incandescent bulb.
- Depending on the initial cost of the bulb, the Federal Trade Commission estimates that it costs $2.60 less per year to power a compact fluorescent bulb than an incandescent bulb. The full purchase price of the bulb will be paid back well within the ten-year life expectancy.

CFLs work in the same way as tubular lamps, but they've been folded and bent into shapes that enable them to replace incandescent bulbs. They are now commonly available with standard Edison screw bases that fit normal sockets, so retrofits are easy, especially in areas where beam control is not important, such as corridors, stairwells, and lobbies.

Choosing the proper CFL can be confusing, and Green Seal recommends a 3:1 ratio: a CFL rated at 20 watts can replace an incandescent of 60 watts. However, the color temperature and CRI must also be considered. Lower temperatures, in the 2700K to 3000K range, will produce a warmer color, while a CRI of 80 or above is preferred for the best color reproduction.

Four-pin CFLs are more efficacious and a better choice

CFLs, both self-ballasted and 4-pin, are available in a variety of shapes. *Source: Compact fluorescent lighting by GE*

when using the lamps in system design: because they use an electronic ballast, start better, produce less flicker, and don't buzz. Their performance and use are dependent on the ballast and luminaire, and many unique products have been developed in order to take advantage of their small size.

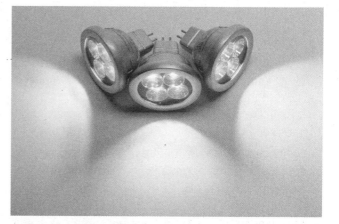

The lamp that is perhaps generating the greatest buzz at the moment is the LED (light-emitting diode). Well-known lighting designer David Nelson of David Nelson Associates says that LEDs are a great light source with many advantages and some disadvantages. On the plus side, they are superdirectional, so light can be placed exactly where it's needed. They are very small, do not generate much heat, and have an extremely long life span—true environmental benefits. Traditionally they have been used as indicators—in electronics, exit signs, toys, traffic signals, and so on—and display panels, but not for general illumination or ambient lighting.

They are, however, beginning to be used in unique ways. A recent study from the Lighting Research Center demonstrated that LEDs can be effective, energy-saving alternatives for incandescent downlights in elevators. A field installation using prototype LED fixtures showed an energy savings of 45 percent compared with the original incandescent lights.[10] Luxo has recently introduced an LED lamp for its Arketto task light. Three 3-watt LEDs will replace the 40-watt halogen lamp.

Although they have a poor CRI, it is their color capabilities that make them so intriguing. LEDs emit colored light without the use of the colored filters that other lighting sources require and can be grouped together to produce combinations of colors that cannot be achieved with other sources. Nelson believes that development of a luminaire that will manipulate and change color temperature throughout the day is on the horizon. In his opinion, Color Kinetics leads the industry in engineering LED products offering great control options for their color change technology and good design support. Although best known for their colored lighting, the company has also introduced white-light LEDs that are a good alternative for retail applications where excessive heat from other light sources is a problem, or in situations where frequent lamp replacement is difficult.

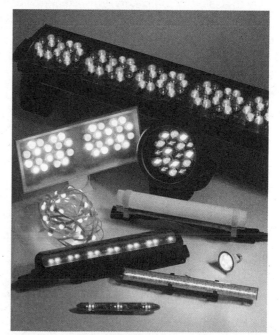

Color Kinetics, a leader in LED technology, manufactures lamps in a multitude of sizes and shapes, from wall-washing fixtures to cove accents. *Photography courtesy of Color Kinetics © 2006*

## Lighting Controls as Part of Integrated Lighting Design

The mantra of green building—integrated design—is a key aspect of most lighting control strategies. It is easy to fall into the trap of thinking of lighting control as the selection of devices to reduce light levels or turn off lights at the right times, but effective lighting control strategies usually must be integrated with the building design, the building's HVAC system, and occupancy patterns. Effective lighting control strategies should be informed by the following factors.

*Lighting requirements.* Different types of spaces have very different lighting requirements—relative both to light levels and to acceptability of different control strategies. The Illuminating Engineering Society of North America publishes standards for light levels in different spaces, but other variables can affect those requirements. Within a given space (an office or classroom, for example), the lighting requirements can vary considerably depending on who is using the space and how it is being used, and as we age, we need higher light levels to function productively.

*Lighting costs.* Electricity costs and demand charges (charges based on time-of-day and peak usage) vary widely by region and by building type. What you pay for electricity and electricity demand has a significant impact on what types of lighting controls make sense.

*Budget.* Some lighting control strategies involve significant first costs. These costs can often be an obstacle to the more sophisticated control strategies or more widespread use of controls throughout a building.

*Commitment of occupants.* How diligent employees or building occupants are relative to energy savings can influence the type lighting controls selected. Somewhat ironically, with the most diligent or committed building occupants, the need for—and benefit of—advanced lighting controls is often the lowest.

*Ability to deal with complexity.* While some lighting control strategies are very simple and intuitive in their operation, there is no getting around the fact that others are very complex. A lighting control strategy should not be employed if it is beyond the abilities of the building occupants to understand, operate, and maintain. This means that some strategies are best left to buildings that have well-trained facility managers. This also means that education of the facilities staff and/or building occupants should be planned for with an advanced lighting control system.

*Source:* Alex Wilson, "Lighting Controls: Beyond the Toggle Switch," *Environmental Building News,* June 2003.

## Controls

Lighting controls can be as simple as a toggle switch or as complicated as a computer-based ballast communication system. They should be used as a lighting management tool to increase occupant comfort and save the maximum amount of energy and money—up to 50 percent or more is attainable. In addition to simply turning lamps on and off, sophisticated control strategies manipulate light in order to achieve desired effects. Devices, on the other hand, are the hardware that is used to implement the strategies. Both will be discussed here and also in Chapter 5 as part of the daylighting section.

Room occupants habitually switch lights on more often than they turn them off, and the objective of controls is to either automate the process of turning them off or at least make it easier, so that energy consumption is minimized. Timed devices and occupancy and daylighting sensors are

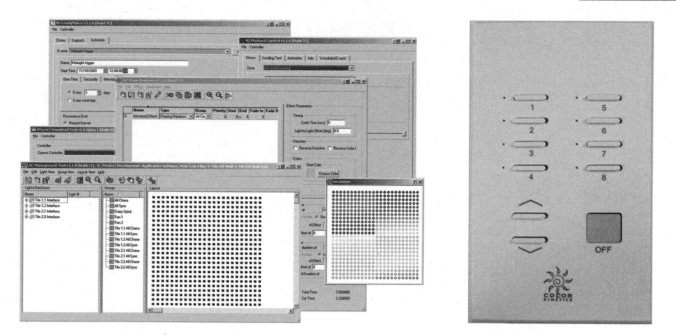

Control devices from Color Kinetics range from simple dimmer-type knobs and keypads to software packages for system control.
*Photography courtesy of Color Kinetics © 2006*

the most common controls used, but new, more sophisticated technologies are also available.

Timers, either manual or preset, that turn lights on and off at specific times are practical for many types of spaces. The manual devices may be useful in trash rooms, for example, where occupants can turn them on for one to fifteen minutes via a rotary dial. Most wall box units are now digital timers that can be set from five minutes to twelve hours or more, are manual-on but auto-off, and have flash or beep warnings. One that is highly recommended is the Watt Stopper TS 400. Time clocks turn lights on and off on a predetermined schedule, and the more sophisticated models are programmable to accommodate weekends and holidays. David Nelson designed a timer-controlled system for the circulation and large open areas of an architectural office (see the Boulder Associates project in Chapter 8) with manual override switches for occupants to turn the lights back on if they need them. Timers installed in restrooms to reduce illumination time from twenty-four to twelve hours per day will result in a 50 percent savings. Even with these devices, lights are likely to be left on far more often than they need to be.

Occupancy sensors are another choice, and they've come a long way from the days when sitting too still at one's desk could plunge a worker into darkness. (A humorous *Dilbert* cartoon depicts a man positioned in a cubicle whose sole job is to wave his arms around to keep the lights on.) Sometimes referred to as motion sensors, a variety of devices with different technologies react to the presence or absence of movement within a given area. They can be used in most space types but are highly recommended in spaces that are not regularly occupied, such as copy, conference, storage, and restroom areas. There are also certain areas such as mechanical rooms that, for safety reasons, should not be controlled by occupancy sensors.

Two characteristics are very important when selecting occupancy sensors: sensitivity and reliability. Sensors that are falsely triggered by air movement, for example, will frustrate occupants, who will likely disable them. The various available sensor technologies and their advantages and disadvantages are listed in Table 3-10.

Occupancy sensors can be sized to fit a standard wall box, similar to a switch, although others should be positioned higher on walls or on the ceiling for best effectiveness.

**Table 3-10: Occupancy Sensor Technologies**

| Type | How They Work | Advantages | Disadvantages |
|---|---|---|---|
| Passive infrared (PIR) | Detect body heat—a direct line of sight is required | • Inexpensive<br>• Resistant to false-on<br>• Can be mounted on ceilings | • Cannot see over obstructions<br>• Sensitivity settings difficult |
| Ultrasonic (US) | Detects high-frequency sound wave signals as motion | • Do not require line of sight<br>• No coverage gaps<br>• Good for oddly shaped and larger spaces | • Prone to false-on<br>• Cannot be mounted as high on ceilings |
| Audible (audio) | Detect noise | • Do not require line of sight<br>• Can be voice-activated<br>• Inexpensive | • Sensitive to false-on from background noise |
| Hybrids | Combines two or more technologies such as PIR and US, or PIR and audible | • Reliable<br>• Wide coverage | • May require more adjustments |

*Source:* Information adapted from Green Seal and *Environmental Building News*

*The Lighting Control Best Practice Guide—Office Buildings,* published by Watt Stopper, a lighting control manufacturer, offers the following control design guidelines:

■ Mount ultrasonic occupancy sensors at least 6 to 8 feet away from HVAC ducts on vibration-free surfaces, and place them so that there is no detection out the door or other opening of the space.

■ In private offices and conference rooms, include switches for manual override control of the lighting.

■ Install night or emergency lighting to insure safe egress if lighting is turned off automatically or manually when people are still in the space.

■ Carefully match the correct voltage and load rating requirements for the specific lighting control devices.

■ For medium and small offices use ceiling-mounted, corner-mounted, or wall-switch passive infrared occupancy sensors; dual-technology sensors are best for larger offices.

■ Smaller lighting control zones are preferable so that fewer lights are turned on by occupants after hours and less energy is used.

Personalized sensors can be positioned at individual workstations to control task lighting, monitors, and other desktop equipment using devices that look like power strips. Essential items such as computers and fax machines that must be on regardless of occupancy are plugged into uncontrolled outlets, as shown in the illustration on the facing page.

Dimming is another control strategy that can increase energy savings as well as provide a way for occupants to adjust lighting levels to their liking. Dimmers, also known as rheostats, vary the current through an electric light in order to control the level of brightness. Manual dimming of incandescent lamps is relatively easy and inexpensive, often with slide or dial wall-mounted controls that also include toggle switching.

Fluorescent dimming is more complicated because the dimming device has to interact with the fixture's ballast. Fluorescent lamps need a ballast controlling the electric current in order to operate. The old magnetic ballasts that made dimming difficult have been replaced with electronic high-frequency ballasts, which typically use 20 percent less energy, are able to operate multiple lamps, are lighter, are quieter, and eliminate lamp flicker. Fluorescent lamps and ballast configurations have been optimized for better performance and greater flexibility.

Some types of lamps are easier to control than others. Screw-base CFLs with integral ballasts and some linear lamp luminaires can be dimmed with simple technology,

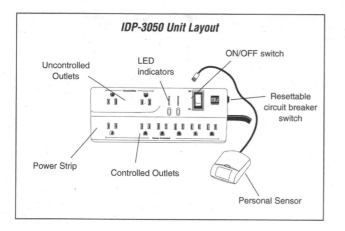

**IDP-3050 Unit Layout**

Uncontrolled Outlets

LED indicators

ON/OFF switch

Resettable circuit breaker switch

Power Strip

Controlled Outlets

Personal Sensor

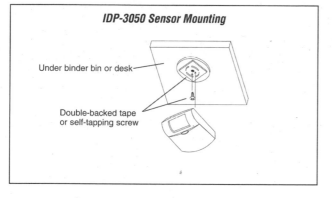

**IDP-3050 Sensor Mounting**

Under binder bin or desk

Double-backed tape or self-tapping screw

Workstation occupancy sensors can be personalized to differentiate between "always on" and "as needed" equipment.
© Wattstopper/Legrand 2006

but sophisticated dimming strategies require dedicated dimmer equipment and lighting control management plans. There are a wide variety of technologies that afford user convenience and comfort while providing energy savings:

- Standard on/off switches and relays can be used to turn groups of lights on and off together. Creative design options can be developed with this simple tool, if the circuiting is properly designed. For example, some of the lamps in each fixture can be switched together, every other fixture can be switched as a group, or lighting near the windows can be turned off when daylight is plentiful.

- Manual hard-wired control consists of a dimmer, connected to a single luminaire or zone, which is operated by the user at the device.

- Preset scene dimming controls change the light level settings for multiple zones simultaneously at the press of a button.

- Remote control dimming is another form of manual dimming that is well suited for retrofit projects to minimize rewiring. Infrared and radio frequency technologies are most successful in these applications. Remote infrared control operates in a similar fashion to other infrared technologies like television, for example.

- Radio frequency controls are equipped with a sender that "talks" to other dimmers' receivers. This allows multi-zone control from a single-zone device.

- Personal control systems are now available that allow users to change levels of lighting, sound, heating/cooling, etc., in their own workspaces.

- Centralized controls can be used to automatically turn on, turn off, and/or dim lighting at specific times or under certain load conditions. This type of control can be used in a conference room or on a building-wide scale. Centralized control strategies can also integrate lighting controls with other building systems such as mechanical or security systems.

- Distributed controls are based on digital communication protocols. These systems are local, or integral, to the luminaire itself, not housed in a central cabinet or enclosure. They integrate with building automation or energy management system. A Digital Addressable Lighting Interface (DALI) system provides a means of control that can speak to an individual ballast or groups of ballasts. The "control wiring" is independent of the "power wiring" and provides the highest degree of flexibility available at this time. When space configuration or occupant needs change, the system can respond by reassigning the ballasts accordingly.

Source: David Nelson, *Whole Building Design Guide*, www.wbdg.org/electriclighting

## Table 3-11: Lighting Control Strategies by Space Type

| Space Type | Typical Use Pattern | If . . . | Then . . . |
|---|---|---|---|
| Cafeterias or lunchrooms | Occasionally occupied | Daylighted | Consider daylight-driven dimming or on/off control. |
| | | Electric lights | Consider ceiling-mounted occupancy sensor(s). Make sure minor motion will be detected in all desired locations. |
| Computer room | Usually occupied | Lights are left on all the time | Consider occupancy sensors with manual dimming. Be sure that minor motion will be detected and that equipment vibration will not falsely trigger the sensor. |
| Conference room | Occasionally occupied | Multiple tasks, from video conferencing to presentations | Consider manual dimming (possibly preset scene control). |
| | | Small conference room | Consider a wall box occupancy sensor. |
| | | Large conference room | Consider ceiling- or wall-mounted occupancy sensor(s). Be sure that minor motion will be detected in all desired locations. |
| Copy rooms | Occasionally occupied | Lights are left on when they are not needed | Consider an occupancy sensor. Be sure that machine vibration will not falsely trigger the sensor. |
| Hallways | Any | Occasionally or usually occupied | Consider occupancy sensors with elongated throw. Be sure that coverage does not extend beyond the desired area. |
| | | Daylighted | Consider daylight on/off control. |
| Lobby or atrium | Usually occupied but no one "owns" the space | Daylighted and lights should always appear on | Consider automatic daylight-driven dimming. |
| | | It isn't a problem if lights go completely off in high daylight | Consider automatic daylight-driven dimming or on/off control. |
| | | Lights are left on all night long, even when no one is in the area for long periods | Consider occupancy sensors. Be sure that minor motion will be detected in all desired areas. |
| Open office | Usually occupied | Daylighted | Consider automatic daylight-driven dimming. |
| | | Varied tasks, from computer usage to reading | Consider manual dimming. |
| | | Lights left on after hours | Consider centralized controls and/or occupancy sensors. |
| Private office | Primarily one person, coming and going | Daylighted | Consider manual dimming, automatic daylight-driven dimming, or automatic on/off. |
| | | Occupants are likely to leave lights on and occupants would be in direct view of a wall box sensor | Consider a wall box occupancy sensor. Add dimming capabilities if appropriate. |
| | | Occupants are likely to leave lights on and partitions or objects could hide an occupant from the sensor | Consider a ceiling- or wall-mounted occupancy sensor. Add dimming capabilities if appropriate. |
| Restroom | Any | Has stalls | Consider a ceiling-mounted ultrasonic occupancy sensor for full coverage. |
| | | Single toilet (no partitions) | Consider a wall switch occupancy sensor. |

*Source:* Information adapted from WBDG, Electric Lighting Controls, David Nelson, www.wbdg.org

Nelson states that in the area of controls, industry is moving toward technology that is smarter on a component by component basis—occupancy sensors that have some artificial intelligence, smart ballasts that can be programmed to do anything, such as indicate when it's time to change the lamp, and wireless systems that will present a lot of interesting opportunities.

The presence of daylight in a building offers the potential for significant energy savings—from 10 to 50 percent—but only if the proper controls are installed. A successful control system integrates electric lighting with daylighting and makes adjustments accordingly through photoelectric technology. Photoswitches and photosensors are the most commonly used. Some switches simply turn lights off when there is ample daylight and are often used for outdoor lighting. However, the abruptness of the change is not well suited for interior applications and should be used only where it makes sense or if cost is a factor. Most people are bothered by rapid changes in light levels, often prompting them to disable the device, but they will barely notice gradual shifts. More expensive photoswitches can provide multilevel switching schemes so that the changes are not perceptible.

Photosensors provide more flexibility such as stepped dimming to intermediate light levels. The choices of commonly available technologies, as explained by Alex Wilson, fall into two categories: open-loop or closed-loop. "With open-loop systems, the photosensor is located remotely from the space being illuminated. The photosensor adjusts the light level based on the available daylight. A single photosensor can control any number of lights in an open-loop system. With a closed-loop system, the photosensor is in the space it controls, so the light level being measured includes both the natural daylight and light provided by electric light fixtures. Because of this configuration, a closed-loop photosensor can control only a small number of lights. In small spaces, such as individual offices and classrooms, closed-loop systems are most commonly used, while open-loop systems are more commonly used for larger spaces such as airports and factories. Most photosensors have time-delay settings that establish how quickly the dimming will respond to changes in light level. A time delay is important with daylighting controls to prevent potentially distracting light level fluctuations as clouds pass over. But if the time delay is too long, a room may get too dark or too bright as daylight levels fluctuate."[11]

The design of a lighting control strategy is dependant on several conditions: the type of the space, how it's used, who uses it, and daylight availability. Table 3-11 offers scenarios for common office spaces.

The success of lighting controls depends upon their performance—do they work as they were intended? This is best determined by commissioning, a process that was fully discussed in Chapter 1; however, the commissioning issues specific to lighting controls often involve adjustments that need to be made after furniture installations or fine tuning for sensitivity and coverage. A play on the old adage could go something like this: if it *is* broke, *do* fix it, otherwise it does you and your energy bill no good.

## Distribution

The types of lamps, luminaires, and controls that are used in an interior space are somewhat irrelevant unless they deliver the appropriate amount of brightness and are properly placed according to function. Lighting plans should be designed to strike the right balance between energy savings and occupant comfort and productivity. Too much or too little brightness can result in long-term eye fatigue, so it's important to get it right. Illumination standards for lighting levels on horizontal surfaces are shown in Table 3-12.

| Table 3-12: Footcandle Recommendations for Common Office Areas | |
| --- | --- |
| Private office | 50 |
| Open office (combination of paper and VDT tasks) | 50 |
| Open office (primarily VDT tasks) | 30 |
| Offices (visually intensive tasks) | 100 + |
| Conference/meeting rooms | 30 |
| Public areas (lobby/lounge/reception) | 10 |
| Corridor/stairway | 5 |
| Elevators | 5 |
| Restrooms | 5 |

*Source:* Excerpted from *IESNA's American National Standard Practice for Office Lighting (RP-1-04),* with permission from IESNA

However, these numbers may be deceptive because others factors must also be considered. According to the Advanced Lighting Guideline (ALG), the determination of lighting level is critical; levels that are too low jeopardize the success of the project, while those that are too high can cause glare and unpleasant light uniformity and result in wasted energy and money.[12] Other factors include the occupants' age. Seniors require almost twice as much illumination as younger people. A school cafeteria may require only 30 footcandles of task illumination, while one in a retirement home may need a light level as high as 50 footcandles. Also, the level of available daylight and controls will guide light level selections as shown in the following ALG example.

"Imagine a private office with a south facing window. Most days the amount of natural light exceeds the 30 footcandles of task light recommended by IESNA for office paperwork. The office may actually average 100 to 300 footcandles and electric light may be unnecessary. However, on particularly dark, cloudy days and at sunrise and sunset on clear days, it's necessary to maintain these task light levels with electric lighting. Later in the evening, a lower task light level may be acceptable, and by the time people arrive to clean the office, task light probably isn't needed and the ambient light level can be reduced to three footcandles. Most importantly, when the space is vacant, the light should be turned off."[13]

Studies show that people, except for the elderly, want lower light levels than the current standards allow, especially in computer/monitor-intensive areas. "Gender, age, background, and expectations of lighting levels and brightness are different among various people due to individual experiences," states David Nelson, citing Malaysia versus the Netherlands as two extremes. "In the past, we've always tried to satisfy the highest common denominator—the person who wanted the highest level of light. In a RPI study when individuals were given the opportunity to dim the lights to where they wanted, the average was from 14 to 17 footcandles, significantly lower than current standards. Lighting design these days looks not only at physiology of our visual system but is starting to address some of the psychology behind how we see. I often design for lower light levels once my clients understand what they're getting."

Most experts agree that optimal lighting results from ambient light provided by electrical sources augmented by available daylight and supplemented by task and accent lighting. The careful manipulation of these sources will deliver pleasing light that supports work performance and delivers good energy savings.

*Ambient* refers to the overall light in the room. Ambient lighting may come from electric lighting, daylight, or both. Ambient lighting luminaires provide downward (direct) lighting, upward (indirect) lighting, or both, as illustrated below, and is most often recessed in, mounted on, or suspended from the ceiling, although panel-mounted fixtures are also a possibility.

If daylight is available to supplement ambient light levels, automatic controls and dimming systems need to be installed within 15 feet of windows and under skylights in order to take advantage of energy conservation opportunities. However, as mentioned in the HVAC section of this chapter, too much daylight can increase cooling loads and can negate any energy savings. Daylighting control strategies are discussed in detail here and also in Chapter 5. On the facing page, the contribution to light levels from both daylight and electric sources is illustrated. As the daylight contribution falls off, electric lighting makes up the differ-

Light output options are (a) direct, (b) indirect, and (c) direct/indirect. The most pleasing results are often achieved through direct/indirect lighting. *Reprinted with permission from the IESNA's American National Standard Practice for Office Lighting (RP-1-04)*

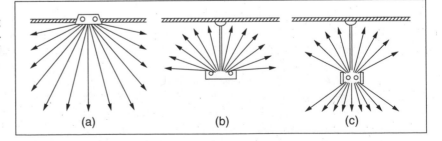

(a)                    (b)                    (c)

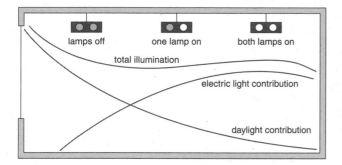

lamps off  one lamp on  both lamps on

total illumination

electric light contribution

daylight contribution

Coordinate daylight and electric lighting controls for maximum energy savings. Electric lighting levels increase as daylight contribution falls off. *Reprinted with permission from the IESNA's American National Standard Practice for Office Lighting (RP-1-04)*

| Table 3-13: Lighting Power Density Models (w/sf) | |
|---|---|
| Whole building: office | 1.0 |
| Space by space | |
| Private office | 1.1 |
| Open office | 1.1 |
| Conference room | 1.3 |
| Training | 1.4 |
| Lobby | 1.3 |
| Corridor | 0.5 |
| Restroom | 0.9 |
| Storage | 0.8 |

*Source:* Information adapted from *ASHRAE/IESNA 90.1-2004 Standard: Lighting Power Density Models,* ©ASHRAE

ence so that total illumination is evenly maintained throughout the room.

While ambient light provides general illumination, task lighting is directed light that is used for specific activities such as reading. Task lights can be hardwired into panel systems or used as portable lamps on the desktop. Pendant fixtures suspended over a dining table or pantry counter are another example. Task lights can and should be adjustable to suit the user's needs and to contribute to energy conservation. Ambient light levels can be reduced significantly when task lighting is used and, according to the Advanced Lighting Guidelines, task-ambient lighting strategies produce energy savings in three additional ways. First, locating the task light source close to the task will efficiently provide the appropriate illumination levels without overlighting surrounding areas. Second, unlike ambient levels, task lighting levels are intermittent. Last, empty workstations and offices may be dark or only dimly lit.[14] For best occupant comfort, the contrast between the ambient and task light shouldn't be too great. A rule of thumb for the brightness ratio is 3:1, such as an ambient light level of 25 footcandles and a task light level of 75 footcandles.

While footcandles are a good measurement of light levels, energy use is measured in watts, and energy savings can best be calculated through lighting power density (LPD) for a building or a space. The ASHRAE/IESNA 90.1-2004 standard establishes LPD models for whole buildings and for individual spaces, as shown in Table 3-13.

These energy code limits are useful in determining if enough light is being provided and also serve as a benchmark for achieving greater energy savings. Good—in fact, excellent—office lighting is possible at 1 watt per square foot or less.

# ■ Heating and Cooling

Architects and interior designers often avoid the HVAC system of a tenant space and its energy efficiency, leaving the entire issue in the hands of the mechanical engineers, which, quite frankly, is where its design belongs. They will be familiar with the building's system and can advise the other members of the design team on the best optimization strategies. However, in order to achieve a high-quality environment at a lower cost, the team must integrate its efforts and recognize that the space functions as a whole, not as a collection of parts. Even the most finely tuned mechanical system can be overwhelmed if sunlight penetration isn't controlled.

Tenants are most often stuck with the system they inherit and should evaluate conditions prior to committing to a space in order to determine what can be done within

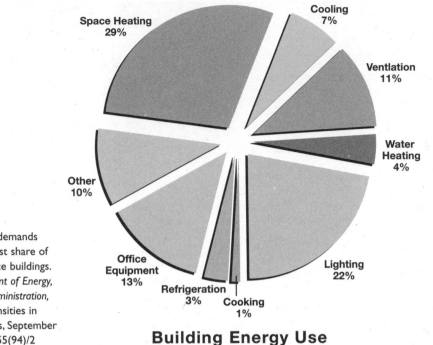

Heating and cooling demands account for the largest share of electricity use in office buildings. *Source: U.S. Department of Energy, Energy Information Administration, Energy End Use Intensities in Commercial Buildings, September 1994, DOE/ELA-05555(94)/2*

**Building Energy Use**

its limits. The decision is an important one because heating and cooling account for the largest share of office building electricity use, as shown in the Building Energy Use illustration above.

Two of the most common systems are constant volume, which delivers a constant airflow to each space, and variable air volume (VAV), which varies the amount of delivered air depending on the heating or cooling loads. The system, in other words, will adjust according to demand, reducing power requirements and saving energy and costs. These and many other considerations are detailed in the *Energy Star Building Upgrade Manual*. [15]

Of course, the best and easiest way to achieve optimal heating and cooling is to select a good building, sometimes referred to as a high-performance building, defined by Beth Brummitt of Brummitt Energy Associates as a "building that provides a comfortable and high-quality environment for its occupants while using less energy and having lower operating costs than a typical building. For example, a building with energy-efficient glass and lighting will stay comfortable even with less air-condition-

ing installed. The increased cost of windows and lights are offset by the reduced initial cost of the air-conditioning equipment." The human health and well-being benefits of high-performance buildings include better thermal comfort, improved indoor air quality, and good daylighting, all of which will be discussed in detail in Chapter 5.

## Zoning and Controls

Within the boundaries of an interior space, heating and cooling variables fall into two broad categories: zoning and controls. Tenants moving into cold, dark spaces—raw space that has not been built out—may have the opportunity to implement some innovative strategies, while those occupying warm, lit space that is already configured to their liking will find it a better choice to leave things as is, even if conditions are not optimal. Implementing change would be expensive and disruptive and would create waste.

How an interior space is zoned for heating and cooling will depend on several factors: use type, space configura-

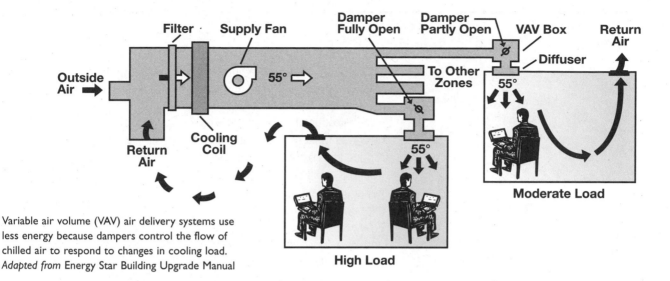

Variable air volume (VAV) air delivery systems use less energy because dampers control the flow of chilled air to respond to changes in cooling load. *Adapted from* Energy Star Building Upgrade Manual

tion, and solar orientation. According to the *G/Rated Tenant Improvement Guide*, heating and cooling needs must be clearly identified when considering the interior layout. " For example, a typical office floor has five primary heating/cooling zones: an internal zone and four perimeter zones, one along each side of the building. Because the internal zone is separated from the windows and packed with heat producing lights, electronic equipment, and people, it typically requires cooling all day long throughout the year. The four perimeter zones are affected by heat gain and heat loss through the windows, and internal heat gains. The zone on the south side, exposed to solar heat gain through the windows for most of the day, will require primarily cooling, even in winter months. The north zone, by contrast, will be losing heat through the windows and may require heating throughout the winter. The zone on the east side may require more cooling in the morning as the sun warms that side of the building, but may need heating in the afternoon during winter months. The west zone will be just the opposite.

"In addition to these primary zones, some areas in the workspace should be considered separate zones. Large conference rooms and workrooms with concentrations of equipment (high-volume copiers and computer servers, for example) will have special cooling and ventilation needs. Enclosed private offices will likely have different heating and cooling needs than open office areas." [16]

Along with thermostats to control temperature, sophisticated automatic controls will return a space to a predetermined setting when unoccupied. Another technology, direct digital control (DDC) systems, is full-blown energy management controlled by a computer that allows all the components in the system to talk to each other. Although more affordable than they used to be, DDC systems are more appropriate for larger interiors projects.

Demand ventilation to control the amount of outside air supply should be considered as part of the mechanical plan. "Standard ventilation specifications," explains the *Energy Star Building Upgrade Manual*, "are based on introducing a prescribed volume of outside air to an interior space. However, building occupants are rarely evenly distributed. Some areas, such as cafeterias, auditoriums, conference rooms, and gymnasiums, may be empty during some portions of the day but full at others to the point that indoor air quality would suffer. The solution to this problem is demand ventilation. By only supplying outside air when and where it is needed, proper air quality is ensured while not wasting energy by supplying the area with outside air during other parts of the day. A popular way to do this is by

## The ENERGY STAR Program

"ENERGY STAR is a government-backed program helping business-es and individuals protect the environment through superior energy efficiency." In 1992 the U.S. Environmental Protection Agency (EPA) introduced ENERGY STAR as a voluntary labeling program designed to identify and promote energy-efficient products to reduce greenhouse gas emissions. Computers and monitors were the first labeled products. In 1995, EPA expanded the label to additional office equipment products and residential heating and cooling equipment. In 1996, EPA partnered with the U.S. Department of Energy for particular product categories. The ENERGY STAR label is now on major appliances, office equipment, lighting, home electronics, and more. EPA has also extended the label to cover new homes and commercial and industrial buildings.

"Through its partnerships with more than 8,000 private and public sector organizations, ENERGY STAR delivers the technical information and tools that organizations and consumers need to choose energy-efficient solutions and best management practices. ENERGY STAR has successfully delivered energy and cost savings across the country, saving businesses, organizations, and consumers about $12 billion in 2005 alone. Over the past decade, ENERGY STAR has been a driving force behind the more widespread use of such technological innovations as LED traffic lights, efficient fluorescent lighting, power management systems for office equipment, and low standby energy use.

"Recently, energy prices have become a hot news topic and a major concern for consumers. ENERGY STAR provides solutions. ENERGY STAR provides a trustworthy label on over 40 product categories (and thousands of models) for the home and office. These products deliver the same or better performance as comparable models while using less energy and saving money. ENERGY STAR also provides easy-to-use home and building assessment tools so that homeowners and building managers can start down the path to greater efficiency and cost savings."

monitoring $CO_2$ concentrations, a good indicator of a space's population. As more people exhale, the concentration of $CO_2$ increases. By controlling the quantity of outside air based on a $CO_2$ set point, an area can be ventilated on a demand basis."[17]

Displacement ventilation systems, such as underfloor air systems, can generate energy savings because they operate at lower pressures, which require less fan energy. Other benefits, such as greater thermal comfort, and implementation strategies will be covered in Chapter 5.

## ■ Equipment and Appliances

Reducing the plug load, defined as everything plugged into the electrical system, is an energy reduction strategy easily achieved by the interiors project. Office equipment, task lights, and appliances such as refrigerators and dishwashers are the largest contributors to electrical loads. Luckily, their impact can be reduced by the use of Energy Star–rated products through power management features.

When the equipment is not in use, it automatically enters a low-power "sleep" mode. An Energy Star–qualified computer in sleep mode consumes about 80 percent less electricity than it does in full-power mode.

Energy Star products cost the same as nonlabeled equipment; however, the estimated savings can be significant, especially in offices with hundreds of units. For example, the estimated annual savings for a computer and monitor is $20 per unit; a printer is $40.

The *Energy Star Building Upgrade Manual,* excerpted on page 94, recommends strategies that organizations should take to ensure that they realize the benefits offered by Energy Star–labeled office equipment.

■ Check Equipment Specifications—Look for and request the Energy Star label when purchasing new equipment....For existing models in the office, check to see if they have power management or other energy-saving features. Although they may not meet the Energy Star specifications, these features will provide some energy savings if activated ...

■ Ensure Proper Equipment Setup—Confirm [with] information systems or support staff that the equipment is installed properly with the power-management features enabled. Each employee has different work habits and should be encouraged to adjust the time settings to accommodate individual work patterns. If the computer power-management feature is not compatible with the network environment, disable the feature on computers, but continue to use it on all of the monitors. Monitors consume 80 percent of the energy used by the two components.

## What's LEED Got to Do with It?

The Energy and Atmosphere section of LEED for Commercial Interiors offers 4 credits and up to 12 points. There are also three prerequisites.

*EAp1: Fundamental Commissioning.* Select a commissioning authority not directly connected to the project to verify that the project's energy and water-related systems are functioning as intended. (Required)

*EAp2: Minimum Energy Performance.* Establish minimum energy efficiency for the tenant systems. (Required)

*EAp3: CFC Reduction in HVAC&R Equipment.* Reduce the amount of ozone generated in tenant systems. (Required)

*EAc1: Optimize Energy Performance.* Decrease energy consumption to reduce environmental impacts associated with excessive energy use. The credit has four parts.

*1.1:* Reduce lighting power density below that allowed by ANSI/ASHRAE/IESNA Standard 90.1-2004. (1 point for a 15 percent reduction, 2 points for a 25 percent reduction, and 3 points for a 35 percent reduction)

*1.2:* Reduce energy consumption by installing daylight-responsive controls in all regularly occupied spaces within 15 feet of windows and under skylights. (1 point)

*1.3:* Reduce energy consumption below the prerequisite via selection of HVAC systems and other building-related strategies such as equipment efficiency and appropriate zoning and controls *or* reduce design energy costs 15 or 30 percent below ANSI/ASHRAE/IESNA Standard 90.1-2004. (2 points)

*1.4:* Reduce energy consumption by installing Energy Star-rated equipment and appliances. (1 point for a 70 percent reduction; 1 additional point for a 90 percent reduction)

*(continued)*

*EAc2: Enhanced Commissioning.* Select an independent commissioning authority to verify that the project's energy and water-related systems are functioning as intended beyond the goals of the commissioning prerequisite. (1 point)

*EAc3: Energy Use, Measurement, and Payment Accountability.* Provide ongoing accountability and optimization of tenant energy and water consumption by submetering or direct payment of energy costs *or* (for larger projects) install continuous metering for the listed equipment and develop a measurement and verification plan as defined by the referenced standard. (2 points)

*EAc4: Green Power.* Encourage use of grid-source, renewable energy technologies with net zero pollution by purchasing a two-year renewable energy contact for at least 50 percent of the tenant's electricity. (1 point)

Adapted from the LEED Green Building Rating System for Commercial Interiors, Version 2.0. Visit ugsbc.org to access the complete rating system.

# 4
# THE MATERIALS
# MAZE

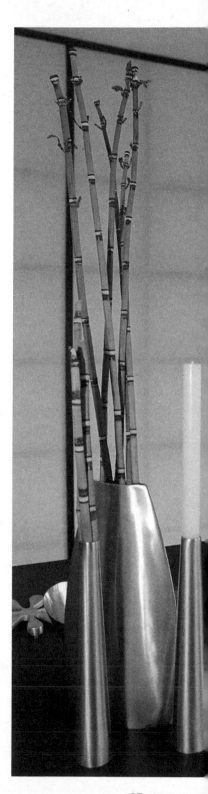

The first question to ask when considering materials selection for a sustainable interiors project is this: is the material or product essential to the success of the project? In general, we are not a society that likes to deny ourselves the luxury of "things." Yet it is becoming increasingly imperative that we rethink our overwhelming desire for stuff. Consider the following statistics offered by physicist Amory B. Lovins of the Rocky Mountain Institute in an essay in the summer 2005 Patagonia catalog:

In 1999, two colleagues and I worked out what it takes to meet a single American family's annual needs. Each year, for a four-person, middle-class household, industry extracts, processes, refines, manufactures, burns, pumps and wastes four million pounds of material. That's approximately 20 times an average person's body weight per day. Of this vast flow of stuff, only 7% gets into products at all, only 1% into durable products and only 0.02% into durable products that later get recycled, remanufactured or reused. Thus, U.S. materials flow is about 99.98% pure waste.[1]

Lovins has spent much of his career studying ways to harness market forces to promote resource efficiency and halt the shocking flow of waste into landfills. In fact, many innovative solutions to this tragedy are documented in the groundbreaking book *Natural Capitalism,* which Lovins coauthored along with Paul Hawken and Hunter Lovins—including remedies to reduce the annual use of an estimated 3 billion tons of raw materials to construct buildings worldwide. Using that statistic as a starting point, one can only extrapolate how many billions of tons of raw materials are subsequently used to manufacture the furnishings for those very same buildings—and how much of that is ending up in a landfill. Consider this: the U.S. EPA estimated that nearly 5 billion pounds of carpet were landfilled in 2005.

So what can designers do to help encourage resource efficiency? How can designers ensure that the materials they choose have the fewest negative ecological impacts? How can designers begin to navigate the materials maze? Unfortunately, as is the case with much of the emerging sustainable design process, there is no single answer when selecting concrete, masonry, wood, metals, insulation, wallboard, floor substrates, carpet, hard-surface flooring, resilient flooring, base and trims, paints and wall finishes, ceiling tiles and framing, lighting, adhesives, furnishings, and fabrics.

First and foremost, designers must remember that sustainable materials must have certain attributes: they must be healthy, durable, appropriate, and easily maintained with minimal environmental impacts throughout their life cycle. The next step, advocates Nadav Malin, editor of *Environmental Building News,* is to ask questions—lots of them—as well as focus on the environmental priorities you have identified as most crucial.

## Ask More Questions

### By Nadav Malin

*Is the look right?*

*Will it do the job?*

*Does it fit in the budget?*

*These are the questions that you probably ask about the materials and products you consider for a project. Once you start looking with a green perspective, however, you will find whole new sets of questions to ask.*

*You might start by inquiring about the materials and resources used, and how they affect the global environment. For example, you might ask:*

*Where did it come from?*

*What went into making it?*

*Where can it go when it's no longer needed in my project?*

*Can it be used safely to make something else?*

*You might also start thinking more broadly about the environment that you are creating—the indoor environment:*

*Does it nurture the health and well-being of its occupants?*

*Will it be comfortable without requiring a lot of energy for heating, cooling, and lighting?*

*These questions can also trickle down into your product evaluations:*

*What chemicals might this product release into the space, and how might the occupants be affected?*

*Does it have a color or a texture that can lead to reduced lighting energy or an expanded range of thermal comfort conditions?*

*Can it be maintained easily without hazardous cleaning chemicals?*

*Asking useful questions requires a lot of knowledge, as does interpreting the responses in a meaningful way. Even researchers who study these issues intensively still have more questions than answers about the complex interactions between material flows and the environment, and between indoor chemical emissions and human health.*

*Fortunately, an increasing number of initiatives and resources can help you make product choices without researching each question exhaustively.*

Once you know what's important to you and your clients, you can focus on the questions you care about most, and then lean on these emerging programs to help you answer them. How might that work? Here are a couple of examples.

"I care about global environmental impacts over the product's entire life cycle, from its inception as raw materials to the end of its service life." To consider the ecological global impacts of any products under consideration, you have to ask questions such as what a product is made of, how it's made, and what possibilities might exist for reusing it. These questions, and the information that they elicit, can quickly become overwhelming. You might find a shortcut in one or more of the following programs.

- **Cradle to Cradle certification from McDonough Braungart Design Chemistry (MBDC).** Based on the compelling notion that everything we use should be reusable indefinitely and safely, this program certifies products that conform to its principles. MBDC also consults to many of the companies whose products it certifies. While this helps with the dissemination of Cradle to Cradle principles, it could be seen as compromising the integrity of the certification program.

- **Sustainable Textile Standard from the Institute for Market Transformation to Sustainability (MTS).** Developed through long negotiations with manufacturers and other interested parties, this standard measures a product's performance on a broad range of sustainability agendas. Claims about achievements in relation to this standard should be backed up by a reputable third party.

- **Environmentally Preferable Product (EPP) certification from Scientific Certification Systems (SCS).** SCS serves as a third-party certifier of standards developed by others, but it also creates standards in cases where they don't otherwise exist. Its EPP certification standard was created to fill such a gap.

- **Listing in the GreenSpec Directory from BuildingGreen, Inc.** GreenSpec lists products that meet BuildingGreen's internally developed guidelines, which are targeted at the greenest 5 to 10 percent of products for each application. While GreenSpec's screening process is not rigorous enough to be considered a true certification program, it allows the company to include more listings than are available from other programs. BuildingGreen accepts no fees from manufacturers. (Full disclosure—the author is a principal at BuildingGreen, Inc.)

"I'm concerned about chemicals released to the indoor environment." Many types of compounds can off-gas from products and contribute to the chemical soup in the air we breathe. The experts don't always agree as to which chemicals we should be concerned about, or what safe exposure levels might be. They also disagree regarding testing protocols, analyzing the data, and how much information to report. Several programs certify products as low emitters of chemicals. They are helpful in simplifying the choices, though you should keep in mind that they don't claim to guarantee healthy indoor air.

When it comes to measuring chemicals associated with products, it is important to understand what is being measured. Three different types of measurements are commonly used:

- The amount of volatile organic compounds (VOCs) in a product, measured as grams per liter or pounds per gallon

- The rate at which chemicals off-gas, typically measured in milligrams per square meter of surface area (this rate usually drops off over time)

- The expected indoor concentration of a chemical, which is based on the off-gassing rate, the amount of the product in a space, the size of the space, and the amount of ventilation

Although the resulting concentration is the most difficult to estimate, it comes the closest to addressing what we are actually concerned about (exposure *of occupants to the chemicals), so it is what most serious indoor air certification programs use. Three programs to consider are:*

- **Greenguard Environmental Institute.** *Greenguard certifies products that have been tested not to exceed established levels of indoor concentrations of a set of chemicals. The thresholds that Greenguard uses and its testing protocols are well suited to screening products that might cause immediate, short-term reactions in building occupants.*

- **California's High Performance Schools Specification Section 01350.** *The California specification is similar to Greenguard but is oriented more toward long-term, chronic health effects as opposed to immediate effects. An early version of this specification seemed to require testing products separately for each project, but it has since been revised so that products can be certified for compliance with the specification. Scientific Certification Systems is one company that provides that certification.*

- **The Carpet and Rug Institute's Green Label Plus program.** *The Carpet and Rug Institute was involved from the early days of emissions testing, with its Green Label Carpet program. Concerned about having to meet competing standards from Greenguard and California, the institute brought the two parties together to create Green Label Plus, which supersedes its original labeling program. In many ways, Green Label Plus brings together the best of the two other programs, although a label from the industry trade association is not as reliable as true third-party certification.*

*Green design is not something to get into unless you enjoy learning new things as you practice. Everyone in the field is still learning, and the end is nowhere in sight. But the tools for making good choices, even with limited information, are improving.*

*Certification and labeling programs go a long way toward simplifying the designer's job by replacing the need to interpret a lot of data with a single seal or label. They don't eliminate the need to learn about the environmental and health impacts of products, but they can certainly allow you to get by with less research. If you're going to rely on a certification program, however, you need to understand what's behind that label . . . so the questions start all over again.*

---

Nadav Malin is vice president of BuildingGreen, Inc. and serves as editor of *Environmental Building News*, a monthly newsletter on environmentally responsible design and construction, and coeditor of the GreenSpec product directory.

## ■ Starting the Dialogue

Many designers have found it helpful to start an informative and intelligent conversation with suppliers about the environmental impacts of the products they sell by using the ASTM Standard E-2129 (Standard Practice for Data Collection for Sustainability Assessment of Building Products), which is organized according to the Construction Specification Institute's (CSI) MasterFormat section to promote consistency in the evaluation of building products. ASTM E-2129 specifically references five main categories, with numerous subcategories:

- *Materials (product feedstock).* Addresses issues such as environmental impacts, recycled content, recyclability, toxicity, renewable resource use, and volatile organic compounds.
- *Manufacturing process.* Addresses issues such as clean versus "dirty" energy usage, waste reclamation, greenhouse gas emissions, effluents, toxic chemical usage, waste usage, water usage, and environmental impacts.
- *Operational performance of installed product.* Addresses energy efficiency, durability, and maintenance procedures of the finished product.
- *Indoor environmental quality.* Addresses positive or negative contributions to indoor air quality.
- *Corporate environmental policy.* Addresses manufacturers' written statements, packaging programs, end-of-life programs, and documentation to support environmental claims.

Wool is a natural and renewable material sheared primarily from commercial sheep flocks, although goat hair and llama hair are also used for textiles. © *Photographer: Marek Gucwa*

The ASTM E-2129 Standard provides an excellent foundation upon which to formulate questions about many of the critical issues pertaining to a product's environmental impacts. When you start asking intelligent, thoughtful questions, such as the ones included in this standard, it encourages responsible manufacturers to respond likewise.

# ▌Natural versus Synthetic ▌Materials

The debate whether natural or synthetic materials are better for the environment ideally illustrates the complexity of choosing appropriate sustainable materials. At first glance, one might automatically assume that natural is better. After all, nearly 70,000 new synthetic chemicals and materials were introduced in the twentieth century, and less than 2 percent of them have been tested for their effects on human health, while more than 70 percent have not been tested at all.[2] This staggering statistic makes the product specification process all the more difficult when a designer attempts to responsibly choose interior components that are considered sustainable. Competition between products—both natural and man-made—is fierce.

Yet the same technological know-how that made possible the development of these 70,000 new synthetic chemicals has also contributed to cleaner production processes for them, thus adding to the confusion over which products are good, which are better, and which are best. Are natural fibers (cotton, jute, silk, wool, linen, hemp) more ecofriendly than their man-made counterparts (nylon, polyester) made from petroleum?

Under certain manufacturing conditions, the answer is no. A brief examination of some of the big-picture issues related to the manufacturing process for a textile made of natural fibers versus one made from synthetic fibers underscores the tough trade-offs when deciding between the two.

But a textile is composed of more than just its fibers. Dyes, additives, and residues of process chemicals are other important components. In fact, textile production's most

| Table 4-1: A Comparison of Fibers | |
|---|---|
| **Natural Fibers** | **Man-made Fibers** |
| Biodegradable. | Not biodegradable, but often can be recycled. |
| Manufactured from renewable resources. Often produced, however, by agricultural and/or farming processes in which petroleum-derived pesticides and fertilizers harmful to the environment are widely used. Conventional farming processes also can result in soil erosion and salinization, aquifer depletion, nutrient loading, and toxic chemical runoff. | Manufactured using petroleum, a depletable resource; however, relatively little petroleum is used to manufacture synthetics. A problematic heavy metal called antimony, needed as a catalyst in making most polyester, creates environmental and human health risks, particularly during production, disposal, and recycling. |
| Many natural fibers, especially cotton, require cleaning, transporting and extensive dyeing and finishing, resulting in significant water pollution hazards. | Water and energy are used in all the processing stages of all fibers, most extensively in man-made fibers. The production process for most man-made fibers is essentially clean. |

Corn is the primary crop used to produce polylactic polymers (PLA), which are spun into fibers. © *Photomorgana*

harmful procedure is the finishing process: dyeing, sizing, treating for stain and wrinkle resistance, and the application of mildew, fire, and moth damage retardants. Many of the chemicals used in these treatments, such as formaldehyde and latex polymers, can cause respiratory problems and skin rashes. Conventional cotton (as opposed to organic cotton) tends to be the most treated. Dyes present another problem. Natural dyes are available, but they can only be used on natural fabrics. They also can't compare in many instances with the performance or appearance of the synthetic dyes so popular in both the clothing and furnishings industries. Also, natural dyes are not completely pollution free. In order to make them more stable, they often require the use of very toxic metallic compounds.

Organically grown fibers, such as cotton, also present inherent problems. First, they are expensive, in large part because the process is so labor-intensive. Farmers must work the fields constantly. Weeding, composting, and defo-

liation must be done naturally, without toxic chemicals. Like its conventional counterpart, organic cotton also uses extremely high quantities of water and cannot be grown year after year without permanently depleting the soil.

Further complicating the natural-versus-synthetic debate is the introduction of new plastics made from plants rather than petroleum. These bio-based fibers are derived from agricultural products such as corn, rice, and beets. The starch portion of these crops are converted into sugar and fermented to produce lactic acid, when is then processed and polymerized to form polylactic acid (PLA). PLA polymers are then spun into fibers. Proponents argue that these biopolymers reduce reliance on mineral resources, use no antimony, and are completely biodegradable back into lactic acid at the end of their service lives. Concerns, however, have been raised about whether the subsequent dyes and chemicals (such as adhesives, fillers, UV inhibitors, stabilizers, plasticizers, bleaching agents, and binders) used on the PLA fibers by textile manufacturers are safe or suitable for recycling, thus negating any environmental benefits. Additional arguments have been raised about the ethics of using food for nonfood products while millions of people are without adequate nutrition. Last, if genetically modified corn is used as the building block for PLA, questions also come into play regarding the unknown long-term consequences of using bioengineered products.

Then there are the end-of-life issues to consider. What happens to any material once it has served a useful life? In the regenerative Cradle to Cradle design paradigm proposed by architect Bill McDonough and chemist Michael Braungart, the ideal answer lies in intelligent synthetic fibers (and fabrics made from them) or the design of materials that can circulate perpetually in a closed-loop production/use/recovery cycle.[3] This means petroleum-based synthetics (technical nutrients) that can be recycled perpetually and safely, or plant-based fibers (biological nutrients) that can safely return to the soil to nourish new plant growth. Of course, the chemicals used to treat fibers, as well as the base fibers themselves, affect these possibilities.

The bottom line is that designers must possess a wealth of data before they can make informed decisions about the materials they select. Fortunately, the past decade has seen a spectacular rise in the awareness of important ecological issues as they relate to all aspects of a product, and the subsequent development of a number of sophisticated tools that address many of the critical issues that need to be considered.

## Toxins

The question of whether a material or substance is toxic or not is complicated, and the answer often will be that it depends. In sufficient quantity, anything—even water—can be harmful; conversely, there are substances too dangerous for use under any circumstances. Asbestos has proven to be one of those materials despite its outstanding insulating characteristics. The problem facing designers is determining which products are safe and which are to be avoided even though they may have desirable attributes.

### Formaldehyde

Formaldehyde is a colorless gas with a pungent odor and irritant properties that is emitted from many materials. It will irritate eyes, skin, and the upper respiratory tract and is lethal at high levels of exposure. However, it has properties that make it useful as a preservative, as a disinfectant, and as a resin in such products as molded plastic items, particleboard, plywood, paper, sealants, paints, textiles, foam mattresses, building insulation, and upholstery stuffing, but its ill effects are clear. Many of these items will off-gas appreciable amounts of formaldehyde for five or more years after manufacture. Worse yet, the evaporating fumes will tend to be absorbed and then rereleased over time by large interior surfaces such as ceiling tiles, wallboard, and carpeting. The EPA has classified formaldehyde as a potential human carcinogen.

It is incumbent upon the designer to search for safer options, and manufacturers have responded by developing alternative products. Conventional plywood and particleboard, for example, are laden with formaldehyde, but many products have come on the market that are acceptable substitutes for use as substrates in countertop and casework applications. One of these, wheatboard, is manufactured using agricultural waste from wheat straw bound

| Table 4-2: Common Sources of Formaldehyde in Building Materials | |
|---|---|
| Composite wood products | Plywood Particleboard Chipboard Medium-density fiberboard (MDF) Furniture and millwork |
| Adhesives and glues | Laminated products Furniture Floors Paneling and millwork |
| Insulation | Fiberglass Foam |
| Acoustic ceiling tiles | Panels Tiles |
| Finishes | Fabrics (permanent-press finishes) Floor (especially acid-cured) Paints (including some latex) Paper |

together with formaldehyde-free MDI (polymeric diphenylmethane diisocyanate) resins and is comparable in both performance and cost. Be aware that urea formaldehyde resins are higher emitters than those made with phenol formaldehyde, which are used primarily in outdoor construction products.

### Flame Retardants

Flame retardants present similar dilemmas. While they play an important role in fire prevention, concerns about their risks have been around for decades. In fact, some, such as PCBs and PBBs, were banned in the 1970s after they were found to be carcinogenic as well as persistent bioaccumulative toxins (PBTs)—substances that build up in the food chain and do not break down easily. PCBs, for example, can still be found in soil and water samples around the world even though their use has been illegal in the U.S. for more than thirty years. Case in point: the Healthy Building Network reported "PCB releases increased from 2 million pounds in 2002 to 22 million in 2003, mostly from PCB waste sent to landfills." PBTs cause developmental damage to children and affect the nervous and reproductive systems of humans and other animals.

# Flame Retardants: A Checklist for Action

1. *Ask manufacturers about halogenated flame retardants in their products.* Even if products free from halogenated flame retardants cannot be obtained today, simply asking manufacturers or manufacturers' reps about these additives will raise awareness and lead to changes in the future.

2. *Avoid combustible materials where feasible.* Instead of using inherently flammable materials that have to be treated with flame retardants, such as foamed-plastic insulation, use inherently nonflammable materials, such as fiberglass or mineral wool insulation. (To avoid an energy penalty for such substitutions, thicker wall sections may be required.) Avoid foam cushioning in furniture in favor of mesh, as in some new office chairs.

3. *Rely on separation of combustible materials to provide fire protection.* Combustible materials can be used with fairly low risk by providing adequate separation from occupied spaces or potential combustion sources.

4. *Install sprinklers in all buildings.* Full sprinklering should be provided in all occupied buildings, including single-family homes, to provide protection from fire.

5. *Where feasible and where there will not be energy penalties, avoid foam insulation.* Avoid foam insulation in most applications unless the manufacturer can provide assurance that halogenated flame retardants are not used. Most foam insulation today is made with halogenated flame retardants, though polyisocyanurate and spray polyurethane insulation is typically made with TCPP, which contains chlorine rather than bromine and is probably less of a health and environmental risk. Rigid fiberglass, rigid mineral wool, and all cavity-fill insulation (fiberglass, mineral wool, and cellulose) is made without halogenated flame retardants.

6. *Do not use polyurethane foam carpet padding.* Soft polyurethane foam carpet padding is produced with pentaBDE or other brominated flame retardants. As the padding disintegrates, dust may become airborne or be ingested. This dust can be particularly dangerous to infants. In place of polyurethane padding, use more traditional materials, such as jute and horse-hair padding.

7. *Remove polyurethane foam insulation from beneath carpeting.* Polyurethane foam padding disintegrates over time, releasing PBDEs into the building. Removing this padding should be a moderately high priority. Use great care to minimize the release of dust into the building, wear a respirator, and clean up thoroughly with a HEPA vacuum.

8. *Specify office and household furniture that does not contain polyurethane foam padding.* A number of leading office furniture manufacturers, including Herman Miller, are trying to eliminate halogenated compounds from their products. The retailer IKEA has eliminated BFRs from all of its furniture.

9. *If polyurethane foam is used in furniture, specify foam with nonhalogenated flame retardants.* Unfortunately, it is very difficult to find out exactly which flame retardants are used in a particular product, so this may not be feasible. With large orders of office furniture, the specifier may wield enough influence to obtain this information from potential suppliers.

10. *Specify office equipment with metal cases rather than plastic.* Because most plastics are inherently flammable, flame retardants are commonly added. By switching to inherently flame-resistant materials, the need for flame retardants can be avoided. (This is the approach Apple Computer has taken in eliminating brominated flame retardants from all plastic components larger than 25 grams—substituting aluminum for plastic in computer casing, for example.)

11. *Specify halogen-free wire and cable.* Polyethylene and polypropylene insulated wire and cable that is produced using nonhalogenated flame retardants is available, though such materials may be difficult to find, and they may need to be installed in metal conduit to provide fire separation.

*Source:* Alex Wilson, "Flame Retardants Under Fire," *Environmental Building News,* June 2004.

Currently, approved and widely used flame retardants are posing similar concerns, as recent reports from the United States, Europe, and Japan have found evidence of accumulation of the chemicals in the environment and human bodies. Known as brominated (or halogenated) flame retardants (BFRs), they are popular because of their effectiveness in stopping or slowing combustion. Found in most polymer-based materials, they are especially prevalent in the polyurethane foam cushioning found in upholstered furniture, carpet cushion, and textile coatings. Their use is pervasive and hard to avoid. Unfortunately, it is very difficult to uncover which flame retardants are being used in specific products because loopholes in labeling laws mean that manufacturers are not required to divulge their use. However, some product producers such as Herman Miller and Interface are upfront about their efforts to eliminate BFRs, and the designer should be persistent in asking questions. *Environmental Building News* published an exhaustive study of this issue that includes a list of strategies on how to move away from BFRs.[4]

There are nonhalogenated flame retardants available that will become more widely used only when customers begin demanding them or when regulatory action prohibits the use of BFRs. In the interim, flame retardants in products should be labeled so that consumers can be fully informed about their environments.

## Mercury

Liquid mercury, although found in small amounts in buildings, is highly toxic to humans when exposed to the air. Items such as fluorescent and HID lamps, thermostats, and certain kinds of switches may have mercury-containing parts that must be removed by experienced personnel prior to demolition and replaced with mercury-free alternatives, if possible.

The most common source of mercury in the atmosphere is produced at power plants where mercury is given off by coal and oil combustion. Energy reduction strategies will, therefore, also help reduce mercury levels. The use of fluorescent lamps over incandescent lighting is a good example, however, of the conflicting choices facing designers. Although incandescent bulbs contain no mercury, they are far less energy-efficient and thus, in that sense, a less desirable environmental choice. Newer long-life fluorescent

lamps are available that contain such a small amount of mercury—10 mg or less—that they are no longer considered a hazardous waste.

Mercury-free HID lamps have been developed and are becoming increasing available. Electronic versions of thermostats and switches are good alternatives to the mercury-containing models.

## Endocrine Disruptors and PVC

Another category of chemicals thought to be dangerous to human hormone systems and fetal development are called endocrine disruptors. So named because they mimic the hormones that control the functions of our bodies, they are especially hazardous to fetuses and children. Phthalates, found in many personal care products, medical supplies, toys, and other soft vinyl products, are an example of endocrine disruptors. In the buildings industry they are commonly found in flooring, wall covering, upholstery, and shower curtains as the additive that gives these products their flexibility. They become dangerous when they leach out of the plastics.

Phthalates have come under attack in recent years, and manufacturers have begun to phase them out of their products. They are also one of the components of polyvinyl chloride (PVC) that critics cite as part of vinyl's triple threat. The others are vinyl chloride and dioxin, a highly potent carcinogen and a persistent, bioaccumulative toxin. Created during the production and disposal of PVC, dioxin is believed to be one of the most environmentally harmful substances known. Vinyl chloride, a deadly gas, is also a by-product of the PVC manufacturing process.

Because of the potential hazards of PVC and because it is neither biodegradable nor effectively recyclable, many companies and government agencies have banned its use or are in the process of phasing it out. The Nike Corp., for example, "is striving to eliminate all substances known or suspected to be harmful to the health of biological or ecological systems at any stage in their life cycle" and is removing PVC from all Nike-brand products.[5] Others such as Kaiser Permanente, the City of San Francisco, and many foreign auto manufacturers are doing the same.

However, in addition to its foes, PVC also has its supporters who argue that the plastic's performance, low cost, and durability offset the negative phases of its life cycle, an issue that will be discussed more fully in the following sections. The vinyl industry is particularly protective of PVC, pointing out that its production process is highly regulated and that its impact on human health and the environment is minimal. They also deny the connection between the vinyl life cycle and dioxin emissions.

As in any controversial debate, it is difficult for the layperson to sort through the myriad of conflicting claims. Design professionals are bombarded by messages both denouncing vinyl and supporting it. In 2004 the USGBC issued a draft report from its task force formed to evaluate the feasibility of a PVC-related credit in LEED. The report, which stated that "available evidence does not support a conclusion that PVC is consistently worse than alternative materials," has been controversial, welcomed by the vinyl industry and product producers but roundly criticized by environmental groups. The Healthy Building Network, for example, called the study flawed for using an inappropriate model, misinterpreting and ignoring important data and scientific studies, and missing critical PVC environmental health issues. According to one of the task force members, the USGBC task group's work was an empirical study that was meant to break through the emotional claims on both sides of the issue. The report has shown that the way a credit is written has a lot to do with its ability to promote market transformation. By providing credit for not using any particular material, according to one of the task force members, "it has become clear that incentive could indeed be given for an alternative that has worse environmental or human health impacts. These complexities are often ignored but must be considered if we are to associate our desire to transform markets with true improvements in health for the environment and for people."

## Material Safety Data Sheet

Another tool available to the designer is the Material Safety Data Sheet (MSDS), although its value is problematic. Regulated by the U.S. government under the Occupational Safety and Health Administration (OSHA), an MSDS is required for all materials that are hazardous or even potentially hazardous. Manufacturers of such products must pre-pare the reports and make them available to workers who may be occupationally exposed to harmful substances, such as painting contractors. They are not meant for consumers, and the layperson will likely have difficulty interpreting the data. Also, the manufacturer of an assembled product, such as a chair, is not required to produce an MSDS; however, one is required from the manufacturer of the foam used to make the chair.

Most reputable manufacturers will gladly provide designers the MSDS applicable to their products even though they are under no legal obligation to do so. Each sheet will identify the manufacturer and their contact information, the name of the chemical, its hazardous ingredients, details of the health and safety issues presented by the substance and recommended precautions for safe handling and use. The sample shown on the facing page clearly establishes that the product is free of hazards. The data provided in other MSDSs, however, is quite technical and will be most useful to specifiers looking for a particular chemical in a product, such the flame retardants discussed earlier.

## Life Cycle Assessment

As we delve into such issues as natural versus synthetic or the use of toxic chemicals in the production process, it becomes increasingly obvious that it is no longer enough for a designer to consider the environmental impact of the products only during the time these goods are being used. Responsibility now extends to the product's entire life span.

But this responsibility, too, has some intricate trade-offs that must be considered. The designer's job is not unlike that of a young child faced with the task of coloring a picture green and having to choose a crayon from the 96-pack Crayola carton. How green should it be? Most likely the child will use daily experiences (grass is dark green, lime is light green) to make the decision.

Designers pursuing sustainable interiors face a similar question: how green do materials need to be? And like our young student above, they too will use their experiences or assumptions, as described by Scot Horst in the following essay, to help formulate their decisions.

## SAFETY DATA SHEET

In accordance with 91/155/EEC and ISO 11014-1

Date: 26 June 2001                                                    Page: 1 of 3

**1.   Product and company identification**

Product name:              Marmoleum, Artoleum, Walton
Manufacturer/supplier:     Forbo-Krommenie BV
Address:                   Industrieweg 12
City:                      1566 JP ASSENDELFT
Telephone:                 +31 75 6477477
Telefax:                   +31 75 6215466

**2.   Composition/Information on ingredients**

Composition: Floor covering based on a binder composed of linseed oil and (natural) rosin, mixed with wood flour and limestone and pressed on a jute backing.

Hazardous ingredients:     None

**3.   Hazards identification**

No health danger.
No environmental effect.

**4.   First-aid measures**

Eyes:              N.a.
Skin:              N.a.
Inhalation:        N.a.
Ingestion:         N.a.

**5.   Fire-fighting measures**

Suitable fire-fighting media:    Water, foam, CO2, powder
Specific hazards:                None

**6.   Accidental release measures**

Personal precautions:        N.a.
Environmental precautions:   N.a.
Methods for cleaning up:     N.a.

## SAFETY DATA SHEET

In accordance with 91/155/EEC and ISO 11014-1

Date: 26 June 2001                                                    Page: 2 of 3

**7.   Handling and storage**

7.1   Handling:    No special requirements
7.2   Storage:     No special requirements

**8.   Exposure controls/personal protection**

8.2   Personal protective equipment:
      Respiratory protection:      N.a.
      Hand protection:             N.a.
      Eye protection:              N.a.
      Skin and body protection:  N.a.

**9.   Physical and chemical properties**

Physical state:            solid, flexible floor covering
Form:                      sheet or tile
Colour:                    various colours and/or patterns
Odour:                     weak "linseed oil" smell
pH:                        N.a.
Decomposition temperature: Approx. 450°C
Flashpoint:                N.a.
Explosion properties:      N.a.
Density:                   $1.15 - 1.25 \text{ g/cm}^3$
Solubility:                not solvable in water or conventional
                           solvents

**10.  Stability and reactivity**

10.1  Hazardous decomposition products: Product is stable.
      No hazardous reactions.

**11.  Toxicological information**

No toxicological effects on human health.

## SAFETY DATA SHEET

In accordance with 91/155/EEC and ISO 11014-1

Date: 26 June 2001                                                    Page: 3 of 3

**12.  Ecological information**

Not solvable in water.
No negative ecological effects are known.

**13.  Disposal considerations**

In accordance with local or state regulations.

**14.  Transport information**

The product is not considered as dangerous and is not submitted to transport regulations.

**15.  Regulatory information**

No special information obliged.

**16.  Further information**

Safety Data Sheet made by:     F.W. Seifert

Third version:                 26 June 2001

The information in this Safety Data Sheet is based upon the present knowledge and experience. The actual facts do not give any information about the qualities and properties of the product.

Forbo's Marmoleum, Artoleum and Walton Material Safety Data Sheet lists product physical and chemical attributes and negative impacts, if any.

## Understanding Environmental Trade-offs

By Scot Horst

*We live in a highly complex world. As we have begun to understand the impacts of the built environment on nature, we have created a series of assumptions about the environmental preferability of certain materials, products and processes. Most of these assumptions come from our understanding of what damages nature or is highly wasteful, an understanding that is defined by those things or issues that are obvious in our own lives. For example, we know we throw a lot of things away, and therefore waste is often on the forefront of our environmental thinking. Because of this, we have established recycled content as a major way to choose environmentally beneficial materials. In this manner we have defined our environmentally preferable choices based on the attributes of a product (e.g., if it is recycled, if it contains waste fiber, etc.) rather than on its full environmental impact through its life cycle.*

*It is important to understand that all human economic activity has some sort of environmental impact. We must also understand that when we choose a material, we do not choose it in a vacuum. Rather, all choices are made relative to an alternative material, and each alternative has a different set of environmental impacts. Making sound choices is a process of understanding the environmental trade-offs associated with each alternative. The most sustainable material is the one that we do not use at all. When we oversimplify the benefits of our material choices, we undermine our ability to know whether our choices are creating better environmental performance.*

*Life cycle assessment (LCA) is a scientific pursuit that attempts to chart the environmental impacts of materials, products, and processes as they flow from and to nature. LCA is a methodology for holistic thinking. It is defined by the International Organization of Standardization (ISO) as "a compilation and evaluation of the inputs, outputs and the potential environmental impacts of a product system throughout its life cycle."[6] In LCA, the cycle that a material or product goes through is broken down into* stages. *The definition of these stages can vary, but when reviewing building materials they typically include the following:*

1. ***Cradle to gate***. *This stage includes all of the impacts of extraction of a material from nature or from other processes (including recycling), up to the point that the material leaves a manufacturing facility.*

2. ***Construction***. *This stage includes transportation from the manufacturing facility and all of the impacts that occur during construction such as emissions from adhesives.*

3. ***Use***. *This stage includes the impacts that occur during the use of the material or product, such as emissions that impact indoor air quality, and maintenance of the material or product.*

4. ***End of life***. *This stage tracks the impacts that occur when the material or product is either sent back for manufacturing, reused, or disposed of, including the impacts of landfills and solid waste.*

*LCA is based on life cycle inventory (LCI) data. LCI is a collection of information about a material or product as it flows through its life cycle. The goal and the scope of the LCI must be carefully defined. All LCA is reliant on the quality of the LCI, so incorrect or missing data can result in improper or incorrect assessments. Further, it should be noted that LCI information can be difficult to obtain for nonquantifiable impacts. As an example, an issue such as land use may be difficult to accurately quantify and assess. For this reason, it is important to understand what LCA can and cannot do. As a decision-making tool, LCA should be considered as a way to begin to understand the complexities of material flows in nature. However, it should not be considered the final answer on all environmental issues.*

*Different types of LCA tools exist; these tools are used in different ways by different tool users. Tools such as GABI and SimaPro are often used by manufacturers to improve the environmental performance of their products. Changes to the product and/or process (e.g., various material or chemical inputs)* can be modeled in the tool to weigh the trade-offs of an input or output alteration and identify any environmental benefits that might occur due to the changes.

In a similar way, designers can use specific tools to see where they can make improvements in their building design by choosing alternative materials. Currently, two tools are available for this use in North America. The Athena Institute, a sustainable materials institute, has a tool called the Athena Environmental Impact Estimator, which is designed primarily for understanding the impacts of structural and envelope materials. In the Athena tool, the designer inputs data about the planned building into the model and can then alter the building and evaluate the differing environmental impacts of different material choices. The designer can change structural characteristics or choose alternative materials in order to improve the performance of the overall design. In LCA, decisions are not set in the context of right and wrong; a good decision using LCA is an improvement over what would have been decided otherwise.

The other tool available in North America was developed by the National Institute of Standards and Technology (NIST). Called Building for Environmental and Economic Sustainabilty (BEES), it is most applicable to interior designers since it includes specific finish materials options. The BEES program allows designers to set parameters of their choosing. These parameters include the weight of importance of different impact categories as well as the general distance a product has to be transported. The model then provides a score for the product and selected alternatives. (See a detailed review in Chapter 6.)

Nature is a system that has evolved through a myriad of complex relationships to work with itself so each process works with neighboring processes to create ecosystems. These ecosystems are natural systems. We, as humans, are part of these systems whether we understand them or not. We have spent many centuries creating our own unnatural systems. When we build a building, whether it is green or not, whether we like it or not, we are impacting natural systems through the imposition of our unnatural systems. Life cycle assessment can provide a road map, a thorough understanding of the impacts of our unnatural systems on ecosystems. If we can learn these relationships, we can begin to understand how to attempt to make both unnatural and natural systems work together. LCA provides hope for the designer by not assigning a doctrine of right and wrong about material choices based on old assumptions of good and bad. Instead LCA helps us understand how we can once again become a part of nature by providing a methodology for understanding how our activity impacts it.

Scot Horst founded Horst, Inc., a sustainable materials consulting firm, which develops innovative environmental programs relating to materials technologies and testing. He also cofounded and serves as president of 7group, a multiservice green building consulting partnership.

As Horst explains, a life cycle assessment (LCA) is currently the most comprehensive method for determining the cumulative global environmental impact of a given product, process, or service, from the raw materials used in manufacturing to the packaging and transport of a finished product to its installation, operation, and use and, finally, to its disposal. Many manufacturers are incorporating LCA into their product development process (often referred to as "design for the environment" or DfE) to meet market demands for greener products as well as their own internal corporate social responsibility standards.

As explained in LCAccess—LCA 101, a publication of the U.S. EPA, the LCA process includes the following activities[7]:

- Compiling an inventory of relevant energy and material inputs and environmental releases (life cycle inventory)
- Evaluating the potential human health and environmental impacts associated with identified inputs and releases (impact assessment)
- Interpreting the results to help make a more informed decision (life cycle interpretation). This process, notes the EPA, is a systematic, phased approach and consists of four components: goal definition and scoping, inventory analysis, impact assessment, and interpretation, as illustrated on page 110.[8]

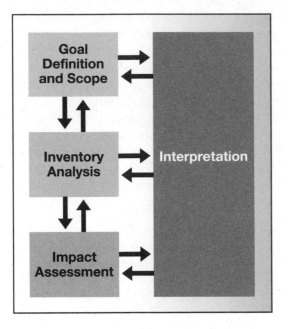

The phases of a life cycle assessment. *Source: ISO, 1997*

■ *Goal definition and scoping.* Define the purpose and method of including life cycle environmental impacts into the decision-making process. In this phase, the following items must be determined: the type of information that is needed to add value to the decision-making process, how accurate the results must be to add value, and how the results should be interpreted and displayed in order to be meaningful and usable.

■ *Inventory analysis.* Identify and quantify energy, water and materials usage, and environmental releases (e.g., air emissions, solid waste disposal, wastewater discharge). The steps in this process include developing a flow diagram of the processes being evaluated, developing a data collection plan, collecting data, and evaluating and reporting the results.

■ *Impact assessment.* Evaluate the potential human health and ecological impacts of the environmental resources and releases identified during the life cycle inventory. Impact assessment should address ecological and human health effects; it can also address

resource depletion. Common impact categories include global warming, stratospheric ozone depletion, acidification, eutrophication, photochemical smog, terrestrial toxicity, aquatic toxicity, human health, resource depletion, and land use. A life cycle impact assessment attempts to establish a link between the product or process and the potential environmental impacts on the above categories. For example, what are the impacts of 9,000 tons of $CO_2$ or 5,000 tons of methane emissions released into the atmosphere? Which is worse? What are their potential impacts on smog? On global warming?

■ *Interpretation.* Evaluate the results of the inventory analysis and impact assessment to select the preferred product, process, or service with a clear understanding of the uncertainty and the assumptions used to generate the results.

When deciding between two alternatives, LCA can help decision makers compare all major environmental impacts caused by products, processes, or services. However, the EPA process outlined above is complex and beyond the capabilities of most designers without the use of a software tool such as Athena or BEES. The following examination of some of the factors associated with the five life cycle stages, illustrated on page 111, underscores the complexity of the holistic assessment provided by an LCA but also restates the issues as a series of questions about typical inputs/outputs, simplifying the concepts a bit.

## RAW MATERIALS

■ Are the raw materials biodegradable? Do they break down into natural constituents?

■ Are the raw materials available in abundance, such as those needed to manufacture linoleum: linseed oil, rosin, wood flour, cork flour, limestone, and jute?

■ Are the materials harvested or extracted with little energy consumption other than that from the sun? Examples include products made from agricultural waste, often referred to as rapidly renewable resources, such as the straw used to make wheatboard.

■ Is it possible to reduce the amount of material needed in a product? Face weights of carpet (the number of

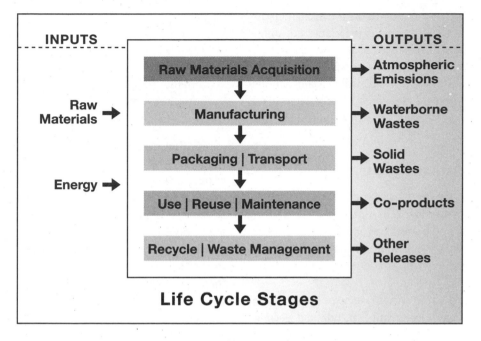

**Life Cycle Stages**

The five life cycle stages. *Source: Adapted from EPA Life Cycle Assessments, 1993.*

ounces of fiber in a square yard) have come down significantly in the past few years. With improvements in fiber quality and manufacturing techniques, face weights of 17 to 20 ounces per square yard have replaced the heavier 24- to 26-ounce carpets without compromising durability or appearance. The amount of energy and water consumed in manufacturing has also decreased.

■ Is the product derived from recycled materials, either postconsumer (tires, soda bottles) or postindustrial waste (fly ash, sawdust)? Old timbers, removed from barns and other sources, have become a popular flooring material.

■ Are the materials extracted locally to minimize the environmental impacts of transport? Bamboo, for example, harvested in Asia for use in the United States, requires energy-intensive transport with its accompanying pollution to deliver it to the job site.

■ Have the materials been obtained responsibly? For example, wood should come only from sources that adhere to responsible forestry practices.

## MANUFACTURING

■ Where is the product manufactured and where are its distribution centers? This point speaks to both the embodied energy contained within the product and whether the factory is in an environmentally sensitive area.

■ Does the manufacturing process have any negative effects on water and air quality? Are ozone-depleting substances produced to manufacture the product? Pollutants generated from toxic materials should be minimal and securely contained. Hazardous production processes should be redesigned.

■ Has the manufacturer employed green energy strategies such as solar, wind, geothermal, and biomass as alternatives to conventional fuels such as coal, oil, or gas?

■ Is the waste produced in making the product reclaimed on-site? If not, how is that waste handled?

## PACKAGING AND TRANSPORT

■ What materials are used in packaging? Are they reusable or recyclable? Many furniture manufacturers blanket-wrap their products. Another popular packaging material, polypropylene wrapping, is recyclable, but only if the infrastructure is in place to reclaim and reprocess it.

- Is the manufacturer moving its goods as efficiently as possible? Freight transporters consume a large amount of energy and create a large amount of pollution. Fully loaded trucks are certainly a better choice than ones that go out half empty.

## INSTALLATION, OPERATIONS/USE/MAINTENANCE

- What solvents or adhesives are necessary to install the product? Do they emit VOCs? In the past, low-emitting adhesives did not perform as well as their noxious counterparts. However, adhesives that provide exceptional performance while meeting tough emissions standards are now available.
- Is the product durable? What is its expected life span? Materials that easily wear out—or "ugly out"—create waste, use excessive resources, and are a poor economic choice.
- Is it easily maintained?
- Does the product contribute to office flexibility and support worker productivity? For example, raised floor systems assist in handling churn with minimal resource waste. They also enable occupants to have more control over their thermal comfort, and they offer significant energy savings and improved indoor air quality.
- If applicable, does the product qualify for an EPA Energy Star rating?
- Can the product be updated if technology improves?

## END OF LIFE: RECYCLE/WASTE MANAGEMENT

- Is the product recyclable at the end of its useful life? Can the product be easily disassembled, making it simpler to sort individual parts into their proper recycling channels?
- If it is recyclable, do facilities exist locally that can recycle it?
- Does the product come with a take-back guarantee?
- Is there a market for the product once it is past its useful life? Can it be used as feedstock for new products rather than landfilled or incinerated?

- Can the product be disposed of safely? For example, fluorescent and many types of HID lamps contain mercury, a highly toxic heavy metal. Although lighting manufacturers have been successful in reducing the mercury content, the lamps must be carefully reprocessed by one of the companies in the United States that specialize in mercury recovery.

LCA is not a perfect science, in part because assigning weights or values to each of the categories during the impact assessment stage usually reflects the subjective values of the stakeholders involved in the process. So how are decisions made using an LCA? Ideally, the LCA results are obvious and one alternative is clearly better in at least one impact area and equal in all others. In other situations, the first step is to identify local and regional environmental threats in an effort to prioritize issues. It is likely that two companies evaluating the same set of data might come to two very different conclusions when deciding between alternative products. A company located in a region with severe air quality issues might weight those issues more heavily than another company that is more concerned about protecting local watersheds.

It's also important to note that an LCA will not determine which product or process is the most cost-effective or performs the best. This information is often derived from a process called a life cycle cost analysis (LCCA), which examines the economics of owning, operating, maintaining, and disposing of a product over a period of time. As a result, an LCA oftentimes is used as one part of the larger decision-making process, many times in conjunction with LCCA.

# Life Cycle Studies: A Comparison

Two studies on resilient flooring illustrate how an LCA and an LCCA may yield similar yet slightly different conclusions about material selection. The first study, "Resilient Flooring: A Comparison of Vinyl, Linoleum and Cork," was conducted by Sheila Bosch, Georgia Tech Research Institute, in 1999 and evaluated the life cycles of these three commonly used floor coverings with a focus on the environmental impacts of production, installation, maintenance, and end-of-life issues.[9] The second study compares the costs of purchasing, installing and maintaining common resilient flooring products, including VCT, sheet vinyl, linoleum, cork, and rubber.[10] The following summaries underscore the similarities and differences between the significant issues raised in an LCA versus an LCCA study.

■ *Vinyl LCA.* In her study, Bosch reported that vinyl flooring is a durable flooring solution with a long service life. Available in many attractive colors and patterns, it is often very inexpensive. However, the production of PVC requires petroleum and releases known carcinogens during the manufacturing process. Plant worker exposure is carefully regulated to protect employees. Individual compounds in vinyl flooring typically do not have high VOC emissions, but the choice of adhesives is important in reducing risks to occupants from off-gassing. Vinyl is seldom recycled, as the non-vinyl backings usually found on them make recycling difficult, so it is more commonly landfilled, creating a rather large solid waste stream. The top diagram on this page by Bosch charts the LCA analysis as vinyl travels from raw materials to finished product to disposal.

■ *Linoleum LCA.* Bosch reports that all of the materials used to produce linoleum flooring (linseed oil, limestone, cork flour, rosin, wood flour, pigments, and jute), including its backing, are natural and abundant resources. When incinerated, linoleum provides a source of energy without producing toxic emissions of its own. It is a low-maintenance, durable material that hardens as it ages, giving it a lifespan of 30 to 40 years. More expensive than vinyl, linoleum is manufactured in Europe and imported to the United States, adding an embodied energy impact. It is biodegradable, but the length of time for degradation under anaerobic conditions in a landfill is likely rather long. The bottom diagram on this page charts the life cycle process for linoleum.

An LCA study of linoleum. *Graphics reproduced with permission from "Creating Sustainable Interiors,"* © 2005 NCIDQ, Inc.

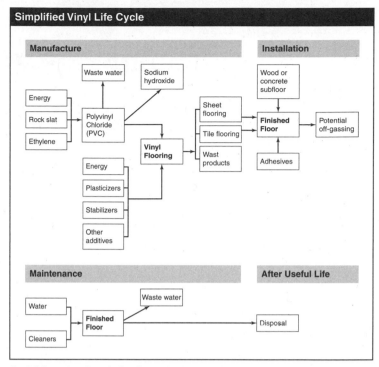

An LCA study of vinyl. *Graphics reproduced with permission from "Creating Sustainable Interiors,"* © 2005 NCIDQ, Inc.

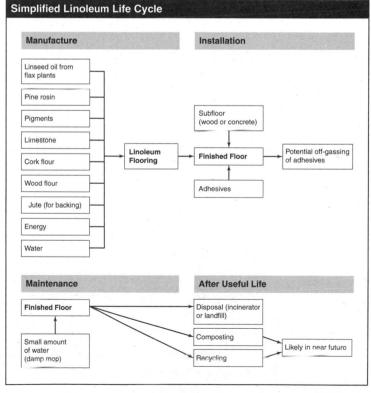

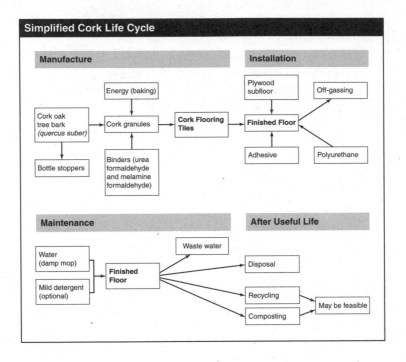

An LCA study of cork.
*Graphics reproduced with
permission from "Creating
Sustainable Interiors,"*
© 2005 NCIDQ, Inc.

■ *Cork LCA.* As reported in the Bosch study, cork flooring is relatively benign with respect to environmental impacts. No fertilizers or pesticides are used to promote tree growth or kill pests. Cork forests are managed carefully and most countries tightly regulate how often cork can be harvested, usually every nine years. The off-gassing of the binders used to agglomerate cork, however, may have negative effects on indoor air quality. Although it is more expensive than vinyl or linoleum, cork is compressible, strong, insulating, acoustical, and resistant to moisture damage, making it an attractive floor covering solution. It is susceptible to abrasion damage but is otherwise very durable, and it is biodegradable and potentially recyclable. Waste cork is often burned to produce energy for the factories. Because of its popularity, cork is not always readily available in the United States. Bosch documents the life cycle analysis of cork in the above diagram.

The second study compared five flooring materials beyond the characteristics examined by Bosch and includ-ed an analysis of the initial cost, the costs of operations, maintenance, and replacement. The study looked at twenty interior and exterior flooring materials, both synthetic and natural. Information regarding construction, performance, cleaning procedures, repair, maintenance, and replacement of building materials was collected by the Florida Department of Education from twelve case study schools. For this discussion we will examine the results for resilient floors only.

The results of the five resilient flooring systems (installed on a concrete subfloor with the appropriate adhesives and substrate materials) are shown in Table 4-3. The dollar amounts, expressed as per square foot, are those cited in the 1999 study and should be used for comparison only. The authors have used a common reference, net present worth (NPW)—the life cycle cost of the system based on a fifty-year building service life—to establish its rankings.

The Bosch report concludes that linoleum flooring appears to be the most sustainable choice when compared to vinyl and cork, with vinyl being the least sustain-

## Table 4-3: Life Cycle Costing for Resilient Flooring

| Ranking | Flooring System | Capital Cost | System Service Life | # of Replacement Systems | Maintenance as a % of Capital Cost | Maintenance Cost | Total Cost of System (NPW) |
|---------|-----------------|--------------|---------------------|--------------------------|-------------------------------------|------------------|----------------------------|
| 1 | Linoleum (.125") | $4.50 | 30 | 1 | 20% | $0.90 | $116.94 |
| 2 | VCT | $1.43 | 15 | 3 | 86% | $1.23 | $151.25 |
| 3 | Sheet Vinyl | $2.05 | 15 | 3 | 60% | $1.23 | $156.71 |
| 4 | Rubber Sheet (1/8") | $5.30 | 10 | 4 | 23% | $1.22 | $189.65 |
| 5 | Cork (1/8") | $3.43 | 6 | 8 | 36% | $1.23 | $208.82 |

Source: "Flooring Materials: Life-cycle Costing for Educational Facilities," by Helena Moussatche and Jennifer Languell

able. The Florida study also ranks linoleum first because of its low maintenance expense and long service life despite its higher capital costs. The initial cost savings from vinyl are counterbalanced by the high costs of its life cycle. Although cork does not fare well in the Florida report, some cork floors that were installed in the early twentieth century are still in use. It is obvious that while life cycle comparisons are useful and informative, they are not reliably conclusive. Asking key questions about a product, the reliability of the data, and the source of that data, as well as critically examining all the environmental impacts, is the responsibility of the design team.

# Furnishings and Finishes: An Overview

The following is an overview of some of the ecofriendly products available on the market today in the area of furnishings and finishes (lighting, appliance, and toilet and faucet options were covered in Chapter 3, while products relating to indoor air quality, thermal comfort, and daylighting—such as paints, ceilings, and automated window shading systems—are covered more extensively in Chapter 5). As underscored in those earlier chapters, and especially in Scot Horst's essay in this chapter, the process

of making an ecologically sound choice requires an informed insight into the environmental trade-offs associated with each alternative. However, designers can follow some general guidelines when selecting interior furnishings and finishes.

- Select products with low or no VOC content, and choose water-based finishes whenever possible, to address indoor air quality issues.
- Use precious materials, such as tropical hardwoods, sparingly and only when certified to be from a sustainably managed forest. Specify wood harvested from sustainably managed forests as well.
- Choose products based on their total life cycle cost, including maintenance, durability, and embodied energy.
- Use products with a high recycled material content, or products that can be recycled, salvaged, or reused, to address end-of-life issues.
- If possible, use products that consist of naturally renewable resources, which can be more easily recycled at the end of their useful life or are biodegradable if landfilled.

Additionally, designers should be familiar with the various third-party certification programs in place (examined in Chapter 6) to fully evaluate the specific benefits each environmental claim offers to their project. Finally, it is

## Myths and Misperceptions

Despite widespread product advancements, a few key misperceptions about sustainable products linger and may hinder their use. Here's a review of the current status of some of the more prevalent myths and misperceptions.

*Sustainable products are inferior in quality than standard products.* Sustainable products today meet the same performance requirements as any other product. In the early days of the green building movement, some products may have had quality-related problems; however, these issues rarely stemmed from the sustainable characteristics of the product. A decade or more of research and development as well as the modern manufacturing processes in place today ensure that most sustainable products now available meet, and often exceed, high performance standards.

*Sustainable products don't meet aesthetic standards.* While some sustainable products may look like they are environmentally friendly, it is most often because they are deliberately designed to present that kind of appearance and/or image. Today, few sustainable products are identifiable based solely on their appearance, as is evidenced by the products featured in this chapter.

*Sustainable products cost more.* Some sustainable products do cost more than their conventional counterparts. However, this additional first cost is often offset by the increased durability of the product, reduced maintenance costs, or other benefits to building occupants such as enhanced indoor air quality. For the most part, though, manufacturing technologies and economies of scale have resulted in a wide array of sustainable products that do not cost any more than standard products.

*Sustainable products are not readily available.* Not only have manufacturers taken note of the potential for sales opportunities associated with the increasing prevalence of green building practices, but many are also paying attention to their own responsibilities in the area of environmental stewardship. As a result, concerns regarding the availability of sustainable products are quickly diminishing. Increasingly, companies are moving away from energy- and waste-intensive manufacturing processes that utilize questionable chemicals and instead are investing in the research and development of a whole new generation of sustainable products.

*Sustainable products are proprietary or are not offered by competitive manufacturers.* As is the case in any industry segment, there are of course some sustainable products manufactured according to proprietary processes. However, a contributing factor to the impressive momentum experienced by the green building movement has been the willingness of all parties involved to share information and the insights gained from lessons learned. The result is a plethora of products that are competitive not only in price but also in performance and aesthetics.

important to note that the products highlighted here represent only a handful of the ecofriendly products available and in no way epitomize the universe of green product options—which, happily, is too large to include within the pages of this book. The following products are simply ones that have come across our radar screen and provide some interesting alternative choices for designers pursuing sustainable commercial interiors. Resources that provide more detailed information on supply options are listed in Chapter 9.

## Textiles

The perfect life cycle has come closest to being achieved by an upholstery fabric. Climatex Lifecycle, developed by Swiss manufacturer Rohner Textile in partnership with Designtex, McDonough Braungart Design Chemistry (MBDC), and the Ciba-Geigy chemical company, was the first fabric to embrace the credo "waste equals food" and remains today the standard by which other green products are judged.

The wool, ramie, and other components of the fabric are completely compostable, so much so that trimming waste is used as mulch in nearby gardens. The entire manufacturing process was scrutinized for environmental optimization and redesigned to completely eliminate all toxins and waste. The factory itself has become a water filtering plant, with the water coming out actually cleaner than the water going in. Standing in the way of achieving a completely closed loop life cycle is the use of fossil fuels both in the manufacturing of the product and in its transportation from factory to end user.

In 1998 Designtex opened its protocols to others, and today the Rohner factory produces a growing line of Climatex Lifecycle upholstery fabrics for other fabric houses. The first to take advantage of this unusual business strategy was Carnegie Fabrics, which had already developed its own environmentally friendly product line. Xorel, fabric woven from polyethylene, is chlorine- and plasticizer-free and is often used as an environmentally friendly alternative to vinyl.

Carnegie has also entered into eco-cooperation ventures with other textile innovators. For example, it is producing a line of Eco Intelligent Polyester (EIP) fabrics developed by Canadian textile manufacturer Victor Innovatex in collaboration with MBDC. EIP, designed for office furniture seating and panels, matches traditional polyester in aesthetics and performance but is made from an optimized fiber that replaces the heavy metal antimony as a catalyst with a safer substance. (Antimony, a known carcinogen, is toxic to the heart, lungs, liver, and skin. Long-term inhalation of antimony trioxide, a by-product of polymer production, can cause bronchitis and emphysema.) It is also chlorine-free, with no chlorinated dyes, auxiliaries, or other inputs either present in the product or used in its manu-

Climatex textiles are made of a compostable biological nutrient designed to turn back into soil at the end of its useful life. Every dye chemical is nontoxic. The water flowing out of the plant at the end of the manufacturing process is pure, and all waste trimmings are pressed into felt, which is sold to farmers for use as mulch. The industry's first collection was introduced in collaboration with William McDonough in 1995.

Incredibly durable, easily maintained, and inherently flame resistant, Carnegie's Xorel is appropriate as a wall covering or upholstery fabric.

facture, and it is also free of PBTs. It is considered a true "technical nutrient," meaning that it remains in a closed-loop system of manufacture, reuse, and recovery, maintaining its value through many product life cycles.

Terratex, a division of Interface Fabrics, was the first to launch a line of commercial fabrics made from Ingeo bio-based synthetic fibers from Cargill Dow. Bio-based fibers are made from organic, rapidly renewable resources where the starch from corn is converted into a thermoplastic fiber with performance characteristics similar to oil-based polyester. Eco-advantages derive from a reduction in the use of fossil fuels, as well as fewer greenhouse emissions produced by their combustion. Additionally, bio-based fabrics are completely biodegradable. Interface Fabrics is developing a new chemical and dye protocol, a scientific assessment of all chemical components contained in its dyes and finishing chemicals to determine which are most environmentally preferable. The protocol is significant because it requires the disclosure by its suppliers of all chemical ingredients contained in the products and not just those ingredients required to be disclosed by governmental regulations.

The company's initiatives also include other minimal-impact fabrics as well as the ReSKU textile reclamation program. The goal is to emulate nature by taking waste fabrics

Eco Intelligent Polyester fabrics by Victor Innovatex represent a closed-loop technical nutrient suitable for panel and seating applications. Shown is Asana, an open-line fabric designed and manufactured to work across a wide range of panel applications, featuring a refined and structural look with an underlying dimensional surface texture.

Interface Fabrics' Terratex fabrics are made from 100 percent recycled or compostable materials, are made with increasingly sustainable manufacturing processes, meet or exceed industry standards, and are recyclable at the end of their useful life. Interface Fabrics, in alliance with Haworth, features this collection of five proprietary fabrics, which are designated Green-e, meaning that credits offset the electricity used to manufacture these Terratex fabrics with the equivalent in certified renewable energy.

and turning them into materials that will continue to feed diverse applications such as seat cushions with recycled content. In a currently operating pilot program, Interface Fabrics is working with a targeted group of furniture manufacturers to return polyester fabrics to the recycling stream. These include regional collection centers starting with Interface's fabric facilities in Michigan, Massachusetts, and North Carolina, with potential expansion to Interface carpet locations in Georgia and on the West Coast. Interface Fabrics is also identifying third-party processors who have systems in place for storing, sorting, and shredding recycled fibers. By reducing the distance recycled fabrics are shipped, they will be able to realize significant cost savings.

Interface Fabrics has also been involved in the development of a coating designed to replace acrylic and rubber latex backing for upholstery, wall covering, and panel fabrics. Industry performance requirements have made it necessary for some panel fabrics, nearly half of all contract upholstery fabrics, and almost all woven wall covering to have a backing, usually made from latex. This is environmentally problematic, however, in that the process of backing fabric creates a permanent bond that is difficult to separate for recycling. The newly developed BioBac coating, however, is made of 100 percent bio-based annually renewable and biodegradable materials. This helps facilitate appropriate fabric disposal because under certain prescribed heat and water conditions, it breaks down to a non-polluting lactic acid that is biodegradable in wastewater treatment systems. To meet industry codes, BioBac is fire-neutral; it also helps reduce glue bleed-through and seam slippage, and it provides dimensional stability and fray resistance.

Many other fabric mills and jobbers have taken on the challenge of developing high-performance, stylish, and sustainable textiles. Arc-Com Fabrics, for example, offers the Eco-tex line of sustainable upholstery and panel fabrics. Made from 100 percent recycled polyester, these textiles are woven from a single fiber type with a recyclable backing or no backing and so are 100 percent recyclable.

HBF Textiles, working in cooperation with TVS Interiors, one of the nation's leading sustainable design firms, developed the Re:Stitch Collection, made from recycled and recyclable polyester.

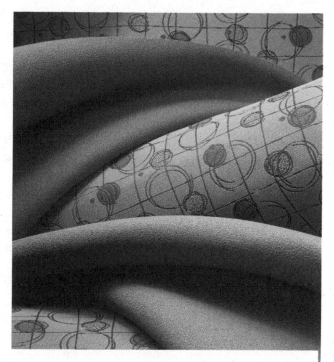

From the Eco-tex collection, patterns Hopscotch and Playground, designed by the Arc-Com Design Studio, are made from a single type of 100 percent recycled polyester and so are considered 100 percent recyclable. © 2003 Arc-Com Design Studio

Pattern Nubby is from the Re:stitch Collection Design by TVS Interiors for HBF Textiles. Re-Stitch is a sustainable fabric collection manufactured from recycled and recyclable polyester.

# The Environmental Attributes of Commercial Interior Textiles

During the 2005 NeoCon World's Trade Fair, Penny Bonda and Nadav Malin, along with a small group of participants, visited top manufacturers, grilling their key staff about the green aspects of their products and discussing the pros and cons of each manufacturer's approach. Carnegie Fabrics, one of the manufacturers on the tour, prepared the following discussion guide to examine ten key points designers should consider when evaluating the environmental claims of companies offering commercial interior textiles.

1. *Textile companies have latitude.* You should understand first and foremost that the textile companies (jobbers) who service the A&D market do not have manufacturing facilities. Therefore they have great latitude in sourcing and designing products to their specifications.

2. *Safety first.* There are fire codes that must be met for interior textiles. They will take precedence over any environmental concern. Fortunately a number of excellent environmental choices meet both criteria.

3. *A journey, not a destination.* Incremental improvements in the sustainability of interior textiles [are] being made on a regular basis. This will continue so as long as the clients (designers, architects, and end-users) demand healthier buildings, finishes and workplaces for their employees and occupants.

4. *Avoid certain materials.* The #1 culprit here would be PVC products. All the anecdotal and scientific information points to chlorine chemistry being a poor environmental choice. From dioxin production to plasticizers, vinyl is at the very least a highly controversial material, no matter what the Vinyl Institute says.

5. *Avoid textile finishes when possible.* The addition of finishes to achieve flame retardance or performance is an overall environmental negative. You have to consider that the extra processing often contains chemicals such as fluoropolymers, which add environmental impact to a textile.

6. *It's not always obvious.* Often designers assume that natural yarn fabrics are more environmentally sound than synthetic products. It is much more complex than that. Many natural fibers require extensive land use and pesticide control that negatively impact air, soil and ground water. Cotton would be a prime example. Synthetic yarns such as polyester can often require less processing and energy use than natural fabrics.

7. *Be careful of vague labeling.* Some textile companies will put wording on their products such as "Environmental Benefit" without any further explanation. They take the position that if a fabric is 100% wool, that fact is enough to state that it is eco-friendly. This issue is much more complex; moth proofing, heavy metal dyestuff and the scouring of wool are all major concerns.

8. *Not all third-party certifications are equal.* Again you need to dig below the surface. Getting an "independent" organization to validate a product's environmental claims can be good, but it's necessary to understand how they are testing and exactly what they're validating.

9. *LEED-CI is only a small start.* If you only base your environmental decisions on the LEED-CI point system, you are barely scratching the surface. This is a superficial system that often only measures one characteristic of a material to gain points.

10. *"Specifier beware."* Treat your specifications no differently than when you plan to purchase something for yourself. Ask the hard questions and don't settle for vague or superficial answers. Manufacturers that are fully behind an environmental protocol will rise to the top.

Reprinted with permission by Carnegie Fabrics.

# Fibers

Antron by Invista was the first carpet fiber to be independently certified, and now recertified, as an Environmentally Preferable Product. Among the criteria used to determine EPP status are manufacturing processes, an area in which Antron has reduced the need for fiber finishes by nearly 50 percent, reduced climate change emissions by 40 percent, and reduced nylon manufacturing waste to zero. Additionally, Invista reports that over 38 percent of the combined energy use of the six plants that produce its fibers and intermediates comes from green energy, including efforts such as co-generation (using heat generated in the manufacturing process to heat a facility) and waste-to-energy (using wastes to power a plant). Invista also operates the successful Antron Reclamation Program (see sidebar). Antron is a type 6,6 nylon polymer that combines fiber engineering technology, a patented soil resistant treatment for dry soil and liquid stains, pile height retention, and resistance to matting, crushing, and abrasive wear.

Zeftron's Savant nylon has been independently certified for recycled content. Regular dye bulk continuous filament yarn is certified to contain a minimum 50 percent recycled Nylon 6ix fiber with a minimum 25 percent postconsumer content and up to 25 percent postindustrial recycled Nylon 6ix content. Through the company's 6ix Again recycling program (see sidebar on page 122), Savant is also fully recyclable. Savant comes with ten-year limited warranties covering carpet wear, stain removal, and colorfastness.

Solutia offers Ultron Renew nylon 6,6, available in a variety of fiber types with up to 100 percent recycled content. Ultron Renew utilizes postindustrial fiber and polymer products created during the nylon manufacturing process before they enter the waste stream, recycling them into premium nylon 6,6 carpet fiber. Carpet manufacturers use these solution-dyed or white dyeable fibers to make carpets with a minimum of 25 percent recycled content, with the opportunity to use the full 100 percent.

Ingeo bio-based fibers from NatureWorks LLC are fibers made from renewable plants, not petrochemical resources. The company essentially harvests the carbon stored in the sugars of corn plants to make a polylactic acid resin called NatureWorks PLA. This resin can then be spun or otherwise processed into Ingeo fiber for use in apparel, bedding, baby and facial wipes, a wide range of furnishing applications such as carpets and rugs, upholstery, wall coverings, and drapery textiles. The fiber's properties provide for flame resistance, high ultraviolet resistance, and stain resistance. In addition, NatureWorks PLA is the world's first greenhouse-gas-neutral polymer, and products made with Ingeo fiber are compostable where that attribute is desired. From cradle to resin, production of Ingeo fiber uses 68 percent less fossil fuel resources than resins for traditional synthetic fibers.

One of the arguments opposing NatureWorks PLA as a leading environmental performer cites the questionable long-term health consequences associated with the use of genetically modified (GM) corn as the building block for PLA. This debate resulted in a September 2005 decision by NatureWorks to offer customers three source options: have the NatureWorks PLA resin they order certified as having no genetically modified content; participate in a source offset program for non-GM field maize purchases; or purchase identity-preserved NatureWorks PLA with specified seed-to-finished-product traceability. Minimum order volume and multiyear supply contracts are required for the manufacture and delivery of identity-preserved NatureWorks PLA.

> "About 80 percent of a product's environmental costs are established in the conceptual-design phase. The sooner in the design phase you start analyzing the environmental impact, the better the results."
>
> —Agis Veroutis, environmental consultant, Roy F. Weston Co.

# Carpet

Most carpet is made to last, but once soiled, matted, or out of style, it is often thrown away well before the end of its useful life. Fiber and carpet manufacturers—a group that came under early scrutiny from environmental groups worldwide—are developing efficient ways to reuse and recycle these materials.

# Reclamation and Reuse

The floor coverings industry was targeted first—and very aggressively—by environmental groups, citing the industry's negative environmental impacts in the areas of materials usage, poor indoor air quality, and disposal—most especially the billions of pounds of floor coverings that were going to landfills. The bulky nature of carpet and the variety of materials used in its manufacture create handling, collection, and recycling problems. The industry responded quickly to these concerns and has devoted much effort during the past fifteen years to not only address but also help solve the environmental problems associated with the use of their products. The following is an overview of some of the efforts and their associated milestones under way by both industry groups and individual manufacturers.

◆ The Carpet America Recovery Effort (CARE) is a joint industry–government effort to increase the amount of recycling and reuse of postconsumer carpet and reduce the amount of waste carpet going to landfills—more than 5 billion pounds annually, according to the most recent estimates offered by the U.S. EPA. Its mission is to identify and encourage market-based solutions for recovering value from discarded carpet, with the goal of diverting 40 percent of waste carpet by 2012. Funded and administered by the carpet industry, CARE also works with stakeholders outside the industry to assist with data collection, analysis, and program evaluation to ensure transparency in the reporting of the group's activities. While numbers to date have fallen a little short of the group's initial ambitious goals, impressive progress is being made: a total of 108.2 million pounds of postconsumer carpet was reported to be diverted from landfills in 2004, with 98.4 million pounds being recycled. This represents a 15.5 percent increase in diversion and a 13.6 percent increase in recycling. Since its creation, a total of 260 million pounds of carpet have been diverted, and 231 million pounds have been recycled.

◆ In 1991, Invista initiated a program to find new ways to put used carpet back to work, which led to the establishment of the Antron Reclamation Program. Since its inception, the program has collected over 100 million pounds of carpet, resulting in more than 400,000 cubic yards of conserved landfill space. In 2002, the Invista Reclamation Center in Calhoun, Georgia, was certified by Scientific Certification Systems' Environmental Claims Certification Program. After a second evaluation, the Invista Reclamation Center was recertified in 2004.

◆ Launched by Zeftron in 1994, the 6ix Again carpet recycling program is based on a closed-loop recycling system. Using a patented recycling process, used Nylon 6ix carpet is converted into pure caprolactam, the precursor of nylon 6, ready for repolymerization into virgin-quality carpet fiber. To date, millions of pounds of used carpet have been diverted from the nation's landfills, filling the increasing demand for postconsumer recycled content by upcycling new nylon back into premium nylon fiber systems. The 6ix Again program, which fuels the recycled content for Zeftron Savant, a 100 percent sustainable Nylon 6ix fiber, has also evolved to include not only products Zeftron manufactures but also those manufactured by others. It guarantees that any recovered face fiber will not be landfilled.

◆ More than 100 million pounds of reclaimed vinyl and vinyl-backed carpet have been recycled by C&A Floorcoverings since the company introduced its Infinity Initiative program ten years ago. Infinity Initiative recycles any postconsumer vinyl-backed carpet, regardless of original manufacturer, into 100 percent recycled-content backing for C&A's ER3 floor coverings. Containing a minimum of 25 percent postconsumer carpet, the remaining 75 percent of the ER3 backing system consists of postindustrial waste generated during carpet manufacturing and industrial waste from the automotive industry.

◆ Like many of its competitors, the success of Shaw's environmental programs depends on receiving back used carpeting; as such, its take-back program includes pickup of any EcoWorx product at no charge, which is then recycled into more EcoWorx, saving the customer not only shipping but also landfill tipping fees. EcoWorx backing, Shaw promises, will always be recycled into more EcoWorx, free of charge. EcoWorx contains 40 percent recycled content.

◆ The Los Angeles Fiber Co., a private West Coast textile and carpet recycler, recycles carpet from four different states, averaging over 7 million pounds of carpet a month. It accepts postconsumer carpet and recycles it into synthetic carpet cushion and other thermoplastic products. To better illustrate the quantity of carpet recycled by this firm, consider that if the Pasadena Rose Bowl was a landfill, L.A. Fiber diverts enough material annually to fill it three times.

◆ The Carpet and Rug Institute has developed an identification system for carpet materials, thus making the sorting of fiber and backing compounds easier and more efficient for recyclers. This identification system, called the Carpet Component Identification Code (CCIC), is currently being used by many of the institute's member companies. Information about carpet composition is printed, stamped, or bar-coded on the back of the carpet backing.

The resilient flooring industry also is paying close attention to end-of-life-issues. Johnsonite's RESTART program began with the reclamation of rePLACE demountable wall base and track and is targeting the eventual reclamation of rubber tile and treads as well. Customers simply request a return goods authorization number from Johnsonite after the product is removed and ready to be shipped back to the manufacturer. Upon receipt, Johnsonite prepares a certificate that verifies the reclamation of the product and the pounds of material diverted from a landfill.

A decade ago, Ray Anderson, the CEO of Interface, declared his intention of making his flooring division environmentally sustainable. What has followed is nothing less than remarkable. Not only has Interface made enormous strides toward reaching the top of "Mount Sustainability," as Anderson characterizes his journey, but many of his competitors in the commercial carpet industry have followed suit. No other product segment has made environmental progress as quickly as this one. As a result, the life cycle impacts of the production, use, and disposal of carpets have lessened across the board, but the most impressive progress seems to have been made in end-of-life strategies.

Interface, for example, launched its ReENTRY Carpet Reclamation Program in 1994 in order to recover used products to use in the recycling process and since that time has diverted more than 66 million pounds of carpet from landfills—52 percent was recycled, 40 percent was used for energy capture and conversion, and 8 percent was collected and reinstalled elsewhere. (See sidebar for information on other carpet reclamation programs.)

Another innovative program for waste reduction was introduced with the invention of the i2 product line. Inspired by nature's random patterns, no two tiles are alike, so no matter how the modules are laid out, they all work together. The company reports that installations are aver-

From the i2 collection from Interface. No matter how the modular Sole Mates tiles are laid out, they all work together, thus eliminating waste and making replacement easier. *Photography: Bruce Quist © 2005*

Twelve-inch square from the Shaw Contract Group's L7 Collection builds on the concept of a pixel to express color. L7 is a cradle-to-cradle product that was designed in collaboration with Bruce Mau and features sustainable EcoSolution Q nylon and EcoWorx backing.

C&A's Ethos is a nonchlorinated, high-performance backing for commercial carpet that is made from the polyvinyl butyral (PVB) film that is recovered when automotive windshields are recycled.

aging less than 2 percent waste versus up to 20 percent waste for broadloom. Because the i2 tiles' patterns always match, replacing damaged tiles is easy and whole installations can stay on the floor longer.

C&A Floorcoverings, part of the Tandus group of floor coverings, has rolled out FLOORE, an innovative buy-back program. Because old vinyl-backed carpet and vinyl waste is the only feedstock for its C&A's ER3 backings, the FLOORE program offers customers financial incentives to return and recycle their old vinyl-backed carpet, which the company then guarantees will be recycled in its entirety, with no portion landfilled, incinerated (including waste-to-energy), or disposed of in any other way.

In 2004, C&A introduced Ethos, a PVC-alternative carpet backing that is made from an abundant waste source—the polyvinyl butyral film that is recovered when automotive windshields are recycled. Until now, there has been no commercial use for this material, which accounts for millions of pounds of landfill waste. Ethos backing is durable and 100 percent recyclable using existing technologies and equipment.

The Shaw carpet company has turned to the MBDC Cradle to Cradle program for its end-of-life protocol. Carpets, it suggests, should be designed as technical nutrients—that is, waste that nature doesn't have a use for but industry does. Also, technical nutrients must be able to be used again and again, never going to the landfill. To make that possible, Shaw has designed its EcoSolution Q fiber and its EcoWorx tile carpet backing to be broken down at the end of their useful lives and reassembled into carpet products that are indistinguishable from carpeting made from virgin materials. The process earned Shaw a Presidential Green Chemistry Award.

Lees Carpets' Unibond and Unibond RE backing systems have earned Environmentally Preferable Product certification on the basis of life-cycle impact assessment (in the categories of resource consumption, product manufacturing, product use, and end of life) as well as operation performance, indoor environmental quality, and corporate environmental policy. Unibond RE, which debuted in 2002, contains 20 percent postconsumer recycled content measured in terms of total product weight and, like its predecessor, incorporates a renewable bio-based resource that Lees says has reduced its dependence on raw materials from petrochemical products by 10 million pounds annually. Unibond RE also eliminates the need for toxic seam welds or seam sealers, yet provides a bond estimated to be three times stronger than conventional latex-backed carpets. Additionally, the system does not require water and uses less than half the energy needed to produce latex systems.

Both Unibond and Unibond RE provide a moisture barrier that is totally synthetic.

Continuing its emphasis on the use of recycled materials, Lees offers the Visio Collection, a broadloom that consists of 20 percent postconsumer recycled content, 19.4 percent postindustrial recycled content, and 12.4 percent rapidly renewable bio-based resin. It is manufactured with Antron Legacy EPP Nylon with high recycled content. All of Lees broadloom carpets are totally recyclable using standard reclamation techniques. Visio was designed in collaboration with Ken Wilson, founder, and Colleen Waguespack, interior designer, of Envision Design.

Milliken Carpet has chosen a different tactic on carpet disposal strategies. "Rethink recycling, think reuse" is the philosophy behind Earth Square, its program that renews existing modular carpet for another installation life. The five-step process begins when old carpet squares are returned to Milliken, supercleaned, retextured, redesigned, and colored and then reinstalled either in the same location or in another. At about half the cost of new carpeting, Earth Square is an economical way to rejuvenate flooring materials. In addition, Milliken's ES backing system is PVC-free and contains up to 35 percent recycled content. The Earth Square process creates less waste and pollution than the manufacturing of new carpet or Milliken's competitors' recycling programs. However, only Milliken modular carpet can be used.

The Future Links pattern in Beach Color is one of the patterns available in Lees' Visio Collection of broadloom carpeting, designed by Ken Wilson and Colleen Waguespack of Envision Design, and composed of recycled and renewable content. *Photography © Envision Design PLLC*

Milliken's Earth Square program supercleans, retextures, redesigns, and colors old and worn modular carpets, giving them a new life for half the original cost and with a new warranty. *© 2005 Milliken Carpet*

## What Is Environmentally Preferable Purchasing?

The U.S. federal government is the single largest consumer of goods and services in the U.S. and, probably, in the world—spending more than $200 billion annually on goods and services. The federal government also spends an additional $240 billion a year, indirectly, through grant disbursements. This incredible purchasing power comes with a responsibility, says the U.S. EPA, to ensure that the products and services it purchases minimize environmental burdens. To that end, the EPA's Environmentally Preferable Purchasing Program is a federal initiative that encourages and assists executive agencies in the purchasing of environmentally preferable products and services. Its goal is fourfold:

◆ Help increase the availability of products and services that are environmentally preferable

◆ Protect human health

◆ Save money

◆ Improve the overall quality of government purchases

Environmentally preferable products and services are defined by Executive Order 13101 as those that "have a lesser or reduced effect on human health and the environment when compared to other products and services that serve the same purpose. This comparison may consider raw materials acquisition, production, manufacturing, packaging, distribution, reuse, operation, maintenance or disposal of the product or service." Because of the comparative, rather than absolute, nature of this definition, EPA has developed additional guiding principles that provide further meaning to this definition, which are detailed in the online report "Final Guidance on Environmentally Preferable Purchasing."

*Source*: U.S. EPA, www.epa.gov.

For those designers interested in exploring carpet options that do not include synthetic materials, Earthweave Carpet Mills offers the Bio-Floor Collection, including hemp and wool broadloom carpets and area rugs that are completely biodegradable. The face fiber is 100 percent naturally pigmented wool fiber with a natural primary (the material that the tufting machine places the wool yarn into, and which holds the yarn in place) of hemp and cotton, versus traditional synthetic polypropylene primary. The carpet's adhesive is made of natural rubber from the rubber tree, while the back of the carpet is made from jute, a hardy fiber-producing plant. The padding is a blend of coarse, naturally pigmented wood mechanically needled, not glued, into a cotton scrim, and it is free of dyes, fire retardants, glues, or mothproofing. Some vegetable matter may be present. Earth Weave recommends that individuals who have a sensitivity to animal fibers should obtain a sample before ordering. Additionally, when the carpet needs to be replaced, the company encourages customers to recycle it to the garden, where it will safely biodegrade while serving as an effective weed barrier and mulch. After an estimated two to three seasons, the padding should completely disappear, adding nitrogen and other nutrients plants need to the soil, essentially returning to grass.

## Resilient Flooring

The flooring industry's resilient segment, which includes linoleum, rubber, cork, and vinyl products, also is embracing the concepts of sustainability. Many manufacturers have developed advanced generations of floor coverings that feature naturally renewable ingredients and/or recycled content. For example, linoleum, a popular flooring in the 1960s and 1970s (although it was first invented in England in the mid-1800s), has enjoyed a resurgence in the past decade, in large part due to its environmental benefits—the product is made with both recycled and renewable ingredients, including linseed oil (extracted from flax plants), cork dust (harvested from the dead outer bark of trees), natural jute fiber, and wood powder (salvaged from sawdust)—and to the development of technologies to increase both its aesthetics and performance. One of the product's environmental drawbacks, however, is that since 1975, when the last linoleum plant in the United States

## Toward Sustainable Sampling

Applying new technologies to conventional processes is a hallmark of sustainable thinking and is exemplified in the new sampling process developed by Tricycle to help eliminate the estimated $1 billion carpet manufacturers spend each year on samples—products that are used only briefly, then discarded to live in the landfill. Tricycle's paper simulation tool (SIM) combines CAD and CAM data with fiber color information to create fully textured, digitally tufted carpet samples that are output as first generation, rich media images on screen and as paper prints.

Customarily, a designer, after selecting the carpet samples she would like to consider, calls her rep and orders actual samples from the mill, a costly, time-consuming process. Using the Tricycle SIM process, however, she calls her rep, who orders the SIM samples on 100 percent recyclable paper using zero oil, which are then shipped to her (in a smaller and less costly package) within twenty-four hours. After previewing the SIM samples, the designer is able to more narrowly select a limited number of actual tufted samples to show to the client. Designers who have used the program give high marks to the samples' color rendition, reporting high degrees of accuracy between the original paper samples and the resulting tufted samples.

Nearly twenty commercial and hospitality carpet brands use the award-winning SIM technology to replace samples in the early rounds of specification. Lees Carpet, for example, offers 135 patterns in 35 colorways as "techno images" through its Web site. The carpets can be custom-colored and viewed online in six unique room scenes; sample images can be on a designer's desk the next day. Mannington is using Tricycle's Apso Jet Set, a product development suite and prototyping engine, to offer designers the ability to collaborate, archive, view, and prototype carpet products as well. Tandus also uses the SIM technology in its online sampling process for modular and broadloom carpet, Blink, which takes designers through a simple four-step process that allows them to choose from hundreds of patterns and colors from the three Tandus brands—Monterey, C&A, and Crossley. Tandus estimates

that prints generated through Blink require 95 percent less energy and water to produce than an average carpet sample. The packaging in which Blink prints are delivered, which also serves as a project folder, is made of 100 percent postconsumer fibers (20 percent FSC-certified), manufactured with energy from wind power.

Other notable sampling initiatives include:

◆ Tarkett Commercial's ReUse Reclamation program provides for the recycling of its own carry boards, chip boxes, and architectural folders. Customers simply ship old samples to Tarkett's recycling center; all can be returned with postage prepaid so that no additional cost is incurred by Tarkett customers. One hundred percent of the returned materials are recycled into future Tarkett flooring or sample vehicles.

◆ Many local chapters of design organizations sponsor "sample round-ups," where professional firms donate excess or unwanted materials to design students in their community. These kinds of programs provide valuable learning tools for students while also extending the life cycle of samples beyond their typical usage.

Tricycle's SIM sampling process provides fully textured, digitally tufted carpet samples that can be viewed online or as color-accurate prints on 100 percent recyclable paper using zero oil. They replace costly and wasteful carpet samples that find their way to a landfill after only a short time of use. © 2005 Tricycle, Inc. Photography by Ben Horner

Flowers Hospital in Dothan, Alabama features Forbo's Marmoleum sheet and tile linoleum flooring. Made from readily renewable natural ingredients, Marmoleum has naturally occurring antistatic and antimicrobial properties, and features Forbo's Topshield finish. *Photography by Michael Parker*

Healthcare and other environmentally conscious specifiers choose Amtico's Stratica flooring products for their looks, durability, and ease of maintenance. Stratica is an eco-polymeric flooring that is virtually VOC- and chlorine-free, and does not require dressing or cleaning with caustic chemicals. © 2005 Amtico International

closed, linoleum is now primarily manufactured in Europe and so has the embodied energy costs associated with overseas shipping.

A leading supplier of linoleum is Forbo, which offers two collections: Marmoleum and Artoleum. Both feature oxidized linseed oil (or a combination of oxidized linseed oil and tall oil) and rosin mixed with other raw materials to form linoleum granules, which are then pressed onto a jute backing to make Marmoleum and Artoleum sheets. No heavy metals are used, and the products have a water-based finish. Adhesives also are 100 percent solvent-free and meet all low-VOC requirements. (The Marmoleum/Artoleum MSDS is illustrated on page 107. At the end of its useful life, Forbo reports that linoleum can be incinerated in an energy-recycling incineration plant, producing a residual calorific value comparable to that of coal. The amount of $CO_2$ released during incineration is roughly equivalent to that taken up by the natural raw materials it uses (flax plants, trees, and jute plants). Therefore, Forbo says, linoleum can be considered a closed-loop system: the energy obtained from incinerating linoleum is roughly equivalent to or even more than that used in production. Another option is landfilling, where Forbo says natural decomposition takes place without the release of harmful substances or gases such as chlorine and dioxins.

Technology has dramatically increased the aesthetic options now available in linoleum. Forbo's Marmoleum, for example, is offered in a number of solid and multicolored options such as Global 2 (marbleized patterns) and Colourful Greys, in which designs appear subtle—at first all one sees is gray—but on closer inspection a marvel of color opens up. Artoleum is a visually striking, highly textured linoleum floor covering designed to hide the daily dirt in heavy-traffic areas where a low-maintenance floor is desired.

Amtico International offers Stratica, a non-PVC, chlorine-free resilient tile flooring for commercial projects, with a realistic range of replica woods, granites, marbles, and stones. Stratica is an eco-polymeric, a term Amtico uses to distinguish products that are engineered from modern synthetic materials to give environmental benefits. Stratica, for example, is made with Surlyn, a durable plastic that is recommended by Greenpeace as an alternative to PVC.

Another benefit is its ability to be installed during occupancy. For example, because Stratica comes in plank form, the Fresno Surgery Center in California was able to carry out an installation of Stratica in stages, thus maintaining the healthcare facility's normal routine.

Rubber flooring is also generally considered a "low-impact" environmental flooring choice. Flooring made from virgin natural rubber comes from a renewable raw material extracted from the sap of the tropical rubber plant. There are also numerous choices of rubber flooring made from recycled rubber, typically from used and discarded tires.

One option, ECOsurfaces, is a collection of eight indoor and outdoor product families manufactured by Dodge-Regupol out of 100 percent postconsumer tire rubber. All are made of recycled SBR (styrene-butadiene rubber) and colored using flecks of ethylene propylene diene monomer (EPDM), an organic synthetic elastomer that, when cured, has many properties equivalent to or better than those of natural virgin rubber. (Dodge-Regupol uses the scrap derived from the manufacturing of virgin EPDM, which it cleans and reprocesses to eliminate any contamination from water, metals, and other by-products.) The SBR and EPDM are then bound with a water-based polymer. ECOsurfaces is available in both tile and roll forms.

From the international sales and marketing organization To Market comes the EarthShapes addition to the Atmosphere recycled rubber flooring series: resilient and recyclable rubber floors made from reclaimed car tires. Three flecked styles—Discovery, Structure, and Exploration—are available in a wide spectrum of shades and in either a 38-inch straight-edge square or a 37-inch interlocking tile. EarthShapes are manufactured from 100 percent postconsumer recycled tire rubber SBR granules along with 100 percent postindustrial colored EPDM granules homogeneously mixed throughout.

Nora Rubber Flooring offers a number of rubber flooring alternatives, including Noraplan Fossil, with a smooth, nonglare finish that reinforces the natural look of the line. Its name is derived from the multicolor granules that resemble fossil inclusions found in nature. Like all Nora products, Noraplan Fossil is PVC-free, made instead from rubber, mineral fillers, and environmentally compatible color pigments. Noraplan Fossil is also made using the Nora Cleanguard manufacturing process, which eliminates the need for waxing or sealing, thus contributing to healthier indoor air and easy, less expensive cleaning with lower maintenance costs.

As discussed earlier in this chapter, cork is another ecofriendly flooring alternative. It actually comes from the

Made from 100 percent recycled tire rubber and colorful EPDM flecks, ECOsurfaces Commercial Flooring boasts an extensive array of 70 color combinations for a variety of applications such as retail, corporate, education, and hospitality. © *EcoSurfaces Commercial Flooring*

Manufactured from 100 percent postconsumer recycled tire rubber SBR granules along with 100 percent postindustrial colored EPDM granules homogeneously mixed throughout, To Market's Earthshapes Collection features three coordinated styles that are suitable for use in office, educational, institutional, healthcare, and retail environments. © *2003 Unicork*

bark of the cork oak tree, which is grown and harvested predominantly in Portugal and Spain, where it is a native species. Cork bark is harvested only from mature trees, typically every nine years, in a continuous cycle that goes on and on—some cork oak trees have been known to live up

The cork used in the Unicork Naturals collection offered by To Market is harvested by hand and the natural habitat is not disturbed at harvest time.

to five hundred years. Cork flooring is made by grinding the bark into small pieces, which are coated with a non-toxic resin binder, and then manufactured as tiles or planks in various thicknesses.

Color variances are achieved when cork is baked in ovens—the longer it bakes, the darker it becomes. Unfinished cork can be painted or stained as well. Cork's cellular structure (50 percent of the volume of cork material is air) makes it not only resilient but also a great sound and thermal absorber. Suberin, the basic substance of cork, discourages microbe growth and is resistant to moisture, fire, and insects. Cork also delivers long-term aesthetics and performance; public buildings designed by architect Frank Lloyd Wright still feature the original cork floors installed in the early twentieth century.

One U.S. cork flooring supplier is To Market, which offers the Unicork Naturals product line, a collection of nine flooring patterns featuring organic and geometric styles in rich neutral tones. Because Unicork Naturals is designed and engineered from the bark of cork trees (and harvested by hand), no trees are destroyed during the manufacturing process.

Wicanders is another leading cork supplier, offering four collections, including one, Motion, that combines cork with rubber for a bolder look. Wicanders also offers Xtreme WRT, a new cork flooring with a matte finish that's based on a compound of tiny ceramic microbeads to protect the floor against abrasion and scratches. Wicanders notes that Xtreme WRT enhances the natural features of wood and cork while considerably improving UV protection.

## Hard Flooring

Concrete is enjoying a resurgence of sorts in commercial applications in large part because it is considered a natural material—composed of cement, water, gravel, stone, and sand—that can be 100 percent recycled indefinitely. Old concrete can be crushed and used for new concrete or as road-building material. For contemporary flooring applications, minimal additives improve the characteristics of the concrete, such as in the case of polished concrete, where it is ground, densified (with a silicate compound considered environmentally benign), and polished to produce a durable, highly reflective surface. (This process can be used on both existing and new concrete floors.) Polished concrete flooring also can be stained or colored to produce an attractive, versatile aesthetic. On average, a polished concrete floor has a ten-year-plus life cycle, typically requiring only stone soap and water for cleaning. Also, little energy is required for manufacturing, and the product is considered chemical- and VOC-free.

*"The longer I research green building practices, the more I appreciate innovations that are not just functional and environmentally responsible, but also cost-effective. Such is the case with polished, densified concrete flooring."*

—Alex Wilson, executive editor, *Environmental Building News,* February 2006

A number of suppliers offer polished concrete systems, including RetroPlate, which uses a water-based sodium silicate that chemically interacts with the calcium hydroxide in the cement to permanently strengthen concrete floors, whether old or new, and to deliver a highly abrasion-resistant, dustproof floor with increased impact resistance and reflectivity. The RetroPlate process uses no solvents or VOCs and is odorless and nonflammable. The company's recent applications have included retail, restaurant, office, school, healthcare, and industrial installations.

Estrie Products International, a division of American Biltrite Canada Ltd., began offering Stonescape in September 2005, marketing it as a flooring alternative made from limestone and ethylene acrylic polymers, naturally abundant resources. Stonescape is PVC-free, emits no VOCs, and contains no plasticizers. Beyond its environmental benefits, the manufacturer notes that Stonescape offers dimensional stability and can help bridge minor subfloor irregularities, is smoke- and flame-resistant, and is designed with inherent antifatigue, sound-deadening, and sound-absorption properties, which reduce noise generation and actively suppress sound resonance.

Touchstone large-format tiles are composed of natural materials such as limestone and quartz bound together with white cement. About 50 percent of Touchstone Tile's raw materials can be considered postindustrial in content, which

means they're materials left over from other stone production, and are sourced locally. Large slabs are formed in special molds, which are then subjected to a process of high-frequency vibration that results in the finest particles gravitating to the bottom of the mold to form a unique surface.

Touchstone Tiles contain no resins or artificial materials and cure naturally, continuing to strengthen and harden over many years. The product is not baked, autoclaved, or heated in any way, thus minimizing the energy consumed in the manufacturing process. Any waste material from batching or curing is recyclable, as are the tiles themselves when replaced.

St. Peter Hospital chose RetroPlate and acid stain for a new, vibrant, yet low-maintenance flooring for its new Emergency Center and the renovation of its main entrance lobby. *Photography by Peter Wagner*

Stonescape, from the Estrie product division of American Biltrite, is a flooring alternative made from a polymeric compound that is environmentally friendly. It is free from PVC, emits no VOCs, contains no plasticizers, and can sustain up to 2,000 psi. *Photography courtesy of American Biltrite*

## Recycled Content: What Does It Mean?

"Buying recycled" means purchasing recycled products (products made with recovered materials). A necessary precedent to "buying recycled" is that manufacturers purchase recovered materials and use them in lieu of virgin materials in the manufacture of new products. Purchasing recycled products or recovered materials for manufacturing conserves valuable landfill space by using goods made from materials that otherwise would have been discarded. Using recycled products and packaging also conserves natural resources and energy. In addition, purchasing recycled products promotes the continued manufacture of these products and helps strengthen markets for collected materials. (It is worthwhile to note that in the early stages of the green building movement, specifying products with recycled content was the predominant priority. The design industry has since evolved its decision making process beyond this sole environmental goal and now considers a broader and more comprehensive set of environmental priorities when selecting products.)

The terminology used to refer to recycling, recycled products, and recovered raw materials can seem confusing. The following definitions are provided to help clarify some of these terms.

◆ *Recycled content.* The portion of a product, by weight or volume, that is composed of preconsumer and/or postconsumer recovered materials.

◆ *Preconsumer materials.* Materials recovered for recycling prior to use by the consumer, including materials and by-products generated from the manufacturing process to be used as feedstock for another process. Examples of preconsumer recovered materials are envelope cuttings and scrap from plastic manufacturing.

◆ *Postconsumer materials.* Materials that have served their intended use as consumer items and have been recovered or diverted from solid waste for recycling. Examples of postconsumer recovered materials include used beverage containers and old computer printouts. The percentage of recovered materials used in a product or within product categories can vary significantly. For example, corrugated boxes can be made from 0 to 40 percent postconsumer materials. Generally, higher levels of recycled content are desirable, but other factors, such as performance requirements, will likely need to be considered in your purchase decision.

The cost-competitiveness of recovered materials and products is highly variable and dependent on the specific product or material, and supply and demand market forces. For example, in the past, paper made with recovered content was often considerably more expensive than virgin paper. Today, however, the price of many types of recycled paper is comparable to that of virgin paper. As more recycled products of all types are purchased, manufacturers increasingly will realize economies of scale, and prices should tend to decrease and stabilize.

In the past, some recycled products did not perform as well as their virgin counterparts. Today, however, recycled products are manufactured to meet the same performance standards as virgin products. Work with your vendors to purchase recycled products that meet your needs and specifications.

*Source: WasteWi$e Tip Sheet: Buying or Manufacturing Recycled Products*, a publication of the U.S. Environmental Protection Agency.

# Wood Flooring

Wood flooring has enjoyed a tremendous resurgence in popularity in the past two decades, after experiencing a substantial decline when advances in the production of carpet in the mid-1960s led to widespread affordable choices in that product segment. Traditionally considered a residential product, wood flooring is increasingly being found in commercial spaces as the introduction of high-performance finishes make the product more durable and easily maintained in high-traffic areas. Much of its newfound appeal lies in the warmth it brings to a space. Most wood floors today are manufactured using North American hardwoods—with increasing numbers of those options being made from wood certified as having been grown in sustainable, well-managed forests that have been certified by outside inspectors accredited by the Forest Stewardship Council (FSC). This means the forests are being managed in a way that ensures long-term productivity and protects local economies, wildlife, recreation, and other uses. Consider that an individual hardwood tree takes anywhere from three decades to more than a hundred years to mature, depending on the species, and the long-term consequences of management become apparent.

Another wood option in flooring that is gaining in popularity is bamboo, made from a rapidly renewable source. Bamboo (which is actually a grass rather than a tree) offers a distinctive finished appearance that comes from the slightly darker bands produced by its nodes, the tightness of its grain, and the uniformity of its color. It offers both hardness and resilience and is both dimensionally stable and moisture-resistant. It is considered an environmentally friendly choice in wood flooring because bamboo is extremely fast-growing; on average it reaches maturity, at heights well over fifty feet, in about five years. Additionally, since bamboo is a grass (some call it a weed), it is harvested again and again from the same plant. On the other side of the environmental coin, however, lies the fact that most bamboo is grown in Asia, Central America, and South America and thus necessitates overseas transportation and its attendant environmental impacts. However, experiments are proving that some bamboo species can thrive in North American climates, although at this point it is being grown primarily for ornamental rather than commercial purposes.

Bamboo flooring is often chosen for high-end applications because of its distinctive appearance as well as its hardness, resiliency, stability, and moisture resistance. EcoTimber bamboo flooring is shown here in the Dahesh Museum in New York City. © 2005 EcoTimber

Bamboo flooring manufacturer EcoTimber recommends the following elements to consider when evaluating the quality of a particular bamboo flooring option: raw materials, adhesives, milling equipment, board lengths, and finishes. From an environmental standpoint, EcoTimber cites the importance of using bamboo that is sourced from bamboo plantations and not from wild habitats, which could lead to too-early and thus unsustainable harvesting practices and also an inferior finished product. EcoTimber offers solid bamboo flooring in 3⅝-inch-wide planks that can be nailed to plywood or glued to concrete subfloors, and engineered bamboo flooring, which consists of a sandable wear layer of bamboo on top of a backing made of plantation pine and fir. This can be nailed to plywood, glued to concrete, or floated. EcoTimber uses a low-VOC European adhesive.

Teragren, another leading bamboo flooring manufacturer, uses the Moso bamboo species, plantation-grown in managed agricultural plots by independent farmers in China's Zhejiang province. Two of the company's recent developments in this product category include the introduction of Synergy, a compressed-strand bamboo flooring

Teragren's durable and renewable bamboo flooring, stair treads, risers, and panels in Vertical Grain Natural grace the foyer of Fallon Worldwide Advertising in Minneapolis. Design by Perkins + Will Architects. *Photography © Hedrich Blessing*

product that is 43 percent harder than traditional bamboo, and Signature Colors, a collection featuring machine-applied water-based stains (espresso, cherry, walnut, and charcoal) applied to the flat grain for interesting colors. All Teragren coating materials are water-based, solvent-free, and non-off-gassing.

Wood flooring made from reclaimed wood is yet another product segment with inherent eco-advantages. These flooring options are manufactured using old-growth wood that has been found in centuries-old barns, recovered from buildings slated to be demolished, or salvaged from the bottoms of rivers.

Aged Woods brand flooring, for example, is milled from old, destined-for-the-dump barn wood, ranging in age from seventy-five years to as much as two hundred years. Proper kiln-drying before milling ensures a stable, bug-free floor. The look of these antique woods is natural, resulting from many decades of weathering the wind, rain, and sun, contributing to the rugged, rustic feel of Early Americana. Additionally, because many of these planks are from the trees of virgin forests, the wood has a tighter grain because it grew during a period of unique ecological balance. Aged Woods categorizes its planks as "antique" or "antique distressed" according to the degree of weathering that has occurred.

Goodwin HeartPine reclaims the heart pine and heart cypress wood used for its product offerings from the waters of the rivers in the southern United States, left over from the 1800s when the rivers were used by many timber operations to raft their logs to nearby sawmills. As Goodwin HeartPine explains, some of the densest, heaviest logs felled by hand more than a century ago rolled off the rafts during the float trip to the mills. Today, Goodwin recovers these abandoned antique logs from the waters (where they have been well preserved due to the oxygen-free conditions) and processes them into river-recovered antique woods for flooring, millwork, and stair parts. Goodwin guarantees 100 percent heart face on every river-recovered board.

Gaylan's passion for sports and its love of the great outdoors is exhibited throughout its store located at the Washingtonian in Gaithersburg, Maryland. The dramatic Aged Woods Antique Oak reclaimed barn wood floor featured here is set down into the surrounding concrete floor and bordered with a one-inch cork strip to allow for expansion. Installation by Syracuse Floor Systems. *Photography by Hayman Studios.*

Beautiful hardwood flooring, millwork, and stair parts are being made from abandoned antique logs rescued from southern river waters by Goodwin HeartPine.

## Wood and Millwork

You may not see it, but particleboard and medium-density fiberboard (MDF) are all around you—floors, walls, cabinets, and doors most likely are made of one or the other. Particleboard has become since World War II one of the nation's leading building materials, primarily because it is a more affordable alternative to solid woods. Another alternative, however, is agriboard—a term used for agricultural-based products such as wheatboard or strawboard. These products do not contain formaldehyde, as most particleboard does, yet they are as durable.

PrimeBoard is one supplier of such "tree-free" particleboard. Using only annually renewable agricultural fibers from wheat and sunflowers, PrimeBoard is bound with emissions-free synthetic resins instead of traditional resins that contain urea formaldehyde. (Urea formaldehyde is used in the majority of North American and imported hardwood plywood panels and has recently been classified by the International Agency for Research on Cancer as carcinogenic to humans.) As a result, no VOCs are emitted into the air, which creates a healthier environment. The company's PrimeBoard Premium Wheat line is an interior-grade engineered panel commonly specified for work surfaces, high-end cabinetry and casegoods, furniture, store fixtures, and any other type of particleboard or laminated products. PrimeBoard Supreme Wheat offers the same properties but with increased moisture resistance.

Sierra Pine offers Medite II, an SCS-certified, no-added-formaldehyde MDF panel engineered for nonstructural applications, which can be used in place of sanded plywood and solid wood. This panel provides the flexibility of a composite panel with the low emissions of solid wood. Its fire-retardant option, Medite FR2, gets its fire-retardant properties not via a topical treatment but rather through an additive that is blended with the wood fibers to provide flame-retardant properties throughout the board. Sierra Pine's Medex is an SCS-certified, no-added-formaldehyde, moisture-resistant MDF panel engineered for interior high-moisture areas.

Columbia Forest Products is currently converting all its veneer-core hardwood plywood plants to formaldehyde-free manufacturing processes, using a patented, soy-based adhesive cooperatively developed by Columbia, the College of Forestry at Oregon State University, and Hercules Inc. Called PureBond, the new adhesive, made up primarily of soy flour, will allow Columbia to completely eliminate formaldehyde from its standard veneer-core decorative panel production. The new binder is 87 percent soy protein, with the remainder a proprietary petrochemical-based polyamide resin. It is water-based, nonflammable, and nontoxic; water vapor is the only emission during curing. The company's agrifiber-core panels are made from straw, a waste agricultural product, and among the wood veneers offered are those that are certified according to Forest Stewardship Council standards.

# Furniture

The multibillion-dollar office furniture industry has received much criticism over the years for many negative environmental impacts, not just in the area of forest depletion regarding the wood used for manufacture, but also for the emission of VOCs during the manufacturing process, as well as the VOCs associated with installation. End-of-life issues have also been a fervent source of criticism in that desks, chairs, panel systems, and filing cabinets traditionally end up in the landfill to make way for the newer/better/cooler options that find their way to the highly competitive marketplace each year. In recent years, though, as awareness of the LEED Green Building Rating System has grown, and as many manufacturers have become actively engaged in corporate social responsibility initiatives, the industry has addressed many of these concerns, as explored in the following summaries of green furniture options.

For example, three of the largest furniture manufacturers—Herman Miller, Steelcase, and Haworth—have used their sustainable design know-how to bring to market an array of attractive, competitive choices in green seating. Herman Miller offers the Mirra Chair, designed according to the company's internal Design for the Environment protocols regarding material chemistry, recyclability, manufacturability, packaging, and ease of disassembly. Up to 96 percent of Mirra'a materials can be recycled at the end of the chair's useful life; in the upholstered version, the Latitude fabric is made from polyester that is 100 percent recyclable at the end of its useful life.

Haworth's Zody, a midpriced task chair, is made with up to 51 percent recycled content and up to 98 percent recyclable materials. Zody is also PVC-free, chrome-free, and CFC-free and has earned a Gold Cradle to Cradle product certification from McDonough Braungart Design Chemistry. The chair features a patent-pending asymmetrical lumbar adjustment, 4-D arms, and optional gel-foam seat. Additionally, Haworth uses 100 percent Green-e windpower credits to manufacture the chair.

Steelcase also offers a Silver Cradle to Cradle certified chair. The Think work/task chair is 99 percent recyclable content by weight and is made of up to 41 percent recycled material. According to MBDC's materials classification protocol, the Think chair uses only materials deemed safe

Mirra is an innovative, high-performing, environmentally advanced work chair. It is the first chair designed to meet Herman Miller's stringent Design for the Environment (DfE) protocol, and was scrutinized to assure that its material chemistry, recyclability, manufacturability, packaging, and ease of disassembly are environmentally friendly.

The first chair to achieve a Gold Cradle to Cradle certification, Haworth's Zody is a midpriced task chair made with up to 51 percent recycled content and up to 98 percent recyclable materials. It is manufactured with 100 percent Green-e wind power credits and is PVC-, chrome-, and CFC-free.

The smart, simple Think chair is comprised of 99 percent recyclable content and can be made up of up to 41 percent recycled material. It is both Cradle to Cradle and Greenguard certified.

Knoll's Dividends systems furniture line is made with high contents of recycled material, features 100 percent recycled content fabric, and contains wood and reconstituted veneers from FSC-certified forests.

Bruce Sienkowski of 2B Studio designed the Rendezvous chair, available from Integra, with a frame made from WoodStalk, an annually renewable wheat straw fiber rather than from wood. A patented parts connection system uses leftovers from the manufacturing in molding.

to the environment. Powder-coat paint is free of VOCs and heavy metals, urethane foam is water-based, and no gluing processes are used in assembly. To extend the chair's life, seat and back cushions, arms, headrest, and lumbar support can be added or replaced. Disassembly for recycling takes only about five minutes using common hand tools. To reduce the negative impacts associated with shipping, the lightweight chairs are manufactured close to customers in North America, Europe, and Asia and shipped ready-to-assemble, which uses less packaging and allows more chairs per shipment.

The upholstered frames of Integra's Rendezvous line of lounge and reception seating, designed by Bruce Sienkowski of 2B Studio, are made with WoodStalk, an annually renewable wheat straw fiber, rather than wood. The company's patented connection system, known as tube-and-plug, uses regrind material (the scraps left over from a main manufacturing process) in molding the nylon plug. All foam and filling materials are CA-117-approved for low toxicity and flammability content, and only CFC-free foam is used. Finally, a water-based, nontoxic glue is used for the foam adhesive.

An examination of two systems furniture options from Knoll underscore some of the environmental progress being made in this furniture category. Its Currents line, for example, contains between 20 and 30 percent recycled-content steel, between 70 and 100 percent recycled-content aluminum, and 100 percent recycled-content particleboard, and the steel and aluminum components are recyclable. Additionally, Knoll offers FSC-certified materials as an option, as well as 100 percent recycled-content fabric. Knoll reports that powder coatings on metal and wood components are virtually 100 percent VOC-free, as are the water-based adhesives used to adhere laminate to substrate, and that the powder coating on metal components has a resin usage rate of up to 95 percent.

Knoll's Dividends system offers similar statistics: 15 to 30 percent recycled-content steel, 20 percent recycled-content aluminum, and 100 percent recycled-content particleboard, with steel and aluminum components recyclable. Water and powder adhesives are virtually VOC-free, as are the powder coatings used on steel components. Dividends is available with 100 percent recycled-content fabric. All hardwoods and reconstituted veneers used in the furniture come from FSC-certified, well-managed forests in North America. Finally, a lease program is available that provides for the product to be returned to Knoll for recycling or refurbishing for a second life.

Teknion's Origami wood casegoods line is the company's most thorough application of design-for-the-environment principles to date. Its environmental parameters include modular product design to increase manufacturing, assembly, and shipping process opportunities and reduce energy requirements and waste; Greenguard certification to support indoor air quality and LEED; FSC-certified veneers, particle core, and MDF options as part of product offerings; integrated-edge design to reduce the need to introduce additional materials and process steps; water-based and powder-coat finishing to reduce VOC emissions; and the use of software that automatically configures part programs to optimize the raw material usage, thus minimizing waste and production scrap.

Origami represents Teknion's most thorough application of Design for the Environment practices to date, meeting stringent environmental and performance goals. © *Teknion*

Sustainable ZUMAfrd furniture items by Virco with Fortified Recycled Wood are 98 percent recyclable through Virco's take-back program and contain significant postindustrial/postconsumer recycled content materials. © *2006 Virco. All rights reserved*

In the classroom furniture arena, Virco offers the ZUMAfrd collection, featuring ergonomically contoured seats, backrests, and work surfaces made from Fortified Recycled Wood, the primary raw ingredients of which are wood products reclaimed from Virco's own manufacturing operations and other sources. This scrap is then reconstituted into a wood flour used for making compression-molded furniture components. (Fortified Recycled Wood helps Virco reduce its own waste stream and, since it can include discarded items obtained through the company's take-back program, ZUMAfrd products may contain high percentages of postconsumer recycled-content materials.) Other environmental features include 40 to 50 percent renewable materials (wood and agricultural fibers), 65 to 75 percent postconsumer/postindustrial recycled-content material, and 98 percent recyclability. The company also promotes that all steel, shipping cartons, foam upholstery material, and plastics used in Virco products are recyclable.

The EcoSystem collection from Baltix Furniture consists of desking components, partitions, storage elements, and a complete table program, all manufactured using recycled and biocomposite materials such as ecowheat, an alternative to MDF for panels and cores; ecosunflower, from sunflower husks, which gives panels a burled-wood look;

This reception workstation from Baltix Sustainable Furniture, Inc. uses wheatboard cores with linoleum laminate for work surfaces and filing, recycled-content aluminum framing, privacy panels of sustainably harvested wood and wheatboard, and daylighting panels of lightweight polycarbonate to create an attractive, functional, durable, fun commercial office unit. © *2005, Baltix Furniture, Inc.*

ecowood harvested from sustainable forests; recyclable aluminum specified at 75 percent postindustrial content; and linoleum components.

Since it was formed in 1998, Olive Designs has been incorporating organic or recycled materials into its lobby, lounge, and other contract seating and table applications. For example, it uses recycled textiles that are limited to a single material content, as well as hemp textiles, which consist of a low-impact renewable fiber grown without herbicides or pesticides and processed into a textile with minimal environmental impact. Colored tops are made from discarded glass bottles, so each furniture piece is an original and cannot be matched perfectly in texture or consistency of color. The use of postindustrial foam ensures that no off-gassing occurs during the recycling process, as can occur with the use of virgin foams. Other recycled components include a 99 percent recycled rubber-surface top made from postindustrial tires and a recycled durable nylon composite made from 100 percent postindustrial scrap. Formaldehyde-free glue is used in the wood lamination process for seating, while a water-based adhesive is used in the upholstery process to adhere foam to plywood. Finally, water-based, powder-coat, and nickel-plated finishes are used to minimize the environmental impacts associated with those processes.

From Environmental Language comes a number of individual furniture pieces that the company has designed to "prove that furniture can be both elegant and environmentally sound." Natural latex foam, organic cotton, and nontoxic glues are used in its upholstered items, while woods include locally reclaimed wood, FSC-certified wood, palm wood, and bamboo. Their Pava side table, for example, is made with sustainably harvested walnut, rift-cut oak, or cherry. Finishes are derived from tree sap and come in ebony wash, dark ebony, and clear.

> "I've been influenced by Biomimicry and have realized the benefit of looking at nature and being inspired by systems that have been in place long before we came along."
>
> —Jill Salisbury, el: Environmental Language Furniture

Olive Designs seating and tables are shown here in a natural balance of materials in the lobby of the Gilman Ordway Campus of the Woods Hole Research Center in Falmouth, Massachusetts. *Photography by Judy Watts Wilson, used by permission of the Woods Hole Research Center*

The Pava Side Table, designed by Jill Salisbury of el: Environmental Language, is available in sustainably harvested walnut, rift-cut oak, or cherry; finishes are nontoxic and derived from tree sap. *Photography by Jeff Schindler, 2005*

## Wall Coverings and Wall Finishes

As with the production of any textile or paper, many of the key environmental impacts of wall coverings occur during the production process. Of particular concern are gaseous emissions and effluent discharges from the printing and coating processes that may be harmful to the environment. There is also the issue of off-gassing during and after a wall covering or interior wall finish is installed, as a result of the adhesives and solvents used. (See Chapter 5 for detailed information regarding indoor air quality and

DialTones is a Pallas Textiles collection made of 50 to 70 percent recycled Japanese telephone book paper. Six colorways bloom from tints found in diverse natural elements. *Photography by Edward Addeo, 1998*

Murano is the newest addition to the Innvironments collection from Innovations in Wallcoverings, a line of wall coverings composed of either natural and renewable or recyclable materials, using water-based inks that neither contain heavy metals nor off-gas harmful pollutants. *Photography by Fumiaki Odaka*

these products.) During use, many products continue to release VOCs, thus lowering the quality of indoor air. Gaseous and toxic chemicals may be required for cleaning. Final considerations involve durability and disposal that impact resource consumption.

Today's ecofriendly wall covering options vary greatly in pattern, texture, and hue and are suitable for an equally varied range of application. One interesting wall covering introduction comes from Pallas Textiles: the DialTones collection, made of 50 to 70 percent recycled Japanese telephone book paper. Mixed with paper pulp, six colorways bloom from tints found in diverse natural elements. DialTones are made in Japan under strict pollution laws and incorporate a minimum amount of dye. It has an easy-care finish and a Class A fire rating. Pallas Textiles also offers Earth Paper, a densely textured wall covering with a soft stucco-like appearance. It consists of 65 percent pulp, 25 percent stone powder, 8 percent straw, and 2 percent polyvinyl alcohol and is available in five colorways.

More than five years ago, Innovations in Wallcoverings introduced Innvironments, a line of wall coverings composed of either natural and renewable or recyclable materials, using water-based inks that neither contain heavy metals nor off-gas harmful pollutants. All wood products are harvested in managed forests, and all polyester components have a recyclable quality. Additionally, Innovations has implemented a number of environmentally responsi-

ble manufacturing processes, including the reduction of water consumption through a closed cooling system; reduction in manufacturing waste; the use of recycled cardboard drums, rather than metal drums, for transporting water-based inks and adhesives; and the use of shipping pallets and packaging materials made from recycled materials. Murano, one of the newest additions to the Innvironments line, is a glass-beaded wall covering from Italy. Refined glass beads are applied to a flexible nonwoven backing, enabling it to be used on the inside and outside of right angles. Available in seven colors, Murano captures the interplay of light and color.

Wolf-Gordon Inc. now offers an Ecological Reclamation Program for its EarthSafe Strata collection of wall coverings. At the end of the product's useful life, the wall coverings can be returned (for credit) and applied to a variety of alternative, secondary uses. Strata is composed of natural, renewable, or recyclable materials and cellulose harvested from managed forests. Additional EarthSafe product offerings include Europa and Esquire, both of which offer a wide range of products, from cellulose and polyester blends to natural wovens, grass cloths, and strings.

Looking at wall coverings in a new way, Milliken & Co. offers 180 Walls, a self-adhesive textile wall covering that the company reports hangs without paste; experiences no wet movement, shrinkage, or corner peel; and can be removed years later without damage to walls. 180 Walls is especially suited for application in humid environments, as air and moisture are able to pass through its breathable, 100 percent polyester textile face fabric. Additionally, a dry pressure-sensitive adhesive is used on the product instead of a wet paste, which is typically a food source for mold and spores. Finally, an antimicrobial agent incorporated into the product reduces the risk of mold and mildew, which typically grow in warm, moist environments. 180 Walls passes industry voluntary specifications for flame spread, smoke development, washability, and stain resistance. All 180 Walls products carry a Class A fire rating. Additionally, industry testing reports that 180 Walls emission levels are 90 percent below accepted standards, and the 180 Walls product has a 25 U.S. perm rating for moisture transport.

Answering the need for more environmentally sensitive interior paints, many of the leading brands are now available in no-odor and low-to-zero-VOC choices. Benjamin Moore, for example, offers Eco Spec interior latex paints and primer in a number of different finishes. Sherwin-Williams offers Harmony water-based interior latex coatings, designed with antimicrobial properties and available as both primer and topcoat. ICI/Dulux offers LifeMaster 2000 paints that are virtually odor-free and contain no VOCs, suitable for use on interior walls and ceilings. Additional paints include Horizon from Rodda Paint Co. and Earth Coat from Vista Paint. Kelly-Moore features Enviro-Cote zero-VOC interior wall paint, as well as E-Coat Recycled Latex, which contains 50 percent minimum postconsumer waste.

Increasing numbers of manufacturers are also offering "natural" paint lines. For example, the Old Fashioned Milk Paint Co. produces a milk paint that combines milk protein, lime, clay, and earth pigments, such as ochre, umber, iron oxide, and lampblack. (The lime is alkaline but becomes inert when mixed with the slightly acid milk.) The company uses no lead, chemical preservatives, or fungicides, and the paint contains no hydrocarbons or any other petroleum derivatives. The company does report a slight milky odor when the paint is applied but says it is VOC-free and safe for occupants with multiple chemical sensitivity.

The Bioshield collection of paints, stains, thinners, and waxes is made from naturally derived and renewable raw materials, including citrus peel extracts, essential oils, seed oils, tree resins, inert mineral fillers, tree and bee waxes, lead-free driers, and natural pigments.

180 Walls by Milliken is a collection of beautiful, innovative textile wall coverings. These PVC-free and Greenguard-certified products revolutionize installation and removal while creating breathable, mold-inhibiting, paste-free, durable surfaces.

YOLO Colorhouse created its paint line with naturally occurring elements. Certified by Green Seal, it is available in forty colors in flat, satin, and semigloss finishes. *Photography courtesy of Yam Studio*

A new line of paints from YOLO Colorhouse was created with naturally occurring elements and has been certified by Green Seal. Its Earth's Color Collection is available in forty colors designed specifically for interiors, and comes in flat, satin, and semigloss finishes. The paint line features zero VOCs and a durable, washable finish. A zero-VOC primer also is offered.

American Clay Earth Plaster is an award-winning, ecologically conscious finish for interior walls and ceilings that takes green to the finer level. Multiple finishes and hues are available. *Photography by David Villy*

Another option for wall finishes is veneer plasters, such as those from American Clay, which feature a combination of natural clays, aggregates, and pigments found within the boundaries of the United States and available in thirty nature-inspired colors and textures. The company explains that unlike some traditional plasters whose manufacture requires high heat, the chemical properties of American Clay plasters are not altered in any way by the manufacturing process. Because its earth plasters are formulated from materials found in the United States and manufactured in the Southwest, less energy is used during the manufacturing process and virtually no building site waste occurs in application. Clay naturally controls the interior climate by absorbing and releasing moisture in response to environmental changes, so walls are warm to the touch in winter and cool in summer. Additionally, natural earth finishes do not provide a home for mold growth, nor do they emit potentially harmful gases from petroleum-based additives or formaldehyde.

Lime paints are another option for producing interesting wall textures. Lime paints are generally mineral-based and dry, with a matte surface that can be rubbed to a gloss finish.

PaperStone and PaperStone Certified composite surface materials from Kliptech Composites feature an 100 percent water-based resin system and utilize a proprietary paper made with postconsumer recycled paper. Shown here is slate black PaperStone Certified in the home of designer Ellen Nipport, White Salmon, Washington.

## Surfacing Materials

A number of interesting surfacing options are now available that provide a wide range of textures and patterns for interior furnishings. One option is the PaperStone composite surface material with a stonelike feel from Kliptech Composites. PaperStone features a 100 percent water-based resin system and utilizes a proprietary paper made with a guaranteed minimum of 50 percent postconsumer recycled paper. PaperStone Certified features 100 percent postconsumer recycled paper and is FSC-certified by SmartWood. Kliptech reports that a 1-inch by 5-foot by 12-

foot sheet of PaperStone Certified (versus a regular pheno-lic composite manufactured from virgin fiber and a regular, commercially available, solvent-based resin) saves 1,233 gallons of water, 2.03 million BTUs of energy, 131 pounds of solid waste, 254 pounds of greenhouse gases, 55 pounds of petroleum-based phenol, and 22 pounds of natural-gas-based methanol. Although the manufacturer says that it is water-safe, certain chemicals such as bleach will cause damage.

Coverings Etc. offers a wide variety of floor and wall panels that are reproduced by means of a high-tech indus-trial process, making it possible to create natural compos-ites with superior features while maintaining the allure of natural beauty and the practicality of environmental con-servation. Its Eco-Cem line, for example, features slabs and tiles made of compound silicon-calcium cement (80 per-cent) that are strengthened with cellulose fibers (20 per-cent wood pulp). Eco-Tek, Eco-Terr Slabs, and Eco-Terr Tiles are slab and tile agglomerates made of natural stone aggregate materials with a cement binder. Coverings also offers Eco-Gres, part of its Ecoverings family of hard surfac-ing materials, which is a twenty-four-color mosaic of recy-cled and porcelain tiles.

3form's Varia Collection is a dynamic resin system engi-neered by encapsulating textured, colored, and natural interlayers (such as thatch and fossil leaves) within high-performance polymer skins to create vibrant translucent panels. Shatterproof, formable, and flame- and smoke-rated, Varia is lightweight and can be cut and drilled with common hand tools. Made of 100 percent 3form ecoresin, Varia features 40 percent recycled content and is recycla-ble. It does not off-gas and contains neither plasticizers nor stabilizers. The company's Full Circle collection of Varia products works with artisan communities around the world to encourage the development of local indigenous economies. For example, the Ithemba collection (which means "hope" in the Xhosa language) features a master-piece of woven wire mesh that has been meticulously cre-ated by African women artisans who are affected by HIV or AIDS. Through a partnership with a local nonprofit group, 3form helps provide a market for their talents.

Bedrock Industries' Blazestone tiles are crafted entirely from postindustrial and postconsumer stained glass, with no added oxides or colorants. Each tile is handmade from

unique combinations of glass that give the tiles their dis-tinctive appearance and subtle color variation. A variety of sizes and shapes include 4-inch diamonds, 2-inch mini-triangles, and 8-inch rosettes, plus circles, leaf shapes, and cat's-eyes.

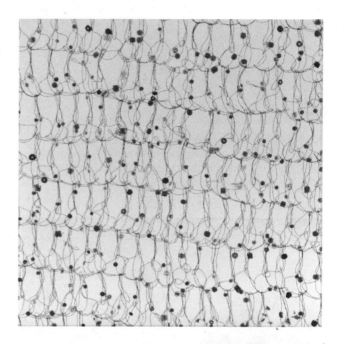

Ithemba, part of the 2005 Full Circle Varia collection from 3Form, features a masterpiece of woven wire mesh that has been meticulously created by African women artisans who are affected by HIV or AIDS. © 3form, Inc.

Blazestone tiles from Bedrock Industries are made from postindustrial and postcon-sumer stained glass, with no added oxides or colorants. Each tile is hand-made and is available in a variety of sizes and shapes.

Armstrong ceilings can contain up to 78 percent recycled content. The company's successful take-back program has resulted in more than 10,000 tons of used tiles being diverted from landfills. © *Armstrong World Industries*

USG's Sandrift acoustical ceiling tiles contain recycled paper, binders derived from corn and wheat starch, and low VOCs.

# Ceilings

Armstrong Ceilings offers an expanding portfolio of sustainable design ceiling choices. Its ceilings can contain up to 78 percent recycled content (which means, based on typical 2002 production statistics and information, Armstrong used in excess of 4 million pounds of post-industrial recycled content—previously installed acoustical ceiling tile and board—in the production of its ceiling materials during the twelve-month reporting period). Recycled content varies by product: mineral fiber ceilings range from 22 to 78 percent, fiberglass ceilings contain 25 percent postindustrial recycled glass, wood panels contain 50 percent recycled content, and metal ceilings have an average of 25 percent recycled content. Many of its ceiling products also can be ordered with higher levels of recycled content. Additionally, the company operates the Armstrong Ceiling Recycling Program, which enables building owners to ship old ceilings from renovation projects to an Armstrong ceiling plant as an alternative to landfill disposal. Under the program, Armstrong pays freight costs for shipping the old ceilings (30,000-square-foot minimum), which it uses as raw materials in the manufacture of new ceilings. Since it introduced the program in 1999, Armstrong has recycled over 30 million square feet of discarded ceiling tiles, or enough tiles to cover 525 football fields. This total represents nearly 21 million pounds of construction waste that would have normally been dumped in landfills.

The use of recycled and renewable raw materials in USG acoustical ceiling tile contributes to reduced consumption of energy and resources without diminishing long-term performance. USG ceiling tiles contain mineral wool derived from slag, a by-product of steelmaking, which reduces the need to mine and process raw materials and minimizes landfill waste. Ceiling tiles also contain recycled paper. Binders are derived from corn and wheat starch, both renewable agricultural resources. In addition to recycled content, USG acoustical ceiling tiles contribute to high-quality indoor environments with their low VOCs. USG ceiling tiles are classified as either low-formaldehyde or formaldehyde-free, based on recognized standards of evaluation and testing. Many of USG's acoustical ceiling panels have also been designed to efficiently reflect light within a space, which enhances indirect lighting, reduces energy consumption, and creates a warm, luminous aesthetic.

EcoVeil solar shade cloth from MechoShade incorporates a material called EarthTex that allows the cloth to be recycled back into new shade cloth in a continuous cradle-to-cradle cycle. EcoVeil shades are shown here in the West Midtown Intermodal Ferry Terminal. *Photography by Jim Roof, 2005*

DesignerLine Window Shades, Weave No. M03C, is made of natural wood-pulp fibers that provide textured elegance and filtered sun control, as shown here in the interior of the LaCroix Restaurant at the Rittenhouse in Philadelphia. Design by Marguerite Rogers, Ltd. *Photography by Matt Wargo. © 2005 Conrad Imports*

## Window Coverings

Historically valued primarily for their aesthetic appeal, window coverings are now recognized for their ability to offer dramatic opportunities for manipulating the quality and quantity of light that enters a space. Window coverings also provide benefits in the area of energy savings, privacy, and the ability of a room's occupants to visually connect to the natural world.

MechoShade Systems' EcoVeil solar shade cloth incorporates a material constructed with a thermoplastic olefin-based yarn called EarthTex (developed by Twitchell) that allows the cloth to be recycled back into new shade cloth in a continuous cradle-to-cradle cycle. (The coating on the EarthTex yarn is essentially the same polymer as the core yarn, which allows it to be melted down, reprocessed, and made into new, first-quality product.) A take-back program allows customers to return their EcoVeil shade bands to MechoShade after they are done using them. The material is then reconstituted into raw materials and made into new EcoVeil shade cloth or other EarthTex-based products. MechoShade also recaptures scraps and cut-offs for imme-

diate recycling, a process the company estimates saves more than 1 million pounds of scrap from going to a landfill or incinerator every year.

Interestingly, while EcoVeil and its components were developed and evaluated for health and safety according to MBDC's Cradle to Cradle protocol, the finished product delivered some unexpected benefits as well. It is less prone to edge fraying, and its lighter weight—about a third less than traditional PVC/polyester screen cloth—allows some larger shades to be lifted manually rather than requiring a motor. EcoVeil is washable, UV-resistant, flame-retardant, and antimicrobial.

A trip to Asia in the 1960s inspired Edie Conrad to bring back to the United States a collection of hand-woven window coverings featuring exotic natural fibers. Today, Conrad Imports offers draperies, a versatile sliding panel shade system, and an outdoor fabric collection, in addition to over eighty custom-woven shades of natural grasses, reeds, and fibers in a Roman-fold design. Its Original Sunshades collection features a line of natural grasses, reed, and fibers, while its DesignerLine Window Shades are crafted of natural wood-pulp fibers. Conrad's Double Density Weaves—which

Hunter Douglas' Duette shades offer increased energy performance because of their unique accordion-fold design that creates a honeycomb-like pocket of air. When lowered, the pocket traps air to help retain heat in winter and reflect heat in summer.

feature two fiber strands, rather than the standard single strand—provide additional sun control and privacy as well as a spectacular visual effect. Conrad also offers Sheerweave Roller Shades featuring a translucent mesh roller shade behind a Conrad Roman-fold sunshade to deliver additional sun control and a reduction in heat gain and glare while preserving exterior views.

Duette honeycomb shades from Hunter Douglas offer significantly better energy performance than standard shades because of their unique accordion-fold design. When lowered, the fabric opens up, providing pockets of trapped air that assist in retaining heat in winter and reflecting it in summer. Duette shades provide different degrees of privacy and light control, from semiopaque for filtered light to opaque fabrics for complete privacy. Opaque Duette shades include a reflective layer to boost energy performance. Duette's accordion-fold design also provides significant acoustic properties, while fabrics provide stringent flame retardance. Shadings are duotone, with a neutral tone facing the exterior and a color facing the interior. Specialty angles and shapes are available for nonstandard windows.

# ▮ From Trash Comes Treasure

Casting a creative light on a serious problem—the enormous amount of waste that is cluttering our landscape—was the impetus behind the creation of Trash to Treasure, an exhibition/competition element of the EnvironDesign conferences. The brainchild of Tama Duffy, ASID, formerly at OPX, and her colleagues at the design firm in Washington, D.C., Trash to Treasure was first introduced at EnvironDesign7, and has since become a popular addition to the event. Through this event the "waste = food" concept epitomizes how ordinary trash becomes the raw materials for offbeat creations, thereby avoiding the landfill. And while the amount of trash rescued from landfills to date may be small, the resulting treasures that have been showcased at each of the three Trash to Treasure events have amply demonstrated how cleverness and determination can help turn ordinary trash into cherished objets d'art. The following are a handful of the favorites, as voted on by the conference attendees.

Doug Sonsalla and Jennifer Books of the Architectural Alliance took the ubiquitous cardboard tubes that architectural papers come wrapped around and constructed the handsome and sturdy S-Q chair and ottoman. People's Choice Award Winner, EnvironDesign8. *Photography by Jim Robinette © Interiors & Sources*

What to do with worn-out underwear? Holly Nelson and Jennifer Paist, two University of Minnesota students, strung together old (but washed) bras and pantyhose to make "The Brammock." Funky Trash Award Winner, EnvironDesign8. *Photography by Jim Robinette © Interiors & Sources*

Signa Weise, Amy Crowder, and Allison Wiese (not pictured), three students from the University of Minnesota, created couture with their striking and wearable Bottle Cap Jacket, fashioned from discarded bottle caps, window screen, pop tabs, paper clips, and brass fasteners. Best of Show Award Winner, EnvironDesign8. *Photography by Jim Robinette © Interiors & Sources*

How many of us have thrown away boxes of old business cards? Jennifer Davis, a designer at Einhorn Yaffee Prescott, found a better use for hers: she constructed a lamp that was functional, beautiful, and a real crowd-pleaser. People's Choice Award Winner, EnvironDesign7. *Photography by Jim Robinette © Interiors & Sources*

Sarah Barnard and Jessica Tarazona salvaged a bit of automotive history in this creation entitled "The Driver's Seat." The chair was made of rescued automobile parts and scrap metal. The seat sports a 1930s Ford truck steering wheel, the feet are made from 1970 Volkswagen Beetle side mirrors, and the backrest is from a late-model Toyota. Best in Show Award Winner, EnvironDesign9. *Photography by Jim Robinette © Interiors & Sources*

# What's LEED Got to Do with It?

The Materials and Resources section of LEED for Commercial Interiors offers 7 credits and up to 14 points. There is also 1 prerequisite.

*MRp1: Storage and Collection of Recyclables.* Facilitate waste reduction by providing a convenient recyclable collection and storage area. (Required)

*MRc1: Reduce the Environmental Impacts of Tenancy.* The credit has three parts.

*1.1 Tenant space, long-term commitment.* Occupant commits to remain in the same location for not less than ten years. (1 point)

*1.2, 1.3: Building reuse, maintain 40/60 percent (by area) of interior nonstructural components.* Retain existing nonshell, nonstructural interior elements such as walls, floors, and ceilings. Earn 1 point for 40 percent and 1 additional point for 60 percent.

*MRc2: Construction Waste Management.* Redirect construction debris from the waste stream. The credit has two parts.

*2.1, 2.2. Divert 50/75 percent from landfill.* Recycle and/or salvage (by weight or volume) of construction, demolition, and packaging debris from the landfill by developing and implementing a construction waste management plan that includes recycling and salvaging materials. Earn 1 point for 50 percent and 1 additional point for 75 percent.

*MRc3: Resource Reuse.* Reuse materials and products to reduce demand for virgin materials. The credit has three parts.

*3.1, 3.2: 5/10 percent.* Incorporate salvaged, refurbished, or reused materials such as doors, frames, cabinetry, and bricks in the project design. Earn 1 point for 5 percent of building materials and 1 additional point for 10 percent (by value).

*3.3: 30 percent furniture and furnishings.* Use salvaged, refurbished, or reused furnishings such as systems furniture, seating, storage pieces, and decorative lighting for 30 percent of the F&F budget. (1 point)

*MRc4: Recycled Content.* Incorporate building products with recycled content to reduce the demand for virgin materials. The credit has two parts.

*4.1, 4.2: 10/20 percent (postconsumer + one-half preconsumer.* Use products with postconsumer plus one-half preconsumer recycled content for at least 10/20 percent (by value) of project materials including furniture. Earn 1 point for 10 percent of building materials and 1 additional point for 20 percent.

*MRc5: Regional Materials.* Specify locally sourced products. The credit has two parts.

*5.1: 20 percent (by value) manufactured regionally.* Specify products that are manufactured (assembled) within 500 miles of the project site. (1 point)

*5.2: 10 percent (by value) extracted and manufactured regionally.* Specify products that are extracted, harvested, or recovered and manufactured within 500 miles of the project site. (1 point)

*MRc6: Rapidly Renewable Materials.* Specify 5 percent (by value) of the project products made from materials that are harvested within a ten-year or shorter cycle, such as bamboo, linoleum, wool, strawboard, and sunflower seeds. (1 point)

*MRc7: Certified Wood.* Specify a minimum of 50 percent (by value) of the new wood products that are certified by the Forest Stewardship Council. (1 point)

Adapted from the LEED Green Building Rating System for Commercial Interiors, version 2.0. Visit www.usbc.org to access the complete rating system.

# 5
# THE INDOOR
# ENVIRONMENT

any discussions on the subject of indoor environmental quality (IEQ) begin with the statistic that people, especially in the United States, spend 80 to 95 pecent of their time indoors. According to a study funded by the California Air Resources Board, Californians spend, on average, 87 percent of their time indoors, 7 percent in enclosed transit, and 6 percent outdoors.[1]

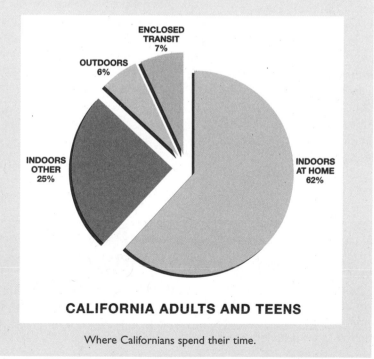

ENCLOSED
TRANSIT
7%

OUTDOORS
6%

INDOORS
OTHER
25%

INDOORS
AT HOME
62%

**CALIFORNIA ADULTS AND TEENS**

Where Californians spend their time.

The Mithun reception area on the north side is daylight by clerestory windows. *Photography by Robert Pisano*

Community spaces at Mithun are placed near the windows and the best views. *Photography by Robert Pisano*

Given these figures, the importance of good IEQ in our buildings is clear, but for many, exactly what that means is vague. Certainly indoor air quality (IAQ) plays a major role. The healthier the air human beings inhale, the better they are going to thrive. As important as it is, however, IAQ is just a part of IEQ. Other considerations include thermal comfort, acoustical comfort, and daylighting and views. This chapter will examine them all, beginning with a quick look at the offices of Mithun Architects + Designers + Planners, an exemplary example of indoor environmental quality as a design priority.

The 160-person firm is housed on the second floor of the Pier 56 building in Seattle with views to the city on the east and across Puget Sound to the Olympic Mountains on the west. Clerestory windows and an increased glazing area provide an abundance of daylight. Shading devices are used on all but the north windows. The office, designed with minimal permanent partitions, located public spaces and circulation areas along the perimeter so all could enjoy the best views. Workstation panel heights, kept to 52 inches, contribute to the open and collaborative work environment. An operations strategy for opening different windows and clerestories is part of a passive cooling system that takes advantage of prevailing winds and provides fresh air and breezes from the water. This natural ventilation contributes to excellent indoor air quality, as do formaldehyde-free plywood and low-VOC paints, sealers, and glues. Thermal comfort is variable—temperatures fluctuate six to eight degrees within the space depending on the location and the time of day—but controlled.

# ■ The Air That We Breathe

Unhealthy air, aka indoor air pollution, is often more dangerous to human health than outdoor air pollution. Because bad air is trapped within the building, there is more concentrated pollutant exposure than generally found outside. Also, indoor air pollution is invisible, unlike the outdoor smog that periodically hangs over our big cities. Dr. Marilyn Black, founder of the Greenguard Environmental Institute and CEO of Air Quality Sciences, Inc., in Atlanta, is a leading expert on characterizing indoor air pollution and its sources. Her essay examines the sources and impacts of poor IAQ and offers suggestions for minimizing its effects.

### *Interior Design: First Step Toward Providing Good IAQ*

By Marilyn Black, PhD

*Sustainable green building is fast gaining momentum in commercial, educational, and residential building sectors. Often the primary focus is on energy efficiency, waste reduction, the use of recycled materials, and outdoor environmental concerns, with the significant benefits associated with good indoor air quality undervalued or ignored. As a result, many buildings today are designed and built without a clear understanding of how the indoor environment affects building occu-*

pants, and consequently indoor environments are created that inhibit productivity, learning, comfort, and health rather than enhancing them. Consider these facts:

- More than ten years have passed since the U.S. Environmental Protection Agency (EPA) ranked indoor air pollution as one of the top five environmental threats to public health and one of the largest remaining health risks in the United States. Yet indoor pollutant levels inside can be two to five times higher and sometimes as much as a hundred times higher than outside air.[2]

- Indoor levels of VOCs can be up to a hundred times higher than outdoors. As many as a thousand different VOCs may be in the indoor environment, where people can easily inhale them.

- The National Academy of Sciences estimated that 15 percent of Americans experience symptoms from indoor air pollution, but an official with the U.S. EPA thinks that about 40 percent of the population experiences one or more symptoms weekly as a result of exposure to poor IAQ in buildings.[3]

- Children are at greater risk for adverse health effect from poor IAQ, as they breathe in more air with respect to their body mass than adults and thus have higher exposure to indoor environmental pollutants.

- More than 20 million Americans have asthma, including 9 million children. From 1980 to 1994, the proportion of Americans with asthma increased by 75 percent. In children under the age of five, the proportion grew by 160 percent.[4] Public health experts advise minimizing exposure to indoor pollutants as a key step in controlling asthma and reducing the severity of attacks and symptoms.

- The annual direct health care costs of asthma are approximately $9.4 billion; indirect costs (such as lost productivity) add another $4.6 billion, for a total of $14 billion.[5]

- In a wider context, the annual economic costs of common respiratory illnesses (reported in 1996 U.S. dollars) are 180 million lost workdays, 120 million additional days of restricted activity, approximately $36 billion ($140 per person) in health care costs, and approximately $70 billion ($270 per person) total cost.[6]

What follows is an overview of IAQ, including potential health risks from poor IAQ, sources of indoor environmental pollutants, and strategies for controlling these sources.

## Impact of Poor IAQ on Building Occupants

Indoor air is very crowded, complicated, and dynamic, full of chemicals, such as pesticides, formaldehyde and other aldehydes, and VOCs; particles; viruses and bacteria; allergens and endotoxins; microscopic organisms, such as dust mites; water vapor molecules (moisture); dust; and mold hyphae and spores, to name a few examples. Table 5-1 lists the major types of indoor air pollutants, their sources, and possible health impacts.

Exposure to any of these indoor pollutants does not automatically mean adverse health effects will occur. There are many factors that determine if building occupants may become ill, including:

- The concentration and amount of the pollutant
- Personal characteristics, such as age, gender, weight, and general health status
- Method of exposure—inhaled or direct contact to the skin
- Length of time of exposure

In general, the longer the exposure, the more risk. Health problems may be acute, occurring immediately or within a few days of exposure, or they can be chronic, perhaps not showing up for many years.

## Strategies for Minimizing Indoor Pollutants

In general, three key strategies minimize indoor environmental pollutants, as follows:

- Ventilation. Ensure the HVAC system is designed, operated, and maintained in such a way that it

## Table 5-1: Major Categories of Indoor Pollutants, Sources, Health Impacts

| Indoor Pollutants | Sources | Possible Health Impacts |
|---|---|---|
| Formaldehyde, aldehydes | Building materials | Cancer |
| VOCs | Building materials, textiles, furnishings, finishes, consumer products, pesticides, fragrances, personal care products, cleaning products and processes, dust | Sensory, respiratory, gastrointestinal irritation; neurotoxicity; hormone disruption; autism; cancer; reproductive and developmental toxicity |
| Viruses, bacteria | HVAC systems, surfaces, people | Respiratory and gastrointestinal illnesses |
| Allergens, endotoxins | Dust mites, cockroaches, pets, mice, indoor mold growth | Allergy, asthma attacks |
| Dust | Ubiquitous | Allergy, asthma attacks |
| Indoor mold growth | Walls, ceilings, HVAC systems, basements, crawlspaces | Allergy, asthma attacks, sensory and respiratory irritation, respiratory infection |

brings in enough outdoor air to dilute the concentration of indoor pollutants. It should also be kept clean so that biological pollutants, such as mold, bacteria, and viruses, cannot grow in ducts and dust does not accumulate. Flushing out the building prior to occupancy is an excellent strategy for ridding buildings of high VOC levels from new building materials, furnishings, and finishes. Operate the HVAC system at slightly positive pressure relative to the outdoors to inhibit moisture intrusion and condensation, key factors for indoor mold growth.

■ **Filtration.** Ensure the HVAC system uses high-efficiency particle (HEPA) filters to capture smaller particles that could be irritating to building occupants. Some HVAC systems also employ ultraviolet light equipment to kill viruses and bacteria. Also, ensure the filters are cleaned and changed regularly.

■ **Source control.** Specify products and materials that emit low levels of VOCs. Be careful, as many products, even those certified as green or environmentally friendly, are rated by their VOC content (weight), not by their VOC emissions. The only way to be sure a product emits low VOCs is to actually measure VOC emissions. For a listing of products

certified to be low-emitting, visit the Greenguard Environmental Institute Web site.[7]

### Preventing and Controlling Indoor Mold Growth

In recent years, indoor mold growth has grabbed news headlines and been at the root of thousands of legal and insurance claims. Mold is ubiquitous both indoors and outdoors. Mold needs three things to grow inside: warmth, an organic food source, and moisture.

Buildings are typically maintained at a temperature that is hospitable to indoor mold growth. Also, interiors are full of numerous sources of food, including materials containing cellulose, such as some wall coverings, gypsum wallboard, paint, wood paneling, plywood, oriented strand board, precast panels and ceiling tiles, fabrics, carpets, upholstered furniture, fiberglass-lined air ducts, and other porous materials where mold breaks down the material itself or uses organic debris that has collected.

Buildings with indoor mold growth also have a sufficient source of moisture. Four primary factors influence the amount of moisture available for indoor mold growth:

1. Building tightness, which does not allow moisture to escape to the outside or to be removed from the inside air through dehumidification

2. *Liquid water infiltration from the outside as a result of a leaky building envelope or structural failure*

3. *Moisture condensation on or near mold-susceptible building materials or components, which originates from water vapor inside or outside the structure*

4. *Moisture generation within the interior by building occupants and their activities*

*Preventing indoor mold growth requires finding the source(s) of moisture and eliminating it. Also important is to select materials and finishes that allow air and moisture to move freely through the wall system. Using highly permeable materials on the cold side and low-permeability materials on the warm side of the wall system maximizes vapor pressure diffusion from the wall, meaning that water vapor inside the wall system will migrate from the wall cavity into the interior space.[8] The Greenguard Environmental Institute's Mold Protection Program offers building certification for the design, construction, and ongoing maintenance of newly constructed buildings implementing best practices for preventing mold growth.*

*Indoor air quality can have a profound impact on the safety, well-being, and productivity of all building occupants. Certain occupants, such as children, elderly, and those on drug therapies, have heightened sensitivities that are exacerbated by the plethora of indoor pollutants. Interior design professionals have the unique opportunity in their daily work to make decisions for improving indoor air quality. Together with many available resources on building systems and material selection from the American Lung Association, the U.S. EPA, Greenguard, and key professional organizations, project design teams have a wealth of information available for designing and maintaining healthy indoor environments.*

---

Dr. Marilyn Black, founder of the Greenguard Environmental Institute and CEO of Air Quality Sciences, Inc. is a leading expert on characterizing indoor air pollution and its sources, with more than twenty years of experience.

The design team's responsibility for providing healthful indoor air is clear and should begin at the very beginning of the project with the selection of a good building. One with a poorly designed or maintained mechanical system will cause air quality problems that are difficult to overcome. For example, a building designed with its air intakes located on the loading dock (it happens!) exposes the occupants to toxic vehicle emissions. Buildings that allow smoking should be avoided unless it is permitted only in designated areas that have been carefully designed and constructed.

Investigate whether a building has had any air quality problems, such as sick building syndrome (SBS), prior to signing a lease. As discussed in Chapters 2 and 7, SBS is a term that is used to describe situations where airborne contaminants cause illness or acute discomfort that can be debilitating and pose a liability risk for both the tenant organization and the landlord. Strategies for identifying the causes of SBS and implementing solutions are available through the EPA's Indoor Air Quality Web site.[9]

Prevention of poor air quality and SBS in the first place is, of course, preferred and involves the three-pronged approach advocated by Marilyn Black—ventilation, filtration, and source control strategies. This section of the chapter presents design considerations and some solutions.

## Ventilation

Ventilation is the supply of outdoor air to a space. It may enter naturally through open doors and windows or it may infiltrate through cracks and crevices in the building envelope. Mechanical ventilation uses fans to draw air from outside and force it through ducts to the places where occupants are located. Ventilation is measured by the flow rate of outside air brought into a building and can be expressed by the volume of space being ventilated (air changes per hour), by the area of the floor being ventilated (cubic feet per minute per square foot, cfm/sf) or by the number of people being served (cfm per person). Standards and codes, such as ASHRAE 62.1-2004, establish minimum ventilation rates that vary with the type of building or space usage. These standards serve not only to optimize indoor air quality but also to balance health and productivity benefits of increased ventilation with energy use.[10] Exceeding the ASHRAE standard will provide superior ventilation—a benefit to the occupants—but it also may lead to larger HVAC systems and increased energy costs.

Although ASHRAE currently recommends 20 cfm per person for office space, it may not be enough. Generally, 50 cfm per person is considered an excellent ventilation level, while less than 15 cfm per person is considered poor, yet not unprecedented. According to a 2001 Aerias report, the requirements for outdoor air were reduced to 5 cfm per occupant during the 1973 oil embargo in order to save energy.[11] At the same time buildings were "tightened up" to prevent leaks and new buildings were built with windows that did not open. This tightening of the building along with reduced ventilation rates began causing discomfort and health problems in building occupants.

Ventilation rates are also influenced by $CO_2$ concentrations in buildings. The higher the levels of $CO_2$ the more outdoor air will be needed to maintain acceptable air quality levels. Installing permanent $CO_2$ monitoring and alarm systems, especially in densely occupied spaces, is highly recommended not only for air quality but also to prevent excessive energy use and the overventilation of spaces. Correct placement of the monitors is important to ensure that representative readings are obtained; multiple devices, though more expensive, will do a better job than a central sensor.

Paul O'Brien, president of GHT Ltd., an engineering firm in Arlington, Virginia, likes to utilize a ventilation control system that separates the outside air from the standard cooling system using a simple VAV box controlled with a $CO_2$ sensor rather than a thermostat. "That allows us to only bring in the outside air that's needed but still maintain a really high air quality. Outside air is very expensive to heat and cool, but on the other hand, you've got to have plenty of it to have a good space. This is a strategy we use that makes financial sense as well as provides great energy savings and great interior air."

> *"No one ever comes in and says, 'I've got a bunch of money so let's design a really nice system.' We don't separate green clients from nongreen clients, but if the budgets allow us to go a little further on things, that's good."*
>
> —Paul O'Brien, president, GHT, Ltd.

O'Brien says he doesn't install $CO_2$ sensors in regularly occupied spaces unless the project is going for LEED points. "In the open office areas it's hard to justify financially because most of the time the system will be running at normal and won't accrue the energy savings. In conference centers, though, the sensors pay back in the first year or two. However, if you're installing them throughout and going for the LEED point, it's a relatively cheap LEED point."

The ventilation effectiveness of naturally ventilated buildings is somewhat dependent on occupant behavior—such as how often and under what conditions windows are opened and closed—but not always. The headquarters of the Chesapeake Bay Foundation in Annapolis, Maryland (and the first LEED Platinum project), uses a combination mechanical and natural HVAC system with a unique system of controls. The building is oriented on its site to capture the bay's breezes, and roof sensors determine when outdoor conditions are optimal, shutting down the mechanical systems and flashing signs alerting the occupants to open the windows. When conditions deteriorate, the signs flash again, signaling that the mechanical system is operating and windows should be closed. This type of system control, though not appropriate for many interiors projects, is a good example of the progressive design solutions that are coming out of the green building movement.

## Filtration

In addition to the appropriate ventilation rates, good indoor air quality depends on the maintenance of the HVAC system to keep it clean and dry. Standing water or organic contamination may lead to microbial growth, for example, but the most important safeguard is the installation and upkeep of filtration devices. Properly fitted and changed regularly, filters play an important role in good indoor air quality, but they are not without controversy. A feature article in *Environmental Building News* explores filtration and presents both the pros and cons.

> "While the concept of air filtration is pretty simple—removing stuff that we don't want from the air we breathe in buildings—the approaches used are diverse, complex, and confusing. . . . Air filtration plays a very important role in many buildings.

"In virtually all buildings with air-handling equipment, some level of filtration is needed to keep ducts, blowers, and other equipment clean. In buildings with specific needs for cleanliness—surgical rooms in hospitals, clean rooms in electronics manufacturing, and homes for people with chemical sensitivity, for example—high levels of air filtration are clearly needed.

"Beyond these specific needs, the requirements for air filtration are not so clear-cut. Clearly there are benefits, but they come at a significant cost—both financial and environmental—through increased energy consumption . . . However, while the filtration efficiency increases, so does the resistance to airflow. This can reduce the delivery of conditioned air, increase energy consumption, and even damage mechanical equipment by overworking blower motors." [12]

Plastic wrap protects the HVAC system from contaminants during construction. *Photography by T.B. Penick & Sons, Inc.*

| Building enclosed | Temperature and humidity control | IAQ testing | Substantial completion | 100% completion |
|---|---|---|---|---|
| **VENTILATE WITH 100% OUTSIDE AIR** | | | | Normal mode |
| Install off-gassing materials | Install fuzzy materials | Indoor air sampling and analysis | Install furnishings | Occupy building |
| Paints | Fabric-covered paints | | | |
| Sealants | Carpet | | | |
| Composites | Ceiling tile | | | |
| Adhesives | | | | |
| Gypsum wallboard | | | | |

**PROJECT TIMELINE AND MILESTONES**

Install off-gassing materials before highly absorptive "sink" materials such as fabrics and carpet. *Source: The Greening Curve: Lessons Learned in the Design of the New EPA Campus in North Carolina, 2001*

LEED has added to the conflict between filtration and energy use by requiring the installation of MERV air filtration to achieve certain points. MERV (minimum efficiency reporting value) is a relatively new standardized method for measuring filter efficiency that uses a scale of 1 to 20 to rate a filter's ability to remove particles. The higher the MERV, the more efficient the filter and the more resistance there will be to airflow. For the cleanest air, a user should select the highest MERV filter that its unit is capable of forcing air through based on the limit of the unit's fan power. A MERV 14, for example, is 95 percent efficient and is often used in hospital HVAC systems. MERV 13 is 85 percent efficient and considered above average for commercial applications.[13] Typically, however, filters in the MERV 4 to 5 ranges are standard in office buildings. The designer hoping to achieve the best IAQ can push for higher MERV values by working with the MEP to determine what level the system can handle and at what cost.

It is imperative to use filtration during construction, especially if the HVAC system is in use. Every precaution should be taken to protect the equipment, ducts, grilles, plenum, access floor, and other openings from moisture, dust, and odors. The most straightforward path to clean indoor air is to prevent contamination in the first place.

Following construction (including the installation of all furnishings and finishes) but before occupancy, both mechanically and naturally ventilated buildings should be flushed out with outside air for approximately two weeks in order to eliminate airborne contaminants. A generic schedule sequence of finishes, according to the EPA, is shown above.

The flush-out procedure and an alternative IAQ test method are fully detailed in the LEED-CI Reference Guide. Many believe, however, that flush-outs are impractical even if they are part of the construction schedule. Delays may eliminate the time allotted, and owners may object to paying rent for unoccupied spaces. Flush-outs may also be ill-advised, especially in humid climates or in those with extreme temperatures. A better strategy is to be extremely diligent about the materials introduced into the project, negating the need for a flush-out and ensuring good IAQ test results. This approach, referred to as source control, is addressed in the following section.

## Pollutant Source Control

Indoor air pollutants come from many sources: tobacco smoke, mold, mildew, building materials, cleaning products, and electronic equipment. In fact, most everything is an emitter, and the challenge is to minimize the level of contaminants within buildings by controlling the source. It isn't an easy task. First, there are no federally regulated standards, only voluntary ones that sometimes conflict with each other. For example, BIFMA International, the commercial furniture industry's trade association, is writing its own emissions standard with different testing protocols than Greenguard, leaving it up to the specifier to sort out and evaluate the differences. See Chapter 6 for summaries of both standards. Next, it is often not easy to get accurate information on some products, either because it doesn't exist or because of "greenwashing" practices on the part of manufacturers. However, removing bad air from buildings can be difficult and expensive; source control—preventing the contaminants introduction into the interior space—is a better strategy.

A case study of two buildings illustrates the impact of source control. Both properties were similar in size, layout, and mechanical design. [14] Building 1, a 160,000-square-foot office building located in Tumwater, Washington, was designed and constructed with a specific source control program in place. Building 2, 140,000 square feet in Atlanta, made no attempts to improve or control indoor air quality. The Building 1 program specified the following:

■ Use of low-emitting interior materials and furnishings

■ Sequenced installation of finishes to ensure that absorptive materials such as carpet and textiles were protected from high-emitting materials
■ The use of temporary ducts during construction
■ A two-week flush-out with 100 percent conditioned outdoor air prior to furniture installation

The results showed that total VOC, formaldehyde, and particle levels were significantly elevated in Building 2 relative to Building 1. The total VOCs ranged from 1,500 to 250 ug/m$^3$ (micrograms per cubic meter of air) for the building with source controls versus 28,000 to 3,200 ug/m$^3$ for the one without. Comparisons of formaldehyde and particle levels were similar.

## VOCs: What Are They and Why Do They Matter?

The EPA has defined VOC to include in effect "any volatile compound of carbon" that is not specifically exempted—a definition not terribly useful to the designer whose main concern is to exclude them from projects. The list of what is considered a VOC (decane, butoxyethanol, isopentane, limonene, styrene, xylene, perchloroethylene, methylene chloride, toluene, vinyl chloride, etc.) and what is not (carbon monoxide, methane, ethane, carbon dioxide, etc.) sounds more like a chemistry book than a design guide. However, the definition isn't so confusing when broken down: *volatile* refers to the ability to evaporate at room temperature, and *organic compound* refers to the carbon connection. As contributors to ground-level ozone, VOCs are harmful to the atmosphere. Indoors, where they are often highly concentrated, they are irritants and can result in health problems. Runny noses, itchy eyes, raspy throats, and headaches are common reactions.

Collectively, all the VOCs measured in an air sample are referred to as TVOCs (total volatile organic compounds) and can be an indicator of the quality of the indoor air. Concentrations are likely to be higher in newly constructed spaces before materials have had an opportunity to off-gas and dissipate. Obviously TVOC levels will vary as products are brought in or removed. In the case study of the two buildings mentioned earlier, an increase in TVOCs after the flush-out period was attributed to the installation and sub-

## The State of Washington Program and IAQ Standards

In the early 1980s, one of Washington state's office buildings fell victim to sick building syndrome. After numerous corrective measures failed, the structure was turned into a warehouse. Because of this incident and the awareness of other indoor air issues in additional state buildings, the state's Department of General Administration recognized IAQ as a primary concern. As it began to plan for construction of four new office buildings for the Capitol Campus in Olympia and the surrounding area, the State of Washington, working with Air Quality Sciences, Inc., incorporated IAQ guidelines into the buildings and designs to ensure creation of healthy and productive environments for its employees. This was the first state-initiated program to ensure the design of buildings with acceptable indoor air quality.

These IAQ guidelines were written into the design and construction specifications for the buildings and were known as the IAQ Program. Pollutant source control was included in the specifications and required the use of low-emitting construction materials, interior finishes, and furnishings in the building. Pollutant specifications were made for general construction materials, systems office furniture, seating, and carpet along with a provision to identify VOCs known to be carcinogens, mutagens, reproductive toxins, or compounds that emit above identified thresholds. Manufacturers were given the opportunity to remove these from their products or to ensure that levels were below health concerns.

In order to meet these specifications, manufacturers were required to test their products' emissions using environmental chamber methodology following ASTM and EPA testing guidelines. Using specific building assumptions supplied by the state, a computer exposure model was used for predicting the contaminated concentrations that would result from use of the specified products. Product compliance sheets were required from the manufacturers indicating product compliance or noncompliance with the pollutant specifications.

As a cooperative project involving the State of Washington and the EPA, a pilot study was undertaken to evaluate the effectiveness of the state's IAQ construction program in meeting its goal of ensuring good indoor air quality in office buildings. The data showed that the process worked. Within thirty days of initial furniture installation, the indoor formaldehyde and VOC levels were found to be acceptable. The use of qualified, low-emitting products and appropriate installation techniques resulted in low, acceptable indoor pollutant levels. Because of the success of this program, other states and construction projects continue to adopt Washington State's pollutant control program. The EPA adopted similar emissions criteria and test methodology for their headquarters construction project. These specifications are now used by EPA in most of its own facilities for materials and building management.

*Source:* Information adapted from Aerias, www.aerias.org.

sequent emissions of office furnishings, a problem that could have been avoided by also holding the furniture off-site for a flush-out period.

VOCs are ubiquitous, found in hundreds of products ranging from building materials and furnishings to cleaning products and cosmetics. Often associated with an odor, VOCs are sometimes referred to as the "new-car smell," making them easy to identify. Formaldehyde, for example, is a very common VOC with a distinct odor. It is found in many products and serves a number of unique purposes.

Widely used as a preservative in paints and personal care products, it also adds permanent-press qualities to fabrics. However, its most common use in building products is as urea formaldehyde resins that serve as binders for plywood, particleboard, and other composite products. Although formaldehyde is naturally occurring in plants and animals, it is an irritant and potentially carcinogenic when present in high indoor concentrations.

## Low-emitting Materials

Pollutant source control is easier to implement than it used to be, primarily due to many low-emitting materials that have recently come on the market. Products such as paints, coatings, adhesives, floor coverings, and substrates that had been high emitters have been replaced with ones that off-gas very little, if at all. These changes have come about, in part, as a response to incidences of severe reactions to poor indoor air.

Products can be evaluated for VOC emissions in a number of ways: measurement of content, emission rates, or performance. The content approach is used by Green Seal and the South Coast Air Quality Management District (SCAQMD) to set VOC limits for paints, coatings, adhesives, and sealants, and are the referenced standards that are used to evaluate these product categories in LEED.

VOC limits are expressed in grams per liter (g/L), as shown for interior paints in Table 5-2 and for interior adhesives in Table 5-3. Critics maintain that this approach isn't valid because it measures only what's in the product, not what's being emitted. However, in the absence of other data, content limits are a decent guide.

The emissions rate protocol is best known as the standard used by the Carpet and Rug Institute (CRI), the industry's trade association, for its Green Label Plus program. Emission rates are expressed as micrograms of contaminant per square meter of carpet per hour. The products are small-chamber-tested for a range of chemicals within seventy-two hours after manufacture with protocols in place for sample acquisition, handling, test specimen preparation, test conditions, methods, and procedures. CRI Green Label Plus was developed in collaboration with California sustainability and health agencies and the Collaborative for High Performance Schools. The carpets

### Table 5-2: VOC Limits for Interior Paints

| Interior Paints | VOC Limit (g/L) |
| --- | --- |
| Flat | 50 |
| Non-flat | 150 |

Source: Green Seal GS-11 limits for interior paints minus water

### Table 5-3: VOC Limits for Adhesives

| Interior Architectural Adhesives | VOC Limit (g/L) |
| --- | --- |
| Indoor carpet adhesives | 50 |
| Carpet pad adhesives | 50 |
| Wood flooring adhesives | 100 |
| Rubber floor adhesives | 60 |
| Subfloor adhesives | 50 |
| Ceramic tile adhesives | 65 |
| VCT and asphalt tile adhesives | 50 |
| Drywall and panel adhesives | 50 |
| Cove base adhesives | 50 |
| Multipurpose construction adhesives | 70 |

Source: Information adapted from South Coast Rule #1168, VOC limits less water and exempt compounds

must meet certain emission rate criteria established for carpet specific chemicals.

Performance-based testing is similar to the emissions rate procedures, but large chambers are typically used that are capable of testing more complex assemblies, such as full installations of systems furniture and flooring. Products are tested over a one-week period in chambers that simulate a standard indoor environment for TVOCs, formaldehyde, particles, ozone, and other regulated pollutants. This procedure is used by Greenguard, a referenced standard in LEED-CI for furniture and seating products.

How, then, does the design team choose low-emitting products for its projects? A good first step is to be aware of the high-emitting materials and avoid them by selecting low-emitting substitutions. Following are some of the interior products most likely to cause indoor air quality problems. Manufacturers offering better alternatives are listed

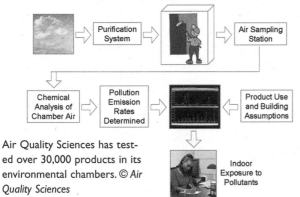

**Determining Emissions Using Environmental Chamber Testing (ECT™)**

Air Quality Sciences has tested over 30,000 products in its environmental chambers. © *Air Quality Sciences*

## The Problems with Mold and Mildew

There are differences between mold and mildew, but for this discussion, the two will be grouped together, and the text will refer to mold. Each grows on different types of materials, but both are microscopic organisms containing enzymes and spores. They are actually very useful in the universe by aiding in the decomposition of dead matter, for example, in forests. In our buildings, however, neither is welcome.

Mold contamination in buildings has always been a problem, but its prevalence seems to be greater in recent years. This may be due to the growing recognition of the associated health and economic risks. Respiratory problems including asthma, allergies, and infection have been shown to increase when mold is present, even driving families from their homes in some cases. Office buildings and schools have had to close because their occupants became sick.

*"Molds gradually destroy the things they grow on; they can grow on virtually any organic substance, as long as moisture and oxygen are present."*

—EPA

Mold contamination has also led to lengthy and expensive litigation. An article in *USA Today*, quoting the Texas Department of Insurance, stated that the top five insurance carriers in Texas alone saw their mold claims quintuple in a year and paid more than $1 billion on mold settlements the past two years.[16] More information on mold-related litigation can be found in Chapter 7.

The presence of mold is a symptom of the larger problem of unwanted moisture, but it's not always easy to find the cause: condensation, leaks in the building envelope, improperly maintained mechanical systems, leaks from water pipes, poor air circulation, and poor humidity control. Lessen the probability of occurrence by planning for prevention early in the design phase of the project. For example, poorly designed or constructed exterior walls may provide conditions that allow moisture to accumulate. If not corrected or repaired prior to the installation of vinyl wallpaper, wood paneling, or other impermeable materials,

in parentheses, with the caveat that this list, drawn selectively from the BuildingGreen online resource GreenSpec, can and will change over time.[15]

- Pressed wood products such as particleboard, medium-density fiberboard, plywood paneling, and oriented strand board. Look for products that use non-formaldehyde-based resins. (Sierra Pine Medex and Medite II; Allied Building Products Viroc Cement-Bonded Particleboard; Rodman Industries ResinCore1 Particleboard)
- Paints and coatings, especially alkyd-based, can be high emitters. Low- or no-VOC products have improved immeasurably in recent years and are now comparable in both price and performance to their high-emitting counterparts. (Benjamin Moore Pristine Eco-Spec; The Real Milk Paint Co.; Sherwin-Williams Harmony Coating System; Devoe Paint Wonder–Pure No-VOC/Odor)
- Adhesives used to install flooring products, including carpets, resilient flooring, and base, have long been an air quality problem. New latex products are on the market offering superior bonding without the VOCs. (W.W. Henry Co. Henry GreenLine Flooring Adhesives; W. F. Taylor Co. Envirotec Floor Covering Adhesives; EcoTimber Zero-VOC Adhesive; Johnsonite #965 Flooring and Tread Adhesive)
- The solvent-based lacquers, coatings, and stains on solid wood furniture and millwork can give off VOCs. Consider water-based polyurethane alternatives. (AFM Hard Seal and Safecoat Clear Finishes; BioShield Interior Transparent Finishes and Stains; Aglaia Natural Finishes and Stains)

moisture may be trapped and mold will grow. Mold remediation is extremely costly and may involve removal of walls, carpets, millwork, and other expensive finishes.

Mold is most toxic when it grows unseen behind walls or in ceiling plenums. Not only is it hidden out of view, but plenums house ducts and pipes, both likely sources of leaks. Ceiling tile manufacturers such as USG and Armstrong have introduced products with antimicrobial treatments that inhibit or retard the growth of mold and mildew. However, antimicrobials are pesticides and their use should be avoided if possible. Once optimal growth conditions exist, even the use of these treatments and the mold inhibitors found in some primers, vinyl products, and adhesives will not prevent mold damage.

Prevention is the least expensive and most effective strategy against mold damage and should include, at a minimum, a sequencing plan for the delivery, storage, and installation of susceptible materials. Absorptive products such as carpet and drywall should never be delivered to the job site until the storage area is protected from weather and adequate protection from moisture can be provided. Water-damaged materials or those with evidence of mold should be removed and discarded.

As Marilyn Black mentioned in her essay at the beginning of this chapter, Greenguard has recently introduced a mold risk reduction plan and a certification program that has been proposed as an American National Standards Institute (ANSI) standard. It has also been preliminarily reviewed by the U.S. EPA and piloted with several building owners, including Emory Medical School. ANSI standard approval is expected in late 2006.

# ■ The Elusive Thermal Comfort

*"They walk among us: wearers of long johns, tucked neatly under suit pants, blouses and jackets. Smugglers of space heaters, sneaking the small appliances under parkas to hide under their desks."*

*"On the other end of the thermometer are the office suffocaters. Despite freezing temperatures outside, despite their desk fans and their pleadings to turn that darn heat off, they are the ones stripped down to T-shirts and flip-flops by the afternoon."*

—Amy Joyce and Justin Blum, "For Workers, the Weather Inside Can Be Frightful," *Washington Post,* January 8, 2006

Thermal comfort is hard to define, yet we know it when we feel it. It involves more than just temperature—certainly humidity and air movement play a role. Breezes, for example, help us tolerate higher temperatures and humidity. Indoor thermal experiences are influenced by sunlight penetration, surface materials, and the cardigan sweater hanging over the back of your chair. People are adaptable, within limits, to the ranges of comfort they will accept, which gives designers and engineers some wiggle room with thermal solutions. On the other hand, hot and cold calls by occupants to the building maintenance staff

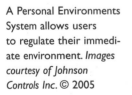

A Personal Environments System allows users to regulate their immediate environment. *Images courtesy of Johnson Controls Inc.* © 2005

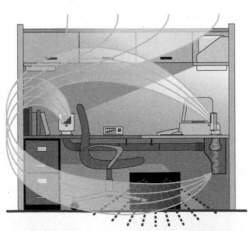

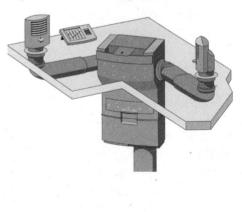

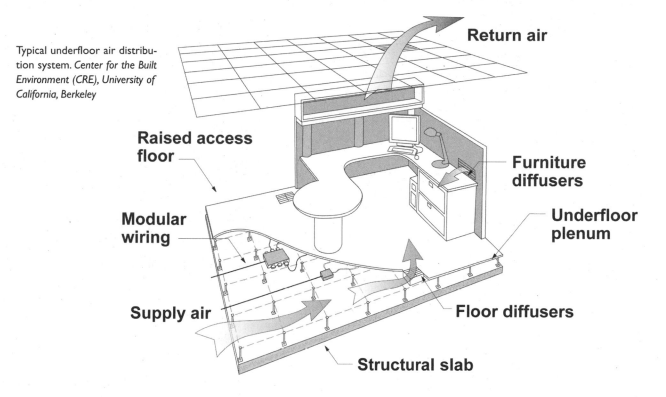

Typical underfloor air distribution system. *Center for the Built Environment (CRE), University of California, Berkeley*

**Return air**

**Raised access floor**

**Furniture diffusers**

**Underfloor plenum**

**Modular wiring**

**Supply air**

**Floor diffusers**

**Structural slab**

are a widespread and expensive problem that can be reduced or even eliminated by better systems.

Thermostat wars, common in many offices, have a negative impact on productivity by causing unnecessary conflict and the waste of a lot of time. These problems can be avoided by providing every office and workstation with its own thermal control. The Personal Environments System, manufactured by Johnson Controls, allows users to regulate temperature and airflow on their desktops as well as other conditions such as task lighting and background noise. The units are available for offices designed for conventional air delivery through the ceiling and for raised-floor systems. It is the latter, however, that offers more benefits.

Raised-floor systems have many economic advantages—a downsized mechanical system, less ductwork, easy access to power and data cabling, and lower churn costs through greater flexibility—but their primary benefit is improved thermal comfort. When air is delivered by an underfloor distribution system, building occupants gain greater control over temperature and velocity. Traditional delivery systems supply conditioned air through a network

of ducts and registers at or near the ceiling. Supply air mixes with the room air and returns through the ceiling into the plenum, providing the entire space, if well designed, with uniformly maintained setpoint temperatures and air movement. However, individual preferences are not uniform, but are influenced by many factors such as gender, clothing, and metabolic rate.

Studies, including one by the Building Owners and Managers Association, show that building occupants rate their ability to control the temperature at their workspace as very important, yet current practice seems to discount the findings.[17] As stated by the Center for the Built Environment, "Current comfort standards specify a 'comfort zone,' representing the optimal range and combinations of thermal factors (air temperature, radiant temperature, air velocity, humidity) and personal factors (clothing and activity level) with which at least 80% of the building occupants are expected to express satisfaction. The standards were developed for mechanically conditioned buildings typically having overhead air distribution systems designed to maintain uniform temperature and ventilation conditions throughout the occupied space. Given the high value placed on the quality of indoor environments, it is rather astonishing that a building HVAC system can be considered in compliance with thermal comfort standards, and yet provide a thermal environment with which up to 20% of the building population will be dissatisfied. This is, however, exactly the case in the conventional 'one-size-fits-all' approach to environmental control in buildings."[18]

In contrast to these traditional systems, underfloor air systems use a raised access floor to deliver a constant flow of fresh air in close proximity to the occupants. As the air enters the space, either through floor diffusers or as part of the furniture system, it mixes with the room air and, as it warms, rises to the ceiling, where it exits through the return. Both desk-mounted and floor-based outlets will provide enough temperature and air velocity variation to satisfy individual thermal preferences. Another benefit is cleaner air, as contaminants are carried up and out.

## ■ Noise: The Other Pollutant

Acoustics are not always included on lists of indoor environmental qualities, but when an office worker, hospital patient, hotel guest, or schoolchild can hear unwanted sounds too loudly, the detrimental effect on well-being and performance is pronounced. The problem is exacerbated because excessive noise—whether from construction site jackhammers outside the window to footsteps from the space above—is often out of the control of the affected individual.

> *"Acoustics doesn't show up in the records of building complaints because people don't complain about acoustics. They don't think the building manager can do anything about it, and that's generally true."*
>
> —Kevin Kampschroer, director, GSA Research and Expert Services

**Contribution to Workspace Distractions Overall**

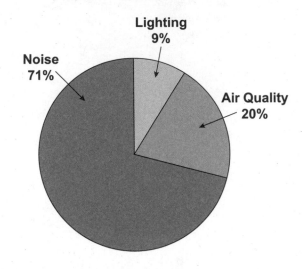

Contributions to workplace distractions overall. © *American Society of Interior Designers*

Multiple studies have shown that office workers regard noise as a major irritant. In 1996, the American Society of Interior Designers (ASID) published *Sound Solutions,* which reported that 71 percent of those surveyed found noise to be a considerable distraction.[19]

A subsequent study, published in 2005, concluded that open collaborative environments, generally smaller workstations, the popularity of unfinished nonacoustical ceilings, raised floors, underfloor air distribution, and the proliferation of electronic devices have increased the negative impacts of noise.[20] The results of numerous research projects are cited, including one from Armstrong World Industries that surveyed knowledge and service workers both prior to and after ceiling systems had been replaced with more absorbent materials and electronic sound masking had been added. The results "consistently indicated that freedom from auditory distractions was the most important feature in efficiently and effectively accomplishing their work tasks."[21] The study results, illustrated on the facing page, further confirm the effect of speech privacy on human productivity.

The good news, according to the ASID report, is that most common acoustical design problems can be resolved by integrated planning, which, as we've learned, is also a basic tenet of green design. Planning for a non-intrusive level of acoustical privacy starts at the beginning of project planning and includes all relevant team members, including the man-ufacturers whose products will play an important role in the solutions: ceiling, sound masking, furniture, and carpet systems.

The ABCs of speech privacy shown below is a recognized approach to acoustical success and includes the performance meas-ures of all installed systems. Ceilings, for example, are rated by their ability to absorb rather than reflect sound, especially in the fre-quency ranges of speech. Lighting fixtures and air diffusers, which are also part of the ceiling system, should be chosen with acoustic properties in mind.

## Improvements Resulting from Increased Speech Privacy

**Focus:** The ability of office workers to focus on their tasks improved by 48%.

**Distractions:** "Conversational distractions" decreased by 51%.

**Error-rates:** Performance of standard "information-worker" tasks (measured in terms of accuracy [error-rates] and short-term memory) improved by 10%.

**Stress:** When measured in terms of the actual physical symptoms of stress, stress was reduced by 27%.

— David M. Sykes, Ph.D.
*How Acoustics Affect Human Productivity*

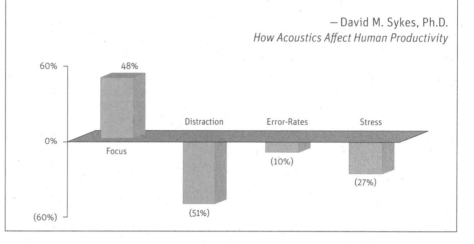

The benefits of speech privacy. David M. Sykes, "How Acoustics Affect Human Productivity," 2004, © American Society of Interior Designers

## The ABCs of Speech Privacy

Acoustical consultants and engineers often refer to three proven methods as the ABCs of balanced acoustical design for achieving a "non-intrusive" level of speech privacy. All three must be used and integrated properly with one another to achieve the desired result.

| Method | Products to Use | Performance Indicators |
| --- | --- | --- |
| Absorb | acoustical ceilings, fabrics, carpet | AC rating, NRC rating |
| | | IIC rating, INR rating |
| Block | furniture systems, panels, walls, partitions, screens, glass | STC rating, CAC rating |
| Cover | sound masking — plenum-mounted or in-ceiling | dB/dBA rating |

The ABCs of speech privacy. © American Society of Interior Designers

In open-plan offices, furniture systems—especially the workstation divider panels—will block sound from migrating from one cubicle to another. Higher panels are obviously going to be better sound blockers, but they will also limit the occupant's access to daylight and views, a conflict to be resolved by consideration of the project priorities. Glass panels may be an effective solution.

Sound masking, sometimes referred to as "white noise," is a good acoustical control strategy and may be as simple as allowing the fan noise from the HVAC system to cover other sounds. However, more sophisticated electronic masking technologies on the market are integrated into the overall design. As stated in *Sound Solutions,* "It is very important that before the sound masking system can be tuned and used, the architectural system must first have been 'robustly' designed to provide the capability of achieving the desired level of speech privacy. If the ceiling and landscape furniture panels are 'value engineered' down to the lowest cost alternative, then it will very likely not be possible to tune the sound masking system to 'make up' for the deficiencies in the architectural selections."[22]

Like ceilings, carpets are rated by their ability to absorb sound. Studies by the Carpet and Rug Institute have shown that products with cut pile and cushions achieve better acoustical control. Permeable carpet backings with greater height and thickness offer better results.[23]

*Sound Solutions* provides details that will help designers integrate acoustical control into their projects; however, elevating the science of sound into the mainstream of green buildings will be furthered by the addition of an acoustics credit into LEED. In 2000 such a credit was written during the development of LEED-CI, but it was subsequently dropped. Many expect that it will be resurrected and included in the next version.

That likelihood is bolstered by the results of an occupant satisfaction survey of the Interface showroom in Atlanta conducted in 2005 by the Center for the Built Environment (CBE). The showroom was originally designed as a touchdown space for its eight employees. However, because it is such a nice place to work, some, including president John Wells, choose to locate their offices there. CBE designed the survey to query the occupants on nine workplace attributes including general satisfaction, office layout and furnishings, thermal comfort, air quality, lighting, and acoustics. The responses were extremely positive as one would expect in a space that had earned a LEED-CI platinum certification, except for one category—acoustics. Fifty-six percent of the respondents said that they were dissatisfied with the sound privacy in their workspace and the poor acoustic quality interfered with their ability to work. The conclusion is obvious—even the greenest interior spaces can be rendered less desirable by bad acoustics. Interface used the survey results to make acoustical improvements in the showroom and to inform the design decisions throughout its portfolio.

# Let There Be (Day)light

Taking advantage of natural light minimizes the need for electric lighting during the daytime, saves energy, saves money, and lifts the spirits of building occupants. When properly controlled and complemented by good views, the combination is a powerful component of green interiors, and few strategies can top it for impact. The experience of daylight in an interior, when done well, is a joy; when not, it can negatively impact the occupant's experience. "Cool daylighting" is both natural and hip, states the Daylighting Collaborative: natural because it "taps into the five-billion-year-old fusion reactor called the sun," and hip because "daylit buildings are just plain more cool—more environmentally, technologically, and anthropologically aware than traditionally lit buildings. Daylit buildings make a statement about their owners: that they know their building science and put it to the best possible use by investing in buildings that use less energy, are more comfortable, and protect our environment."[24]

Many of the details of daylighting and views are intertwined with other design decisions, such as those previously discussed in Chapter 3 on lighting. In her essay that follows, Nancy Clanton further discusses the interconnectedness of the physical characteristics of the building, energy savings opportunities and the lighting/daylighting solutions.

## Why Daylighting?

### By Nancy Clanton

*Designing daylighting into all of our buildings can have lasting benefits, including environmental quality and energy savings. Using free solar energy is very tempting considering energy prices are only increasing. Pre-electricity buildings took full advantage of daylight since this was the only lighting source. Today, we have the advantage of combining basic design knowledge with high-performance materials to enjoy the benefits of daylight while controlling its adverse heat effects. Good design starts with a concept that is developed with solid strategies and techniques.*

### Daylighting Economic Success

*Including quality daylighting in building designs is extremely economical. When longer-term benefits such as energy savings are considered, it can easily be seen as a good investment. Research has shown that additional financial benefits of increased produc-tivity and profitability can dwarf the life cycle costs. For example, a series of studies performed by the Heschong Mahone Group found that grocery stores that incorporated skylights had a 40 percent increase in sales, and students in schools with the most daylight had 20 percent higher math scores and 26 percent higher reading scores. Finally, it is worth noting that when combined with other integrated design techniques, daylighting may not even increase initial construction costs.*

### Conceptual Building Design Strategies

*Building orientation and geometry give a solid foundation to quality daylighting design. Glazing size and location will determine daylight quantity. Taking advantage of views will add to occupant satisfaction.*

Building Orientation . . . Most Light for Your Buck

*Proper building orientation helps the design in many ways by fully taking advantage of daylight potential. Fortunately for us, the sun will not change its path, making it a predictable design element that works for the life of the building.*

Studies have shown that a daylit grocery store will show an increase in sales. *Photography courtesy of Stop & Shop*

Translucent window shades control sunlight and glare while preserving views at the Denver University Law School. *Photography courtesy of Clanton & Associates*

*An orientation that favors maximum southern and northern exposures minimizes solar heat gain and glare in the morning and late afternoon. In the Northern Hemisphere, glazing on southern exposures provides a potential daylight contribution of up to 45 percent, and northern exposures produce glare-free, quality lighting.*

### Daylighting Success Relates to Geometry

*Tall ceilings and high windows will allow the deepest daylight penetration into areas. Typically, daylight will penetrate about 1.5 times the maximum window height into a room. If the window has a light-reflecting shelf or light shelf, then daylight has the potential of penetrating up to 2.5 times the window height. Allowing daylight to come into an area from more than one direction will more deeply penetrate the space and provide better uniformity.*

### Glazing Size and Locations

*Windows on the north and south façades will provide the best-quality daylight. Use larger windows over smaller punched windows in order to reduce contrast between the brighter window and the perimeter walls. Model the daylight availability to optimize glazing quantity depending on typical climate conditions, solar heat gains, and daylight goals.*

*Toplighting strategies are ideal for large single-story buildings and for nonperimeter areas. Three to five percent of the roof area will be needed to provide uniform lighting with standard skylights.*

### Take Advantage of Views

*Quality views are definitely desirable and necessary for a myriad of tasks. Teachers are less stressed if they have views, and healthcare patients recover faster and require less pain medication. Office workers are more productive, take fewer breaks, and complain less about health problems. Corner offices with two windows tend to be the most desirable. Views of nature are more beneficial than overlooking a parking lot. A building site without natural views will be improved by adding landscaping and flowers.*

### Technical Fine-Tuning

*The next step in daylighting design is to select an appropriate glazing type, provide shading to minimize direct sun penetration, and integrate the design with the electric lighting and controls.*

### Glazing Types and Flavors

*In selecting glazing, there are several issues to determine. The first is how much visible light you want to come through the window. View windows shouldn't be too bright, yet not dark enough to change the color of the scene. Windows that are not in the normal field of view and are used primarily for daylight penetration can have a higher visible transmittance value.*

Solar heat gain coefficient (SHGC), the percentage of solar heat from the sun that passes through into the building, is another glazing choice. The lower the SHGC the more thermally comfortable the window becomes. It also lowers the cooling load when sizing HVAC systems.

## Most Windows and Skylights Require Shading

*External shading such as awnings, porches, and light shelves prevent the solar heat gain from ever striking the window. This type of shading is very important for southern façades. East and west façades will have direct sunlight in the early morning and late afternoon. Vertical shading and landscape features can help mitigate this penetration. Northern façades will have minimal direct sunlight penetration in the wintertime.*

*Skylights also require shading in order to minimize the glare and solar heat gain from direct sun penetration. Splayed ceiling openings and reflectors mounted below skylights help in controlling the direct sun. Another option is to use high-performance skylights.*

Since most buildings are not built on orthogonal coordinates, internal user-controlled shading may be necessary for task areas.

## Supplement Daylight . . . Do Not Duplicate It

*An integrated design technique is to take into account the sufficiency of daylighting so that electric lighting never duplicates it but only supplements it. On cloudy days, for example, daylight appears "flat," so some direct lighting is required to add shadows. Fortunately, less lighting is required in most interior spaces at night. If a building's electric lighting system is designed only to meet the building's needs on cloudy days and for nighttime activities, then less equipment is needed. If we consider that many large buildings have cooling loads even in winter because of the internal heat generated by electric lighting, people, and equipment, daylighting offers potential energy and cost savings throughout the life of a building.*

## To Dim or Not to Dim . . . That Is the Question

*The final technique is to control electric lighting. The key is combining personal controls with automatic*

At the offices of Boulder Housing Partners, light shelves aid in distributing daylight deeper into the space. *Photography courtesy of Clanton & Associates*

*controls. Personal controls give occupants the ability to turn on/off or dim the lights according to individual needs. Automatic controls include daylight, motion-sensing, and building energy management controls. Personal controls can be used in areas where people work, meet, or teach, such as offices, classrooms, or conference rooms, whereas automatic controls work well in public areas such as hallways, restrooms, lunch-rooms, and lobbies.*

*A combination of personal and automatic controls works best. A good basic approach would be to pro-vide personal spaces such as individual offices, confer-ence rooms, and classrooms with manual dimming controls that have upper limits when daylight is plenti-ful and occupancy sensors. Public areas also can be effectively and inconspicuously controlled with daylight and occupancy sensors.*

*Building-wide automatic energy management sys-tems should be programmed to control lighting except under emergency conditions, in which case the lighting can be turned off or dimmed as needed. If properly designed, lighting controlled by daylight and occupan-cy sensors will automatically minimize both daytime and nighttime lighting loads as a subsystem of the building energy management system.*

### The Art and Science of Daylighting Design

*Simple techniques can produce great results. With complicated buildings, a daylighting consultant will help with orientation, geometry, glazing locations, size, specification, and shading devices. Additionally, a day-light model can show how the design will behave and help refine the solutions. All great daylighting design begins with these steps:*

*1. Maximize south and north façades.*

*2. Use high ceilings and tall windows.*

*3. Maximize quality views for task areas and share the daylight.*

*4. Calculate the optimal size and number of windows and toplighting for even illuminance while minimiz-ing heat gain.*

*5. Select high-performance glazing.*

Fabric scrims are used to control sunlight penetration at the Missouri Department of Natural Resources. *Photography cour-tesy of Clanton & Associates*

*6. Shade south façades.*

*7. Avoid direct sunlight in task areas such as offices, classrooms, and conference rooms.*

*8. Use high reflectance values for surfaces.*

*9. Integrate the electric lighting and controls for optimal energy savings.*

---

Nancy Clanton is founder and president of Clanton & Associates, a lighting design firm specializing in sus-tainable design.

## Daylighting: Making It Work

"Daylighting is perhaps the most demanding and challenging form of illumination because of its variability and its impact on many aspects of the building. To design daylighting properly, integration of design and coordination among disciplines is essential," states the *Advanced Lighting Guideline*.[25] A poor daylighting system or lack of proper controls can create many energy and occupant comfort problems.

Daylight enters buildings either through windows or skylights, and more often than not the interiors project is stuck with what it gets. In some buildings with northern orientations, set very close to neighboring structures or with small, deep-set windows, the design team can do little to add daylight to the interior. For other buildings with southern, western, and eastern exposures, excellent daylighting opportunities exist but will demand that control strategies are put in place. These include light shelves, shades, louvers, and window films. Automatic photosensors, essential to lowering energy use through daylighting, are discussed in Chapter 3.

## Light Shelves

Windows often let in too much light, creating problems of excessive heat, ultraviolet degradation, and glare at the perimeter, while too little light penetrates deep into the interior space. One solution is the installation of light shelves that reflect light onto the ceiling and then bounce it deep into the room. When combined with louvers or shades, many of the problems of direct sun are avoided. Properly done, light shelves increase a window's useful illumination depth from 1.5 times its height to 2 times or more. Exterior light shelves or a combination are a more effective shading solution than interior shelves alone, but often they are impractical for the interiors project.

Light shelves are constructed out of many different materials. One project used hollow-core doors cut to custom lengths as an inexpensive strategy; others have used particleboard, wheatboard, and stretched fabric panels. Manufactured products, including those from Construction Specialties, are made from an expanded polystyrene foam core covered with aluminum or other facing materials finished to match paint colors, wall covering, and

Light shelves installed in the S. C. Johnson Wax headquarters, designed by HOK, bounce light off the reflective ceiling further into the interior. *Photography by Edward J. Purcell*

other items. Light shelves can be suspended from the ceiling or attached to the walls or window frames and should be angled up from the window to provide better shading and light bounce. The design—size and angle—will be based on the location's latitude, building orientation, and window height. A white or other reflective paint color on the ceiling will help bounce the light further back into space. Matte finishes are best to diffuse light without causing hot spots.

Light shelves are best when incorporated into a daylight management plan such as the one implemented by Luckenbach|Ziegelman Architects at the Malletts Creek Library in Ann Arbor, Michigan. The shelves, installed on the south-facing windows with motorized roller shades mounted below, are computer-controlled by photo-optic

The light shelves at Malletts Creek Library add architectural interest as well as shield occupants from the southern sun. *Photography courtesy of Luckenbach/Ziegelman Architects; Philip Proefrock*

sensors. Originally designed as a stand-alone system, the shade controls have been integrated into the building energy management plan.

## Window Coverings

Glare, defined as excessive and concentrated light, is distractive, annoying, and even disabling. In a study conducted by the Heschong Mahone Group, window glare had a "significant negative effect" on workers, decreasing performance by 15 to 21 percent.[26] Caused by nearby buildings, pavement, or highly reflective objects that bounce too much light into the interior, glare is light that needs to be diminished. Unprotected windows can negate the advantages of daylight by causing UV damage and heat gain in addition to glare. The design team can use many strategies to prevent these problems.

Shadecloths by MechoShade, shown here at the Philips Plastic Origen Center, filter natural light while providing a partial view to the outdoors. *Photography by Don F. Wong*

On tall windows the combination of light shelves and shades, blinds, or louvers delivers a double benefit. The shelves reflect daylight into the interior, while the shading devices, installed to cover only the lower portion of the window, control glare.

Numerous window covering options are available: roller shades, Roman shades, vertical and horizontal blinds (both solid and perforated), draperies, and shutters all will keep out unwanted light, but each should be evaluated for the specific application. Vertical louvers and horizontal miniblinds will block the sun, but they may also block the view. As the sun moves, the blinds must constantly be adjusted and, when partially open, solar gain is reflected back into the room; when closed, the advantages of daylighting are lost. Occupants will often keep the blinds closed rather than making adjustments during the course of the day. One study of offices with light-colored, perforated vertical blinds found that 80 percent remained open during the day on the north side of the building, but on the south side 80 percent remained partially or fully closed. The researchers also found that while the blinds were adjustable, the controls were often difficult to reach.[27]

Roller shades made of visually transparent materials offer increased flexibility by shielding sunlight but protecting occupant views, even when lowered. They can be ordered in a range of openness factors that determine the density of the weave: a 3 percent openness factor would be a tighter, more opaque weave than 10 percent. Specifying

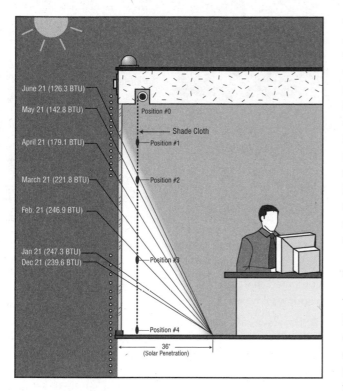

The *New York Times* is employing MechoShade's AAC SolarTrac system with Daylighting Manager Window Management at its new Manhattan headquarters. The system is designed to automatically adjust the window shade position in accordance with the angle of the rays of the sun, resulting in reduced heat gain and control of solar ray penetration. *Illustration courtesy of MechoShade Systems Inc.*

a light-colored surface facing out and a darker color surface on the interior will maximize UV reflection and minimize heat gain. Shade cloths made from PVC-free yarns are also available.

Window coverings are most effective when installed with control systems such as Lutron's Sivoia QED that can be integrated with lighting, security, or climate controls and programmed to preset stop points. Operated by infrared remotes or keypads, this type of user-friendly system provides occupants a convenient way to manage sunlight.

The AAC SolarTrac and Daylighting Manager System by MechoShade provides computerized solar tracking that

will automatically adjust the position of the shades in accordance with the dynamics of the sun's movement and the brightness of the window wall. Usable with all types of windows, including skylights and atria, the system relies on rooftop solar radiometers and window area daylight brightness sensors. This is a new technology that has been chosen for use in the *New York Times'* new Manhattan headquarters. Lawrence Berkeley National Laboratory researched and tested the system at a mock-up built at the site of the newspaper's printing plant in Queens, New York. How well the technology performs and users' acceptance of an automated system are yet to be seen; however, its development demonstrates the importance of building systems integration.

## Window Films

The sun provides 7,000 to 10,000 footcandles of light on bright days and 5,000 to 6,000 footcandles on completely overcast days, considerably more light than what is needed for the majority of tasks. Clear glass windows let too much of that light in, causing glare and sharp contrasts that are uncomfortable and prompting occupants to close the blinds and turn on electric lighting.

A better solution is to replace clear glass with low-emissivity (low-e) glass or, when replacing the windows is not feasible, to apply film on the interior surface to achieve many of the same results—reduced heat gain, glare, protection against sun damage and fading to furniture, fabrics, carpets and artwork. According to the International Window Film Association, "clear single pane glass (1/8" to 1/4") will reject 23–28% of the ultraviolet light from the sun. Insulated glass is slightly better, rejecting 36–41%. Window films installed on glass reject 95–99% of solar ultraviolet light." [28]

Changing out single-pane windows to high-performance units offers additional insulating benefits, but this type of building alteration is often outside the interior project's scope of work. Window films, however, can be retrofitted on almost any type of window if permitted by the building owner. Some types of films change the appearance of the exterior glass, causing a mirrored effect that limits their use as an aftermarket application. However, newer products on the market offer excellent solar block-

Biosphere 2 chose Vista Luminance window film to reduce glare and control heat gain. *Photography courtesy of Vista Window Film/CP Films Inc.*

ing, UV protection, and reduced heat loss without altering the look of the façade. Window films also provide shatter resistance in case of storms, earthquakes, vandalism, or terrorist attacks.

In order to select the correct product it is necessary to understand how window films work and to define which properties are most important to the project. Window films are a laminate composed of a polyester substrate and a metal scratch-resistant coating bonded together by an adhesive. Older products worked by absorption, whereas newer, spectrally selective high-performance films rely on reflectivity and emissivity, filtering out heat while allowing more light transmittance. The performance properties and metrics of three window films and ⅛-inch clear glass are compared in Table 5-4. The films, manufactured by Vista Window Films, are: .

- Dayview V45, a good choice for high-visibility display windows such as showrooms because of its higher visible light transmittance and low reflectance properties.
- Luminance V28, which has a reflective exterior appearance and is an option for applications where heat and glare are major problems, as demonstrated by the film's solar heat gain coefficient.
- SpectraSelect 70, a spectrally selective film with performance numbers that excel in every category. The film offers extremely low reflectance and excellent solar energy rejection while admitting a very high percentage of visible light.

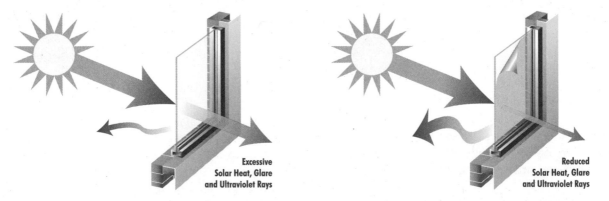

Windows with low-e glass or window films applied to them will allow light transmittance while screening out heat and ultraviolet rays. *Image courtesy of Vista Window Film/CP Films Inc.*

## Table 5-4: Performance Properties and Metrics of Window Films

| Window Film Properties | Clear Glass | V45 | V 28 | VS70 |
|---|---|---|---|---|
| **Visible light transmittance**: how much visible light passes through the film. A low percentage helps with glare control, while a higher percentage maintains natural light conditions. | 89% | 45% | 27% | 70% |
| **Visible light reflectance**: how much visible light the film reflects. This property is what makes windows look like mirrors; the higher the percentage, the "shinier" the window. | 8% | 17% ext. 14% int. | 34% ext. 20% int. | 8% ext. 8% int. |
| **Solar heat gain coefficient**: the total amount of solar heat that is transmitted directly, plus what is absorbed by the film and then radiated into the building, expressed as a number between 0 and 1. | .81 | .54 | .35 | .45 |
| **Total solar energy rejected**: basically, the inverse of the solar heat gain coefficient, expressed as a percentage. It's the amount of solar energy across the entire spectrum rejected by the film. | 19% | 46% | 65% | 55% |
| **U value**: a measure of heat conductance (the inverse of R value). Differences between indoor and outdoor temperatures are typically greatest in heating climates, making the U value more important than in cooling climates. A lower U value means less heat loss, as well as less condensation. | 1.06 | 1.03 | 1.00 | .90 |
| **Ultraviolet light blocking**: the amount of UV light blocked by the film—98 to 99% for most films. UV inhibition is required for the longevity of the film; fade prevention of carpets, furnishings, and fabric window treatments is a bonus. | 35% | 99.9% | 99.9% | 99.9% |
| **Emissivity**: the film's ability to reflect heat back into a room. The lower the number, the better the film is at preventing interior heat loss. | .84 | .84 | .81 | .66 |

*Sources:* Definitions adapted from "Comparison of High-Performance Window Films," *Environmental Building News,* June 2005; metrics from Vista Window Films

# Skylights

Sixty-two percent of commercial floor space is directly under the roof and is available for toplighting, versus 25 percent of the square footage located within 20 feet of the perimeter that can be sidelit from windows.[29] Thus, toplighting presents a far greater opportunity to introduce daylight into buildings than is generally assumed, especially in areas with a preponderance of single-story or low-rise construction. Big-box retail stores, for example, have successfully used skylights to draw customers deeper into center areas and highlight merchandise. Atria, designed into high-rise buildings, also effectively distribute daylighting into the core.

> *"Skylights aren't usually needed to achieve good results until you get beyond 25 feet of the perimeter windows."*
>
> —The Daylighting Collaborative, Energy Center of Wisconsin

Skylights, especially those positioned directly over regularly occupied areas, need to be shielded through the use of diffuse glazing, blinds, louvers, or other materials in order to prevent too much light, or hot spots of light. This opens the door to creative solutions such as that developed by Envision Design for a nonprofit client in Washington, D.C. The challenge was to introduce natural light into a dark 1950s-era warehouse in order to create a cheerful, engaging, and welcoming environment for an organization working with people with severe and persistent mental illness.

Two tactics were employed. The building's perimeter window area was increased by 300 percent, and four large skylights were added to the roof, allowing 99 percent of the permanent workforce to have access to natural light.

A stretched polyester fabric ceiling system was installed to disguise the simple strip fluorescent fixtures and to diffuse the natural light pouring in from the skylights. This handsome solution, achieved on a modest budget, contributed to an environmentally friendly, non-stereotypical office that expresses respect for the people served by the organization.

A workstation situated under a skylight in the offices of the non-profit organization Green Door is shielded by a scrim of stretched fabric. © *Envision Design, PLLC. Photography by Michael Moran*

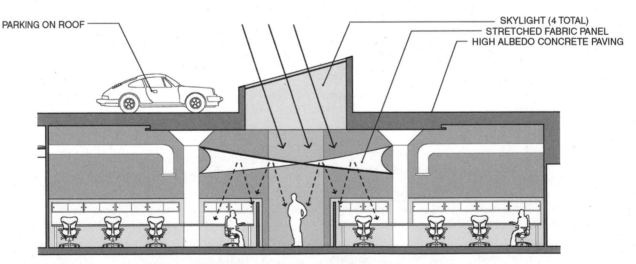

PARKING ON ROOF

SKYLIGHT (4 TOTAL)
STRETCHED FABRIC PANEL
HIGH ALBEDO CONCRETE PAVING

Skylights provide diffused lighting to centrally located workstations. © *Envision Design, PLLC*

Tenant spaces without adequate windows or those located below the top floor, where skylights are not possible, may be able to import daylight through some of the exciting emerging technologies. Light pipes, as an example, are cylindrical devices with transparent domes and highly reflective interior surfaces. Easier to install in existing buildings than skylights, they are just beginning to become commercially available. The Oikos Green Building Source Web site offers good information on light pipes as well as traditional skylights. [30]

# The Importance of Views

Windows are a central and complex component of buildings. As the Heschong Mahone Group's report states, of all the functions of windows, "the most interesting and most controversial is the importance of view. In office buildings, it has long been a truism that the senior executives are rewarded with corner offices, with the biggest boss getting the best view." [31] Hotel rooms with good views cost more, and many a real estate deal has hinged on the sights that can be seen through the windows.

Numerous studies point to the contribution of view and a connection to nature to increased performance and feelings of well-being: schoolchildren achieve higher test scores, hospital patients go home sooner, and even prisoners are happier. However, the benefits vary depending on the view's angle, content, and absence of glare. For example, one of the most important benefits of a good view is helping to prevent eye fatigue. Frequent changes of focus from close work on the computer screen or reading to distance viewing is very beneficial, making it likely that the company president overlooking the boulevard will have less eyestrain than his secretary with a view of the alley.

The Heschong Mahone Group's study found that "having a better view out of a window, gauged primarily by the size of the view and secondarily by greater vegetation content, was most consistently associated with better worker performance in six out of eight outcomes considered. Workers in call centers were found to process calls 6 percent to 12 percent faster when they had the best possible view versus those with no view. Office workers were found to per-

form 10 percent to 25 percent better on tests of mental function and memory recall when they had the best possible view versus those with no view. . . . Reports of increased fatigue were most strongly associated with a lack of view." [32]

Even the best of views will not benefit building occupants unless easily seen from regularly seated positions. Given their importance, it is essential that interiors be designed to optimize views, requiring a difference approach from standard practice. Typically, workers in private perimeter offices enjoy views, while others located away from the windows do not. In open office plans, high cubicle partitions block the view when occupants are seated.

Maintaining a view should be one of the primary objectives of space design. In many situations, successful views are most easily achieved through the use of one material—glass. Consider the use of transparent glazing for the walls of private offices located around the perimeter or those pulled back toward the core. Envision Design used glass to its best advantage at the Environmental Defense headquarters in Washington, D.C. The introduction of natural light and views to the outside for all staff members was critical to fulfilling the client's program and in many ways guided the design decisions for the layout and the materials selection. The long and narrow footprint of the space provided an excellent opportunity to achieve the desired transparency with the extensive use of glass. Every office has floor-to-ceiling glass panels that permit light to penetrate deep into the space, and each full-time staff member has a view to the outside from a seated position. [33]

> *"I love it, but I can't explain to you why. It's obviously not one thing, but a whole combination of things."*
>
> —Staff member, Environmental Defense, Washington, D.C.

Credit 8.3 in LEED-CI requires a direct line of sight to perimeter vision glazing, defined as that portion of exterior windows above 2 feet 6 inches and below 7 feet 6 inches. In other words, clerestory windows, although an excellent source of daylighting, do not qualify as view windows. The design team should plot out views to the vision windows as they plan the partition and furniture layouts. The

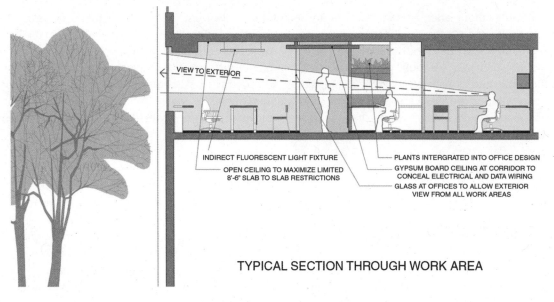

INDIRECT FLUORESCENT LIGHT FIXTURE

OPEN CEILING TO MAXIMIZE LIMITED
8'-6" SLAB TO SLAB RESTRICTIONS

VIEW TO EXTERIOR

PLANTS INTERGRATED INTO OFFICE DESIGN

GYPSUM BOARD CEILING AT CORRIDOR TO
CONCEAL ELECTRICAL AND DATA WIRING

GLASS AT OFFICES TO ALLOW EXTERIOR
VIEW FROM ALL WORK AREAS

## TYPICAL SECTION THROUGH WORK AREA

Workers seated in the interior offices have a clear line of sight to the perimeter window glazing. © *Envision Design, PLLC*

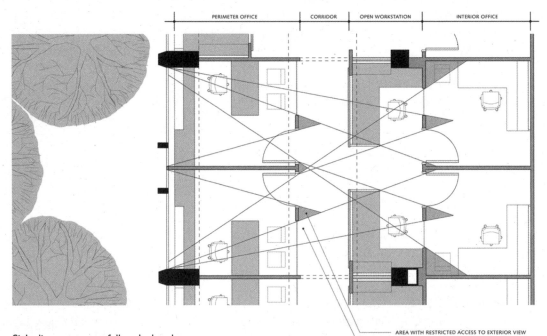

PERIMETER OFFICE | CORRIDOR | OPEN WORKSTATION | INTERIOR OFFICE

AREA WITH RESTRICTED ACCESS TO EXTERIOR VIEW

AREA WITH CLEAR ACCESS TO EXTERIOR VIEW

Sight lines were carefully calculated to provide access to natural light and views through glass partitions and low panel heights. © *Envision Design, PLLC*

## TYPICAL PLAN AT WORK AREA

The AutoStrada office system by Knoll offers a frameless window add-on panel. *Photography courtesy of Knoll, Inc.*

In collaborative and call center applications the perpendicular placement of the Knoll work surfaces is an asset to good views. *Photography courtesy of Knoll, Inc.*

plan and section drawings shown on the facing page demonstrate how Envision Design achieved compliance with the LEED credit requirement at Environmental Defense, which attained LEED-CI Silver certification.

Open office systems present unique problems. The higher panel heights offer better privacy and acoustics, yet block views—the worker may as well be sitting in a windowless room. Some manufacturers are providing solutions by designing their panels with vision glazing inserts at eye level, as shown above.

A successful strategy, especially for call centers like the one above—positions the workstations perpendicular to the window wall to minimize view blockage.

There are times when the building configuration, space needs, furniture characteristics, or budget make it impossible to give all workers a good view from their desk chair. In these cases, the designers should make every attempt to place the common areas, corridors, lounges, break rooms, and cafeteria such that these spaces will provide occupants with excellent views—at least for a while.

## What's LEED Got to Do with It?

The Indoor Environmental Quality section of LEED for Commercial Interiors offers 8 credits and up to 17 points. There are also 2 prerequisites.

*EQp1: Minimum IAQ Performance.* Enhance indoor air quality in the occupant space by meeting the requirements of the applicable sections of ASHRAE 62.1-2004. (Required)

*EQp2. Environmental Tobacco Smoke (ETS) Control.* Prevent or minimize the exposure of occupants to ETS by locating in a smoke-free building or, in buildings where smoking is permitted, implement strategies to prevent migration of ETS from designated smoking areas. (Required)

*EQc1: Outdoor Air Delivery Monitoring.* Install permanent monitoring and alarm systems, such as $CO_2$ sensors, that provide feedback on the ventilation system performance. (1 point)

*EQc2: Increased Ventilation.* Provide additional air ventilation above the referenced standards for mechanically ventilated buildings (ASHRAE 62.1-2004) or naturally ventilated buildings (CIBSE). (1 point)

*(continued)*

*EQc3: Construction IAQ Management Plan.* Reduce IAQ problems resulting from the construction/renovation process. The credit has two parts.

> *3.1: During construction.* Develop and implement an IAQ management plan for the construction phase that includes compliance with the referenced standards and protects the HVAC systems and absorptive materials. (1 point)

> *3.2: Before occupancy.* Develop and implement an IAQ management plan for the preoccupancy phase that includes a flush-out procedure or an IAQ test procedure following a recognized protocol. (1 point)

*EQc4: Low-Emitting Materials.* Reduce indoor air contaminants. The credit has five parts.

> *4.1: Adhesives and sealants.* Specify low-VOC materials in compliance with the referenced standards from SCAQMD and Green Seal. (1 point)

> *4.2: Paints and coatings.* Specify low-VOC materials in compliance with the referenced standards from SCAQMD and Green Seal. (1 point)

> *4.3: Carpet systems.* Specify low-VOC materials in compliance with the referenced standard from Carpet and Rug Institute's Green Label Plus. (1 point)

> *4.4: Composite wood and laminate adhesives.* Specify materials with no added urea formaldehyde. (1 point)

> *4.5: Systems furniture and seating.* Specify low-VOC materials in compliance with the referenced standard from Greenguard or EPA's ETV protocol. (1 point)

*EQc5: Indoor Chemical and Pollutant Source Control.* Design to minimize and control hazardous particulates, contaminants, and pollutants from entry into tenant spaces and to achieve physical isolation from the rest of the building. (1 point)

*EQc6: Controllability of Systems.* Provide high levels of lighting and thermal control for individuals and groups. The credit has two parts.

> *6.1: Lighting.* Provide lighting controls for at least 90 percent of occupants and for all shared multi-occupant spaces. (1 point)

> *6.2: Temperature and ventilation.* Provide thermal controls for at least 50 percent of occupants and for all shared multi-occupant spaces. (1 point)

*EQc7: Thermal Comfort.* Provide a thermally comfortable environment. The credit has two parts.

> *7.1: Compliance.* Establish comfort criteria through compliance with ASHRAE 55-2004. (1 point)

> *7.2: Monitoring.* Maintain thermal comfort with a permanent monitoring system and a process for corrective action. (1 point)

*EQc8: Daylight and Views.* Provide occupant connection to the outdoors. The credit has three parts.

> *8.1, 8.2: Daylight 75/90 percent of spaces.* Design the space to achieve maximum daylight effectiveness and to control glare. Earn 1 point for 75 percent of regularly occupied spaces and 1 additional point for 90 percent.

> *8.3: Views for 90 percent of seated spaces.* Design the space to maximize direct line-of-sight view opportunities. (1 point)

Adapted from the LEED Green Building Rating System for Commercial Interiors, Version 2.0. Visit ugsbc.org to access the complete rating system.

# 6
# THE TOOLS OF
# OUR TRADE

n January 1998, *Interiors & Sources* magazine published an article on green resources that began with this quote from Theodore Roosevelt. "Do what you can, with what you have, where you are." The article went on to observe how difficult it is to find, investigate, specify, or order green building materials. Various sources were cited and reviewed to aid designers entering and struggling with this fledging discipline, and in retrospect, there wasn't all that much. Design professionals did, indeed, have to make do with what little they had.

Times have certainly changed. Today's green building practitioner can draw from an impressive reservoir of tools: rating systems, research data, product standards and certifications, assessment guides, publications, and Web sites galore. Many of the sources referenced in the 1998 article are either no longer available or hopelessly out of date. Amazingly, LEED wasn't even mentioned. Under development by the U.S. Green Building Council (USGBC), an organization in its infancy at the time, the green building rating system that we now know as LEED for New Construction was little known and far from certifying the first project. However, the meteoric rise of USGBC and LEED since that time has fueled a similarly explosive growth throughout the green building industry. Green design is widely viewed as the hottest design specialty, and organizations from the government, the NGO world, and the private sector are eager to take part.

Below we present the predominant available tools, beginning with rating systems and design guides, followed by product standards and certifications. This list is comprehensive but hardly complete. New resources are constantly being introduced. In February 2006, for example, USGBC, the American Society of Heating, Refrigerating and Air-Conditioning Engineers (ASHRAE), and the Illuminating Engineering Society of North America (IESNA) announced the development of a new minimum standard for high-performance green buildings. Proposed Standard 189P, Standard for the Design of High-Performance Green Buildings Except Low-Rise Residential Buildings, will bring high-performance green building practices to the mainstream. Using LEED as a key resource, it will be an ANSI-accredited standard that can be incorporated into building codes. It is intended that 189P will eventually become a prerequisite under LEED. Scheduled for completion in 2007, this collaboration is exciting for the industry and for all involved.

> "My goal has always been for USGBC to make the term 'green building' redundant—because all buildings will be green. With Standard 189P, we are taking a huge step towards making that goal a reality."
>
> —Rick Fedrizzi, president, CEO, and founding chairman, U.S. Green Building Council

Each of the reviews that follow is presented in the same format—an opening section pulled from the organization's Web site describing who it is "In Its Own Words." Next is a summary of its offerings, followed by "The Buzz," subjective observations about the group's methodologies, achievements, successes, and disappointments. "The Last Word" offers final comments and reflections. USGBC and LEED are listed first and in more detail than the others in recognition of their prominence and influence.

# Green Building Organizations, Rating Systems, and Design Guides

## *U.S. Green Building Council (USGBC)*

**www.usgbc.org**

### In Its Own Words

The U.S. Green Building Council (USGBC) is the nation's leading nonprofit coalition for advancing buildings that are environmentally responsible, profitable and healthy places to live and work. Major programs supporting its mission include the Council's Leadership in Energy and Environmental Design (LEED) Green Building Rating Systems for New Construction, Existing Buildings, Commercial Interiors and Homes; LEED Workshops; LEED Professional Accreditation; the Greenbuild International Conference & Expo; and a robust local chapter program.

Since its founding in 1993, USGBC has been focused on fulfilling the building and construction industry's vision for its own transformation to high-performance green buildings. Today, it includes nearly 6,000 member companies and organizations —representing more than 1,000% growth in the past four years alone. During that same period, more than 574 million square feet of building space has been registered or certified under LEED, and the annual U.S. market in green building products and services has grown to $7 billion.

Industry-led and consensus-driven, the Council is as diverse as the marketplace itself. Membership includes building owners and end-users, real estate developers, facility managers, architects, designers, engineers, general contractors, subcontractors, product and building system manufacturers, government agencies, and nonprofits. Leaders from within each of these sectors participate in the development of the LEED Rating Systems and the direction of the Council through volunteer service on USGBC's open committees.

Text and logo reprinted with permission, U.S. Green Building Council.

## What It Offers

For many, USGBC is synonymous with LEED. The rating system is the organization's primary product; however, the development process and LEED's introduction into the marketplace has required USGBC to set up a support infrastructure—one that has evolved into an impressive list of additional products, services, and strategic industry alliances.

■ Committees, populated by volunteers with staff support, are at the heart of USGBC. With their unbelievable enthusiasm, depth of knowledge, and commitment, volunteers fuel the Council's growth.

  ■ *Product committees.* Each of the rating systems is written and governed by a core committee made up of both appointed and elected members. The membership at large may participate through corresponding committees. Product committees are also in place for the development of market sector guides— retail, schools, healthcare, labs, lodging, and multiple buildings/campuses.

  ■ *Technical advisory groups (TAGs).* The LEED credit categories—Sustainable Sites, Water Efficiency, Energy and Atmosphere, Materials and Resources, Indoor Environmental Quality—are each supported by a TAG to advise the product committees and to assist with credit interpretation requests and credit ruling appeals. Members of the TAGs are appointed and are required to have specialized knowledge in the relevant subject area.

  ■ *Technical science advisory committees (TSACs).* Established to "provide an independent and impartial forum for vetting the technical (and controversial) aspects of LEED," these provisional committees are appointed by the USGBC Board of Directors. TSACs have been formed to study issues such as PVC and HCFC.

  ■ *Organizational committees.* Established to manage the programs and relationships of the Council, these committees include Government, Education, Emerging Green Builders, Greenbuild, Curriculum and Accreditation, and Greening the Codes.

■ Chapters are the conduit between the national organization and its grassroots members, serving as an important communications link to green building information and advocacy through local programs and outreach. Individuals who work for a USGBC member company may join chapters as full members; others may join as associates. To date, there are sixty-seven chapters and organizing groups in the United States.

■ LEED education is available through the LEED Training Workshops. Full-day workshops and half-day modules are offered on a wide variety of LEED topics, including credit-by-credit instruction in the LEED products as well as specialized subjects such as specification, commissioning, and energy modeling.

■ The LEED Accredited Professional Exam tests knowledge and understanding of green building practices, familiarity with LEED requirements, and the ability to apply them in practice. Successful candidates earn the LEED Accredited Professional (LEED AP) designation. The exam is offered nationwide for LEED-NC (new construction), -CI (commercial interiors), and -EB (existing buildings).

- Greenbuild is USGBC's remarkably successful annual conference and exposition. High-profile keynote speeches, an educational program of seminars and workshops, and a sprawling product expo drew over 10,000 people to the 2005 event, making it likely that networking is Greenbuild's most popular activity.
- Strategic alliances with federal agencies such as the U.S. Department of Energy and the U.S. General Services Administration, professional associations and industry partners have yielded important benefits to the Council and other stakeholders. For example, the annual Federal Summit provides a forum for the Council membership to interact with the government sector. Also, the *Green Building SmartMarket Report,* developed in partnership with McGraw-Hill Construction, provides valuable never-before-seen database information to the green building community.

**The Buzz**

As is to be expected with an industry Goliath, USGBC is both praised and criticized. Admirers point to the market transformation that has occurred, largely through the presence and actions of the organization. As the Council has grown, so has the green building movement, and the connection is not accidental. Prior to the founding of the Council, green buildings were few and far between— Audubon House, the Natural Resources Defense Council's New York office, and the Washington, D.C. office of the Environmental Defense Fund come to mind. The early pioneers—Bob Berkebile, Bill McDonough, and the Randy Croxton/Kirsten Childs team—were struggling for recognition for their work. Today, there are in excess of 4,773 LEED-certified or -registered buildings and interior spaces, in every U.S. state, representing more than one-half billion square feet. More than 25,000 people have sat for and passed the LEED Accreditation Exam.

The Council's growth has been swift—old-timers remember when the entire membership fit into a rather smallish banquet hall—and not without growing pains. There were fewer than ten people on staff when USGBC moved its headquarters to Washington, D.C., in 2000; today the number tops seventy. Problems were inevitable as the staff ramped up and volunteers and paid personnel

learned to work together effectively. Strategic blunders, confusing policies, and bureaucratic nightmares confounded the green community. Design teams struggled with LEED, stymied by a lack of resources and timely responses. Although the metrics were impressive, LEED certifications were falling below expectations. LEED itself was being criticized for being too cumbersome, for being expensive, and, in the case of some credits, for setting an unacceptably low benchmark and, alternatively, too high in other instances. Competing products appeared in the market, and the USGBC began to look vulnerable.

The Council responded to both its critics and its competition with staff and policy changes that have been well received. Most significant are the modifications to the LEED submission, documentation, and certification processes with an online tool developed with Adobe LiveCycle technology. The new system will streamline procedures, practically eliminate paperwork, and offer design teams new options such as documentation submission in two separate phases.

**The Last Word**

USGBC dominates the green building industry and, despite the very public display of its warts and wrinkles, is a strong and growing organization. One of the Council's trademarks is transparency, which has likely contributed to its success and vulnerability. Hopefully the organization will continue to creatively and astutely adapt to the ever-changing green building landscape.

**LEED (Leadership in Energy and Environmental Design) Green Building Rating System**

LEED

Build green. Everyone profits.

**www.usgbc.org**

## In Its Own Words

The LEED Green Building Rating System is a voluntary, consensus-based national standard for developing high-performance, sustainable buildings. USGBC's members, representing every sector of the building industry, developed and continue to refine LEED.

LEED was created to:

- Define "green building" by establishing a common standard of measurement
- Promote integrated, whole-building design practices
- Recognize environmental leadership in the building industry
- Stimulate green competition
- Raise consumer awareness of green building benefits
- Transform the building market

LEED provides a complete framework for assessing building performance and meeting sustainability goals. Based on well-founded scientific standards, LEED emphasizes state-of-the-art strategies for sustainable site development, water savings, energy efficiency, materials selection and indoor environmental quality. LEED recognizes achievements and promotes expertise in green building through a comprehensive system offering project certification, professional accreditation, training and practical resources.

Text and logo reprinted with permission, U.S. Green Building Council.

## What It Offers

There are currently six LEED Rating Systems available or under development:

- LEED for New Construction (NC) is the "original" LEED and is used for new buildings and major renovations. LEED was first introduced in August 1998 and officially launched in March 2000; the most recent edition, Version 2.2, was released in November 2005.
- LEED for Commercial Interiors (CI) was developed for use by the tenant improvement market and others who do not have control over the building shell and major systems. The credits only address items within the project's scope. Committee work on CI began in 1999 and was launched in November 2004.
- LEED for Existing Buildings (EB) addresses whole-building operations and maintenance for facility managers, building owners, and operators; unlike NC and CI, it is intended to be used after construction is complete. EB was launched in November 2004.
- LEED for Core and Shell (CS) is intended for speculative commercial buildings in which the owner does not control the interior fit-out. CS responds to the developer's need for market differentiation through LEED prior to project completion by allowing for precertification. CS was launched in summer 2006.
- LEED for Homes (H) is being developed by USGBC in cooperation with selected "Home Providers"—local and regional organizations that are working with homebuilders during the pilot phase of the program. A rating system for single-family and low-rise residential communities, LEED Homes is scheduled for launch in 2007.
- LEED for Neighborhood Development (ND), a cooperative venture of the USGBC, the Congress for the New Urbanism, and the Natural Resources Defense Council, will address the issues of smart growth and urbanism as they apply to neighborhood design. Still in its pilot phase, ND is expected to launch in 2008.

In addition to the rating systems, USGBC is developing specialized products for retail, labs, campuses and other multiple building projects, schools, lodging, and healthcare to focus on the specific needs of different building types. LEED for Labs, for example, will address the unique ventilation and process load requirements for laboratories.

The LEED rating systems are only the beginning. USGBC provides multiple resources to aid in documentation and certification of each product.

- The Reference Guide is the design team's bible, providing details about credit intents, achieving the credit requirements and complying with the documentation requirements. It also includes summaries of reference standards, calculation methods, formulas, and recommended design strategies and technologies.

**LEED·CI**

FOR COMMERCIAL INTERIORS

REFERENCE GUIDE

Version 2.0

Second Edition
December 2005

The LEED for Commercial Interiors Reference Guide

- LEED-Online is a user-friendly interface that has allowed the LEED process to go paperless. Powered by Adobe LiveCycle technology, team members are able to upload credit templates, view CIRs, manage the project details, and submit 100 percent of their documentation online.

### The Buzz

Developing a LEED product is like giving birth—painful, but ultimately rewarding. The process is long and arduous due partly to the USGBC's consensus process, one of its virtues yet also one of its shortcomings. In an effort to get it right, the folks writing the rating systems labor over every credit, ad infinitum, to ensure that all constituent voices are heard, which is critical for success. The lengthy process is also due to the fact that many green building issues are fuzzy, with no obvious resolution, and different stakeholders will, in good faith, argue widely divergent opinions.

> "A blissfulness of ignorance pervaded this band of people who started out thinking that all we had to do was put a few criteria down and that would be it. We didn't know what we didn't know and we just forged ahead and assumed that somehow the problems would resolve themselves. Not to downgrade the importance of the technical issues, but the biggest challenges have been implementation, diffusion and operations."
>
> —Rob Watson, senior scientist, Natural Resources Defense Council, on the writing of the first LEED rating system in 1995

- The Scorecard is a checklist of all the prerequisites and credits with their point totals. It is a handy way to set goals during the early planning stages of the project and to track progress.
- Letter Templates are customized spreadsheets, available online, to simplify the documentation process. Information prompts, easy-to-use data fields, and integrated calculators are built in and user-friendly.
- Credit Interpretation Rulings (CIRs) allow project teams to seek guidance and feedback on the likely outcome of a proposed strategy prior to submitting documentation. Registered project design teams have access to prior inquiries through a searchable database.

LEED is, and always will be, in a constant state of refinement. Minor changes are made as needed, but major changes must go through a public comment and ballot process. However, to ensure that the LEED credits remain flexible, technically relevant, and market savvy, Performance/Intent Equivalent Alternative Compliance Paths (PIEACPs) are now accepted in lieu of the "as written" compliance path, provided a lengthy list of procedures are followed. Also, aligning credit changes within

# Easy Credits/Not-So-Easy Credits

Many of the users of LEED have a love/hate relationship with the rating system, with much of the emotion centered on the credits. Some are affectionately labeled "low-hanging fruit" because they are considered "easy." Others strike fear in the hearts of design teams.

Which credits are most often and least often achieved? Table 6-1 lists the percentage of the first thirty-two LEED-CI certified pilot projects and the points attained from credits at both ends of the spectrum.

### Table 6-1: LEED-CI Credits Achieved by 32 Pilot Participants

| Most Often Achieved (by percentage) | | Least Often Achieved (by percentage) | |
|---|---|---|---|
| 100% | EQc4.3: Low-Emitting Materials—Carpet Systems | 12.5% | EQc4.5: Low-Emitting Materials, Systems Furniture and Seating |
| 100% | Innovation c2: LEED-AP | 12.5% | EQc5: Indoor Chemical and Pollutant Source Control |
| 96.9% | Innovation c1 (varies by project) | 12.5% | EQc6: Controllability of Systems* |
| 93.8% | SSc3.1: Alternative Transportation—Public Transportation Access | 15.6% | MRc1.1: Tenant Space, Long-Term Commitment |
| 90.6% | MRc2.1: Construction Waste Management—Divert 50% from Landfill | 18.8% | MRc3.2: Resource Reuse, 10% |
| 90.6% | MRc5.1: Regional Materials—20% Manufactured Locally | 21.9% | EAc5: Measurement & Verification* |
| 90.6% | EQc4.2: Low-Emitting Materials—Paints and Coatings | | |

\* Credit has been revised since the pilot version.

the different rating systems is challenging and can be confusing to the public. For example, LEED-NC Version 2.2 altered some of the credits that are also found, but haven't changed, in LEED-CI. Conversely, CI Version 2.0 introduced changes to credits a full year before NC adopted them.

There has to be a better way to manage change within LEED. USGBC, recognizing some of the process problems and complaints, announced refinements and enhancements in November 2005. For example, the Council is placing more trust in its customers by eliminating credit audits and limiting documentation requirements to the instruments of service that are typically created in the course of project work rather than asking for additional documents created specifically for LEED.

Work has just begun on LEED Version 3.0, a far-reaching revision that is already being viewed as the panacea—the LEED we've always dreamed about. Tom Hicks, the vice president of LEED for USGBC, anticipating a two- to three-year development cycle, won't promise that level of perfection. "The timetable, scope, etc. are not explicitly known at this point," commented Hicks. "V3 will serve as a platform for all of the LEED rating systems and will likely include LCA and regional weighting; however, until the scope is nailed down these are not certainties."

**The Last Word**

Michael Arny, founding chair of LEED-EB, has said that LEED is the triumph of good over perfect—an apt description.

# LEED-CI in the Real World: Getting It Done

CTG, Inc. is an environmental engineering firm based in Irvine, California. Its founder, Malcolm Lewis, has participated in the development of LEED since its inception, and he and his colleagues have worked on more than fifty LEED projects. It was logical, then, that they would register in the LEED-CI pilot program when the firm decided to expand and renovate its offices. The project is interesting because it illustrates both the opportunities and pitfalls encountered by design teams, even ones as experienced and knowledgeable in green buildings as the CTG folks.

Located in a one-story, chevron-shaped concrete tilt-up building in an office park, the firm decided to expand into attached vacant suites to either side of their existing location. The expansion area included an 1,800-square-foot warehouse space. This new space presented new design challenges and possibilities. Whereas the offices that it had occupied for the last eight years and the majority of the new office space were built out in a typical fashion, with 9-foot ceilings, standard windows, and an overhead HVAC distribution system, the warehouse addition was unconditioned space with a 15-foot ceiling height and two truck bays with roll-up doors.

CTG approached LEED-CI by making project decisions that made sense for the firm, rather than arbitrarily selecting a certification level and designing to it. "We didn't make decisions based on getting points," said project manager Marc Cohen, "but on what was feasible. We looked at the scorecard [see facing page] and realistically assessed which of the points would work for this project. Silver seemed achievable."

Once a design team determines that it can get the prerequisites, the next step is to identify which of the credits are easily attained. For CTG they included:

◆ *Water efficiency points.* Low-flow lavatories and toilets by several different manufacturers were installed.

◆ *Enhanced commissioning.* CTG provides this service to clients, after all!

◆ *Energy use measurement and payment accountability.* CTG pays its own utility bills separate from rent payments.

◆ *Building reuse.* Only a few walls were removed, and the interior nonstructural components were maintained.

◆ *Resource reuse.* Furniture and furnishings were reused or salvaged.

◆ *Low-emitting materials.* CTG rejected the standard paint and carpet from the property owner and paid a cost premium for low-VOC products.

Other credits were more difficult due to building limitations and contractor and owner resistance. The landlord, for example, would not allow penetration of the roof membrane, so skylights, which would have helped achieve the daylighting credits, were not installed. However, other strategies were employed that make the CTG workplace a more pleasant and healthier environment, whether or not they contributed to the LEED point totals.

The lighting design plan is one of the most successful elements in the office, in both the old and new sections. Light power density levels average .85 to .9 W/sf across the entire suite, with 20 to 25 footcandles at the desktops. In the low-ceiling (nine-foot) areas, pendant-mounted direct/indirect fixtures with single T5HO lamps are suspended 18 inches down from ceiling. The ceiling tiles are an extremely smooth high reflectance white, creating a glowing effect and providing a uniform ambient light. On the warehouse side, the fixtures are similar but use two T8 lamps with wing reflectors made from a thin, flexible plastic; they illuminate the workstations while also providing illumination for the high-bay warehouse ceiling. Foil-backed batt insulation is installed between

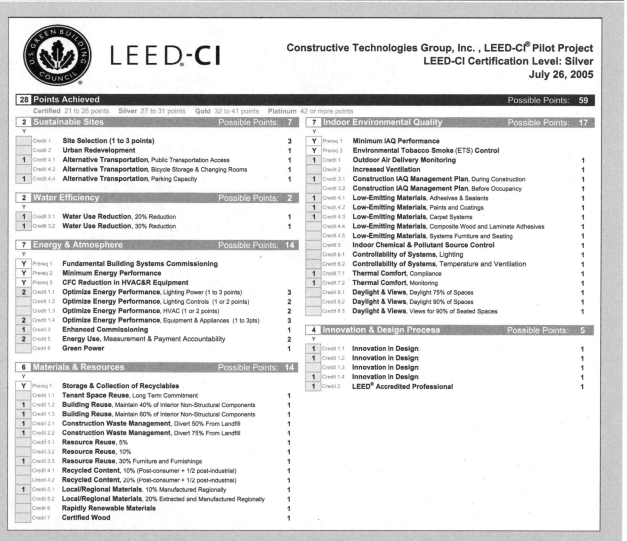

**LEED-CI**

Constructive Technologies Group, Inc. , LEED-CI® Pilot Project
LEED-CI Certification Level: Silver
July 26, 2005

| **28** | **Points Achieved** | | | Possible Points: | **59** |
|---|---|---|---|---|---|

**Certified** 21 to 26 points    **Silver** 27 to 31 points    **Gold** 32 to 41 points    **Platinum** 42 or more points

| **2** | **Sustainable Sites** | Possible Points: | **7** |
|---|---|---|---|
| Y | | | |
| | Credit 1 | Site Selection (1 to 3 points) | 3 |
| | Credit 2 | Urban Redevelopment | 1 |
| 1 | Credit 4.1 | Alternative Transportation, Public Transportation Access | 1 |
| | Credit 4.2 | Alternative Transportation, Bicycle Storage & Changing Rooms | 1 |
| 1 | Credit 4.4 | Alternative Transportation, Parking Capacity | 1 |

| **2** | **Water Efficiency** | Possible Points: | **2** |
|---|---|---|---|
| Y | | | |
| 1 | Credit 3.1 | Water Use Reduction, 20% Reduction | 1 |
| 1 | Credit 3.2 | Water Use Reduction, 30% Reduction | 1 |

| **7** | **Energy & Atmosphere** | Possible Points: | **14** |
|---|---|---|---|
| Y | | | |
| Y | Prereq 1 | Fundamental Building Systems Commissioning | |
| Y | Prereq 2 | Minimum Energy Performance | |
| Y | Prereq 3 | CFC Reduction in HVAC&R Equipment | |
| 2 | Credit 1.1 | Optimize Energy Performance, Lighting Power (1 to 3 points) | 3 |
| | Credit 1.2 | Optimize Energy Performance, Lighting Controls (1 or 2 points) | 2 |
| | Credit 1.3 | Optimize Energy Performance, HVAC (1 or 2 points) | 2 |
| 2 | Credit 1.4 | Optimize Energy Performance, Equipment & Appliances (1 to 3pts) | 3 |
| 1 | Credit 3 | Enhanced Commissioning | 1 |
| 2 | Credit 5 | Energy Use, Measurement & Payment Accountability | 2 |
| | Credit 6 | Green Power | 1 |

| **6** | **Materials & Resources** | Possible Points: | **14** |
|---|---|---|---|
| Y | | | |
| Y | Prereq 1 | Storage & Collection of Recyclables | |
| | Credit 1.1 | Tenant Space Reuse, Long Term Commitment | 1 |
| 1 | Credit 1.2 | Building Reuse, Maintain 40% of Interior Non-Structural Components | 1 |
| 1 | Credit 1.3 | Building Reuse, Maintain 60% of Interior Non-Structural Components | 1 |
| 1 | Credit 2.1 | Construction Waste Management, Divert 50% From Landfill | 1 |
| 1 | Credit 2.2 | Construction Waste Management, Divert 75% From Landfill | 1 |
| | Credit 3.1 | Resource Reuse, 5% | 1 |
| | Credit 3.2 | Resource Reuse, 10% | 1 |
| 1 | Credit 3.3 | Resource Reuse, 30% Furniture and Furnishings | 1 |
| | Credit 4.1 | Recycled Content, 10% (Post-consumer + 1/2 post-industrial) | 1 |
| | Credit 4.2 | Recycled Content, 20% (Post-consumer + 1/2 post-industrial) | 1 |
| 1 | Credit 5.1 | Local/Regional Materials, 10% Manufactured Regionally | 1 |
| | Credit 5.2 | Local/Regional Materials, 20% Extracted and Manufactured Regionally | 1 |
| | Credit 6 | Rapidly Renewable Materials | 1 |
| | Credit 7 | Certified Wood | 1 |

| **7** | **Indoor Environmental Quality** | Possible Points: | **17** |
|---|---|---|---|
| Y | | | |
| Y | Prereq 1 | Minimum IAQ Performance | |
| Y | Prereq 2 | Environmental Tobacco Smoke (ETS) Control | |
| 1 | Credit 1 | Outdoor Air Delivery Monitoring | 1 |
| | Credit 2 | Increased Ventilation | 1 |
| | Credit 3.1 | Construction IAQ Management Plan, During Construction | 1 |
| | Credit 3.2 | Construction IAQ Management Plan, Before Occupancy | 1 |
| 1 | Credit 4.1 | Low-Emitting Materials, Adhesives & Sealants | 1 |
| 1 | Credit 4.2 | Low-Emitting Materials, Paints and Coatings | 1 |
| 1 | Credit 4.3 | Low-Emitting Materials, Carpet Systems | 1 |
| | Credit 4.4 | Low-Emitting Materials, Composite Wood and Laminate Adhesives | 1 |
| | Credit 4.5 | Low-Emitting Materials, Systems Furniture and Seating | 1 |
| | Credit 5 | Indoor Chemical & Pollutant Source Control | 1 |
| | Credit 6.1 | Controllability of Systems, Lighting | 1 |
| | Credit 6.2 | Controllability of Systems, Temperature and Ventilation | 1 |
| 1 | Credit 7.1 | Thermal Comfort, Compliance | 1 |
| 1 | Credit 7.2 | Thermal Comfort, Monitoring | 1 |
| | Credit 8.1 | Daylight & Views, Daylight 75% of Spaces | 1 |
| | Credit 8.2 | Daylight & Views, Daylight 90% of Spaces | 1 |
| | Credit 8.3 | Daylight & Views, Views for 90% of Seated Spaces | 1 |

| **4** | **Innovation & Design Process** | Possible Points: | **5** |
|---|---|---|---|
| Y | | | |
| 1 | Credit 1.1 | Innovation in Design: | 1 |
| 1 | Credit 1.2 | Innovation in Design: | 1 |
| | Credit 1.3 | Innovation in Design: | 1 |
| 1 | Credit 1.4 | Innovation in Design: | 1 |
| 1 | Credit 2 | LEED® Accredited Professional | 1 |

CTG's LEED-CI Scorecard reflects the points earned on the way to a Silver Rating. © *Constructive Technologies Group, Inc.*
*All rights reserved*

the exposed truss joists and has been sprayed with two coats of white low-VOC paint to maximize light reflectance from the suspended fixtures. Light levels don't feel as low as they are because no high-contrast areas exist and shadows on the desks are minimized. Although task lights are provided, very few people use them on a regular basis. Two points were achieved for EA credit 1.1, lighting power; however, although occupancy sensors were installed, the lighting fixtures in the majority of the office spaces didn't lend themselves to daylight dimming and the designers were not able to put enough controls into the suite to achieve the threshold of EA credit 1.2, lighting controls.

*(continued)*

In the new space CTG chose to test a HVAC technology not common in buildings in the area before recommending it to clients. As shown in the photograph, a displacement ventilation system was designed with fabric ducts that run vertically, bringing air down from the ceiling into two perforated metal thermal displacement diffusers and delivering it to the occupied zones. The air is delivered at a fairly low velocity and at warmer temperatures than would be required with a traditional overhead system, which would have used a lot more energy driving cooler conditioned air down from the high ceilings. "We have a moderate climate," said Cohen, "and rather than sizing the system to accommodate temperature extremes, as an engineer would typically do, we cut back to achieve thermal comfort for 99 percent of the time. We didn't want to take the energy hit for oversizing."

CTG's newly expanded offices include a renovated warehouse space with 15-foot ceilings and two truck bays converted into large windows. © *Constructive Technologies Group, Inc. All rights reserved*

Despite this inventive mechanical solution, CTG was not able to achieve the LEED-CI energy credit (EA1.3) for optimizing HVAC performance because the displacement ventilation system serves only a small percentage of the office. EQ credit 2, increased ventilation, was also thwarted by the overhead system's air-handling units, proving that even the best engineering firms run into building limitations that prevent their projects from achieving higher point totals.

EQ credit 7.1, thermal comfort compliance, was fairly easy to achieve for this project and any others located in a mild climate zone. The second part of the credit, thermal comfort monitoring, relies on a system called Aircuity, a Web-based monitoring tool with sensors installed throughout the space that gather information on temperature, humidity, $CO_2$, and particulates at approximately one-minute intervals. CTG is beta-testing the product in its office and is pleased with its monitoring ability. However, LEED reviewers denied the submission of this system as an innovation point because of its reliance on a single product and because it had been used to achieve the thermal comfort credits. Double dipping, as it's called, is not allowed in LEED.

Three innovation points were granted, one for educational signage throughout the building, another for green housekeeping, and the third for use of a climate-neutral carpet certified by a third-party program to lessen the life cycle global warming impact of major building materials through greenhouse gas reduction.

CTG would have liked to have had other opportunities for higher point totals, as would most every LEED project. But the firm is delighted with its handsome and healthy new offices and with the LEED-CI Silver certification plaque on the wall.

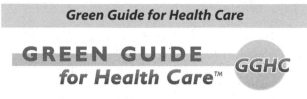

### Green Guide for Health Care

www.gghc.org

## In Its Own Words

The Green Guide for Health Care is the healthcare sector's first quantifiable sustainable design toolkit integrating enhanced environmental and health principles and practices into the planning, design, construction, operations and maintenance of their facilities. This Guide provides the healthcare sector with a voluntary, self-certifying metric toolkit of best practices that designers, owners, and operators can use to guide and evaluate their progress toward high performance healing environments.

Healthcare facilities present both a challenge and opportunity in the development and implementation of sustainable design, construction and operations practices. Issues such as 24/7 operations, energy and water use intensity, chemical use, infection control requirements and formidable regulatory requirements can pose significant obstacles to the implementation of currently accepted sustainability protocols. Furthermore, it is appropriate that guidelines customized for the healthcare sector reflect the fundamental organizational mission to protect and enhance individual and community health, and acknowledge the intrinsic relationship between the built environment and ecological health. As the healthcare sector develops a design language for high performance healing environments, it has the opportunity to highlight the associated health-based benefits. This, in turn, can inspire the broader adoption of health-based design principles in other building sectors.

Text and logo reprinted with permission, GGHC.

## What It Offers

The current version of the Green Guide for Health Care (GGHC) 2.1 Pilot looks somewhat like LEED, having borrowed the credit structure and numbering scheme; however, there are differences. Obviously directed at one mar-

ket segment, the Green Guide identifies the specific health concerns addressed by the credits with oversight by a medical expert, Dr. Ted Schettler, MD, MPH. Recognizing the importance of maintaining the environmental profile of the healthcare facility, a separate section addresses operations and maintenance protocols. More significantly, the GGHC is a voluntary self-certifying tool for users to internally track compliance with the system's requirements and goals. While the GGHC does not intend to establish a separate certification system, the pilot phase will be used to determine appropriate threshold designations to distinguish self-certifying achievement levels for GGHC 2.2.

The checklist looks very similar to LEED, with many of the same credits, but has added prerequisites for an integrated design program and an environmental health program. Requirements have also been added for healthcare-related issues such as contaminant prevention and medical equipment efficiency. Another difference is the "not applicable" column available for credits that are physically unattainable by a project.

In addition to the Green Guide, GGHC has set up a Web-based online resource for peer-to-peer discussions of how to "green" healthcare facilities. This forum is also being used as a dialogue to explore refinements to the program. Participation in the forum is currently limited to members of teams directly involved in the design, construction, and/or management of projects registered in the GGHC pilot program.

## The Buzz

Although the GGHC is being promoted as a best-practices guide rather than a consensus-based standard, the development process has been rigorous, aboveboard, and complete, including a public comment period. A steering committee of well-respected, independent, and diverse industry leaders guides the direction of the program and prohibits participation by organizations with direct financial interests in the products or certification services addressed by the Green Guide.

Conversations between GGHC and USGBC have explored the possibility of linking the Green Guide to the LEED system, but some credit incompatibilities may present obstacles. However, both organizations support, in principle, a partnership reflecting their long-standing collaborative relationship—one that is in good hands with Gail Vittori, GGHC's steering committee convener, who also heads up USGBC's LEED healthcare product committee.

### The Last Word

Healthcare facilities have come under attack for being unhealthy environments, adding to the stress and even illness of occupants. The Green Guide for Healthcare, though still a work in progress, is a valuable road map for the designers and operators of these buildings.

## The Collaborative for High Performance Schools (CHPS)

the

collaborative

for high

performance

schools

**www.chps.net**

### In Its Own Words

The Collaborative for High Performance Schools (CHPS, often pronounced "chips") aims to increase the energy efficiency of schools in California by marketing information, services, and incentive programs directly to school districts and designers.

CHPS can help school districts and their design teams bring better performance into the classroom. Its goal is to improve the quality of education for California's children and facilitate the design of learning environments that are resource efficient, healthy, comfortable, well lit, and contain the amenities needed for a quality education.

High performance schools achieve these goals by using a whole building, integrated design strategy that incorporates the best of today's ideas and technologies. From the beginning of the design process, each of the building elements (windows, walls, building materials, air-conditioning, landscaping, etc.) is considered part of an integrated system of interacting components. Choices in one area often affect other building systems; integrated design leverages these interactions to maximize the overall building performance.

Text and logo reprinted with permission, CHPS.

### What It Offers

CHPS provides resources to school districts and the design community to aid in the development of high-performance schools through *Best Practice Manuals,* a reference guide offered in four volumes:

- *Volume I—Planning* assists the people in the school district with developing the necessary design strategies to build a high-performance school.
- *Volume II—Design* is a set of technical guidelines providing information and recommendations on building systems and design.
- *Volume III—Criteria* establishes the standards that define a high-performance school as listed on a scorecard with six sections: Sites, Water, Energy, Materials, Indoor Environmental Quality, and District Resolutions (which institutionalize high-performance goals at a local level).
- *Volume IV—Maintenance and Operations* contains guidelines to help schools continue to perform as they were intended throughout the life of the facility.

CHPS offers many other resources such as trainings, seminars, and publications. One example is the list of products for use in classrooms that have been certified to meet the low-emitting materials criteria in California's Section 01350 governing indoor air quality in buildings.

### The Buzz

CHPS is a California design guide that has found a nationwide audience. Originally developed in 1999 to improve the performance of California schools, CHPS has expanded to include national and state specific versions of the manuals. However, the guide does remain California-centric, using Title 24 as its energy baseline rather than ASHRAE 90.1, the referenced energy standard in LEED. Recognized and respected as a very rigorous standard, CHPS may one day align with LEED for Schools. Charles Eley, CHPS executive director, is an active USGBC member and functions as a valuable link between the two organizations.

## The Last Word

California educates one out of every eight students in America, but its current building infrastructure is aging, and more than 30 percent of existing facilities need a major renovation. CHPS is improving the odds that the state's students will learn in high-performance environments.

## The Green Building Initiative (GBI) and Green Globes

www.thegbi.org

## In Its Own Words

*Who We Are:* The Green Building Initiative is a non-profit network of building industry leaders committed to bringing green to mainstream residential and commercial construction. The GBI believes in building approaches that are environmentally progressive, but also practical and affordable for builders to implement.

*What We Do:* The Green Building Initiative works with builders, architects, developers, engineers, and their associations to facilitate understanding and acceptance of sensible green building practices.

*Vision:* The Green Building Initiative envisions a future in which energy-efficient, healthy and environmentally conscious construction, commonly known as green building, becomes the norm instead of the exception within the residential and commercial building industries.

*Mission:* The mission of the Green Building Initiative is to promote practical green building approaches to energy efficient and environmentally sustainable building practices commonly referred to as "green building." The Green Building Initiative is focused on ensuring the availability of credible and practical green building approaches within the residential and commercial construction industries.

Text and logo reprinted with permission, GBI.

## What It Offers

Green Globes, a product of the Green Building Initiative (GBI), is a green management tool for the building design and construction industry. Half of GBI's work is residential, in partnership with the National Association of Home Builders (NAHB) and its Model Green Home Building Guidelines. Adapted from a Canadian protocol, Green Globes was introduced into the United States in 2004. Designed for new commercial buildings, the process begins as a self-assessment using a 150-item questionnaire with yes/no/not applicable check boxes. Green design attributes are listed in the following categories: project management, site, energy, water, resources, emissions/effluents and indoor environment. The use of the checklist encourages design teams to consider green building strategies such as integrated design, acoustics, and life cycle analysis, whereas the "not applicable" option recognizes that some points may be out of reach for some projects.

The questionnaire may be used during the design phase and then again during construction. A Green Globes–trained architect or engineer may grant certification following a review of the questionnaire at the project's end and award a rating of one to four globes.

The American National Standards Institute (ANSI) has formally recognized the Green Building Initiative as an accredited national standards developer. In turn, the organization has submitted an application to establish Green Globes as an American National Standard.

### The Buzz

Critics refer to Green Globes as "LEED light," rewarding intent rather than achievement or building performance. GBI's lack of transparency—who are its members and how is it funded?—and the hassles of actually gaining access to the questionnaire are in sharp contrast to the openness of LEED and ready accessibility of most of its resources.

However, GBI has a well-financed and active advocacy effort in place, and some state governments are considering recognizing Green Globes in addition to or even in place of LEED. In early 2006 the U.S. federal government announced its intent to remain rating-system-neutral.

### The Last Word

Green Globes, the first serious competitor to LEED, is viewed as a useful tool that has not to date earned widespread acceptance or credibility.

# Product Standards and Certifications

Product certifications have been around for decades, providing first-, second-, and third-party audits and verifications. They make the designer's work easier by establishing standards and guidelines that certify compliance with codes and laws and contribute to making the development, manufacturing, and supply of products and services safer and more reliable. A terrific example with which almost everyone is familiar is Underwriters Laboratories Inc. (UL), an independent, not-for-profit product safety testing and certification organization whose labels can be found on electrical products. It describes itself not only as a household name in the United States but as "one of the most recognized, reputable conformity assessment providers in the world."

Few would argue with its success. Seventeen billion UL marks have appeared on products since their founding in 1894. Most consumers know what the UL mark means, depend upon it to verify product safety, and don't question its value. However, not all product certifications are as easy to trust. They haven't been around as long, they have not yet achieved widespread acceptance, or their authenticity may be challenged by others. However, independent, tech-

nically expert evaluations by a third party without a financial interest in the product are enormously important, and the green building industry should be encouraged by their development.[1]

## General Product Standards and Certifications

> ### BEES (Building for Environmental and Economic Sustainability)

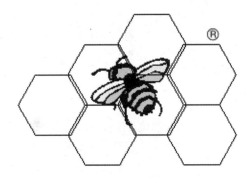

www.bfrl.nist.gov

### In Its Own Words

The Building and Fire Research Laboratory of the National Institute of Standards and Technology (NIST) has developed and automated an approach for measuring the life cycle environmental and economic performance of building products. Known as BEES, the tool is based on consensus standards and designed to be practical, flexible, and transparent. BEES reduces complex, science-based technical content (e.g., over 400 material and energy flows from raw material extraction through product disposal) to decision-enabling results and delivers them in a visually intuitive graphical format.

Text and logo reprinted with permission, NIST.

### What It Offers

NIST is the driving force behind BEES, a product life cycle assessment software tool that measures and compares the environmental and economic performance of building products. Aimed at designers, builders, and product manufacturers, BEES includes actual environmental and economic performance data for 118 generic products and 80 brand-specific products from 14 companies.

The purpose of BEES is to develop and implement a systematic methodology for selecting building products that achieve the most appropriate balance between environmental and economic performance based on the decision maker's values. The methodology is based on consensus standards and is designed to be practical, flexible, and transparent.

BEES measures the environmental performance of building products by using the life cycle assessment approach specified in the ISO 14040 series of standards. All stages in the life of a product are analyzed: raw material acquisition, manufacture, transportation, installation, use, and recycling and waste management. Economic performance is measured using the ASTM standard life cycle cost method, which covers the costs of initial investment, replacement, operation, maintenance and repair, and disposal. Environmental and economic performance are combined into an overall performance measure using the ASTM standard for Multi-Attribute Decision Analysis. For the entire BEES analysis, building products are defined and classified according to the ASTM standard classification for building elements known as UNIFORMAT II.

## The Buzz

Reviewers have praised BEES Version 3.0, released in 2002. With this new version, BEES "incorporates new systems for calculating aggregated LCA scores, introduces additional impact categories, and adds a whole new feature in the form of brand-specific products," comments Nadav Malin in *Environmental Building News*. However, Malin continues, "Regardless of the tool used, we strongly recommend taking LCA results with a grain of salt, and questioning the underlying assumptions before relying on the outcomes. BEES results are still heavily dependent on many debatable assumptions, and they are subject to very large margins of error. But the remaining drawbacks are more a reflection of the state of life cycle analysis today than they are a problem with BEES itself." [2]

## The Last Word

Life cycle assessments are complex. BEES software simplifies the process, but the concepts remain difficult.

## MBDC: Cradle to Cradle (C2C)

**△ MBDC**

www.mbdc.com

### Its Own Words

MBDC is articulating and putting into practice a new design paradigm, what *Time* calls "a unified philosophy that—in demonstrable and practical ways—is changing the design of the world." Instead of designing cradle-to-grave products, dumped in landfills at the end of their "life," MBDC transforms industry by creating products for cradle-to-cradle cycles, whose materials are perpetually circulated in closed loops. Maintaining materials in closed loops maximizes material value without damaging ecosystems.

Cradle to Cradle Certification provides a company with a means to differentiate its product within the marketplace, defining tangible achievement and providing credibility. Within the certification process, MBDC evaluates a material or product's ingredients and the complete formulation for human and environmental health impacts throughout its lifecycle and its potential for being truly recycled or safely composted. Certification of a finished product also requires the evaluation of energy-use quantity and quality (i.e., relative proportion of renewable energy), water-use quantity, water-effluent quality, and workplace ethics associated with manufacturing.

If a candidate material or product is found to achieve the necessary criteria, it is certified as a Silver, Gold, or Platinum product, or as a Technical/Biological Nutrient (a classification available for homogeneous materials or less complex products). MBDC is developing a system and guidelines by which companies who have certified products can license the use of the Cradle to Cradle brand for marketing.

Text and logo reprinted with permission, MBDC

### What It Offers

As an alternative to the cradle-to-grave legacy of the industrial revolution (built on a linear, take-make-waste model of material flows), Cradle to Cradle (C2C) presents a new vision based on three basic principles:

- *Waste equals food.* Materials can be continually reused as either a biological or technical nutrient.
- *Use current solar income.* Sunlight is the earth's one perpetual source of energy.
- *Celebrate diversity.* Natural systems thrive on diversity and complexity. Life burgeons with rich variety in response to evolving niches.

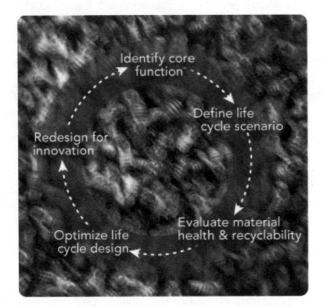

Cradle to Cradle design includes the evaluation and optimization of all chemical and material inputs throughout product life cycles.

MBDC offers two Cradle to Cradle tracks for certifying a product:

- *Cradle to Cradle Technical/Biological Nutrient Certification.* A pass-fail approach for materials and products homogeneous in nature using Material and Nutrient (Re)utilization criteria.
- *Cradle to Cradle Product Certification.* A three-tiered approach consisting of Silver, Gold, and Platinum levels and five categories of metrics: Materials, Nutrient (Re)utilization, Energy, Water, and Social Responsibility.[3]

Certified products are reviewed annually by MBDC to assure that no major changes have been made prior to re-certification.

### The Buzz

C2C began with the 1995 collaboration between McDonough Braungart Design Chemistry, the Rohner textile factory in Switzerland, chemical giant Ciba-Geigy, and Susan Lyons, a former design director for Designtex when they developed the first commercially viable and compostable textile—the McDonough Collection of Lifecycle Climatex fabrics. The group made news again when it offered the technology to competitors.

The C2C protocol is very intensive and though it examines water, energy, and social responsibility, its primary focus is on materials. All material components are identified (down to the 100 ppm level), classified, and color-coded: green indicates little or no risk, yellow indicates low to moderate risk, and red indicates a high hazard associated with the use of the substance.

Examples of certified products include Haworth's Zody chair (Gold) and Steelcase's Think chair (Silver). Solutia Ultron Fiber has been certified as a technical nutrient and Classic Wool Flannel by Pendleton Woolen Mills as a biological nutrient. (See Chapter 4 for more information on many of these C2C certified products.)

### The Last Word

Though McDonough and Braungart are viewed within the green design field as among the earliest and most prolific pioneers, the C2C protocol is only now emerging as a practical design paradigm.

## *Scientific Certification Systems (SCS)*

SCIENTIFIC CERTIFICATION SYSTEMS

**www.scscertified.com**

## In Its Own Words

SCS was established in 1984 as the nation's first third-party certifier for testing pesticide residues in fresh produce. Over 20 years the company has become a leading standards developer and independent certifier of multiple facets of the food industry and of the environmentally sound management of forests, marine habitats, and a wide variety of manufacturing-related businesses.

### HOW WE'RE DIFFERENT

SCS takes very seriously its independence and credibility as a third-party certifier. We follow established and recognized guidelines to ensure our objectivity in granting certification. No member of our team, including our contract consultants, has any financial, management, or ownership connections with any of the clients we certify. All SCS certification programs are based upon three key principles:

- *Independent*—Certification should be granted by an independent, third-party with no vested interest in the product that is being certified. Following the tradition of auditors in other industries, SCS charges strictly for the professional services that it delivers, but makes no guarantee that a certification will be granted.
- *Scientifically Verifiable*—All claims must be scientifically verifiable; the results must be reproducible by others using the same predetermined criteria and procedures set forth in the standard—with assurance of data reliability. If a claim cannot be verified using scientific methods of evaluation, then it should not be certified.
- *Transparent*—The standard and certification process—e.g., details regarding required sample collection, laboratory testing, and declaration of modeling parameters—must be publicly available.

Text and logo reprinted with permission, SCS.

## What It Offers

Founded in 1984 as third-party certifier in the food industry, SCS moved into the certification of green buildings and products in the late 1980s. A for-profit multidisciplinary scientific organization, SCS works with hundreds of companies and other organizations to evaluate and certify environmental programs and products. Its work is based on scientifically defensible, field-verifiable, performance measurement systems developed by SCS and others such as ISO, ASTM, and NSF.

SCS certifies specific single-attribute claims, such as recycled content, indoor air quality performance, and biodegradability. Hundreds of companies have put their products through the process. SCS is also known for its more comprehensive certification programs such as Environmentally Preferable Products and Services (EPP). EPP was established in response to Executive Order 13101, which directs federal agencies and their contractors to identify and purchase "products and services that have a lesser or reduced effect on human health and the environment when compared to other products and services that serve the same purpose." Some companies have utilized both single-attribute and EPP claims. For example, C&A Floorcoverings began with certification of recycled content of its ER3 carpet tile products and then sought certification under the EPP program when it became available in 2003.

The EPP designation is also used by the EPA for its environmentally preferable purchasing program to identify materials in its database. SCS's program is independent from that established by the federal government but is consistent with its guidance.

EPP certifications are based on a detailed and stringent five-step certification process including an audit and an on-site inspection of manufacturing facilities, along with upstream suppliers as necessary. Twenty-eight different attributes in four life cycle stages are examined before an applicant's environmental claims are verified and a certificate is issued. Products must receive 75 out of a possible 100 points, earning at least 50 percent of the points available in each of the four areas. Annual reviews are required to ensure that the certified claim remains valid.

### The Buzz

Building upon a decade of expertise in the certification of low-emitting products, SCS launched a new program, Indoor Advantage, in late 2005 covering a broad array of nonfloor interior building products: wall coverings, ceiling tiles, furniture, casework, and insulation. Indoor Advantage is consistent with the requirements of the LEED credits for low-emitting materials other than flooring. A second program, Indoor Advantage Gold, includes additional criteria to certify compliance with California's Section 01350 Specification and CHPS.

SCS has also introduced Sustainable Choice, a new program to promote social responsibility as well as environmentally favorable products. The first product category available for certification is carpet floor covering. Like EPP certification, SCS evaluates multiple attributes across the product's life cycle. SCS is expected to announce programs in sustainable furniture, floor covering, and textiles.

### The Last Word

Due to its use by EPA, the State of California, and SCS, there is some confusion in the marketplace over the EPP designation; in some quarters, the label Environmentally Preferable Product is becoming synonymous with green materials. However, Scientific Certification Systems is emerging as the leading third-party certifier in the United States.

## Green Seal

www.greenseal.org

### In Its Own Words

Green Seal is an independent, nonprofit organization that strives to achieve a healthier and cleaner environment by identifying and promoting products and services that cause less toxic pollution and waste, conserve resources and habitats, and minimize global warming and ozone depletion. Green Seal has no financial interest in the products that it certifies or recommends or in any manufacturer or company. Green Seal's evaluations are based on state-of-the-art science and information using internationally recognized methods and procedures. Thus, Green Seal provides credible, objective, and unbiased information whose only purpose is to direct the purchaser to environmentally responsible products and services.

Green Seal works with manufacturers, industry sectors, purchasing groups, and governments at all levels to "green" the production and purchasing chain. Among the tools Green Seal uses are product certification; purchasing guidance, including product recommendations; special projects and evaluations of products and purchasing; and policy recommendations. Thus, purchasers may use Green Seal's assistance in a variety of forms—certified or recommended products, manuals on best practices and product criteria, environmental specifications and standards for products, and evaluations of specific cases or situations.

Text and logo reprinted with permission, Green Seal.

### What It Offers

Founded in 1989, Green Seal provides multiple-attribute third-party certifications to a variety of products, including paints, compact fluorescent lamps, commercial adhesives, occupancy sensors, windows, and window films. Unlike many of the other standards, Green Seal is recognized by consumers, especially for its labeling program for cleaning products.

The rigorous standard-setting process begins with a stakeholder committee of manufacturers and trade associations, product users, government agencies, academia, and environmental and public interest groups. Using ISO environmental principles and life cycle evaluations, criteria are drafted to address the most significant environmental impacts. The process concludes with a public comment period followed by responses and an appeals policy.

Once a standard has been established, Green Seal accepts applications for certification. The evaluation process includes test data review and plant visits; the bar is set high so that only the best products will be awarded the Green Seal.

Green Seal identifies and makes product recommendations in several categories—an opportunity for market differentiation between brands for the best environmental choices. Selected manufacturers are asked to submit information on products for peer review. Based on the results, Green Seal recommends specific brands and models that meet its criteria, which are published as Choose Green reports.

### The Buzz

Green Seal uses an open consensus-based process to establish its standards, award certifications, and make product recommendations. More than 300 products have received Green Seal Certification and may use the logo on packaging and marketing materials; however, manufacturers listed in Choose Green Reports may not use Green Seal's recommendation in advertising, promotion, or selling.

### The Last Word

Green Seal is well regarded for its processes, its products, and especially for its contribution to green product awareness.

## Specific Product Standards and Certifications

**FloorScore**

www.rfci.com

### In Its Own Words

The FloorScore program, developed by the Resilient Floor Covering Institute (RFCI) in conjunction with Scientific Certification Systems (SCS), tests and certifies flooring products for compliance with indoor air quality emission requirements adopted in California. Flooring products include vinyl, linoleum, laminate flooring, wood flooring, ceramic flooring, rubber flooring, wall base, and associated sundries. A flooring product bearing the FloorScore seal has been independently certified by SCS to comply with the volatile organic compound emissions criteria of the California Section 01350 program. These flooring products qualify for use in high performance schools and office buildings in California. Thus, products with the FloorScore seal have passed a third party certification process and are recognized as contributing to good indoor air quality in order to protect human health.

Text and logo reprinted with permission, FloorScore.

### What It Offers

FloorScore, a single-attribute certification program measuring VOC emissions for certain flooring products, was developed by the trade association representing the resilient flooring industry. Using small-scale environmental chamber testing, the procedures test product samples for their emissions of individual VOCs to calculate VOC emission factors rather than testing for TVOCs. According to RFCI, "It's not an issue of simply measuring total VOCs in the air you're breathing. What matters is the nature of particular VOCs that may be in the air."

FloorScore is open to all manufacturers of hard surface flooring; certified products include vinyl tile, vinyl composition tile, vinyl sheet flooring, linoleum, and polymeric and laminate flooring.

### The Buzz

The certification program, four years in the making, is California-centric, originating from the 01350-based protocols and thresholds from the California Department of Health Services' Standard Practice for the Testing of Volatile Organic Emissions from Various Sources Using Small-Scale Environmental Chambers. FloorScore has used Berkeley Analytical Associates for testing. The program measures a single attribute, emissions, and does not evaluate the environmental effects of other material issues such as PVC content.

### The Last Word

The Resilient Floor Covering Institute, an industry trade association, took the high road and partnered with SCS, a third-party certifier, to provide air emissions labeling for hard surface flooring. USGBC has approved recognition of FloorScore as an alternative compliance path for the low-emitting materials credit for carpet in LEED.

---

## The Carpet and Rug Institute (CRI)

THE CARPET AND RUG INSTITUTE

CRI GREEN LABEL +PLUS™
carpet-rug.org

**www.carpet-rug.org**

### In Its Own Words

The Carpet and Rug Institute is the national trade association representing the carpet and rug industry. The Institute's membership consists of manufacturers representing over 90% of all carpet produced in the United States, and suppliers of raw materials and services to the industry. There is continued coordination with other segments of the industry, such as distributors, retailers, and installers. CRI is a source of extensive carpet information for consumers, writers, interior designers, specifiers, facility managers, architects, builders, and building owners and managers, installation contractors, and retailers.

Text and logo reprinted with permission, CRI.

### What It Offers

CRI's Indoor Air Quality Testing and Labeling Program is a voluntary industry effort to monitor carpet and rug emissions. Carpet, carpet adhesives, and cushions that meet the standards will earn the CRI Green Label or Green Label Plus. The latter is the more stringent of the two and was developed to meet the CHPS requirements defined in California's Section 01350 Specification. Products are tested by the Air Quality Sciences laboratories in Atlanta, with quarterly and annual retesting required. Additional chemicals have been added to those being tested under the earlier Green Label program.

### The Buzz

Indoor air quality experts criticized the original Green Label standard as being too lenient. As an example, the LEED-CI credit for low-emitting carpets is the only non-innovation point to be achieved by 100 percent of the pilot projects. The organization responded with a tougher standard and partnered with others to ensure the measure's credibility.

### The Last Word

Despite the welcome introduction and acceptance of Green Label Plus, critics continue to voice concern that the certification is controlled by a trade organization rather than a third party.

---

## Greenguard Environmental Institute (GEI)

GREENGUARD® Indoor Air Quality Certified

**www.greenguard.org**

### In Its Own Words

The Greenguard Environmental Institute is an industry-independent, non-profit organization that oversees the Greenguard Certification Program. As an ANSI Accredited Standards Developer, GEI establishes acceptable indoor air standards for indoor products, environments, and buildings. GEI's mission is to improve public health and quality of life through programs that improve indoor air.

*About the Greenguard Indoor Air Quality Certification Program for Low Emitting Products*—The Greenguard Certification Program is an industry independent, third-party testing program for low-emitting products and materials. Access to the Greenguard Product Guide, an indoor air quality (IAQ) resource, is provided at no charge. The guide features products, which are regularly tested to ensure that their chemical and particle emissions meet acceptable IAQ pollutant guidelines and standards.

*About the Greenguard Mold Protection Program*— The Greenguard Mold Protection Program protects lenders, insurers and building developers from mold risk by ensuring that buildings use industries' best practices for safeguarding against the damage and resulting losses caused by mold. The Greenguard Mold Protection Program "certifies" those buildings that meet this standard and monitors their compliance throughout the term of the loan or building life.

Text and logo reprinted with permission, GEI.

### What It Offers

Greenguard Certification is a valuable tool for designers, product specifiers, and purchasing organizations that want to locate off-the-shelf, low-emitting products for indoor environments. It is a voluntary program available to all manufacturers and their suppliers. Founded in 1996, the protocol evolved out of the original AQSpec List program developed by Marilyn Black, Ph.D., and Air Quality Sciences, Inc. (AQS). The original AQSpec List program was simply a registry or listing of products that had been tested following specific test protocols and found to meet the EPA and State of Washington emissions standards. GEI and the Greenguard Certification and labeling program evolved from that initial effort and operate as a

separate nonprofit organization. Now over forty-five manufacturers in nine different industries offer Greenguard Indoor Air Quality Certified Products. The Greenguard Mold Protection program was added to GEI's offerings in 2006.

GEI has established performance-based standards to define certification procedures including test methods, allowable emissions levels, product sample collection and handling, testing type and frequency, and program application processes and acceptance. All products are tested in dynamic environmental chambers following ASTM standards D-5116-97 and D-6670-01, the EPA's testing protocol for furniture, and the State of Washington's protocol for interior furnishings and construction materials.

In 2005, GEI published the *Greenguard 2005 Indoor Air Quality Guide,* written to aid design professionals in easily integrating indoor air quality into their projects. It includes general information, facts and figures on emissions, and an IAQ management plan that can be customized for specific projects and inserted into specifications.

An office chair is readied for emissions testing in a large-scale chamber. © *Air Quality Sciences*

## The Buzz

AQS has been testing product emissions for many years in its large and small chamber laboratories. Controversy erupted with the founding of GEI and the Greenguard certification program. Although structured as separate entities, critics—the folks behind California's Section 01350 and BIFMA, the trade association representing the commercial furniture industry—claim the two organizations are too closely connected. The debates escalated in July 2002 when USGBC released its pilot version of LEED-CI, which included a new credit for low-emitting furniture and furnishings and referenced Greenguard as its standard. (Author's note: Penny Bonda is the founding chair of the LEED-CI Steering Committee as well as a member of the Greenguard Advisory Board, a group that was formed after the development of the draft of LEED-CI.) Almost immediately manufacturers began to scramble, recognizing that designers, eager to capture every possible point in their quest for LEED certification, would begin looking for low-emitting furniture that met the Greenguard criteria.[4] The California group argues that its standards are more appropriate IAQ measurements and should be included in LEED. The furniture industry (through BIFMA) rebelled against Greenguard's proprietary tests, pricing, and retesting procedures and created its own furniture emissions standard (discussed next) rather than be subject to requirements by an outside group. Both BIFMA and Greenguard are ANSI-accredited standards developers, and each has submitted applications to ANSI to develop an American National Standard based on their protocols.

Despite the discord, AQS is the predominant emissions testing facility in the United States and has the only large-scale commercial test chambers. Many of the largest commercial furniture manufacturers have received Greenguard certification for their systems furniture and seating lines.

## The Last Word

Greenguard is a legitimate third-party certifier. The organization has resolved many of its differences with the California 01350 folks; however, the conflict has escalated between Greenguard and BIFMA, as the furniture group has received approval from USGBC to incorporate its standard as an alternative compliance path for the low-emitting materials credit for systems furniture and seating in LEED-CI.

## In Its Own Words

Established in 1973, BIFMA International (formerly known as the Business and Institutional Furniture Manufacturers Association) is a not-for-profit trade association of furniture manufacturers and suppliers addressing issues of common concern. The association's membership of over 260 companies represents over 80% of the value of North American shipments of office furniture. BIFMA's mission is to serve the North American office and business furniture manufacturing industry as an information resource, industry advocate and by offering professional and industry-wide trade development opportunities. BIFMA Interna-tional provides an effective forum for cooperation and collaboration for the promotion of the industry. Strategic areas of focus include standards development, statistical data generation, government relations, industry promotion, education, networking and trade development activities.

Text and logo reprinted with permission, BIFMA.

## What It Offers

BIFMA has developed safety and performance standards according to guidelines established by ANSI to provide manufacturers, specifiers, and users a common basis for evaluating safety, durability, and the structural adequacy of commercial furniture, independent of construction materials. The standards define specific tests, laboratory equipment to be used, the conditions of testing, and the minimum acceptance levels to be used in evaluating these products. Some existing standards include color measurement, textile characteristics, and quality standards. BIFMA also provides guidelines on ergonomics and sustainability.

In 2005 BIFMA developed a furniture emissions standard that has been submitted to ANSI as an American National Standard. The effort has involved furniture manufacturers, component suppliers, test laboratories, internationally recognized emissions research scientists and technical experts, and has relied heavily on statistical floor plan analysis of over 5,000 workstation installations.

The proposed standard is actually two documents: a standard test method (BIFMA M7.1-2005) and a standard with acceptance concentration limits for low-emitting furniture that originated with the State of Washington and were later adopted by the EPA (BIFMA X7.1-2005).

### The Buzz

In some respects the BIFMA Furniture Emissions Standard is more stringent that the Greenguard standard, but some specific differences weaken it: less frequent testing intervals and concern with the selection process for representative samples. However, most of the criticism centers on the absence of a requirement for third-party certification. Manufacturers may self-certify that their products meet the BIFMA standard, which some fear might deprive customers of a balanced and trustworthy audit process.

### The Last Word

BIFMA has invested a great deal of time, expense, and intellectual capital into the development of standards that serve its industry well. It should consider making the most of its reputation by enlisting third-party certifiers, as have other trade associations.

## Forest Stewardship Council (FSC)

**www.fsc.org**

The FSC logo identifies products which contain wood from well-managed forests certified in accordance with the rules of the Forest Stewardship Council. © 1996 Forest Stewardship Council A.C.

### In Its Own Words

The Forest Stewardship Council is an international network to promote responsible management of the world's forests. FSC brings people together to find solutions to the problems created by bad forestry practices and to reward good forest management.

- FSC is a stakeholder-owned system for promoting responsible management of the world's forests.
- Through consultative processes, it sets international standards for responsible forest management.
- It accredits independent third party organizations that can certify forest managers and forest product producers to FSC standards.
- Its trademark provides international recognition to organizations that support the growth of responsible forest management.
- Its product label allows consumers worldwide to recognize products that support the growth of responsible forest management worldwide.
- FSC undertakes marketing programs and information services that contributes to the mission of promoting responsible forestry worldwide.
- Over the past 10 years, 50 million hectares in more than 60 countries have been certified according to FSC standards while several thousand products are produced using FSC-certified wood and carrying the FSC trademark. FSC operates through its network of National Initiatives in more than 34 countries.

Text and logo reprinted with permission, FSC.

### What It Offers

With its trademark, FSC provides assurances to those who buy, specify, and use wood and wood products that those materials have come from responsibly managed forests. It also ensures that the harvesting is legal, that ownership rights and the rights of workers and indigenous communities are respected, and that endangered wildlife habitats are not being negatively affected.

FSC itself does not issue certifications, but rather accredits certification bodies in order to maintain its independence from those seeking certification. Two types of certificates are offered. The holder of a Forest Management Certificate can claim that its operations comply with FSC standards. However, it must also obtain a Chain of Custody Certificate before selling products as FSC-certified. Chain of Custody tracks the raw materials through all stages of processing, transformation, manufacturing, and distribution from the forest to the consumer and guarantees the assurances FSC has made to its customers. As of January 2006, 777 Forest Management Certificates had been issued in sixty-six countries.

### The Buzz

FSC is a referenced standard recognized by LEED because it is a true third-party certification, having separating itself from any group or organization with a vested interest in the forestry industry. FSC is highly regarded by environmentalists, but some have criticized its requirements as too onerous. In early 2005, FSC introduced three new labels, FSC Pure, FSC Mixed, and FSC Recycled, to make it easier to certify composite wood products.

### The Last Word

Home Depot determined that its customers will choose certified wood products when given the option and has recognized and promoted FSC certification as its preferred standard.

## Sustainable Forestry Initiative (SFI)

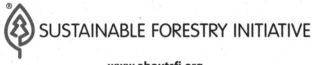

www.aboutsfi.org

### In Its Own Words

The Sustainable Forestry Initiative program is a comprehensive system of principles, objectives and performance measures developed by professional foresters, conservationists and scientists, among others, that combines the perpetual growing and harvesting of trees with the long-term protection of wildlife, plants, soil and water quality. There are currently over 150 million acres of forestland in North America enrolled in the SFI program, making it among the world's largest sustainable forestry programs.

To ensure forests are protected, the American Forest & Paper Association (AF&PA) developed the SFI program to document the commitment of their members and the program's licensees keep our forests healthy and practice the highest level of sustainable forestry. The Sustainable Forestry Initiative program is based on the premise that responsible environmental practices and sound business practices can be integrated to the benefit of landowners, shareholders, customers and the people they serve. The SFI program provides a means for foresters, landowners, loggers and wood and paper producers to satisfy the growing demand of the American people for environmental responsibility while still being able to produce—at an affordable price—the forest products upon which people have come to rely.

Text and logo reprinted with permission, SFI.

### What It Offers

The Sustainable Forestry Initiative program is a forestry management plan that recognizes both environmental responsibility and sound business practices. Following an application process developed by the AF&PA, the program awards four on-product labels to participating companies that have satisfied the SFI Label Use Requirements. The requirements are based upon the SFI Standard, which is defined by a set of principles embracing both environmental and market demands. A list of SFI Objectives translates these principles into action.

The labeling program distinguishes between primary producers, or certified participants—those who receive most of their raw material directly from the forest—and secondary producers, or certified manufacturers for processed wood operations.

### The Buzz

Certification standards should be open and transparent, but sorting through all the different layers of SFI protocols is confusing and frustrating. SFI is most frequently criticized, however, for being too cozy with the forest product companies, including its developer, the American Forest & Paper Association, a trade group that represents a significant majority of the forestry industry. Although steps have been taken over the years to improve the program's credibility, including the addition of a chain of custody standard,

SFI continues to take a backseat to the more stringent FSC certification.

## The Last Word

Furniture manufacturers, among others, are urging USGBC to recognize wood certification programs in addition to FSC. In response, USGBC is considering changes to LEED's wood and bio-based materials credits that will allow certification standards beyond those currently referenced in LEED. The proposal will follow USGBC's consensus process, which includes a public comment period and member balloting.

## Institute for Market Transformation to Sustainability (MTS) and the Sustainable Textile Standard

**www.mts.sustainableproducts.com**

## In Its Own Words

The Institute for Market Transformation to Sustainability believes it is possible to transform manufacturing and retail practices worldwide so that by 2015 sustainable products are available in 90 percent of the global marketplace. Because the 100 largest companies account for more than 90% of the world's products, it believes its mission is attainable. Sustainable products are those products providing environmental, social, and economic benefits while protecting public health, welfare and environment over their full commercial cycle, from the extraction of raw materials to final disposition, providing for the needs of future generations. Sustainable products increase corporate profits while enhancing society as a whole, because they are cheaper to make, have fewer regulatory constraints, less liability, can be introduced to the market quicker, and are preferred by the public.

MTS brings together a powerful coalition of sustainable products manufacturers, environmental groups, and key state and local government leaders using market mechanisms increasing sales and mar-

ket share of sustainable products. It has identified consensus protocols for sustainable products such as FSC Certified Wood, Certified Organic Products, and the Clean Car Standard.

Text and logo reprinted with permission, MTS.

## What It Offers

MTS standards are consensus- and lifecycle–based, focused on specific products. The Unified Sustainable Textile Standard 2.0 for carpet, fabric, and apparel was approved unanimously by the MTS membership following an extensive review and balloting procedure. Its purpose is to provide a market-based definition for sustainable textiles, establish performance requirements for public health and environment, and address the triple bottom line of economic, environmental, and equity values throughout the supply chain. It is intended to help raw material suppliers, converters, manufacturers, and end-users.

The standard identifies six levels of sustainable attribute performance and four levels of achievement by which textile materials and products can be measured with respect to specific attributes that indicate progress toward sustainability. The criteria for certification is comprehensive, divided into five subject categories:

- Safe for Public Health and Environment (PHE)
- Renewable Energy and Energy Efficiency (RE)
- Material, Biobased or Recycled (MATLS)
- Facility or Company Based (MFG)
- Reclamation, Sustainable Reuse and End of Life Management (EOL)

Following a successful documentation review, achievement levels are awarded according to the number of points earned and the product receives the right to use the label. MTS is regarded as a manufacturer's certification in that the manufacturers self-certify that their product has met the standard's criteria.

## The Buzz

MTS took the consensus process to new levels by involving multiple stakeholders in its development process. In late 2005, MTS released the Sustainable/EPP Flooring Standard for all hard-surface flooring and announced its intention to develop an Integrated Design Process Standard Guide for Sustainable Buildings and Communities and the Sustainable/EPP Products Performance Standard.

### The Last Word

Navigating the MTS maze is difficult because the Web site does not provide search capabilities. A Web search failed to find the list of certified textile products.

## The Very Last Word

The state of design guides, standards, and certifications is in a state of flux. Those reviewed here are just the tip of the iceberg, with more coming online almost daily. GreenBlue, for example, is working on sustainable standards for textiles, packaging, and cleaning products. Other products already in the marketplace include Athena's Environmental Impact Estimator, FTC Environmental Market Guidelines, *Consumer Reports'* Greener Choices recommendations, and of course Energy Star, described in Chapter 3. International programs include Blue Angel in Germany, Nordic Swan in Scandinavia, Japan's Ecomark, and the Environmental Choice label in Canada.

These tools are the designer's best defense against greenwash—the proliferation of untruths and half-truths that range from naivety to blatant lies. One of the more outrageous examples is the claim by a carpet manufacturer that use of its product would earn 17 LEED points, a feat that would be downright impossible, if not miraculous. The simple process of asking for verification of material attributes, preferably by a third-party certifier, puts the manufacturer on notice that its customers are demanding accountability and will ultimately lead to greater truth and transparency in product claims.

> *"There are over 95,000 voluntary consensus standards and it is estimated that only 1 percent are being verified by third parties; the rest are self-declared. Not only is it important to leverage existing standards and participate in the development of new ones, but it is also critical to encourage third-party verification."*
>
> —Kirsten Ritchie, director, environmental claims, Scientific Certification Systems

## ▌Specifications

Designers should begin to write green requirements into their specifications in order to ensure the most sustainable outcome. Ross Spiegel, a former president of the Construction Specifications Institute (CSI), believes that it benefits the design team for the specification writer to become involved in the project as early as possible, ideally during the schematic design phase. This allows the spec writer to research product alternatives and contribute his or her findings on such things as innovative technologies, nontoxic and recycled products, and waste reduction procedures.

Spiegel and coauthor Dru Meadows have published the second edition of their book *Green Building Materials: A Guide to Product Selection and Specifications*. It is a valuable resource for design teams wishing to ensure that the environmental goals set for their projects are carried out. In his essay below, Spiegel provides guidance on the four steps to greener materials.

### *Four Steps to Greening Your Specifications*

#### By Ross Spiegel

*A green/sustainable project can become reality only if the contract documents clearly convey the intent of the design. Through the specifications the designer conveys a material's physical, performance, and environmental attributes as well as its installation instructions. By following some basic steps of specification writing, the designer can "green" the specifications to help achieve a project's sustainability goals.*

*The first step is taken long before the specifications are written but is a critical step in ensuring a successful green/sustainable project. Before the material selection process begins, the designer should compile a list of environmental attributes for the materials that might be specified for a project, such as recycled content, low VOC content, certified wood, and so on. Similarly designers should compile a list of attributes that they do not want to see incorporated into the project through product specifications.*

The next step takes place during the development of the project's design, as material options are being compiled and evaluated. Using the list of attributes developed in the first step, the designer evaluates the available options in each category of material. For example, if flooring material options are being considered, the designer should make a list of available materials to evaluate and compare to the attributes compiled in the first step. Of course, the environmental attributes are not the only ones that the designer must take into account in the decision-making process. Fire safety, aesthetics, and life cycle considerations must be added to the list of environmental attributes to make a complete evaluation of the materials. By comparing the attributes of carpet versus resilient flooring versus ceramic tile, the designer will be able to make an informed selection of floor surfacing materials. The designer can also weight the various attributes as a specific project requires. On a green/sustainable project more weight is typically given to the environmental attributes.

Once the designer completes the evaluation of all of the material categories he or she is ready to proceed to the next step in the specification process: identifying, researching, and evaluating the specific materials and manufacturers in each of the categories.

While this is the most intensive step in the process it is also the most important. Working with the entire project team, the designer compiles as much information as possible about the available materials from the manufacturers. Polling other members of the project team to determine their experience with the potential products is a valuable benefit of working with a team. By using the many available building material and environmental Web sites, the designer can quickly identify materials and manufacturers to research. With potential materials identified, the designer then starts to collect technical information that will be important in the decision-making process. A good way to start collecting this information is to develop a questionnaire that can be sent to each manufacturer, requesting specific information about its product's environmental attributes. While this may seem a simple chore,

it is not. Just sending out information requests does not always result in a mailbox full of detailed responses with technical information and samples. Usually several back-and-forth exchanges will be necessary before all of the information requested is received. There will be some instances of disappointment. This is somewhat understandable given the proprietary nature of most products and the manufacturer's desire to maintain an edge over its competitors. Sometimes just finding the right person to ask at a company can be difficult. Nonetheless, the designer must be persistent.

A useful evaluation tool that the designer can develop is a spreadsheet evaluation form, as shown in Table 6-2. It should include a column to list the attributes being evaluated and separate columns to indicate the information for each product within a material category. When the form is completed the designer will have a very detailed chart showing how the products stack up against each other. On publicly bid projects, where the designer must usually list three manufacturers for each product, the evaluation form will make it easier to find more than one manufacturer able to provide an acceptable product.

The completion of the evaluation process sets the stage for the fourth and final step, writing the specification. Using the information compiled in the previous step, the designer selects the appropriate specification sections to include in the project manual. To ensure that the environmental attributes are respected during the bidding and construction phases of the project, the designer must incorporate specific requirements into the specifications. The carpet specification section, for example, could include requirements for recycled content and recyclability as well as limitations on the VOC content of the adhesives. The section could also include guidelines regarding the disposal of excess materials and the submittal of documentation that substantiates the environmental attributes. On publicly bid projects the designer can also specify products based upon their performance and attributes rather than naming manufacturers. This, of course, puts the burden on the designer to have a detailed level of knowledge

## TABLE 6-2: Ceiling Tile Evaluation Form

| Item # | Attribute | Manufacturer No. 1 | Manufacturer No. 2 | Manufacturer No. 3 |
|---|---|---|---|---|
| 1 | Manufacturer's name | Armstrong | BPB Celotex | USG Interiors Inc. |
| 2 | Product name and model number | Ultima no. 1911 | Safetone Cashmere CM-454 | Acoustone Fine Textured Pattern/Frost-440 |
| 3 | Nominal size and thickness | 24 × 24 × ¾ inches | 24 × 24 × ¾ inches | 24 × 24 × ¾ inches |
| 4 | ASTM E1264 classification | Type IV, Form 2, Pattern E | Type III, Form 1, Pattern E | Type III, Form 4, Pattern E |
| 5 | Material | Wet-formed mineral fiber | Wet-felted mineral fiber | Cast mineral fiber |
| 6 | Edge detail | Beveled tegular | Beveled tegular | Beveled tegular |
| 7 | Noise reduction coefficient (NRC) | 0.7 | 0.6 | 0.7 |
| 8 | Sound transmission class (STC) | Not specified | Not specified | Not specified |
| 9 | Ceiling attenuation class (CAC) | 35 | 35 | 40 |
| 10 | Light reflectance (LR) | LR-1; actual 0.90 | LR-1; actual 0.82 | LR-1; actual 0.82 |
| 11 | Surface finish/color | Factory-applied acrylic latex paint | Not specified/white | Not specified/white |
| 12 | Fire resistance | Class A; flame spread 25 | Class A; flame spread 25 | Class A; flame spread 25 |
| 13 | Humidity resistance | Yes | Yes | Yes |
| 14 | Mold/moisture resistance | Yes | Yes | Not specified |
| 15 | Recycled content percentage | 66–79 | 82–88 | 67 |
| 16 | Reclamation program | Yes | Unknown | Unknown |
| 17 | Sustainable manufacturing program | Yes | Unknown | Unknown |
| 18 | Warranty | 10-year limited | 10-year limited, 104°F, 90% RH | 10-year limited, 104°F, 90% RH |
| 19 | Other features | Washable; impact-, scratch-, and soil-resistant | None identified | Impact-, scratch-resistant |

about the products available in each material category. It also requires that the designer employ a very strict substitution policy to ensure that only acceptable products make it into the project. Clearly written and detailed specifications will make the designer's job during the bidding and construction phases much easier.

The steps outlined above employ some of the basic tenets of specification writing that apply equally to both sustainable and nonsustainable projects. They begin at the earliest stages of a project's development and continue through the design, bidding, and construction phases, ending with the project's completion. Following these simple steps will enhance a project's chances of attaining its sustainable goals.

Ross Spiegel, AIA, FCSI, CCS, CCCA, LEED AP, associate/senior specification writer for Fletcher-Thompson, Inc.

It isn't always easy to write specifications for new product, and processes or to make the switch to new language rather than simply reverting to specifications from past projects. When using the common specification format from CSI, the best place to start is to describe sustainable design goals within Division 1 that address general project requirements and procedures. However, as stated in a report by Nadav Malin in *Environmental Building News,* even large firms such as HOK have spent considerable resources on developing language for a Division 1 section on general green requirements, as well as sections on indoor air quality and LEED requirements. Other firms rely on knowledgeable and enthusiastic spec writers, but many are on their own. "Managing specifications," Malin continues, "is an ongoing challenge for nearly all the firms. Greening a common firm specification is challenging enough; getting project managers to use it may be even trickier, unless they are committed to the green agenda."[5] Luckily, there is a terrific tool available to assist designers, simplify the product selection process, and save time.

BuildingGreen's *GreenSpec Directory* contains detailed listings for nearly 2,000 environmentally preferable building products, with descriptions, manufacturer information, and links to additional resources. All listings are screened and written exclusively by the BuildingGreen staff, and unlike other directories, it does not charge for listings or for the review process, nor does it accept advertising. This adds a layer of reliability—and respectability—not found in competing products. The revised Sixth Edition added new or refined criteria and dropped listings for discontinued products and those that failed to meet the *GreenSpec* criteria.

Products that qualify for the guide are evaluated individually for a wide range of environmental traits:

- Products made from environmentally attractive materials such as salvaged goods or those with recycled content, rapidly renewable and agricultural waste materials, and certified wood
- Products that are green because of what isn't there: toxins such as PVC and CCA wood preservatives, fluorescent lamps with low mercury levels, and products that reduce material use
- Products that reduce environmental impacts during construction, renovation, demolition, and ongoing building operation, such as leased carpeting, Energy

The revised Sixth Edition of the *GreenSpec Directory* is part of the BuildingGreen Suite, a resource for reliable environmental information. © 2005 BuildingGreen, Inc.

Star equipment, fixtures that conserve energy or water, and products that have exceptional durability and low maintenance requirements
- Products that contribute to a safe, healthy indoor environment: low- or no-VOC paints, sealants, and adhesives; products that block the spread of contaminants, warn occupants of indoor pollutants, and improve light quality

*GreenSpec* has been written to inform the specification writing process, not as a substitution for it. The new Directory features guideline specification language as well as wide-ranging information on general environmental considerations and on the specifics of the materials and products to take into account. It is available as part of a suite of products from BuildingGreen (www.buildinggreen.com) that also includes *Environmental Building News* (EBN), a monthly newsletter that typically features a lengthy and detailed article on some aspect of green buildings.[6]

# ■ The Sustainable Library

Every designer knows that a good resource library is essential to good design. Finding what you want when you want it often means the difference between a well-executed project and one that falls short. Likewise, becoming a credible environmental designer means having specific knowledge and resources at your fingertips, organized in such a way to be immediately accessible.

The first decision to be made in setting up a green library is to settle on a physical arrangement within the office. Do you incorporate sustainable resources into or separate from the regular library? There are pros and cons to both methods, and the solution may be to do both if space permits, except that there is something inherently non-ecofriendly about duplicating samples. Carpet binders are an obvious example. They are much too bulky to duplicate, but sustainable carpets can be distinguished with a green sticker of some sort to separate green products from the rest. Tricycle, reviewed in detail in Chapter 4, has introduced its SIM technology to reproduce on paper the colors and textures of carpeting that are remarkably accurate. Although primarily used for sampling, some carpet manufacturers may elect to dispense with the binders altogether and supply designers with the SIM paper reproductions instead. A carpet executive who had originally rejected using SIM "got it" when two tractor-trailer loads of architect's folders with out-of-date colors were returned.

Another solution, which is less space-intensive and wasteful than duplicating them, is to store catalogs and samples in the regular library (marked with those identifying stickers) and list the environmental products and resources available in the office in reference notebooks, along with MSDSs, technical information, publications, and papers. This method provides a way for any designer to do the research necessary to design in a sustainable manner without taking up too much room. Also, organize the green library as the standard library. In other words, if the CSI system is used for one, use it for the other as well.

One common problem is how to keep the green library current. Sustainable design is an evolving field. What's best today may not be so tomorrow, requiring vigilance. Small manufacturers, many of whom have excellent products, come and go so quickly that specifying their materials is chancy. Getting and assessing accurate information can also be difficult. Technologies are very complicated, and it sometimes seems that the more research that's done, the more complexities are revealed.

The McGraw-Hill Construction Network for Products (formerly Sweets) is an online database that includes content from 10,000 manufacturers, sortable by various filters such as green attributes as identified by manufacturers or by third-party certifications. McGraw-Hill is also planning to establish procedures for a juried green label program, available online. The site (www.construction.com) is the portal for other McGraw-Hill resources directed toward the green community, such as the Dodge database of projects and an online version of their new magazine, *Green Source*.

Tectonic Studio (www.studio.bluebolt.com) is an online resource library of over 100,000 commercial interior finishes representing more than sixty brands. One of its unique features is its ability to create design boards by dragging samples onto a digital canvas. Searches can be conducted by product type, brand, color/style, and keywords or by environmental attributes. The Green Search feature looks for products in two ways: by rating or certification systems or by area of environmental benefit. For example, a search for modular carpet tile produces pull-down menus for LEED and the four credits that the product may contribute to achieving. The environmental benefit areas include materials, IEQ, and waste management/end-of-life issues as they are addressed in the rating system. Users may select all attributes or just one, and a list of brands meeting the criteria is provided.

Design firms need to be proactive in assembling a viable green library. It helps to have a knowledgeable resource person available to the entire staff, one who is fluent in green-speak and who can weed out the greenwash. Such a person should also be able to establish norms for all product categories against which all products can be measured. Send out product questionnaires, such as the one presented in Nadav Malin's essay in Chapter 4, and request updates from suppliers every six months or so. Hold regular briefings with the entire staff to keep them current. Some firms hold sustainable product lunchtime demonstrations or plan green happy hour gatherings.

The day will come when green libraries are standard. A few firms are already there, but for most it isn't yet practical, although the online availability of product catalogs helps. Supply and demand will drive the process; the more designers demand green products, the quicker the manufacturers will supply them with the goods that will enable the creation of built environments that are nurturing, enduring, and sustainable.[7]

# 7

# THE BUSINESS CASE FOR GREEN DESIGN

The growing awareness of the environmental impacts of how and where we work and the ways in which we conduct business have had a significant impact on the economic landscape of the late twentieth century—influences that will only grow in magnitude as we make our way through the early part of this century. Some argue that the environmental movement has been one of the most significant factors shaping corporate management philosophies in recent years. It is not uncommon these days for CEOs to espouse the concept of corporate social responsibility or to advocate management philosophies such as the triple bottom line, a term coined by SustainAbility's John Elkington that calls for measurement of corporate performance along three interlinked lines: profits, environmental sustainability, and social responsibility. In fact, many environmental advocates believe these and other similar concepts could be the primary drivers in changing public and private sector policies in the coming years. A growing list of NGOs and independent business consultancies have recognized the potential for harnessing market forces to simultaneously achieve both positive environmental gains and attractive bottom lines. What these organizations have discovered is that partnering with corporations—not campaigning against them—is the most effective way to achieve their dual objectives.

For example, SustainAbility has enjoyed much success helping corporations worldwide explore how social and environmental innovation is key to the new market opportunities of the future. The Business Environmental Leadership Council (BELC), created by the Pew Center for Global Climate Change, advocates that business engagement is critical for developing efficient, effective solutions to climate problems and that companies taking early action on climate strategies and policy will gain sustained competitive advantage over their peers. Evidently its forty-one members, representing $2 trillion in market capitalization and more than 3 million employees, agree. In the office furniture industry, three companies considered fierce competitors—Steelcase, Haworth, and Herman Miller—often can be found collaborating and sharing what some may consider proprietary information during the meetings they attend of the West Michigan Sustainable Business Forum, a nonprofit organization whose goal is to encourage the adoption and implementation of sustainable development business practices aimed at improving corporate profitability while simultaneously enhancing the long-term health of the environment.

Helping fuel this trend toward corporate consciousness is a tenet called "stakeholder value," which calls for companies to consider the impacts of their business operations on all parties that might be affected, including not just shareholders but also employees, customers, suppliers, business partners, and surrounding communities. This philosophy greatly expands what has traditionally been perceived as a company's primary responsibility: the bottom line. And while one might think that a company's investors—its coveted shareholders—should be dismayed by this departure from strict bottom-line economics, it is increasingly becoming just the opposite. In fact, more and more consumers are actively engaging in the practice of socially responsible investing (SRI), defined by the U.S. Social Investment Forum (SIF) as an investment process that considers the social and environmental consequences of investments within the context of rigorous financial analysis. Although SRI represents a relatively small portion of total investments (approximately one out of every ten dollars under professional management), it continues to grow and become more mainstream and influential in the United States. According to the *2005 Report on Socially*

## Defining Shareholder Value

From a business perspective, sustainability adds a new dimension into the concept of providing shareholder value, explains Ecos Corp. CEO and founder Paul Gilding. Creating shareholder value is an "essential outcome if we want companies to flourish and build value for society, and in doing so create opportunities for their employees and communities. But, ironically, focusing company strategy on creating shareholder value is actually a lousy way to create it over a sustained period of time.... A company needs to know why it exists. What is its purpose in society? What does it want to achieve? What does it believe? How does its existence improve quality of life for the people it interacts with?" It is only when a company "knows the answers to these kinds of questions," Gilding says, that "it has the framework it needs to make decisions and run its business—and, therefore, the framework it needs to create value for shareholders.... So by defining a company's social purpose, we are really defining its business strategy. Why? Because it answers the question: What real and sustained value will we bring to society, through the hard and inspired work of our people, and how will we gain our fair share of that value?"

*Source:* "Doing Business on Purpose," *green@work*, September/October 2003.

*Responsible Investing Trends in the U.S.*, a biannual report issued by the SIF, socially responsible investment assets grew faster than the entire universe of managed assets in the United States during the last ten years.[1] It estimates that total SRI assets rose more than 258 percent between 1995 and 2005, from $639 billion to $2.29 trillion.

Private investors aren't the only ones filling the ranks of socially responsible investors, either. California state treasurer Phil Angelides launched a landmark initiative called Green Wave in February 2004 to use California pension funds' clout and considerable assets to demand more disclosure of climate change and other environmental risks from portfolio companies and invest in clean energy technologies to encourage job creation and economic growth in the state.

Why are individuals and institutions turning toward social investing? According to Mark Thomsen, research and news director of SRI World Group, Inc., writing in the March/April 2004 issue of *green@work*, one reason is that investors "perceive it as a 'safe haven' from corporate scandal," while investors, on the other hand, are "taking notice of the increasing correlations being drawn between environmental, social, economic and corporate governance performance and share value."

Without a doubt, the successful twenty-first-century CEO needs to capitalize on the intangible assets that increasing numbers of social investors value, Thomsen argues. "Intangible assets can include the company's reputation, employees, brands, patents, research and development prowess, and ideas and processes. Little is known about which intangible assets account for what portions of market value. Nevertheless, reputation, brand value, the ability to retain good employees and other such factors associated with better-than-average environmental, social, economic and corporate governance performance certainly are components."[2]

As evidence of this "awakening" by contemporary CEOs, one need only look at the results of the July 2005 study by the Social Investment Research Analysts Network (SIRAN), which found that more than half of the Standard & Poor's 100 Index (fifty-eight companies) have special sections of their Web sites dedicated to sharing information about their social and environmental policies and performance, and almost 40 percent (thirty-nine companies) now issue annual corporate social responsibility reports.[3]

## ■ Building a Tangible Symbol

So what does all this talk about shareholder value and corporate social responsibility have to do with green building? Quite a lot, actually, because as companies travel the path toward greater corporate responsibility, they have come to realize that their buildings can serve as a first and highly visible symbol in a commitment to sustainability. The built environment offers numerous opportunities for concrete expressions of environmental stewardship: buildings can reduce energy consumption and thus greenhouse gas emissions, reduce precious fresh water consumption, and minimize the use of natural resources in the materials selection process.

National and local programs encouraging a wide range of green building projects have increased dramatically over the past few years, projects that clearly demonstrate what green buildings can accomplish. From all indications, this trend is destined to continue. A 2004 survey of 719 building owners, developers, architects, engineers, and consultants by Turner Construction Co., a subsidiary of the Turner Corp., one of the nation's leading general builders, found that in the coming three years, 93 percent of executives working with green buildings expect their green workload to rise. More than half (51 percent) of them anticipated substantial increases in their green building activities, while another 42 percent expected these activities to increase somewhat. Even among executives not currently working with green buildings, nearly one-third (30 percent) thought it was very or extremely likely that their organization would work on a green project in the next three years. The survey also found that 88 percent of executives currently involved with green buildings have seen their activities with these buildings increase during the last three years, and nearly 40 percent have seen green activity increase substantially during that period.[4] The tremendous growth of the U.S. Green Building Council's voluntary LEED Green Building Rating System underscores this trend: As of June 2006, over one-half billion square feet of building space has been registered or certified under LEED. Forecasts offered by McGraw-Hill Construction indicate that by 2010, between 5 and 10 percent of nonresidential construction starts will be designed using the principles of green design, which translates into a market valued between $10.2 and $20.5 billion.[5]

For green building to be gaining such tremendous traction within the business community, there obviously needed to be more than just the feel-good justification of environmental fairness to sway corporate opinion in its favor. Early environmental advocates knew that solid, compelling evidence—presented in the vernacular business executives understood—was crucial to convince businesses that the best way for them to do well was by doing good. And so in the mid-1990s, pioneers in the green building movement undertook the momentous task of documenting—and most especially communicating—that there was more to sustainable buildings than what met the eye. The bible many of the early champions relied on in their efforts, especially in the commercial buildings industry, was a book entitled *Green Development: Integrating Ecology and Real Estate.* Written by a team of experts in the Green Development Services program at the Rocky Mountain Institute (RMI), and published by John Wiley & Sons in 1998, the book described "an entirely new way of thinking about the goals and the process of creating and modifying the built environment." Based on eighty case studies drawn from Green Development Services' extensive worldwide research and consulting work, it set out to prove that environmental considerations could be viewed as opportunities to create fundamentally better buildings and communities—less wasteful of land and resources, healthier and more comfortable to occupy, cheaper to run, more productive to work in, and ultimately more profitable to build and operate.

The book emphasized that green development is "not an altruistic pursuit carried out by developers willing to forego profit to protect the environment. Rather, it is a way to achieve multiple benefits—for the developer, investors, occupants, and the environment—yielding better market, financial, human, and environmental performance." The benefits identified in *Green Development,* and featured prominently on the organization's Web site[6], include:

- Reduced capital costs
- Reduced operating costs
- Marketing benefits: free press and product differentiation
- Valuation premiums and enhanced absorption rates
- Possibility of streamlined approvals
- Reduced liability risk
- Health and productivity gains
- Staying ahead of regulations
- New business opportunities
- Satisfaction from doing the right thing

Interestingly, three subsequent surveys aimed at ascertaining the specific economic benefits of green building resulted in nearly identical findings. The first occurred five years after the publication of *Green Development,* when the Senate Committee on Environment and Public Works, in conjunction with the USGBC, convened a Green Building Roundtable to educate congressional members and their staff on green building trends. Specifically, private and public sector representatives on the 2002 roundtable discussed the economic and health benefits of green building, the barriers facing its progress, and the opportunities available to federal agencies to further promote sustainable spaces.

During the course of the roundtable discussion, Hines Development and the USGBC were charged with the task of describing the economic arguments for green buildings. The resulting pamphlet, *Making the Business Case for High-Performance Green Buildings,* produced in partnership with the Urban Land Institute and the Real Estate Roundtable, detailed these ten top reasons[7]:

- In the event that up-front costs are higher, they can be recovered through lower operating costs.
- Integrating design features lowers ongoing operating costs.
- Better buildings equate with better employee productivity.
- New technologies enhance health and well-being.
- Healthier buildings can reduce liability.
- Tenant costs can be reduced significantly.
- Property value will increase.
- Many financial incentive programs are available for green buildings.
- Communities will notice your efforts.
- Using best practices yields more predictable results.

A second study, the Turner Construction survey of building owners, developers, architects, engineers, and consultants mentioned earlier, also identified a list of benefits generated by green buildings.[8] A significant percentage of responding executives said that green buildings outperform nongreen buildings in the following categories:

- Greater health and well-being of occupants (86 percent)
- Higher building value (79 percent)

- Higher worker productivity (76 percent)
- Higher return on investment (63 percent)
- Higher asking rents (62 percent)
- Higher occupancy rates (52 percent)
- Higher retail sales (40 percent)

More recently, a survey conducted by the International Facility Management Association (IFMA) further highlights some of the behind-the-scenes reasons why increasing numbers of corporations—70 percent of those responding to its survey—are taking a serious look at their green building strategies. According to findings from the 2005 Sustainability Study, shown in Table 7-1, the motivation behind implementing green policies included concern for improved employee health and productivity, cost savings, environmental responsibility, reduced liability, and life cycle cost strategy. Of slightly less importance were public opinion and corporate or government mandates.

"The rewards of green building, like improved employee health, cost savings and environmental responsibility, have really started to emerge, so we were not surprised that more facility managers are adopting green building policies now," commented Shari Epstein, associate director of research for IFMA.

> "If we think of providing sustainable workplaces as a service, rather than as a commodity, we will build what is most economical for us to maintain and operate, and easiest for occupants to comfortably and productively use."
>
> —William McDonough, FAIA, 1993

## ■ Making the Case

In the years following the publication of *Green Development,* an overwhelming amount of research has been conducted examining in great detail both the hard and soft business benefits of green buildings. The following sections attempt to present a cross section of available research on many of the benefits mentioned above. It is important to note, however, that not all green buildings enjoy the maximum effect of all the benefits explored.

Variations in construction strategies and the degrees to which these actions are employed obviously result in different levels of financial rewards. The Sustainable Commercial Interiors diagram, which first appeared in Chapter 1 and is shown again on page 214, illustrates the three primary areas of concern—economics, environment, and social—and the results/reductions/improvements that can result from their integration into many vital aspects of a company's operations and its culture.

A first step toward appreciating the economic arguments for green building necessarily must begin with an understanding of a building's "real" cost. According to work done by the National Research Council in 1998, a building's first costs (initial construction) typically account for less than 10 percent of the money that must be spent on a facility over its life. That means operating expenses (lighting, heating/cooling, maintenance) constitute the largest cost of owning a building—as much as 85 percent of the building's real cost (also referred to as life cycle cost). Additional costs include land acquisition, conceptual planning, renewal or revitalization, and disposal.

### Table 7-1: 2005 IFMA Sustainability Survey

| Reasons for Greening Your Facility | Very Important | Somewhat Important | Not Important |
|---|---|---|---|
| Improved employee health and productivity | 73% | 26% | 1% |
| Cost savings | 71% | 28% | 1% |
| Environmental responsibility | 65% | 35% | 1% |
| Reduced liability | 47% | 42% | 12% |
| Life cycle cost strategy | 42% | 49% | 10% |
| Public opinion | 35% | 50% | 15% |
| Corporate mandate | 31% | 39% | 30% |
| Government mandate | 28% | 42% | 31% |

*Source:* The International Facility Management Association's 2005 Sustainability Study

Increased productivity
Reduced capital costs
Reduced operating costs
Reduced liability/mitigation costs
Increased property values
Quicker lease-outs/higher occupancy rates
Higher asking rents
Availability of tax incentives
Higher shareholder value
Higher retail sales

Reduced absenteeism
Lower healthcare premiums
Lower turnover rates
Decreased recruitment/
retention costs
Streamlined approvals
Marketing differential

Reduced HVAC costs
Reduced water consumption
Reduced electricity costs
Reduced landfill/tipping fees
Reduced churn rates
Avoiding mitigation hazards

ECONOMIC

SUSTAINABLE
COMMERCIAL
INTERIORS

SOCIAL

ENVIRONMENT

Perception as a good
corporate neighbor

Increased public relations/
marketing opportunities

Strengthened relationships with
community stakeholders

Increased customer loyalty
Satisfaction of doing well
by doing good

Aesthetic harmony
between building and
its natural surrounding

Reduced emissions
Reduced ozone depletion
Waste reduction
Efficient materials usage
Reduced natural resources
consumption
Reduced use of toxic substances
Reduced off-gassing/VOCs
Extended material life cycle

Enhanced employee health and well-being
Improved learning environments
Increased occupant comfort
Improved indoor air quality

Incorporating sustainable interior design strategies can achieve a
number of positive results/reductions/improvements throughout
a company's operations and culture.

## Costs and Benefits of Green Building

It has long been thought that building green means building more expensively, some estimates suggesting anywhere from 10 to 25 percent more than conventional construction. A number of research studies, however, rebut this argument, demonstrating that sustainable buildings don't necessarily have to cost prohibitively more up-front; sometimes first-cost investments of only 2 to 4 percent can earn substantial long-term paybacks. This is especially true if sustainable design goals are integrated into the design process early on.

In 2000, Xenergy Inc. and SERA Architects prepared for the City of Portland, Oregon, one of the first-ever reports examining the costs of green buildings. Titled "Green City Buildings: Applying the LEED Rating System," the study was designed to investigate options open to the city to promote the construction and operations of green buildings.[9] It had two primary objectives: determine how green three recently built city buildings were, and assess how each building could have been built to qualify as green and determine the costs and benefits that would have occurred.

Despite the fact that the three buildings fell short of the point total required for LEED certification at that time, the report suggests that they could have been designed to meet the requirements for a relatively small (if any) increase in first cost. Table 7-2, included in the report's overall findings and recommendations, shows the amounts that the original construction cost would have increased if the building had been designed to meet LEED based on the lowest first cost as well as the lowest life cycle cost. The report notes that these estimates probably overstate the actual costs if an integrated approach to meet the requirements were implemented beginning in the design and planning phase.

A second study, "Examining the Cost of Green," was conducted by Davis Langdon, a consulting firm offering cost planning and sustainable design management services to architects and owners.[10] The study analyzed forty-five library, laboratory, and academic classroom projects that were designed with a goal of meeting some level of the LEED-NC certification, and compared them to ninety-three non-LEED buildings with similar program types. All costs

**Table 7-2: Summary of Costs Required to Qualify as LEED Certified**

| Building | % Increase in First Cost | |
| --- | --- | --- |
| | Lowest First Cost Approach | Lowest Life Cycle Cost Approach |
| 1900 Building | 0.3% | 1% |
| East Precinct | 1.3% | 2.2% |
| Fire Station 17 | –0.3% | 0% |

*Source:* "Green City Buildings: Applying the LEED Rating System," prepared by Xenergy Inc. and SERA Architects for the City of Portland, OR, 2000

were normalized for time and location in order to ensure consistency for the comparisons. The study found that projects were able to achieve LEED within the same cost range as non-LEED buildings.

However, the authors pointed out, it does not necessarily follow that a specific individual building will be able to achieve LEED at no added cost. Rather, the data suggest that there are many factors affecting cost in a building and that LEED tends to have a lesser impact than other factors. What's of particular significance in influencing the cost of green, according to the Davis Langdon study, is the established intent and values of the building owner and design team. "The best and most economical sustainable designs are ones in which the features are incorporated at an early stage into the project, and where the features are integrated, effectively supporting each other, and the owner has the ability and willingness to make decisions affecting aesthetics and operations in the interest of sustainability. If the owner has no expressed desire to incorporate elements of sustainable design, it becomes more difficult to incorporate the necessary modifications into the design."[11]

Another key factor in the cost of sustainable design, notes the Davis Langdon study, is the response of bidders to the green requirements in the contract. "There are some measurable direct costs to be borne by the contractor, including the cost of documentation of the material credits, the application of the construction indoor air quality credits, and some of the schedule impacts of post construction building flush-out. These however, are relatively low costs.

"A far greater impact comes where the contractor perceives the sustainable requirements as onerous or risky," the report continues."Some construction contracts include phrases that transfer the liability for achieving LEED certification to the contractor. Clearly the contractor, when faced with this requirement, will include a greater risk contingency into its bid, if it is willing to bid at all. In order to manage the impact of sustainable design on bid response, it is necessary to write reasonable specifications and contracts, and to engage the contractor in a collaborative process, possibly even including training and bonuses for compliance, rather than transferring risks and applying penalties for failure."[12]

DPR Construction recently discovered some surprising results about the financial impact of green building processes since moving into its new 52,000-square-foot office building in Sacramento, California.[13] The firm, working with architect LPA Sacramento, Inc., designed the new facility to achieve a Silver LEED certification for new construction (LEED-NC) and a Gold rating in the LEED for Commercial Interiors (LEED-CI) program. DPR reports that it managed the LEED certification process with its own customized green building tools and performed extensive analysis of each credit, evaluating which ones offered the greatest return on investment and made the most business sense to pursue. Based on the results of this analysis, shown in Table 7-3, the firm targeted the Silver rating for its base building, which required an additional outlay of $85,000 on a $6.2 million project—just 1.4 percent—and included recycling of construction debris, selecting wood products certified by the Forest Stewardship Council, and using numerous earth-friendly materials chosen for their

### Table 7-3: DPR Construction—LEED-NC Cost and Benefit Impact Breakdown

| | Certified Credit Costs | Credit Subtotal: 10-Year Savings | Silver Rating Credit Costs | Credit Subtotal: 10-Year Savings | Gold Rating Credit Costs | Credit Subtotal: 10-Year Savings | Platinum Rating Credit Costs | Credit Subtotal: 10-Year Savings |
|---|---|---|---|---|---|---|---|---|
| **Summary of Cost Impacts** | | | | | | | | |
| Design and consulting costs | $13,800 | $0 | $13,800 | $0 | $13,800 | $0 | $13,800 | $0 |
| Sustainable site credits | $4,803 | $0 | $15,303 | $15,093 | $100,803 | $15,093 | $175,803 | $15,093 |
| Water efficiency credits | $1,800 | $9,582 | $1,800 | $9,582 | $1,800 | $9,582 | $26,888 | $10,994 |
| Energy and atmosphere credits | $0 | $125,779 | $32,374 | $397,555 | $295,274 | $729,701 | $1,027,274 | $918,370 |
| Materials and resources credits | $0 | $0 | $0 | $0 | $0 | $0 | $50,000 | $0 |
| Indoor environmental quality credits | $0 | $0 | $12,235 | $0 | $12,235 | $0 | $330,235 | $0 |
| Innovation and design process credits | $5,000 | $0 | $9,600 | $22,640 | $9,600 | $22,640 | $9,600 | $22,610 |
| | $25,403 | $135,361 | $85,112 | $444,870 | $433,512 | $777,017 | $1,633,512 | $967,097 |

high content of recycled material, durability, low maintenance, and nontoxicity. DPR also installed a turbo-core compressor, utilizing magnets rather than oil. (In its analysis, only the Platinum LEED rating was associated with higher costs than savings.)

Based on its analysis, the firm anticipated that the additional cost would be recouped in two and a half years through energy and water savings. After one year of occupancy, though, DPR reports that the payback actually exceeded its expectations and is trending toward a full return in just under two years.

Perhaps the most definitive cost-benefit analysis of green building ever conducted was completed by the Capital E Group, Lawrence Berkeley Laboratory, and forty participating California state agencies. The results, published in the October 2003 report *The Costs and Financial Benefits of Green Buildings: A Report to California's Sustainable- Building Task Force,* found that investments in green buildings pay for themselves an impressive ten times over, according to principal author Greg Kats. Additionally, he noted that the University of California Board of Regents drew on the early findings of this study "to adopt a state-wide university policy for the design of green buildings, and the report was cited as the financial rationale in 2004 legislation for New York City to require green design for all public buildings from 2006 on."[14]

This study, drawing on conventional versus green building cost data for forty LEED-registered projects—32 office buildings and eight schools—and an in-depth review of several hundred existing studies as well as conversations with architects and developers, found that sustainable buildings are very cost-effective investments. The financial benefits were found to be in lower energy, waste, and water costs, lower environmental and emissions costs, and lower operational and maintenance costs, as well as increased productivity and health.

As summarized in Table 7-4, Kats reported that the "net financial benefits of green design are estimated to be about $50 per square foot for Certified- and Silver-level green buildings, and about $65 per square foot for Gold- and Platinum-level buildings. This is over ten times larger than the average 2 percent cost premium (about $4 per square foot) for the forty green buildings analyzed."[15] Not only does the study highlight the fact that energy savings

### Table 7-4: Net Financial Benefits

| Category | 20-Year NPR |
|---|---|
| Energy value | $5.79 |
| Emissions value | $1.18 |
| Water value | $0.51 |
| Waste value (construction only)—1 year | $0.03 |
| Commissioning O&M value | $8.47 |
| Productivity and health value (Certified and Silver) | $36.89 |
| Productivity and health value (Gold and Platinum) | $55.33 |
| Less green cost premium | –$4.00 |
| Total 20-year NPV (Certified and Silver) | $48.87 |
| Total 20-year NPV (Gold and Platinum) | $67.31 |

*Source:* "Are Green Buildings Cost Effective?" by Greg Kats, *green@work,* May/June 2004.

exceed the average increased cost associated with building green, but it also illustrates that actions which positively impact employee productivity and health can result in financial gains that are far larger than the cost of construction or energy. "Consequently, even small changes in productivity and health translate into large financial benefits," Kats said. "Despite gaps in data and analysis, the report points to a clear conclusion: building green up to and including the LEED Gold level generally makes financial sense today."

*The bottom line:* In most cases, if the interior design team is brought into the design process early on (during predesign and/or programming), many strategies and materials can be investigated and incorporated that provide long-term paybacks with little to no added first costs versus conventional construction. There are significant environmental impacts associated with furniture and furnishings in an interiors fit-out, and it is crucial that the products specified deliver the best environmental benefits for the money spent. In addition, reuse and recycling efforts can reduce landfill fees as well as waste disposal volume and costs.

## Lower Operating Costs

Surprisingly, while objections to first costs seem to be the primary obstacle to implementing green design, the appeal of lower operating costs is ranked as the number one reason for adopting such practices, according to findings included in the *Green Building SmartMarket Report,* published by McGraw-Hill Construction.[16] Fifty-three percent of respondents to a McGraw-Hill survey cited operating efficiencies as the number one reason, another 14 percent said it was number two, and 11 percent ranked it as third. To the savvy green building marketer, then, any demonstrable savings in operating costs associated with green building can provide a convincing financial argument for implementing such construction practices. Savings that can be forecast to occur within a relatively short period make the argument even more persuasive. For example, using a basic payback equation (which calculates how long it takes for an expenditure to pay for itself) would help a company determine that the payback of a $3,600 expenditure on lighting upgrades that results in $900 in energy savings per year would occur within four years.

Operating efficiencies associated with green building strategies include lower energy and water costs, reduced cleaning and maintenance requirements, and a reduction in churn costs. The last is especially valuable for companies that require frequent space reconfigurations to support the way in which they conduct business. IFMA reports a mean churn rate of 41 percent for all types of facilities, with an average cost per move of $809.[17] A case study of the Rachel Carson State Office Building by the Pennsylvania Department of Environmental Protection illustrates how a single element of green building—a raised-floor system—can substantially increase efficiencies in operations costs related to churn rates. Raised-floor systems are considered an integral component of high-performance sustainable design not only because they create an underfloor plenum for HVAC air distribution (estimated to save between 20 and 35 percent in energy costs compared to conventional ceiling systems) but also because occupant-adjustable air diffusers in the floor allow each employee to adjust temperature and ventilation in work areas while the distribution system provides consistent temperature, superior ventilation and humidification, and good indoor air quality throughout the facility. Additional cost efficiencies are achieved because raised-floor systems, especially when combined with demountable wall systems and systems furniture, allow space configurations to be completed more quickly and conveniently, with little to no ductwork or construction modifications.

At the Carson facility, approximately 23 to 30 percent of the office's 1,500 employees are moved annually. Using conventional design and construction (fixed wall systems), the cost to move each employee was estimated at $2,500 per person. With the raised flooring system, however, it cost only $250 per person to move, as no demolition or construction was required. Consequently, the annual savings, as shown in Table 7-5, totaled nearly $850,000, a sum that exceeds the annual energy cost for the entire building.

*The bottom line:* Through space planning and product specification, interior designers can greatly influence the factors that help lower operating costs. Flexible work spaces that consider both existing and future needs, energy-efficient lighting, air and temperature controls, water-efficient faucets and toilets, automated window coverings, energy-efficient appliances—these are just a few of the areas where designers can help maximize the conservation of natural resources and thus maximize a building's ability to operate most efficiently. Additionally, the specification of durable and low-maintenance materials made from natural materials (sourced locally to offset the embodied energy costs/emissions of transportation) can also yield savings in maintenance and replacement costs.

| Table 7-5: Pennsylvania Department of Environmental Protection, Rachel Carson Building/Churn Case Study Comparison | |
|---|---|
| **Conventional Construction** | **High-Performance Construction** |
| 1,500 employees | 1,500 employees |
| X .25 employees | X .25 employees |
| = | = |
| 375 X $2,500 | 375 X $250 |
| = $937,500 | = $93,750 |
| **Savings of $843,750** | |

# Increased Productivity

It's a fact few companies can dispute: personnel costs, including salaries and benefits, make up by far the biggest portion of total business expenses for building occupants. It only makes sense, then, that any strategy designed to boost productivity provides a greater return on investment and significant savings to a company's bottom line. In the following essay, Bill Browning, one of the founders of RMI's Green Development Services and a contributing author to the Green Development book, as well as one of the green building field's veteran champions, makes a convincing case for the premise that sustainable buildings positively impact any company's best asset: its people.

## *The Economics of a Green Work Space*

### By Bill Browning

*Commercial space is supposed to support commerce. That's a simple enough notion. But how we treat the people in the space is generally abysmal. Indoor environmental quality should be an issue of importance to anyone who spends a lot of time inside. Since most Americans spend more than 85 percent of their lives within buildings, it would seem prudent to determine the effects of indoor environments. There are compelling examples in which improvements to visual acuity, thermal comfort, and indoor air quality have led to measurable increases in worker productivity.*

*In 1994, Rocky Mountain Institute published Greening the Building and the Bottom Line, by Joseph Romm and William Browning. This study documents eight cases in which efficient lighting, heating, and cooling have measurably increased worker productivity, decreased absenteeism, and/or improved the quality of work performed. Productivity gains from energy-efficient design can be as high as 6 to 16 percent, providing savings far in excess of just the energy savings.*

*The companies profiled undertook the energy efficiency retrofits for good economic reasons. For example, a three-year payback, typical of lighting retrofits, is equal to an internal rate of return in excess of 30 percent, well above the hurdle rate of most financial man-*

*agers. By cutting energy use by 50 cents or more per square foot, the retrofit will also significantly increase the net operating income of a building. These gains, however, are tiny compared to the cost of employees.*

*A national survey of the stock of offices available in 1990 showed that energy typically cost about $1.80 per square foot. Office workers' salaries alone, on the other hand, cost approximately $130 per square foot, or about seventy-two times as much as the energy costs. An increase of 1 percent in productivity could save more than the entire annual energy cost. Today the spread is higher. Environmental Building News estimated that salaries and benefits are now around $318 per square foot and total energy at $2.35 per square foot.*

*Productivity increases can be measured in several ways: production rate, quality of production, and changes in absenteeism. All of these can be improved if the workers suffer fewer distractions from eyestrain, poor thermal comfort, or similar factors.*

*It has been generally believed, however, that any change in a worker's environment will increase productivity. Research done at Western Electric's Hawthorne plant in Chicago from 1929 to 1932 has been interpreted to show that experiments to monitor the effect of a workplace change on productivity can be complicated by interaction between workers and researchers. This led to a widespread belief that changes in working conditions affect productivity only because they signal management's concern, the so-called Hawthorne effect. Any gains were believed to be only temporary.*

*What was less well known was that the experimental methods and results from this work were extremely questionable. The research pool included only five subjects, who along with their supervisors could monitor their own production rate on an hourly basis and received a bonus any time their production rate exceeded the plant average. Despite these flaws, for more than sixty years the pervasive mythology of the Hawthorne effect led researchers to ignore the effects of building design on productivity.*

*That's why the 1994 study by RMI is of particular importance. It generated more than 500 articles in print media and national broadcasts. It has also led* to other cases emerging, including a few that were able to link indoor air quality improvements to gains in productivity.

In 1995, a study to determine a protocol for identifying and assessing potential benefits of green buildings was initiated by Battelle Pacific Northwest National Laboratory and the Herman Miller furniture company. Funded by the U.S. Department of Energy, this initiative was an attempt to move beyond ex post facto recording of gains in productivity. This multiyear experiment used a protocol derived from E. O. Wilson's biophilia work. Biophilia posits that humans have an innate desire to be around other living things. The theory implies that since humans emerged on the savannas of Africa, there is a distinct preference for environments with similar conditions. Therefore, if similar conditions can be found in the built environment, then humans should perform better in those places.

The Herman Miller Greenhouse plant is a 300,000-square-foot facility near Zeeland, Michigan. The Battelle study included detailed measurement of light conditions, temperature, VOC and other airborne compounds, acoustics, and layout in both the existing and newly occupied facilities. Healthcare data and existing measures of productivity for the 700 employees were collected for the year prior to the move and then in the new facility. Researchers used the biophilia conditions as predictors for which portions of the new facility might capture gains in productivity. The study also included building energy performance, materials performance, and monitoring of the landscape systems. While the plant had an overall gain in productivity, certain workers did not have measurable gains. These workers tended to be in areas that had thermal and glare issues, or worked during the night shift and thus had no experience of the daylight or a connection to the outside landscape.

Heschong Mahone Group undertook a series of productivity studies for the California Energy Commission. These studies were focused on linkages between daylighting and productivity and looked at retail sales across 100 grocery stores, test performance of schoolchildren, and office workers' productivity. All of these studies involved statistically significant pools and document large increases in retail sales, test performance, and worker productivity. In 2003, as Lisa Heschong delved into the details of this work, she concluded that the quality of daylight makes a difference, and a view to nature also has a very positive influence on productivity, particularly for office workers.

Yale University, in partnership with RMI and others, has a research initiative under way to further define and test the patterns that lead to biophilic responses in buildings. The eventual goal is to create a series of spatial and qualitative templates that lead to better buildings.

Will just any environmental measure produce gains in productivity? No. It appears that only those designs and actions that improve visual acuity, thermal comfort, and IAQ seem to result in these gains. A view to nature is also important. This would then place a greater importance on good design and on a total quality approach that seeks to improve energy efficiency and improve the environmental quality of workplaces.

Companies can improve their workers' output in all sorts of ways that have nothing to do with environmental performance; for that matter, they can increase environmental quality in the work space in ways that won't necessarily improve labor productivity. But if a company is in the market to do one or the other, why not do both? Ultimately we must ask ourselves, what is it worth to be in a healthy, inspiring space?

The results of these case studies indicate the economic benefits measured to date are significant. Even if we assume only a 1 percent gain, with annual salaries at $130 per square foot, then the gain is $1.30 per square foot per year. Given a ten-year life for design measures and a 12 percent hurdle rate, then that 1 percent productivity gain has a present value of $7.36 per square foot. Seven dollars a square foot could then justifiably be added to the project budget. Understanding what measures are important to productivity and how the environmental responsiveness affects workers is an area no designer or building owner should ignore.

Bill Browning is principal of Browning Partners, LLC and a co-founder of Browning + Bannon LLC.

*The bottom line:* It is the interior designer's role to select products that best support people and teams. Poor indoor air quality—which can result from careless specification of interior furnishings and materials—has been estimated to cost U.S. businesses approximately $15 billion in worker productivity annually. Thus, even small improvements in indoor environmental quality can mean regaining millions in lost revenue. Combine those savings with the increases in productivity associated with healthy work places, and it becomes clear that the design of interior environments is essential to a company's long-term success and viability.

## Improved Employee Health and Well-being

No one wants to spend one-third of his or her life working in a building that makes the person feel uncomfortable or, worse, sick. And yet, according to the World Health Organization, one out of every three workers may be toiling away in a workplace that is making them ill.[18] As a result, today's office workers are becoming increasingly sophisticated and knowledgeable about the factors that contribute to both. This trend was clearly illustrated in the results of a 1999 study by the Building Owners and Managers Association (BOMA) and the Urban Land Institute, which analyzed 1,800 office tenants in 126 metropolitan areas. The study, "What Office Tenants Want: 1999 BOMA/ULI Office Tenant Survey Report," found that 95 percent of those responding to the survey ranked comfortable air temperature and 94 percent ranked indoor air quality as among the most important tenant comfort features. What was the number one reason tenants move out? The survey indicated most tenants left because of problems with keeping the indoor temperature comfortable.[19]

Today, it's no longer good enough to provide a functional work space; employers are increasingly focused on providing work environments that make their employees feel good physically and mentally. They have found a willing—albeit unconventional—ally in this endeavor: insurance providers, who, according to *The Kiplinger Letter*, estimate that corporate wellness programs can give employers a 50 to 400 percent return on investment on health care

costs. That means that an employer with more than fifty workers could save anywhere from $1.49 to $4.91 on each healthcare dollar spent.[20]

Vivian Loftness, professor of architecture at Carnegie Mellon University, estimated that treatment for illnesses and health conditions influenced by the indoor environment costs employers about $750 per employee annually, a figure that accounts for approximately 14 percent of all annual health insurance expenditures.[21] That $750 is spent as follows: throat irritations, $19; colds, $68; sinus conditions, $18; asthma, $101; allergies, $95; lower respiratory problems, $244; eye irritations, $18; back pain, $92; headaches, $73; and muscularskeletal disorders, $24.

Two studies reinforce the correlation between improved indoor environmental quality and employee health and well-being. A study conducted by the city of Seattle documented a 40 percent reduction in absenteeism (and a 16 percent increase in productivity) in an evaluation of thirty-one green building case projects.[22] A study by Lawrence Berkeley National Laboratory found that improvements to indoor environments could reduce health care costs and work losses from communicable respiratory diseases by 9 to 20 percent, from allergies and asthma by 18 to 25 percent, and from other nonspecific health and discomfort effects by 20 to 50 percent. That translates into savings of $17 to $58 billion annually for U.S. businesses in lost work and health care costs.[23]

As more and more documented research becomes available that demonstrates proven ties between green buildings and improved employee health, many industry analysts predict that insurance companies will begin offering lower premiums to companies that occupy these buildings.

*The bottom line:* By planning spaces and specifying those systems and amenities that employees rank as top priorities, interior designers can maximize occupants' satisfaction with their work environments. Exposure to daylight, views of the outdoors, and fresh air combine to create a better place to work. Additionally, specifying products with certified low-VOC ratings reduce the health risks associated with sick building syndrome (SBS), helping to reduce costly absenteeism rates and related health insurance premiums.

## Improved Employee Recruitment and Retention

Increased comfort, views to the outdoors, increased daylight, fresh air—these are just a few of the added-value amenities occupants of green buildings enjoy that contribute not only to a general feeling that management cares about their well-being but also to the creation of an immensely satisfying work environment that employees—especially the up-and-coming Gen Xers and Gen Yers—are increasingly reluctant to forgo. Thus, many companies that reside within green buildings are experiencing substantial reductions in employee turnover, resulting in the elimination of hundreds of thousands of dollars previously spent on recruitment and training. The savings can be truly dramatic: estimates for employee recruitment and training average between $10,000 and $12,000 for a nonprofessional employee and between $30,000 and $35,000 for a professional employee. The retention of even a handful of employees annually can easily justify the short-term consequences that might be associated with green building design.

For some companies, especially those in high-tech industries, employee recruitment and retention are top priorities—making the associated benefits of green design especially appealing. For example, the new $140 million, 350,000-square-foot Platinum LEED-rated Genzyme headquarters in Boston was designed by the German firm Behnisch, Behnisch and Partner with more than just the environment in mind. Among the twelve-story building's distinctive features: an animated curtain-wall façade, garden-like interior spaces, exterior garden terraces, flexible work spaces, and automated shading systems—all created to deliver the optimal work environment. "The theory behind it," said Genzyme spokesman Bo Piela, "is that it will be a more pleasant space for our employees to work, which is good for recruitment and retention."[24]

*The bottom line:* Companies with work environments that lead to higher levels of employee satisfaction are finding that turnover rates are decreasing; happy and healthy employees are more likely to stay put. Interior designers play a significant role in specifying many of the amenities that today's workforce values, thus helping reduce the substantial financial burdens associated with recruiting and training workers.

> *"The sustainable workplace … can attract and retain talented workers, instilling dedication and pride-of-ownership when employees can relate to working in a place, and for an organization, that is committed to protecting the earth and demonstrates that commitment through its actions."*
>
> —Guidelines for Creating High-Performance Green Buildings, Pennsylvania Department of Environmental Protection

## Reduced Liability

A startling statistic issued by the Insurance Information Institute (III) provides a glimpse into the increasing importance of indoor air quality issues in the commercial building field, a health-related issue integral to the precept of green building practices. The III reports that IAQ-related lawsuits are on a dramatic rise, with an estimated 10,000-plus lawsuits currently pending across the country alleging mold-related injuries alone. That represents a 300 percent increase since 1999. An independent study of IAQ-related illnesses by the U.S. Department of Energy confirms this trend. While defendants in these lawsuits primarily include insurance companies, property management companies, homeowner associations, designers, contractors, and sellers of single-family residences, almost any party associated with a building's construction or maintenance—building owners, managers, real estate developers, architects and interior designers, engineers, general and HVAC contractors, manufacturers of building products, and leasing agents—can be named. Depending on the relationship between the parties involved (such as employer-employee or landlord-tenant) and the type of damages claimed (such as personal injury or property damage), legal actions available to redress IAQ complaints vary. However, negligence is a frequently used legal theory, although some plaintiffs are also relying on other legal premises such as intentional tort, product liability, employment discrimination, and breach of warranty. The wide scope of such lawsuits affirms the case for increased attention to IAQ issues and the ability of green building practices to help reduce the liability associated with these legal actions.

Because many IAQ-related cases are settled out of court, few settlement figures for total costs due to unfavorable judgments in IAQ lawsuits are available. However, a handful of oft-cited benchmark IAQ cases serve as useful indicators on the dollar range and settlement costs associated with litigation.

One case example, *Call v. Prudential,* was the first major IAQ case argued before a jury and has generated important IAQ-related law even though the case was settled before a verdict was reached (for a sum estimated in the multimillion-dollar range). Claims by the plaintiffs in the case charged acts of negligence, including using building materials that emitted formaldehyde or other noxious substances, failure to warn them that the building was unsuitable for occupancy due to the resultant noxious fumes and chemicals, failure to supply sufficient fresh outside air to the building, failure to heed reports of tight building syndrome and sick building syndrome, and failure to convey information about their attendant health effects. The owner of the building, Prudential Insurance Co., was named in the suit together with the management company, the architect, the engineer, the general contractor, the companies that installed the HVAC components, and the company that built the floor where the problems originally occurred. The principal significance of this case lies in the fact that it was the first time a judge ruled that those involved in the design, construction, and installation of an HVAC system could be held liable under the theory of strict product liability, including not only the manufacturers and sellers of the system but also the architects, engineers, and installers.

In another case, U.S. Environmental Protection Agency employees alleging SBS-related illnesses filed suit against the owners and managing company of the EPA's Waterside Mall headquarters in Washington, D.C., and were awarded a jury verdict against the building owners and managers. The plaintiffs in *Bahura v. S.E.W. Investors* claimed that exposure to VOCs from new carpet installed during a renovation resulted in coughs, scratchy throats, sinus infections, fatigue, and dizziness. In 1993, a jury awarded $948,000 to the plaintiffs; in 1995, however, four of the five disabled plaintiffs' verdicts were set aside because the four could not show any physical injuries.

The DuPage County Courthouse in Illinois was the cause of a number of suits involving hundreds of litigants.

In 1991, shortly after law enforcement and judicial staff began to occupy the building, occupants began to suffer from symptoms characteristic of SBS. In March 1992, when several building occupants were removed by ambulance, the building was temporarily evacuated and eventually closed. Later that year, a number of the building's occupants filed a personal injury lawsuit against the architect, building contractors, and HVAC contractors, alleging that their illnesses were caused by the design of the ventilation system and the presence of volatile organic compounds. The county then sued the architect and contractors, seeking $3 million for fixing the building's ventilation system. The final verdict—that the county's operation of the ventilation system was the problem—meant it received no money for damages. Individual suits were settled out of court. Millions of additional dollars were spent on investigations, legal fees, renovation, and occupant compensation.

In yet another case involving a courthouse, *Martin County, Florida v. Frank Rooney,* a jury awarded $13.7 million in damages against a construction manager and three surety companies. The case involved the Martin County Courthouse, which was constructed in 1989 for $11 million. After experiencing IAQ problems (which occurred, in large part, because the south Florida humidity supported the growth of molds and fungi in building materials, including vinyl wallpaper), a $24 million rehabilitation of the facility was mandated (more than double the building's original cost). The county also had to relocate its employees for two years while the renovation work was being done. The project's original architect, mechanical engineer, and other contractors had also been named in the initial lawsuit but settled out of court.

*The bottom line:* A variety of interior furnishings and materials can contribute to poor indoor air quality and sick building syndrome—the basis for an ever-increasing number of lawsuits in recent years. Through their efforts, interior designers can prevent the specification and/or installation of toxic materials and cleaning products, materials that promote or harbor mold, or materials that emit VOCs. They can also ensure that adequate flushing periods are identified to minimize the level of indoor pollutants during construction and after occupancy. Legal precedents have demonstrated the extension of responsibility to all parties involved in the construction process, setting the standard for an interior designer's legal obligation to maintain safety standards in this regard.

> *"For every dollar invested in energy performance upgrades for leased properties, the return is a $2 to $3 increase in asset value."*
>
> —U.S. Department of Environmental Protection

## Property Value and Income Will Increase

As operating costs of a building diminish, it naturally follows that the property's appraised value increases due to a rise in the building's net operating income—an increase of ten times the annual cost savings for a capitalization rate of 10 percent, reports the New Buildings Institute in its *Benefits Guide: A Design Professional's Guide to High Performance Building Benefits.* Thus, a 75,000-square-foot building that saves 50 cents per square foot per year in operating costs ($37,500) will see the value of the building increase by $375,000.[25]

The report *Hidden Value: Recognizing the Asset Value of High-Performance Buildings,* also delves into the opportunities available for increasing the value of sustainable buildings.[26] The study provides a telling example of how the simple retrofit of an energy-efficient lighting system dramatically increases the building owner's cash flow.

In the example, the owner of an office building is approached by its sole tenant regarding upgrades that include an energy-efficient lighting system. Two lighting strategies (replacement of 14,000 fluorescent lamps with lower-wattage versions and installation of more than 900 motion sensors) are employed to reduce energy costs by approximately 30 percent, which results in a monthly savings of 81 cents per square foot. The owner, seeking an Energy Star label for the building, decides to pay for the entire project, recouping the investment with a rent increase of $390,000 per month (an amount equal to three-fourths of the energy cost savings), which the tenant agrees to. The tenant still reduces its monthly operating

expenses by $130,000 and also benefits from improved lighting. In the end, the owner has improved the long-term marketing quality of the building, reduced the first cost of the retrofit, and increases the building income from $47.95 per square foot to $48.55 per square foot. As illustrated in Table 7-6, the retrofit pays for itself in 1.5 years and provides the owner with a cash flow surplus of $390,000 each month afterward.

*The bottom line:* The efficiency and performance aspects of commercial interior design can greatly contribute to a reduction in the operating costs of a building, thus raising its appraised value due to a rise in net operating income. Tenants are increasingly willing to help pay for any additional costs associated with increased operating efficiencies, as those savings can be carried over into their own direct operating budgets.

| Table 7-6: Cash Analysis of Energy-Saving Lighting Retrofit | | |
|---|---|---|
| | **Owner** | **Tenant** |
| **Before Retrofit** | | |
| Rent | +$30,783,900 | –$30,783,900 |
| Energy costs | — | –$1,733,400 |
| Other operating costs | — | –$2,863,300 |
| Balance (monthly) | +$30,783,900 | –$35,380,600 |
| **After Retrofit** | | |
| Rent | +$31,173,900 | –$31,173,900 |
| Energy costs | — | –$1,213,400 |
| Other operating costs | — | –$2,863,300 |
| Balance (monthly) | +$31,173,900 | –$35,250,600 |
| | (added income of $390,000 per month) | (savings of $130,000 per month) |

*Source: Hidden Value: Recognizing the Asset Value of High-Performance Buildings,* prepared by the Institute for Market Transformation for the New York State Energy Research and Development Authority (NYSERDA)

## Understanding the Value of Value

Traditional methods of valuation have obscured the fact that green buildings bring real business benefits and increased market value. As a result, it's time to reassess our valuation methods, say Chris Corps and Dr. Ross Davies, authors of the article "Green Value: Bringing Real Business Benefits."[27] "Green, or sustainable, buildings present a huge and largely untapped commercial opportunity to valuers and their clients. Demand is rising fast for green new-builds, while the market for green retrofits of existing conventional buildings is larger still. Yet if these commercial opportunities are to be grasped, valuers need to take a fresh look at the ways in which they view the effect of green features and related performance on asset value," the authors note, basing their opinion on the findings of a report entitled *Green Value: Relating the Market Value of a Real Estate Asset to Its Green Features and Related Performance.*[28] The study included case study interviews with developers, owners, and occupiers of green office, industrial, retail, residential, and educational buildings across Canada, the United Kingdom, and the United States. Its objective was to test the assumption of many builders, owners, developers, lenders, and valuers that there is no link between market value and green features and related performance.

Corps and Davies report that the RICS research has concluded that this view is a fallacy, finding that green building features and practices can and do benefit the market value of a real estate asset. However, they note, central to the debate over the link between green building features and asset value itself are the different notions of what constitutes "value."

The authors argue that the green building industry needs a better grasp of the financial methodology used to analyze property investments, while accounting and valuation bodies need to catch up on the benefits of green buildings as well as the costs. Both sides need to agree on consistent valuation measures that better represent a green building's value. They cite as an example one case in which a traditional development failed, while its directly comparable green counterpart thrived. "Such evidence has to start being absorbed into valuations," they propose.

Source: *RICS Business,* November/December 2005.

## Quicker Sales and Lease-outs

The higher-class amenities and increased comfort associated with green buildings oftentimes results in faster property sales or leases, according to many owners and developers—thus minimizing the time for which lease space remains unoccupied. The potential for tenant savings in the areas of energy use and water consumption also capture the attention of prospective tenants. The U.S. Environmental Protection Agency, for example, estimates that a tenant can save about 50 cents per square foot annually through no-cost management and operational strategies that cut energy use by 30 percent—an accumulated savings of $50,000 or more in a five-year lease of 20,000 square feet of office space.[29] As a result of these factors, green properties are oftentimes able to generate higher-than-average prices. "Because people want to live and work in buildings that are good for their health, there are marketing benefits, too. Green office buildings also command rents as much as 10 percent above the norm," said Douglas Durst, president of the Durst Organization.[30]

This competitive advantage is especially attractive during downturns in the real estate market. Because green buildings can differentiate themselves from other properties on the market, they stand out in the virtual crowd, sometimes generating valuable (free) publicity that conventional properties do not.

*The bottom line:* Many of the business benefits derived from green buildings stimulate increased interest in the property on the part of potential buyers and tenants, which often translate into quicker sales and/or lease agreements. In some cases, these come with higher-than-normal price tags. As many of these benefits accrue from high-performance space planning and interior furnishings criteria, commercial interior designers play an important role in helping a company achieve this competitive advantage.

## Attractive Financial Incentives

A variety of financial incentives at the local, state, and national levels provide attractive budgetary enticements to strengthen the business case for building green.

At the federal level, for example, the recently enacted Energy Policy Act of 2005 (EPAct) provides numerous tax deductions for those buildings targeting substantial energy savings. The following summary, provided by the Tax Incentives Assistance Project (TIAP) and current as of March 2006, details the tax savings made available by the new legislation[31]:

> A tax deduction of up to $1.80 per square foot is available to owners or tenants (or designers, in the case of government-owned buildings) of new or existing commercial buildings that are constructed or reconstructed to save at least 50% of the heating, cooling, water heating and interior lighting energy cost of a building that meets ASHRAE Standard 90.1-2001. Partial deductions of up to $.60 per square foot can be taken for comparable reductions from any one of three building systems—the building envelope, lighting, or heating and cooling system—that meets goals consistent with achieving the 50% savings for the entire building. An interim system-specific goal for lighting . . . allows prorated deductions from $.30 to $.60 per square foot for [some] lighting systems.

> The person or organization that makes the expenditures for construction is generally the recipient of the allowed tax deductions. This is usually the building owner, but for some HVAC or lighting efficiency projects, it could be the tenant. For government-owned buildings, the deduction may be taken by the building or system.

The builder (or designer, in the case of publicly-owned buildings) can take the deduction in the year the property was placed in service. The building or system must be certified, with inspection and testing, as meeting the energy cost savings goal according to rules to be issued by the IRS in consultation with the U.S. Department of Energy. . . . In the case of lighting systems, simpler certification methods should be possible.

For lighting systems . . . the law specifies that a deduction of $.30 per square foot can be taken if the lighting system employs dual switching (ability to switch roughly half the lights off and still have fairly uniform light distribution) and reduces installed lighting power by at least 25% from values specified in specific cited tables in ASHRAE Standard 90.1-2001. As lighting power reductions climb from 25% to 40%, the deduction is increased proportionally, up to $0.60 for a 40% power reduction (plus the dual switching). This prorated credit does not apply to warehouse lighting.

TIAP reports that the EPAct also provides for tax incentives for businesses incorporating solar energy systems for their use (including solar water heating, certain solar lighting systems and photovoltaic systems) and "placed in service" in 2006 and 2007. The tax credits are for 30% of the cost of the system.

Many states also provide attractive financial tax savings related to green building. New York was the first state to implement a Green Building Tax Credit, aimed first and foremost at motivating developers to invest in environmentally friendly commercial and multifamily housing units, but also to provide financial motivation for building owners and tenants as well. The 2000 tax credit (which was extended again in 2005) allows for the following:

> Builders who meet energy goals and use environmentally preferable materials can claim up to $3.75 per square foot for interior work and $7.50 per square foot for exterior work against their state tax bill. To qualify for the credit, a building must be certified by a licensed architect or engineer, and must meet specific requirements for energy use, materials selection, indoor air quality, waste disposal and water use. In new buildings, this means energy use cannot exceed 65% of use permitted under the

New York State energy code; in rehabilitated buildings, energy use cannot exceed 75%. Ventilation and thermal comfort must meet certain requirements, and building materials, finishes and furnishings must contain high percentages of recycled content and renewable source material and cannot exceed specified maximum levels of toxicity. Waste disposal and water use must also comply with criteria set forth in the law.

Ten percent of the cost of ozone-friendly air-conditioning equipment, 30% of the installed cost of fuel cells and 100% of the cost of built-in photovoltaics (PV) solar panels may also be recouped through the credit. Fuel cells, which emit only carbon dioxide and water, and photovoltaic panels, which convert sunlight directly to electricity with no emissions at all, both carry high up-front costs compared to conventional energy delivery technologies.[32]

Since the adoption of the New York state legislation, other states have passed similar legislation, including Maryland, Massachusetts, New Jersey, and Oregon, as have a growing number of local municipalities. Additionally, some states have passed legislation offering income, corporate, property, and/or sales tax incentives related to green building. Income tax incentives vary, although most are implemented through tax credits, allowances, and deductions. Like income tax incentives, corporate incentives allow corporations to receive credits for the cost of equipment and related expenditures. In some cases, deductions for any income received from royalties related to patents may be allowed. State property tax incentives typically include straightforward exemptions, although some special assessments may also be included. Finally, sales tax incentives typically exempt purchases of related equipment from the sales tax. Table 7-7 provides an overview of current incentives by state.

A number of state and local initiatives also are available that provide funding for companies seeking to explore green design and building strategies. The intent of many is to increase the competitive advantage of their city and/or region. For example, Pittsburgh's Green Building Fund is available to qualified developers who plan to integrate green design into either new construction or rehabilitation projects. The fund provides a source of flexible financing,

| State | Income Tax | Corporate Tax | Property Tax | Sales Tax |
|---|---|---|---|---|
| Alabama | • | | | |
| Arizona | • | | | • |
| Arkansas | | • | | |
| California | | | • | |
| Colorado | | • | • | |
| Connecticut | | • | | • |
| Florida | | | | • |
| Hawaii | • | • | | • |
| Idaho | • | | | |
| Illinois | | | • | |
| Indiana | | | • | |
| Iowa | | | • | • |
| Kansas | | • | • | |
| Maryland | | | | • |
| Massachusetts | • | • | • | • |
| Minnesota | | | • | • |
| Missouri | | • | | |
| Montana | • | | • | |
| Nevada | | | • | |
| New Hampshire | | | • | |
| New Jersey | | | | • |
| New York | | • | • | |
| North Carolina | • | • | • | |
| North Dakota | • | | • | |
| Ohio | | • | • | • |
| Oregon | • | • | • | |
| Rhode Island | • | • | • | |
| South Dakota | | | • | |
| Texas | | • | • | |
| Utah | | | • | |
| Vermont | | | • | • |
| Virginia | | | • | |
| Washington | | | | • |
| West Virginia | | | • | |
| Wisconsin | | | • | |

Table 7-7: States with Tax Incentives for Green Construction

Source: Office of Energy Efficiency and Renewable Energy, U.S. Department of Energy

## Noteworthy Outcomes

While all environmentally responsible buildings can enjoy the business benefits described in this chapter, some market segments report sector-specific outcomes that are helping to fuel the momentum toward greater integration of green building strategies.

### Healthcare

◆ Studies have shown that cardiac care patients with good views from their beds showed better and faster improvement.
◆ Premature babies gained weight faster in nurseries with natural daylight.
◆ Improved air quality has been demonstrated to decrease hospital-acquired infections.
◆ Studies suggest that brighter light can reduce medication errors.

### Schools

◆ A study of high school students in California reported that schools with good daylighting showed up to 20 percent better test scores in math, and 26 percent better test scores in reading.
◆ A study of schools in North Carolina concluded that children attending schools with full-spectrum light were healthier in general and absent on average three to four days less than students in conventionally-lit classrooms.
◆ Schools with improved indoor air quality demonstrate a reduction in absenteeism among students and teachers, especially those who suffer from asthma and other respiratory ailments.
◆ Schools with green design features, such as solar panels or furnishings made from recycled materials, have found these to be valuable hands-on teaching tools.

### Retail

◆ Wal-Mart and other retailers reported higher sales of merchandise displayed under skylights.
◆ Consumers demonstrate a preference for shopping in stores with skylights, describing them as cleaner, more spacious, and more open.
◆ In October 2005, Wal-Mart unveiled an environmental plan to boost energy efficiency, eliminate waste, and curb greenhouse gases that management hopes will demonstrate the company's commitment to cutting costs while adopting greener practices.

### Hospitality

◆ Hotels with a solid ecofriendly message report increased sales as a result of this positive marketing differential and the press coverage it generates.
◆ Towel and sheet changing cards can save hotels 5 percent on utilities alone.

with loan amounts from $200,000 to $400,000, subordinate collateral positions, fixed market-rate financing for the term of the loan, extended repayment terms when necessary, and potential support for soft costs associated with the LEED rating system (certification with LEED is a requirement).

For nonprofit organizations, the Kresge Foundation is sweetening the proverbial financial pie by providing special funding for green building projects. Through its Green Building Initiative, launched in late 2003, the foundation makes available special planning grants of $50,000 to

$100,000. It also includes bonus grants of $150,000 to $250,000 to Kresge grantees whose building projects become LEED-certified. As of November 2005, the Kresge Foundation reported that it had awarded sixty-three green building planning grants totaling $4,146,000 and another thirty-three grants totaling $5,450,000 as a bonus program for grantee organizations achieving LEED certification. Kresge's planning grants cover some of the costs associated with planning a green building. Grant funds are not meant to cover feasibility studies or routine architectural or development costs. Rather, they should cover the added costs of implementing a full integrated design approach. These costs include professional services to facilitate charrettes during the predesign period that involve stakeholders and members of the design team; energy analysis and modeling; materials analysis, including products and technology that support green building development; ecological site planning, including stormwater management; commissioning expenses associated with the planning process; and costs associated with LEED registration and initial documentation.

*The bottom line:* By working with clients to help them understand the implications of available tax incentives and building grants, interior designers can implement those design strategies that will fully realize the bottom-line benefits of building green.

## Increased Recognition of and Respect for Environmental Efforts

An integral part of the stakeholder concept mentioned earlier in this chapter is the ability of a company to be perceived as a good corporate neighbor. In other words, external parties believe the company is behaving in a respectful manner that is sensitive to the community around them and to the people who inhabit it. Thus, actions that convey a respect for the condition of the natural environment—especially those that appear to go above and beyond ordinary efforts—also appear to respect those who have a stake in it. This contributes to the creation of highly valuable, albeit intangible, assets such as goodwill, a positive image, and enhanced loyalty.

The idea of community, though, can also be extended beyond local geographical boundaries to include parties with which the company has relationships, such as clients, the public, suppliers, media, politicians, and regulators. The resultant benefits—such as increases in publicity coverage and marketing exposure, attractiveness to potential recruits, and stronger community relations—can be highly lucrative. Some municipalities, including Arlington, Virginia, Santa Barbara, California, and Scottsdale, Arizona, even offer streamlined zoning considerations and permit reviews for green projects, helping avoid costly permit delays.

Certainly the new green headquarters for Bank of America that will soar fifty-two stories tall in midtown Manhattan has gained much external traction for the financial services business—and will most likely continue to do so long after it opens in 2008. The Durst Organization and Bank of America broke ground in summer 2005 on One Bryant Park, a steel, aluminum, and glass skyscraper that aims to be the first high-rise office building to achieve a Platinum LEED rating. The bank's new headquarters, designed by Cook+Fox Architects, will showcase how the combination of innovative green design and technology can reduce pollution and operating costs while enhancing the health and productivity of occupants. A $1 billion project, it will include an electricity-generating station (heat generated by the $10 million power plant will be used to make ice at night to help air-condition the building). Translucent, high-performance glass in floor-to-ceiling glazing permits maximum sunlight in interior spaces. The building will capture and reuse all rainwater and wastewater, saving millions of gallons of water each year. Finally, it will be built largely from recycled and recyclable materials sourced from within 500 miles of New York City.

Bank of America has been an active participant in environmental advocacy issues for many years, and thus its new headquarters will serve to put a public face on its efforts. Certainly, the citizens of New York City can't help but feel they are gaining the very best of new neighbors when their governor, George Pataki, proclaims, "The new Tower—which will stand as one of the world's most environmentally responsible high-rise buildings—is a shining example of how we can create jobs while also protecting the environment. I want to commend the Bank of America and The Durst Organization for their commitment to New York. This project will not only help us reach our goal of creating one million jobs in New York by the end of the decade, it will bolster our efforts to provide the safest, cleanest environment possible for future generations of New Yorkers to enjoy."[33]

The retail giant Wal-Mart also captured a plethora of positive press headlines and environmental accolades worldwide when it announced a number of ecological initiatives in 2005, including a pilot plastic recycling project, two experimental green supercenters, a waste reduction strategy, and a number of energy efficiency/greenhouse gas reduction programs. The attention painted a very earth-friendly face on the company, an objective that is oftentimes difficult for such a large corporation to do. In this case, though, basking in the limelight comes with a caveat. A company that garners such incredible levels of publicity lays itself open to scrutiny in all areas. So while many organizations applauded Wal-Mart's efforts in this regard, they did so with a cautionary tone. Explained Carl Pope, executive director of the Sierra Club, in his formal statement about the announcement: "Wal-Mart's new commitments to increase efficiency and reduce pollution and waste are important first steps for a company that has such a profound impact on our environment. More companies should take these positive steps towards safer and healthier communities. While this announcement shows that Wal-Mart can be [a] leader, it also demonstrates that they should be able to take equal steps to protect workers. Wal-Mart should also include in their plans an effort to more-responsibly site their stores, obey our nation's clean water laws, which have been violated in the past, and address community concerns at all of their locations."[34]

*The bottom line:* Environmental issues continue to gain momentum with consumers, and a company's green building provides tangible evidence of corporate concern for the same. Through their design efforts, interior designers can help companies maximize the aesthetic appeal and performance of their green interior spaces, helping them gain valuable exposure with all stakeholders.

## Best Practices Deliver More Predictable Results

The U.S. federal government is actually one of the lead players in the sustainable building movement. The General Services Administration's (GSA) Public Buildings Service (PBS) is a leader in building green not only because of its place in the U.S. real estate market—owning, leasing, and managing nearly 350 million square feet—but because of its level of commitment to incorporating principles of sus-

tainable design and energy efficiency into all of its building projects. In fact, beginning in 2003, the GSA began requiring that all building projects must meet criteria for basic LEED certification.

This mandate underscores GSA's advocacy of "best practices," which is defined as "specific business processes that work for one organization and create ideas, options and insights for other organizations." Specifically, the GSA explores methods, processes, or practices about which one or more of the following pertain: it produces superior results; it leads to exceptional performance; it is recognized by an industry expert; it is deemed so by an organization's customers; and/or it is clearly a new or innovative use of personnel, resources, or technology.

A key advantage of green building—one might argue that it is an inherent advantage—is the use of best practices to achieve more predictable results, largely because the practice of green design necessarily involves a more disciplined and integrated approach that serves to mitigate construction challenges and surprises. The result, then, is the ability to enhance the quality of the final product: a building that delivers environmental, economic, social, and health benefits for all.

Recognizing this advantage, many federal agencies in addition to the GSA adhere to the same best-practices policies it espouses. For example, the Department of Interior supports the use of LEED-EB by its facilities and all partnered projects. The Department of State now requires all embassy construction for the next ten years to use LEED guidelines. The U.S. EPA requires that all facility construction and new building acquisition projects larger than 20,000 square feet meet LEED Silver standards. Two government agencies—the U.S. Air Force and the U.S. Army—have both adopted LEED principles into their construction guidelines.

Green building's best-practices results have also been noted at the state and local levels, where governing bodies are enacting legislation to ensure that their investments in building projects deliver superior performance. Most of the current legislation on the books requires a minimum of LEED certification for projects, while others require LEED Silver. The City of Scottsdale, Arizona, however, took a more stringent approach when in 2005 it became the first city in the nation to adopt a LEED Gold rating requirement for both new city buildings and renovations. Table 7-8 summarizes the green building legislation and recommendations offered by state and municipal agencies as of early 2006.

*The bottom line:* Sustainable design isn't about dos and don'ts as much as it's about context. Interior designers involved with designing and building green offer a funda-mental understanding of the principles of sustainability and then a thorough knowledge of the science and tech-nology necessary to achieve a client's goals (whether pub-lic or private)—as well as the goals of the communities in which projects are located.

| Table 7-8: Green Building Legislation and Government Recommendations (as of June 2006) | | | |
|---|---|---|---|
| State | Re: LEED | Comments | Municipal Initiatives |
| Arizona | All state-funded buildings required to meet LEED Silver. | Newly constructed state-funded buildings also required to incorporate renewable energy. | **Phoenix**—City council encourages projects to follow LEED guidelines, but certification is not required.<br>**Scottsdale**—All new occupied city buildings of any size to achieve LEED Gold. All future renovations and nonoccupied city buildings to be designed and built to include as many principles as possible from LEED and city's own Green Building Program. |
| Arkansas | | State agencies encouraged to use green design strategies including LEED. Legislative Task Force on Sustainable Building Design and Practices reviews and advises on sustainable building issues. | |
| California | LEED Silver required for all new and renovated state-owned facilities. | | **Alameda County**—All county projects must meet LEED Silver.<br>**Berkeley**—Municipal buildings over 5,000 sq. ft. required to meet LEED Silver.<br>**Calabasas**—All nonresidential city and privately-owned buildings between 500 and 5,000 sq. ft. to be LEED certified. Buildings over 5,000 sq. ft. must meet LEED Silver.<br>**Long Beach**—LEED Silver required for new municipal construction over 7,500 sq. ft.<br>**Los Angeles**—All city-funded building projects required to be LEED certified.<br>**Oakland**—All municipals projects (new and renovation) with a minimum construction cost of $3 million to meet LEED Silver.<br>**Pasadena**—All new commercial (25,000 sq. ft. or more; city buildings of 5,000 sq. ft. or more) and residential construction (at least four stories high) to achieve LEED certified at minimum.<br>**Pleasanton**—All new public projects to achieve LEED Gold, and all city-owned, occupied existing projects to achieve LEED-EB Silver. Developers receiving financial assistance from Portland Development Commission must achieve LEED standards.<br>**Sacramento**—All city projects require LEED certification; projects over 5,000 sq. ft. to meet LEED Silver.<br>**San Diego**—LEED certification required for all public projects. Plan review and construction incentives for projects using LEED are available.<br>**San Francisco**—All municipal new construction, additions, and major renovations (both city-owned and leaseholds) over 5,000 sq. ft. to meet LEED Silver, with credits for LEED AP and Commissioning mandated.<br>**San Jose**—LEED certification required for all municipal projects over 10,000 gross sq. ft.<br>**San Mateo County**—New projects and additions built by the county and greater than 5,000 sq. ft. to achieve highest practical LEED rating certification. Smaller projects encouraged to follow LEED standards, but are not required.<br>**Santa Monica**—All new city projects to achieve LEED Silver. Projects registering for LEED certification with proper documentation receive priority plan checks. Buildings eligible for expedited permits are also eligible for grants of $20,000 to $35,000 depending on the level of LEED certification. |

*(continued)*

| State | Re: LEED | Comments | Municipal Initiatives |
|-------|----------|----------|----------------------|
| Colorado | Adopted LEED-EB and incorporated LEED-NC for all state buildings. | Colorado Greening Government Coordinating Council develops and implements conservation policies. | **Boulder**—All new or significantly renovated city facilities required to meet LEED Silver. |
| Connecticut | | Bill passed by Senate, pending in House, requiring new state-funded construction to achieve LEED Silver. | . |
| Florida | | | **Gainesville**—All government county buildings to be LEED certified. Permit-related incentives available. **Sarasota County**—All county government buildings to be LEED certified. Reduced building permit fees and streamlined review available. |
| Georgia | | | **Atlanta**—All city-funded projects over 5,000 sq. ft. or more than $2 million required to meet LEED Silver certification. |
| Illinois | | State of Illinois Capital Development Board considering requirement of LEED certification for public projects. | **Chicago**—All new city-funded construction and major renovations projects must meet LEED certification, with the goal of 25% of existing municipal buildings certified by 2020. Green Tax Increment Financing process and density bonuses under development. **Cook County**—Ordinance proposed requiring LEED certification of all county building projects. **Normal**—LEED certification required in the central business district for public and private new construction over 7,500 sq. ft. at ground level. |
| Maine | All new or expanding state buildings to incorporate LEED guidelines provided that standards can be met on a cost-effective basis. | | |
| Maryland | All capital projects greater than 5,000 gross sq. ft. to be LEED certified. | A green building standard, such as but not necessarily LEED Silver, must be used for state capital projects. | **Bowie**—All municipal projects to adhere to green building criteria and to use LEED guidelines on project-by-project basis. The city's first green demonstration project to be LEED Silver. |
| Massachusetts | | Considering LEED for all state projects. | **Acton**—Density bonus for LEED certification. **Arlington**—All new buildings and major renovations to achieve LEED Silver at minimum. **Boston**—The city's Green Building Task Force aims to establish LEED silver for all city-owned projects, and amend the Boston Zoning Code to require all large projects built in the city are LEED certified. |
| Michigan | All state-funded new construction and major renovations over $1 million to be LEED certified. | | **Grand Rapids**—All new construction, renovations, and building operations to be LEED certified. |
| Missouri | | | **Kansas City**—All new city buildings to meet a minimum LEED Silver. |
| Nebraska | | | **Omaha**—All new Metropolitan Community College construction projects and sites to be at minimum LEED certified. |

| State | Re: LEED | Comments | Municipal Initiatives |
|-------|----------|----------|----------------------|
| New Jersey | All new schools to incorporate LEED guidelines. | New Jersey Economic Schools Construction Corp. encourages LEED but does not require certification under its $12 billion public school construction program. | **Cranford**—All township-funded facilities projects and township-owned buildings to meet LEED Silver. Developers also may apply for density bonus when achieving LEED certification.<br>**Princeton**—Master plan encourages, but does not require, the use of LEED guidelines for public facilities and publicly funded projects. |
| New Mexico | All public buildings over 15,000 sq. ft. to be LEED Silver. | | **Albuquerque**: City-funded projects 5,000 sq. ft. or larger must meet minimum LEED Silver certification. Includes LEED-NC, -EB, -CS, or -CI. |
| New York | | Encourages, but does not require, state projects to seek LEED certification. Financial incentives available through New York State Energy research and Development Authority and New York State Green Building State Credit Program. | **New York City**—New construction, additions, and substantial reconstruction of all city-owned buildings costing $2 million or more to meet LEED Silver. Legislation also applies to private projects that receive $10 million or more in public financing or at least half financed by public money.<br>**Suffolk County**—Capital program pilot project under way to be LEED certified. |
| Nevada | All state-funded buildings required to be LEED certified or higher, in accordance with LEED or equivalent standard. | Each biennium, at least two occupied public buildings whose construction is sponsored or funded by the state must be designated as a demonstration project or be equivalent to a LEED Silver or higher certification, or an equivalent standard. Tax abatements for property that has an eligible LEED Silver building, and tax exemptions for products or materials used in the construction of a LEED Silver building. | |
| Oregon | | Business Energy Tax Credit for sustainable buildings is tied to the LEED certification level achieved. LEED silver is minimum; applies to LEED-NC, -CI, and -CS. | **Eugene**—Uses LEED-NC as guideline for all new city-funded construction. LEED-EB used as assessment tool. |
| Pennsylvania | | Financial incentives available to public school districts meeting LEED Silver. Four state funds provide incentives for investments in energy efficiency and renewable energy projects. | |
| Rhode Island | All new construction or renovation of public buildings to meet minimum LEED Silver. | | |
| Texas | | | **Austin**—LEED certification required for all public projects over 5,000 sq. ft.<br>**Dallas**—All city buildings larger than 10,000 sq. ft. to meet at minimum LEED Silver.<br>**Houston**—All city-owned buildings and facilities over 10,000 sq. ft. to use LEED to the "greatest extent practical and reasonable," with a target of LEED Silver. |
| Utah | | | **Salt Lake City**—All new city-constructed buildings and major renovations over 10,000 sq. ft. to meet LEED Silver. |

*(continued)*

| State | Re: LEED | Comments | Municipal Initiatives |
|---|---|---|---|
| Virginia | | | **Arlington**—Allows higher density for commercial and private developments meeting LEED Silver. All commercial site plan applications required to include LEED Scorecard and LEED AP on project. All projects must contribute to a green building fund for county education and outreach. |
| Washington | All state-funded projects over 5,000 sq. ft., including state-funded schools, to achieve LEED Silver certification. Dept. of Corrections requires LEED Silver for buildings down to 5,000 sq. ft. | LEED Silver is the standard for design and construction by Dept. of Administration, several state colleges and other agencies; certification is not required. New Energy Life Cycle Cost Analysis Guidelines require all new and remodeled public projects over 25,000 sq. ft. to analyze a LEED Silver building (or equivalent rating approved by Dept. of Administration). Scorecard that reflects this analysis required during submittal process. | **Issaquah**—Free professional LEED consultation available to developers, as well as streamlined permit reviews. **King County**—All new public construction projects to be LEED certified. Application of LEED criteria encouraged for building retrofits and tenant improvements. **Seattle**—All city-owned projects (new and renovations) over 5,000 gross sq. ft. to meet minimum LEED Silver. Economic incentives for new and existing private construction projects available. |
| Washington, D.C. | | | LEED Silver at minimum required by Dept. of Parks and Recreation for all new construction and major renovation. |
| Wisconsin | Dept. of Administration working to establish standards based on LEED. | New state facilities to be 30% more energy efficient than required by commercial code. Energy usage in state buildings to be reduced 10% by 2008 and 20% by 2010. | |
| CANADA | | | |
| Alberta | | | **Calgary**—New or significant renovations over 500 sq. m. to achieve LEED Silver or higher. |
| British Columbia | | | **Vancouver**—LEED for British Columbia (adopted in July 2004) required for all new civic buildings greater than 500 sq.m. New public buildings to achieve LEED Gold, with specific energy points mandated. |
| Ontario | | | **Toronto**—committed to installing green roofs "when practical" on new and existing city-owned buildings. For new construction, city targets coverings 50 to 75% of each building's footprint. |

*Sources:* USGBC; federal, state, and municipality websites; various Internet news services

# ▌A Sustainable, Sustaining ▌Workplace

One of the most important lessons to be learned from an examination of the financial implications of green design is that all factors are interrelated. It is nearly impossible, for example, to discuss first-cost issues without considering operating efficiencies and improved productivity. Equally related are the issues of employee health and well-being and employee recruitment and retention, or property values and risk factors.

Central to this whole discussion, according to the Sustainable Buildings Industry Council (SBIC), is that green buildings must be looked at as an integrated whole and their performance—and the performance of their occupants—evaluated over time. Only then, says the SBIC, do you begin to get a true sense of what the sustainable workplace can mean to a company's bottom line, regardless of whether it's measured in economic or human terms. More and more, it notes, people are realizing that one needn't be sacrificed at the expense of the other and, in fact, physical and economic well-being are inextricably linked.

# 8
# SUBSTANCE AND STYLE

*"What you do is to teach a hundred
what I have taught you,
and inspire each of them to teach a hundred.
That's how it's always done."
"Yes ... but is it enough?"
Ishmael frowned. "Of course it's not enough.
But if you begin anywhere else,
there's no hope at all."*

From *Ishmael* by Daniel Quinn

We are a society that loves to learn from example; we especially relish success stories because they reaffirm our belief that it is indeed possible to transform the theories and principles of our ideals into reality. We inwardly cheer when obstacles are overcome and applaud when goals are met—and we think, "If they can do it, so can I."

For that very reason, we include here twelve project case studies that illustrate the "can-do" attitude that's required to transform the emerging principles of sus-tainable interior design into powerful, real-life examples of great green design. The projects are varied in size, scale, and scope, but each one is filled with substance and style—the necessary ingredients to capture the interest, the imagination, and above all the inspiration that will drive home the important lessons that sustainable design has to offer. Each of these projects has transformed environments, attitudes, and cultures—while, of course, being a little kinder to the earth in the process.

## ◼ Greenpeace: Materials Matter

It's not surprising that sustainable design issues were a high priority when Greenpeace—one of the world's most visible organizations campaigning against environmental degradation—was relocating its Washington, D.C., office. Yet, despite its global environmental expertise, the specifics of greening the workplace was not an area where Greenpeace had a lot of knowledge.

A chance meeting between Greenpeace project coordinator Bill Richardson and Ken Wilson, AIA, eventually led to the group selecting EnvisionDesign, Wilson's newly formed design firm with a keen interest in and high enthusiasm for sustainable design, as project architects. Early on, the two parties agreed that Greenpeace's mission should drive the design solutions.

After numerous potential sites were rejected, including typical "glass box" office buildings, Greenpeace decided on a site that was actually five buildings that were subsequent-

Yellow was used throughout to define portals. The Risom furniture with cotton webbing on solid wood frames was special ordered to be fabricated from FSC-certified maple. Visible is the ceiling design scheme combining exposed structural, electrical, and mechanical systems with carefully placed drywall surfaces. *Photography © Michael Moran*

ly joined together and renovated, located in an area of the city undergoing major redevelopment with convenient access to the Metro rail system. Greenpeace liked the idea of "recycling a building by making it functional again." Greenpeace also was blessed in having a developer, Douglas Jemal, who bought into their vision. Amazingly, Greenpeace wrote into the lease that the base building—all of it, not just its own space—would be PVC-free except for the electrical wiring, for which no viable alternative exists.

## Open Office, Casual Culture

An incredible team effort was needed to transform this funky old building. Greenpeace's former offices had been a rabbit warren, sectionalized and inhibiting staff interaction. Meeting the goal of opening up the office and yet maintaining the old building's personality was challenging because each of the five buildings had varying ceiling heights and floor levels to reconcile. Ramps were constructed not only as a connection device but also to provide handicapped access. The handrails on either side of the ramps are an attractive decorative element.

Despite considerable employee resistance to change from its previous private office layout, the decision was made to incorporate an open office plan in part because of the anticipated savings it would achieve. In the end, the project realized a 45 percent savings in drywall not used and a 61 percent savings in unused doors. Lighting, measured in watts, represented a 39 percent savings, not including the additional savings from the light sensors. Open workstations made it possible to increase the number of workspaces by 65 percent, from fifty-seven to ninety-four. Greenpeace also wanted to promote better teamwork and communication among the staff, goals easier to accomplish with the open plan system. Phone closets and huddle rooms were provided for privacy, but they're not used as much as anticipated.

Everyone has views to the outside, with the amount of light equalized via dimming and light sensors set to adjust automatically to daylight conditions. Interior walls in the workspace areas are parallel to the exterior, and shelving is perpendicular to minimize light blockage. A seemingly small detail—transparent risers on the connecting stairs—actually enables the maximum transmittal of light. Energy con-

Ramps reconcile the different floor levels of the five buildings joined together. Drywall portals that intersect the corridor ceilings were created at the penetrations through the masonry party walls of the existing structures. *Photography © Michael Moran*

Built-in workstations were chosen over systems furniture to reflect the Greenpeace culture. All workstations were placed to allow views to the exterior from a seated position. Low vertical dividers permit the built-in workstations to be as flexible as possible. *Photography © Michael Moran*

sumption is minimized through the use of the light sensors, while solar roof panels provide electricity and heated water.

In a nod to Greenpeace's more casual culture, flexible built-in workstations were selected instead of more traditional systems furniture. Requiring minimal installation labor, moveable vertical dividers provide the desired flexibility, while aluminum strips were applied along the back edges as a finishing device and to assist with wire management. All exposed work surface edges were clad with a rubber strip, and high-contact areas were stained black to conceal scuff marks.

A recycling counter made from recycled yogurt containers resides in the lunchroom. Visible in the background are the private phone closets, provided to help employees adjust to the open workstation environment. *Photography © Michael Moran*

## Setting an Example

It was crucial to the design team that this office become a model for others to follow, and so every decision was made under a microscope to ensure environmental correctness. Key material decisions for furniture and furnishings included the following:

- The workstations were constructed exclusively from environmentally friendly primary materials, including a wheatboard and an FSC-certified particleboard, formaldehyde-free and prefinished with a zero-VOC coating.
- Natural cork was installed at each workstation as a tack surface.
- Bamboo flooring was rejected because of the difficulty in verifying the manufacturing processes.
- All woods used were certified as sustainable by the Forest Stewardship Council (FSC), including the wood used to produce the Risom lounge chairs made especially for this project by Knoll.
- PVC-free data cabling was found to replace more commonly used products.
- Pantry countertops were made from recycled yogurt containers.
- Rubber flooring was made from recycled tires.
- A Shaw carpet with recycled face fibers was selected and installed with low-VOC adhesives.
- Bathroom tiles were made of recycled glass.
- Doors and desks were constructed from FSC-certified wheatboard and particleboard, respectively, formed with glues that contain no formaldehyde.
- Perforated metal window coverings were made of aluminum with recycled content.
- One refrigerator runs on butane—no more than that found in two cigarette lighters.
- A large sliding wall and a series of oversized pivot doors, both made from wheatboard panels, separate the main conference room from the reception area and provide flexibility for many types of gatherings.
- As much of the existing masonry as practically possible was left exposed, thus reducing the amount of material needed for the build-out.
- All file cabinets were purchased used and were refurbished and repainted with water-based paint.

The stair treads are milled from recycled oak reclaimed from the demolition of another building. In order to both minimize the amount of material used and maximize natural light penetration, stair risers and guard rails were constructed out of sheets of expanded steel. Visible on the right is the large sliding door separating the main conference room from the corridor. *Photography © Michael Moran*

Open workstations were placed at the perimeter of the building with support functions centrally located on the interior. The two levels of the 15,000-square-foot space are connected by an open staircase. *Photography © Michael Moran*

- Furniture was selected for its recycled content, including an ergonomic chair at each workstation.
- The structural components of the connecting stair were made from steel that contains over 96 percent recycled material. The steel was sandblasted to clean it and to provide a surface receptive to the low-VOC, clear epoxy coating. (The sandblasting process was so effective that Wilson was certain the first time he saw it that the steel had been painted—something he most definitely didn't want.)

## Principles in Action

Richardson describes the new Greenpeace offices as "brilliant," not just because of its aesthetics but also because of its underlying principles and logic. "Our new space argues against the main criticism that environmental design doesn't measure up aesthetically," he says.

It also measures up in numbers. A post-occupancy evaluation, the results of which are shown in the chart on page 240 found that 73 percent of the staff had higher

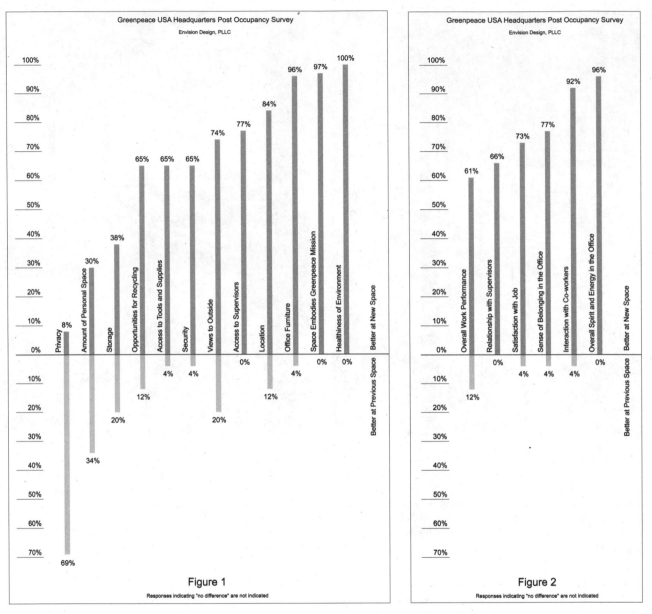

Greenpeace postoccupancy survey results. © *Envision Design PLLC*

job satisfaction, 92 percent reported increased interaction with co-workers, 96 percent felt that the overall spirit and energy in the office were greater, and 100 percent said the space felt "healthier." In fact, turnover was reduced by 60 percent from the year before the build-out to the year after.

One final number speaks to the project's initial goals. When asked if the new space embodied the organization's mission, an overwhelming 97 percent of employees agreed, proud that their new office "is a prototype of both ideals and practice with the Earth in mind...an example of their commitment to a green today and better tomorrow."

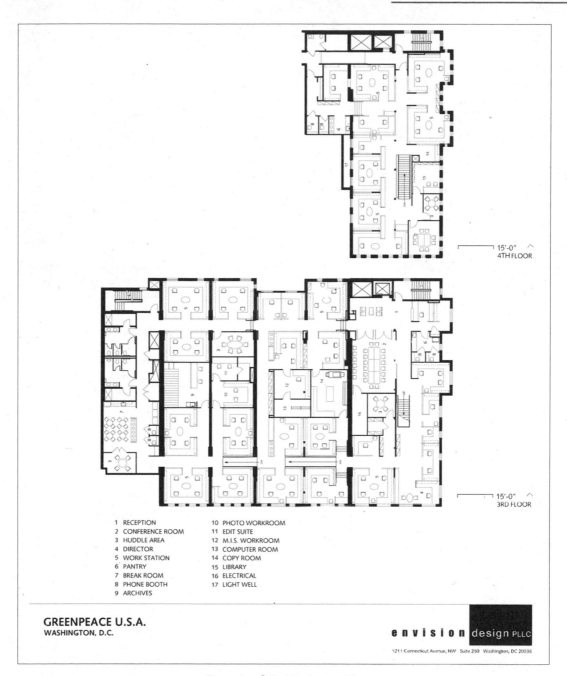

15'-0"
4TH FLOOR

15'-0"
3RD FLOOR

1   RECEPTION
2   CONFERENCE ROOM
3   HUDDLE AREA
4   DIRECTOR
5   WORK STATION
6   PANTRY
7   BREAK ROOM
8   PHONE BOOTH
9   ARCHIVES

10  PHOTO WORKROOM
11  EDIT SUITE
12  M.I.S. WORKROOM
13  COMPUTER ROOM
14  COPY ROOM
15  LIBRARY
16  ELECTRICAL
17  LIGHT WELL

**GREENPEACE U.S.A.**
WASHINGTON, D.C.

envision design PLLC
1211 Connecticut Avenue, NW  Suite 250  Washington, DC 20036

Floor plan. © Envision Design LLC

# HOK: Working in Daylight Downtown

Employees and visitors get an immediate sense of the commitment to sustainable design as soon as they step off the elevator. This view from the elevator lobby shows the HOK founders wall, sealed concrete floors, and daylight from the skylights into a central common area. © *Michelle Litvin*

The new St. Louis, Missouri, offices of Hellmuth Obata Kassabaum (HOK) make a bold statement about sustainable design, innovation, and collaboration in a team environment. From the very beginning of the design process, employees and design directors were involved through design charrettes, reviews, and workstation mock-ups. Among the design strategies that were identified early on:

- Create a unifying space that brings all HOK employees together, with shared functions grouped together to enable interaction.
- Create workspaces that are unique to each type of work function (designers do different work than accountants).
- Provide all employees with direct access to views and daylight.
- Provide for flexibility so that the office can change as the needs of the organization change.
- Provide collaborative spaces throughout the office: enclosed formal conference rooms, huddle rooms to support impromptu meetings and conference calls, and open teaming spaces.

## Increasing Collaboration

The most significant project goal was to increase collaboration while providing flexible and productive space for teamwork. Shared team support spaces are provided at the window wall for impromptu conferencing, reference locations, and technology/support. The totally open environment is acoustically private as a result of the volume of the space, background noise from the air supply, and absorptive materials such as the carpeting. Personal visual and acoustical privacy is provided by unassigned huddle rooms located throughout the space.

As the sole point for services, the community kitchen, located in the heart of the space, reinforces HOK's culture of bringing people together to interact personally and professionally. Active throughout the day, the area serves as a gathering space for events and learning, and it also provides informal seating, banquet seating, and stand-up counters for impromptu meetings and casual conversations.

## Commitment to Place

HOK focused its search for its new office on the downtown area in order to emphasize the importance of keeping business downtown and to act as a leader for other businesses. HOK has been a design leader in St. Louis, serving as the creative force behind new streetscapes, the development of Chouteau's Pond, Ballpark Village, and many other projects that benefit the community. The firm also was the first company to sign up for the Downtown Employee Assisted Housing Program, through which HOK provides forgivable loans to employees buying homes in the downtown area.

Supporting this commitment is HOK's commuter program, which provides employees the opportunity to purchase public transportation fares with pretax dollars to encourage the use of public transportation. In this spirit, and because of the large number of HOK staff who ride bikes to work during the spring, summer, and fall months, HOK provides bike parking for pedaling commuters. Additionally, to support the health and welfare of its

employees, and to do its share in keeping rising health care costs to a minimum, HOK provides shower and locker facilities for those who commute by bike or who wish to walk or run during the lunch hour. HOK also encourages new bike riders during May (National Bike to Work Month) and for the past two years has been the employer with the single largest bike commuting group on National Bike to Work day, according to Trailnet (a not-for-profit organization that promotes bicycle and pedestrian activities through events, advocacy, and education).

## Waste-Wise

Priority was also placed on ensuring that as few building components and furnishings as possible found their way to the waste stream. In the end, HOK estimates that a total of 602,656 pounds of construction waste was recycled or repurposed.

Materials able to be recycled included 90,000 pounds of gypsum wallboard through Peerless Resource & Recovery; 37,714 square feet (26,400 pounds) of ceiling

The most significant project goal was to increase collaboration while providing flexible and productive space where teamwork is a priority over personal space. The totally open environment is acoustically private as a result of the volume of the space, background noise from the air supply, and absorptive materials such as the carpeting.
© Michelle Litvin

tiles through Armstrong Ceilings Recycling Program; 44,000 pounds of carpet and VCT tile with DuPont's Carpet Recovery Program; and 48,480 pounds of metal.

In addition, HOK was able to reuse a significant amount of building materials. Working with Metropolitan Square Building Management, building components saved included 130 doors, 109 aluminum frames, more than 200 large fluorescent lighting fixtures, and 19 HVAC diffusers.

Working with City Museum, a local developer, and local nonprofits provided a second life for many furnishings. Items saved included 32 wood benches, 14 brass pendant light fixtures, 78 can lights, 18 track lights, 48 brass accent light fixtures, 2 bookcases, 4 sink faucets, and 2 toilets, plus numerous cabinets, countertops, and shelving. More than 6,000 pounds of material samples were donated to the St. Louis Teacher's Recycle Center. Finally, through an internal program with HOK employees, tables, lighting, electronics,

filing cabinets, chairs, cabinets, planters, and shelving also found new homes.

In addition, all tenants in the Metropolitan Square Building are offered paper recycling services free of charge. As part of HOK's move to its new office on the seventh floor, lease negotiations with building management and research done on the part of HOK resulted in the provision for comprehensive recycling services (including glass, plastic, aluminum cans, paper, and cardboard) for all tenants, as required by the LEED program for HOK.

## Materials Use

A concerted effort was made to have as many building materials as possible manufactured and/or extracted within 500 miles of St. Louis, with an emphasis on selection of sustainable materials. Products selected for their recycled content included solid-surface countertops, carpet tiles, and homosote tack boards (in lieu of fabric-wrapped tack panels). Materials featuring low VOCs included all paints, adhesives, sealants, carpets, and furniture. Bamboo was selected for its rapidly renewable features, while the ceiling tiles were selected based on the manufacturer's ability to recycle the existing tiles that were discarded.

In addition, minimal gypsum was used, as only a few built-out rooms were created. Ceilings were used for acoustically private spaces only. The design aesthetic of exposed structure and ductwork was fitting, as was sealing the existing concrete slab floor in public circulation areas rather than using a floor finish material.

## Let There Be Light

In order to provide daylight to the inner core, HOK punched two skylights (19 feet 6 inches by 30 feet each) into the intermediate roof. To control the amount of light entering the space, a sophisticated louver system was developed to distribute light evenly and block glare. The louver's daylight control system tracks the sun's movement, providing even coverage throughout the day. The louver surfaces allow light to be bounced uniformly into the space. It was important to design the system to be sim-

A less-is-more approach to the design of the office is employed simultaneously with high design aesthetics. © *Michelle Litvin*

Daylight from one of two skylights is distributed with the use of a sophisticated louver system that tracks the sun's movement through the sky, providing even coverage throughout the day.
© *Michelle Litvin*

Daylight and reflected light are bounced throughout the office.
© *Michelle Litvin*

ple, easy, and locally fabricated. By responding continuously to external conditions and internal needs, this dynamic system defines the character of the space.

Studies ensured that design team expectations translated into real-world solutions. A computer lighting analysis helped assess realistic visual comfort and daylight availability goals. An hourly analysis through all seasons quantified potential daylight-harvesting schemes. Gable window light shelves minimize glare and heat gain while maintaining views. Daylight diffusers transform a disabling glare source into a visual asset.

The low-reflectance ceiling material requires a lighting system that utilizes both direct and indirect components. Luminaires next to windows and skylights use dimmable ballasts with photocells that sense the amount of available daylight, adjusting light levels to conserve energy when daylight is sufficient. All huddle, conference, work, toilet,

copy, and storage rooms are equipped with occupancy sensors that turn lights off when spaces are not in use.

## Indoor Air Quality

Mechanical equipment performance criteria were established to meet ASHRAE 62-1999: Ventilation for Acceptable Indoor Air Quality, to ensure that staff would have plenty of fresh air. IAQ testing was performed by an industrial hygienist prior to occupancy to ensure that all contaminant levels were below established standards. A construction IAQ management plan was carried out to protect on-site materials from moisture damage and mold growth, protect the ventilation system from construction dust and debris, remove contaminants from construction space prior to occupancy, and isolate areas to prevent contamination of other spaces. Furniture selected meets the Greenguard certification for indoor air quality.

In all, the results of the project have been overwhelmingly positive. The endeavors made to "walk the talk" on HOK's sustainable values have created a great place to work and a healthy environment, which is already showing positive effects on workplace productivity and staff quality of life. Since the project was completed, HOK has taken additional steps toward sustainability with its decision to purchase renewable energy credits from wind farms to offset 100 percent of the annual electricity used in all its offices worldwide. This represents more than 4 million kilowatt-hours of wind, and is estimated to be the single largest commitment to wind power by an architectural firm to date.

## Haworth Showroom: Sustainable Thinking, Smart Design

The NeoCon World's Trade Fair is a mecca for interior designers, architects, and owner's representatives—it's a once-a-year chance to preview the innovative products that interior furnishing manufacturers have been developing during the previous year (or sometimes two or three) and dream of the possibilities for their use in future projects. Designers interested in green products have traditionally had to search for what was available—usually just a handful of choices from a few forward-thinking manufacturers.

Such was the state of affairs when, in 2004, Haworth turned the A&D community's world upside down, transforming its 29,000-square-foot showroom and conference center into a utopia of green design strategies and products, showcasing for an entire industry just what's possible when sustainable thinking marries smart design.

Designed by Perkins+Will of Chicago, the showroom reflects Haworth's holistic approach to the working environment, one that is centered on people and ideas. The new showroom was, in fact, the platform used to introduce Haworth's new brand strategy and design philosophy, "Adaptable Workspace, Designed Performance and Global Perspectives," demonstrating its evolution from a company offering workstations to a solutions-driven resource for workspaces. The Perkins+Will team, led by Eva Maddox, Eileen Jones, Rod Vickroy, and Frank Pettinati, served an

Perkins+Will/Eva Maddox Branded Environments worked with Haworth to transform its Chicago showroom into a stunning platform featuring the company's interior architecture and office furniture solutions, emphasizing a "work" and "restore" experience through the use of interactive, multisensory, and mind expansion techniques. *Photography © Craig Dugan, Hedrich Blessing*

A reflecting pool built within raised flooring is calming and beautiful. A clean and airy aesthetic just beyond welcomes visitors into the space, inviting them to explore a world where full-height movable walls seamlessly intersect with furniture, seating, and lighting. Photography © *Craig Dugan, Hedrich Blessing*

Haworth's human-centered design approach is demonstrated by the various work styles that are showcased throughout the entire showroom, from the walls, floor, ceiling, and furniture systems to lighting, sound, power, voice, and data. *Photography © Steve Hall, Hedrich Blessing*

integral role in the development of the strategy, market positioning, image, communications, and sustainability initiatives to properly reflect the new direction of the Haworth brand.

Throughout the showroom, unique spaces feature Haworth's interior architecture and office furniture solutions, emphasizing a "work" and "restore" experience through the use of interactive, multisensory, and mind expansion techniques. Haworth's human-centered design approach (we all work a little differently, after all) is demonstrated by the various work styles that are showcased throughout the entire design, from the walls, floor, and ceiling to furniture systems, lighting, sound, power, voice, and data. "Restore" is achieved through architectural features such as a reflecting pool and "glow" walls that provide glare-free ambient light; the plan layout was also organized to maximize the amount of daylight and its depth of penetration into the space, with materials selected and positioned to reflect light throughout the entire space. "Work" is accomplished through touchdown spaces, casual meeting areas, modular private offices, individual work spaces, and flexible conference spaces.

From the moment a visitor enters the showroom, it's clear there's nothing ordinary about anything within the dramatic space. Perkins+Will created an expansive, open entryway that features sleek modular Indiana limestone flooring, with message boxes that incorporate computer monitors, video animation, graphics, and text in various languages in a nod to the international flavor of NeoCon attendees and Haworth's global presence. A stainless-steel band is embedded in the floor, listing the Haworth headquarters, showrooms, and manufacturing sites around the world.

But it's the reflecting pool that grabs immediate attention. Built within the raised flooring, the pool is calming and beautiful, acting as a welcoming beacon that stands in sharp contrast to the frustrating world of Merchandise Mart hallways left behind. Beyond the pool, a clean and airy aesthetic welcomes visitors into the space, inviting them to explore a world where full-height movable walls seamlessly intersect with furniture, seating, and lighting products to create an adaptable, high-performance work environment.

## More than Meets the Eye

While the stunning design elements make the Haworth showroom visually memorable, there's a rich sustainability story to it as well. The project earned LEED-CI Gold certification in the program's pilot project phase, the first and only showroom in the Merchandise Mart to do so—in large part because of the dedication of all design team members to implementing the innovative and creative strategies needed to meet those high standards. From the beginning, the goal was for the showroom to function as an industry-leading example of sustainability (from social, environmental, and economic perspectives) demonstrating methods of integrating improved quality of life, restorative space, resource preservation, waste elimination, and cost reduction. The combination of good design and engineering did just that.

Not only has the showroom earned a LEED-CI Gold rating, it received the 2005 Best of Competition showroom award at NeoCon 2005 and a 2005 Design Excellence Award from the Chicago chapter of the American Institute of Architects for its clean aesthetic and high-performance green design practices. *Photography © Steve Hall, Hedrich Blessing*

The application of "true fluid" products, allowing full adaptability and reconfiguration, incorporates a "reuse, rewire, retask" philosophy. This prevents waste that might occur with future reconfigurations of the space. *Photography © Craig Dugan, Hedrich Blessing*

For example, Haworth's underfloor HVAC system (CFC- and HCFC-free) reduces energy expenditures and increases thermal comfort and air change effectiveness. Additionally, acknowledging the link between user satisfaction, control of the personal environment, and worker productivity, individual temperature controls at each workstation allow users to manage their own environments. One hundred percent of the showroom's electricity is offset via wind power credits, which is twice the green power requirement under LEED-CI. (Recognizing the environmental impact green power can have, Perkins+Will recently agreed to purchase 100 percent green power for its North American office locations from Renewable Choice Energy's green power program, which subsidizes the generation of renewable energy sources that make cleaner energy available to all consumers.) Haworth also submeters all incoming utilities to help reduce energy costs.

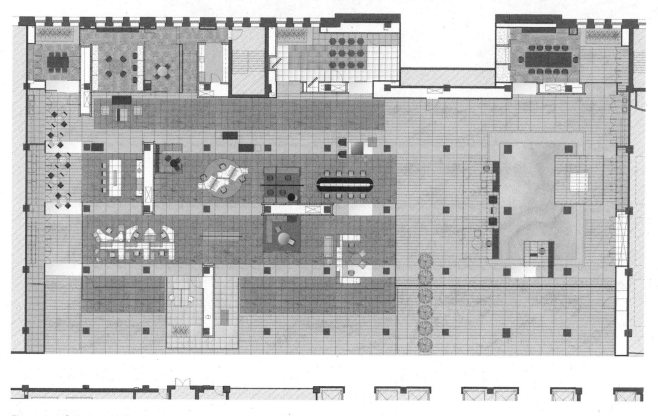

Floor plan. © *Perkins+Will*

The project also served as a showcase for Haworth's Greenguard-certified products. In fact, Haworth floors, walls, and furniture contributed 20 of the 36 points received on the LEED submission. Many of these products use high-recycled-content materials, including wheatboard, a renewable construction material that is used as a substrate throughout the space. Haworth products also feature wood finishes certified by the Forest Stewardship Council.

Other notable green features include:

■ The reuse of materials salvaged and repurposed from the prior showroom. This eliminated construction and demolition waste and reduced the consumption of new resources. An estimated 50 percent of the total demolition materials were recycled, saving them from the typical landfill destination.

■ The use of rapidly renewable materials, such as wheatboard substrate material and cork flooring.

■ Use of materials sourced from local suppliers, such as the reflecting pool (Chicago), glass (Michigan and Ohio), and stone flooring (Wisconsin).

■ Energy Star–rated HVAC equipment for energy efficiency.

■ Underfloor air distribution, contributing to a reduction in energy costs of 20 to 30 percent.

■ A low-voltage lighting system estimated to reduce energy consumption by more than 60 percent.

■ The application of "true fluid" products, allowing full adaptability and reconfiguration, incorporating a "reuse, rewire, retask" philosophy. This prevents waste that might occur with future reconfigurations of the space.

In recognition of the showroom's clean aesthetic and high-performance green design practices, it received the 2005 Best of Competition showroom award at NeoCon 2005. Most recently, it was awarded the 2005 Design Excellence Award from the Chicago chapter of the American Institute of Architects.

Gensler designed the shaped ceiling of the conference center and lighting designers Bliss Fasman added the slotted recesses to house the dot-dash scheme of three-foot sections of cold-cathode and MR sources to light the table below. *Photography by Paul Warchol*

# Toyota: Driving the Path to Sustainability

Toyota, the third-largest automotive manufacturer in North America, embraces the environment as few other companies do—in its products and in its buildings. The success of Toyota's hybrid vehicles, especially the Prius, has prompted other automakers to introduce products with better fuel economy and lower emissions. Given this reputation and record, it makes sense that the company would also strive for the most environmentally responsible spaces in which to house its employees. Toyota has earned LEED-NC Gold certification twice: for its 624,000-square-foot South Campus headquarters in Torrance, California, and for a processing center in Portland, Oregon. A Toyota dealership in Dallas, Texas, is the first of its kind to seek LEED certification.

When the government affairs group in Washington, D.C., made the decision to move its offices, there wasn't any doubt that the new space would be built out according to the standards set by the LEED-CI rating system. The green design process started early by hiring a real estate broker savvy in environmental issues. The details of their careful building selection process, partially based on environmental concerns, are covered in the sites section of Chapter 3.

Project goals were set when Gensler was brought on board for architecture and interior design services. The client's instructions included a requirement for demonstrating Toyota's cultural commitment to the environment, but green goals were to be kept in perspective and attempted for the right reasons—not simply to accumulate LEED points. The entire project team had the credentials to make appropriate sustainable decisions—every member of the Gensler design team was a LEED Accredited Professional, as were others from CBRE real estate/project management services and Rand Construction, the general contractor.

> *"Everyone on the team knew they had to bring something to the party if this was going to work."*
>
> —Jill Goebel, IIDA, LEED AP, senior associate, Gensler

## Lighting: The Essential Element

Toyota chose its building and crafted its lease to support the company's environmental goals; the early determination to build a sustainable space directed every decision. For example, the selection of a light color palette was driven in part by the desire to reduce energy use. According to lighting designers Glen Fasman and Steven Bliss, "Gensler had wanted to use whites from the beginning, but energy requirements helped encourage them to go even further in that direction. It was a requirement for us that they had light finishes, and it worked out very well for the lower light levels we were shooting for."

Lighting power density was reduced to 15 percent below the standard, yet the space looks very well lit because of the balancing strategy used by Bliss Fasman. Most of the office is lit with a combination of T5s and compact fluorescent lamps; however, in high-profile areas with specialized finishes, such as the stainless steel columns in the reception area, incandescent sources were used, but with a twist. A remotely located illuminator feeds into a bundle of fiber-optic cables that run across the plenum and split into eight discrete fixture heads. The effect on the columns is similar to what would be achieved by MR downlighting. However, energy is conserved because instead of using eight separate sources, a lower-wattage single source is providing the power and light is delivered through fiber-optic cables rather than individual luminaires and lamps. "We used the incandescent watts sparingly where we needed them for effect and then balanced with more efficient light sources in the majority of the spaces," explained Fasman and Bliss.

Other energy-saving strategies include occupancy sensors installed throughout, Energy Star equipment and appliances—the dishwashers exceed the energy guideline by 102 percent—and separately metered electricity in order to track lower energy use from efficient design and conservation efforts. Toyota also purchased green power credits.

The office has daylight exposure on four sides and via the central atrium, yet the client decided against daylight-responsive controls due to the additional cost of the system. The floor plan carefully provides daylight exposure and views to all occupants—albeit to the surrounding office buildings in this densely built area. According to project designer Jill Goebel, "Our plan gives people an intu-

A stone wall and neon-lit ceiling cove, plus a view to the structural elements of the building atrium, add interest to the lobby. The white terrazzo floor and other light finishes helped keep light levels low.
*Photography by Paul Warchol*

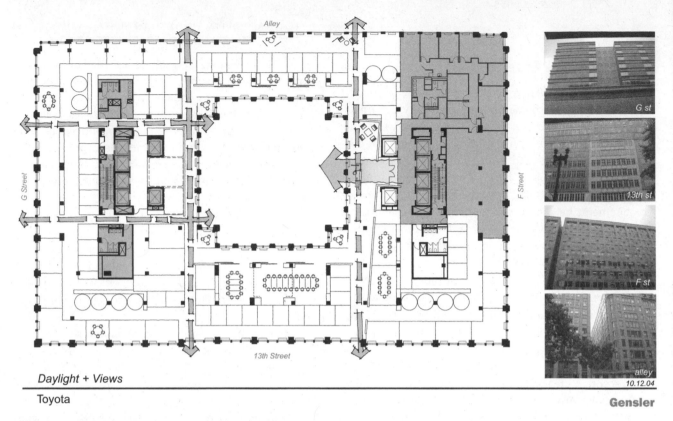

Daylight + Views

Toyota

G st

13th st

F st

alley
10.12.04

Gensler

Sightlines to outside and atrium views are plotted on the floor plan. *Plan courtesy of Gensler*

itive orientation within the space as well as increased comfort through connection to the outdoors. Furthermore, the offices have glass front and wing walls not only to bring in light but also to encourage associate collaboration."

## No New Car Smell

The selection of all materials as well as general construction practices were done to achieve the best possible indoor air quality. Products chosen to minimize the introduction of VOCs and formaldehyde include a glossy white color core laminate used as a wall finish in place of high-emitting lacquers. The matrix used to set the recycled glass and mirror chips in the terrazzo floors is completely VOC-free. Other low-emitting products include the paints, carpets, rubber wall base, and furniture from Knoll, which has been Greenguard-certified. The designers also attempted to eliminate other toxins from the space through the use of

Private offices are pulled back from the perimeter to share natural light with the corridor. *Photography by Paul Warchol*

PVC-free materials such as a vinyl alternative wall covering from Carnegie.

Recycled content was also considered in the material selection criteria for the steel studs, drywall, acrylic backsplashes, and ceiling tiles. A rubber floor, appropriately made from postconsumer auto and truck tires, is used in the support spaces. Rapidly renewable products include agrifiber board as a millwork substrate as well as for the solid doors; bamboo flooring is used in the break room.

Significant efforts were made to use FSC-certified wood as well as locally sourced materials. Modifications were made to the standard specifications, as many of Toyota's preferred products are based on West Coast markets. For example, conference tables were purchased from Toronto and North Carolina rather than Seattle.

## Get Comfortable

A good deal of thought was put into the thermal and acoustic comfort of the staff. Enclosed offices have either a dedicated perimeter heat pump or a thermafuser to control the volume of air delivered to the space, providing each occupant with individual temperature control. High-occupancy areas such as the conference center and break room have dedicated HVAC systems equipped with $CO_2$ sensors to ensure that sufficient outside air is delivered when needed. A superior level of filtering has been provided with MERV 13 filters for all base-building air handlers. The filtration used during construction also prevented dust and smells from affecting other tenants in the building. To control acoustics, steel sound attenuators were installed instead of using standard internal duct sound insulation.

Both the client and the design team believe that sustainable practices should focus not only on the immediate occupants but on the community as well. Unusual and conscientious attention was paid to the disposal of construction waste and debris. At least 50 percent of the demolished space was either recycled, given back to the building, or donated. According to Goebel, "By contributing existing doors, frames, and lighting to Goodwill Industries, over 70 cubic yards of still viable building materials were prevented from going to the landfill. The heat pumps that Toyota removed from its space were given back to the building to be used for maintaining and replacing others in the building."

Simplicity, functionality, durability, and value were listed as project priorities as well as showcasing the client's brand. The design is beautifully rendered, with a significant use of glass and steel to represent the manufacturing image. As one would expect, Toyota's products and concepts are prevalent throughout, in the art, in display cases, and in the model cars on most everyone's desktop.

A large billboard "bus wrap" graphic applied to the glass wall of the break room adds colorful and themed interest yet affords views to the atrium windows beyond. *Photography by Paul Warchol*

The metallic surfaces and color scheme of the Accenture office visually project the desired image of advanced thinking, while contemporary design elements such as the canopies in this network center absorb sound to facilitate collaboration in an open environment.
© Ed Massery

# Accenture: Flexible, Fluid, and Ecofriendly

"Young, progressive and innovative." This description offered by Accenture to describe its corporate culture and ethic applies equally well to the green building movement. Thus it was fitting that when the global management consulting, technology services, and outsourcing company needed a new home for its Pittsburgh office, it turned to the sustainable design experts at Davis Gardner Gannon Pope Architecture (DGGP) to create a contemporary, collaborative work space that incorporated a host of environmentally sensitive attributes.

The 5,000-square-foot tenant build-out project is located in what was at the time a speculative building in Penn Center West, a suburban office park along the highway corridor connecting the airport with downtown Pittsburgh. Accenture desired a space that met the company's new mandates for office culture: it no longer wanted an environment filled with traditional private offices but rather sought a flexible, fluid space that accommodated and facilitated the way day-to-day business is really done—energetically, efficiently, and in teams. With an average employee age of 27.5 years, the project also needed to be hip and contemporary.

The space programming process identified the need for the following areas in the build-out space:

- Reception area
- Network center/café lounge
- Open office area
- Private offices
- Enclosed collaborative/meeting rooms
- Focus rooms
- File and copy area
- Tele/data room

By the nature of the work that it does, most Accenture consultants travel to their work, meeting with clients personally. Thus, the overall design of the office needed to accommodate the more innovative hoteling work methods, which allows consultants to reserve on a daily or project basis an open workstation, private office, or meeting room, depending upon a specific project's needs. Design features such as the canopies provide aids to collaboration in open spaces by absorbing sound. The metallic surfaces and color scheme are part of the visual message of advanced thinking by a progressive group of professionals. The color scheme, material selections, and spatial organization reinforce the youthfulness and creativity that Accenture markets to its customers.

## Environmental Sensitivities

The interior was constructed in a building also designed by DGGP that followed the requirements of a LEED-NC project. The building has raised-floor HVAC and electrical/tele/data systems with the resulting improved ventilation effectiveness and adaptability/flexibility to accommodate future change. The interior took advantage of all the sustainable features that the building shell provided.

However, because the small space is packed with workstations, small private offices, and private meeting rooms, it projected a sardine-can-like feeling. To overcome this,

Frosted glass in varying patterns are used to provide visual privacy, yet the translucency of the glass conveys a sense of the daylight beyond. © *Ed Massery*

Low-emitting materials, paints, and finishes were specified, as well as carpet tile that is Green Seal–certified. Many other materials used were high in recycled content. © *Ed Massery*

DGGP introduced superior access to daylight and, wherever possible, views to the exterior.

The plan was arranged so that all workstations and offices have views to the exterior. The tall deck-to-deck space and tall windows contribute to the effect. Interior borrowed lites were also introduced both above and below eye level to innermost offices and conference rooms in order to provide visual relief to the eye. Again, the tall space and windows offer something interesting to see.

Varying degrees of privacy were achieved through the use of frosted glass with different levels of opacity; however, the translucency of the glass always conveys a sense of the daylight beyond.

Additionally, DGGP selected low-emitting materials, paints, and finishes, as well as carpet tile that is Green Seal–certified. Many of the additional materials used, as well as the furniture selections, were high in recycled content.

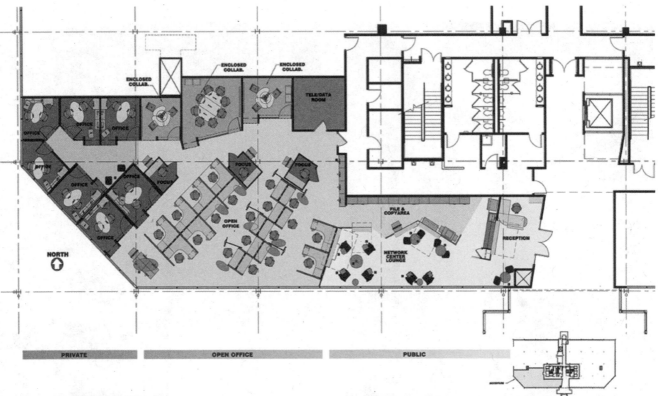

Floor plan. © *DGGP Architecture*

The reception area is located apart from the waiting room, in a circular room that is easily accessible. Patients entering the center are immediately greeted with warm and organic materials designed to calm and soothe.
© Peter Mauss/Esto

# Continuum Center: Natural Healing

The design of the Continuum Center for Health and Healing was a watershed project for Guenther5 Architects and Beth Israel Medical Center, both located in New York. The health center took a leap of faith when opening this 10,000-square-foot healing center in midtown Manhattan, offering alternative medicine to its patients; the design firm, meanwhile, traveled a path paved with new principles of healing design never before put into practice. In the end, both achieved the desired objective: an award-winning space filled with warm colors, organic materials, and an empowering design that enhances patients' physical, emotional, and spiritual well-being. Explains Robin Guenther, principal and founder of Guenther5 Architects, "Patients really understand that the space feels different—the air 'tastes different.' The operable windows, even though it's in the middle of Manhattan, are well used and often opened."

The Continuum Center offers acupuncture, massage therapy, chiropractors, nutritionists, and other nontradi-

tional treatments; as such, it desired that the overall space and internal structures be the antithesis of the mainstream waiting room (sterile and "medical"), seeking instead a space that would be interactive and relaxing. Here, the waiting room serves as a multifunctional space for patients to talk with and learn from one another, an experience facilitated by a large meeting table for group learning, a resource area, individual lounge seats, and Web-ready computer stations. In another departure from tradition, the reception area is located in a circular room that is easily accessible from the waiting area but out of direct view.

## Feng Shui Influences

Contributing a significant influence to the design parameters was the introduction of feng shui principles throughout the entire space. Collaborating with feng shui master Alex Stark, Guenther5 was able to establish construction and design principles that optimized the spaces' potential. Feng shui is an ancient Chinese art built on the belief that *qi*—the vital life force pervasive throughout the universe and existing in all living things—can be affected by the external environment. The Continuum Center chose to

257

adopt feng shui principles for its space in the belief that a positive arrangement of our environment promotes better health because qi is allowed to flow freely. An environment blocking the flow of qi, conversely, negatively impacts both physical and mental health.

The interior spaces of the Continuum Center were guided by the feng shui principles of the "art of placement," believed to improve energy flow through the interior. In accordance with those beliefs, spaces were assigned as follows:

- The consultation, examination, and therapy rooms were placed to the north to promote patient healing and tranquility.
- Staff areas were located to the south to encourage harmonious internal communication.
- The waiting room was placed to the west to provide pleasure and connectivity.

- The OB/GYN rooms were situated to the east to represent new beginnings.

Rooms and areas placed southwest and southeast as well as northwest and northeast also symbolize and foster inner growth and outer potential.

It is especially significant that the building's "prime real estate"—the northwest corner, on the intersection of Fifth Avenue and 28th Street—was designated public space for all to enjoy. In a conventional medical office, this space would have automatically been assigned as a doctor's private office; here, however, giving the space to the patients serves as a symbolic gesture to empower patients, a theme essential to the center's mission.

In another departure from traditional planning models, the waiting space is not visible from the elevator lobby. Instead, patients first travel through a complex spatial sequence intended to relax and calm.

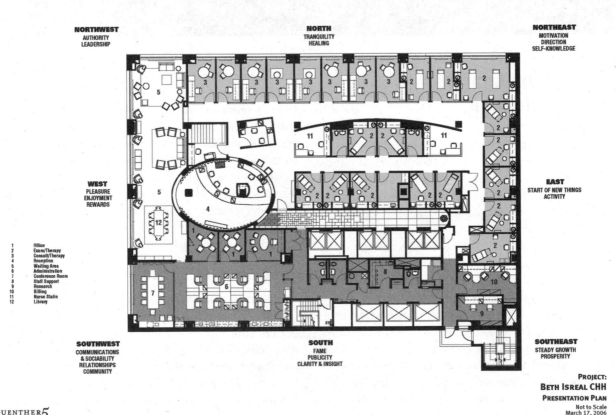

Floor plan. *Courtesy of Guenther5 Architects*

Interior spaces were guided by the feng shui principles of the "art of placement," believed to improve energy flow through the interior. The northwest corner, which typically would be considered the most prestigious location and assigned to doctors, was given instead to patient areas to symbolize a commitment to their well-being. © Peter Mauss/Esto

The waiting room serves as a multifunctional space for patients to talk with and learn from one another. It includes a large meeting table for group learning, a resource area, individual lounge seats, and Web-ready computer stations. © Peter Mauss/Esto

## Living in Harmony with Nature

Feng shui principles impacted the interior design of the space in other ways as well. For example, the belief that living beings should live harmoniously with each other as well as with elements in nature influenced Guenther5's choice of the sustainable furnishings and finishes selected for the interiors, a task Robin Guenther said was not so easy five years ago when the project was being completed. "There was very limited availability of green materials— what a difference now," she commented. "We sent back three shipments of acoustic insulation, for example, until the distributor understood that we were serious about a formaldehyde-free product."

In the end, though, Guenther5 settled on the following sustainable design strategies:

- Material selections (flooring, paint, adhesives, and cabinet substrates) that eliminate the use of formaldehyde and VOCs. (Guenther said this project taught her that sustainable construction sites "smell" different, because they basically don't have VOC odors. "The difference matters to construction workers," she noted. "Painters remarked about it. On one occasion, we came onto the site and noticed a VOC odor . . . which we could track right to an open quart container of adhesive.")

- Minimal carpet is used; products specified included high levels of recycled content or were made from natural fibers. Major flooring materials are cork and linoleum, both natural, biodegradable products.

- Fabric selection focuses on the use of recycled and compostable materials. Materials were selected to be easily maintained with natural cleaning products in order to preserve a high level of indoor air quality.

- Durable, premium-quality, fast-curing, low-VOC paints and stains were used that meet or exceed all federal and state air quality regulations (including California's) and contain no formaldehyde, ammonia, crystalline silica, or ethylene glycol.

- The medium-density fiberboard used for custom cabinetry is made from 100 percent recovered wood from old pallets, construction waste, and manufacturers' outfall, which preserves natural resources and habitats. It is finished with a water-based clear finish that is very low in both odor and VOCs.

- The suspended ceiling's acoustic panels are composed of aspen wood fibers bonded with an inorganic cement, which is then formed under heat and pressure to create uniquely textured, extremely durable flat panels. All of the raw materials used are sustainable.
- Recycled glass tiles were used in restrooms with an appropriate adhesive and grout to make an environmentally friendly wall finish solution.
- Reclaimed antique heart pine is used in the yoga room and for the wood slat wall in the corridor. It is reclaimed from outmoded factories, textile mills, and warehouses as they are demolished. The wood finish is a natural oil product and is 100 percent biodegradable and made without harmful synthetic chemicals.

- Furniture materials, upholstery, and other fabrics also further reflect the center's commitment to environmentally conscious choices. Additional design elements contributing to the space's "organic" composition include soft lighting and calming auditory input.

Because patients often come to the Continuum Center seeking Western and Eastern remedies for health issues that have environmental causes, Guenther explained, practitioners felt strongly that the environment of the office should "do no harm" to patients with allergies, asthma, and chemical sensitivity. And indeed it does not, offering patients instead a welcoming retreat, one that is designed—physically and philosophically—with their very best interests in mind.

Wood reclaimed from abandoned buildings finds new life in the wood slat wall of this corridor. It is finished with a natural oil that is completely biodegradable and emits no VOCs. © *Peter Mauss/Esto*

Furniture and fabrics were chosen for their recycled content and use of biodegradable materials. © *Peter Mauss/Esto*

REI's store facilities serve as visible symbols of the retailer's active support of urban redevelopment, environmental stewardship, and increasing access to outdoor recreation. © Peter Eckert, Eckert and Eckert

# REI Portland: Sustainable Design Hat Trick

An old adage claims, "The third time's the charm," and it appears that REI Inc. is bound and determined to prove it true. The national outdoor gear and clothing co-op first demonstrated a commitment to urban revitalization in 1996 with the opening of its Seattle flagship store. A second project found the retailer an integral player in the renovation of Denver's early 1900s electric trolley power plant into an award-winning retail space. For its hat trick, REI set out to relocate its Portland, Oregon, retail store from the suburbs to a new mixed-use complex in the high-density, industrial Pearl Street district downtown that was undergoing renovation. REI selected the site because it offered easy access for pedestrians, bicyclists, and streetcar riders. Equally important was the opportunity for achieving a secondary goal: demonstrating the co-op's commitment to environmental stewardship values by being one of the first commercial interior projects in the nation to earn a LEED-CI certification—and a Gold rating at that.

REI's longtime partner in these rehabilitation projects is Mithun, an architecture, design, and planning firm based in Seattle. Together the client and design firm transformed the 37,500-square-foot store into a rugged, ecofriendly destination for the neighborhood's urban dwellers. Occupying the first two floors of the Edge Loft building, with residential lofts above, the REI Portland project has become an inviting destination, nestled among restaurants, art galleries, and furniture stores.

> "Values are playing a bigger role in the purchasing decisions for a lot of our clients,"
>
> —Susan McNabb, LEED consultant, Mithun

Because the store site slopes across its 200-foot retail frontage, REI wanted a single-plane floor for maximum display flexibility. This was achieved with the use of a removable concrete floor that will also accommodate future adaptation by smaller tenants, as well as allowing new grade-level entrances with only minor remodeling efforts.

Exposed concrete floors, deconstructable details, and exposed mechanical and electrical systems allow REI the flexibility to reconfigure the retail space quickly, inexpensively, and with minimal environmental impact. © *Peter Eckert, Eckert and Eckert*

Exposed concrete structure within the interior, deconstructable details, and exposed mechanical and electrical systems maximize the ability to recycle and salvage building materials while minimizing waste in future tenant space reuse. It also allows easy reconfiguration during REI's tenancy with minimal environmental impact.

While REI is a tenant within the larger mixed-use building, the choice of building materials does have an impact on overall building quality. The shell consists mostly of concrete and insulated glass—both extremely durable and long-lasting. Concrete was left exposed to the greatest extent possible to reduce material consumption. Additional ecofriendly materials include low-VOC finishes; fixtures constructed of formaldehyde-free engineered wood; timber accents and trellis canopies fashioned of recycled wood and Paralam, an engineered lumber made from a small, fast-growing species; and VOC emissions from carpets below limits set by the Carpet and Rug Institute. Additionally, materials manufactured locally and materials with high recycled content are used extensively throughout the store. REI was also able to recycle an impressive 96 percent of construction waste.

## Eco-efficiencies

While the building occupies the whole block, REI's retail space is oriented along the eastern face to receive maximum exposure to the sun for early morning warm-up hours. Once the store opens, the sun travels in such a way that it provides soft indirect light during the remainder of the day. Two of the primary walls are all glass, so ambient daylight floods the entire retail space. The south face has minimal transparent exposure due to solid walls at security areas and canopy overhangs at the entrances. An open-air parking garage with lofts above shields the west façade.

Other tenants in the mixed-use building occupy the northern exposure; however, REI has indirect north light for office areas. This orientation has allowed REI to minimize start-up heating costs while also reducing the cooling load throughout the afternoon.

Because of Portland's temperate climate, the HVAC system brings in fresh air throughout the day and evening. REI added carbon dioxide sensors for indoor air monitoring, and ventilation airflow controls calculate the adequacy of air distribution to all occupied areas in the retail space. During construction and immediately after, ductwork and HVAC equipment were sealed off and inoperable until the space was clean of dust and fumes.

Energy-efficient fixtures, extensive windows in the space, and use of daylight sensors have resulted in a 26 percent reduction in lighting energy load. All lighting—retail, office, storage, display, track, and general—is controlled by a Novar computer-based system. Photosensors and time clocks keep exterior lighting levels at a minimum with an anticipated savings of 6,106 kWh/yr. Occupancy sensors and photosensors inside are anticipated to provide an energy savings of 9,734 kWh/yr on the retail floor, 3,499 kWh/yr in the offices, and 63,467 kWh/yr in storage areas. Additionally, track lighting provides a further anticipated savings of 13,306 kWh/yr.

High-bay fluorescent light fixtures with three ballasts are circuited to allow three levels for general lighting. A minimum general lighting level is selected for nonbusiness

Two glass window walls flood both levels of the interior space with soft and attractive ambient light, which, combined with energy-efficient light fixtures, reduces energy consumption significantly. © Peter Eckert, Eckert and Eckert

Mithun specified low-VOC finishes and carpeting, fixtures constructed of formaldehyde-free engineered wood, and timber accents and trellis canopies fashioned from ecofriendly or recycled wood. © Peter Eckert, Eckert and Eckert

hours, while the full lighting level is chosen during sales hours (though artificial illumination in those areas infused with daylighting is decreased based on natural light levels). REI uses supplemental track lighting during sales hours and during stocking. Moveable racks with integral lighting, including plug and cord assemblies, follow the track lighting standards.

The REI Portland project meets the LEED prerequisites for thermal efficiency, comfort performance, and ventilation, which represent the baseline standard for modern HVAC design. $CO_2$-sensing equipment provides energy-saving benefits at times of low occupancy under cold and hot weather conditions when the store ventilation systems are able to bring in less fresh air. Other notable green strategies include the specification of efficient plumbing fixtures that have resulted in a 32 percent water use reduction and a recycling program within the store for everything from lunchroom beverage containers to product packaging. In fact, much of the packaging material does not even reach the store, as REI's distribution center consolidates shipments and then reuses the shipping containers.

## Lessons Learned

The REI/Mithun team initially investigated the potential for this project to participate in the LEED for Retail pilot

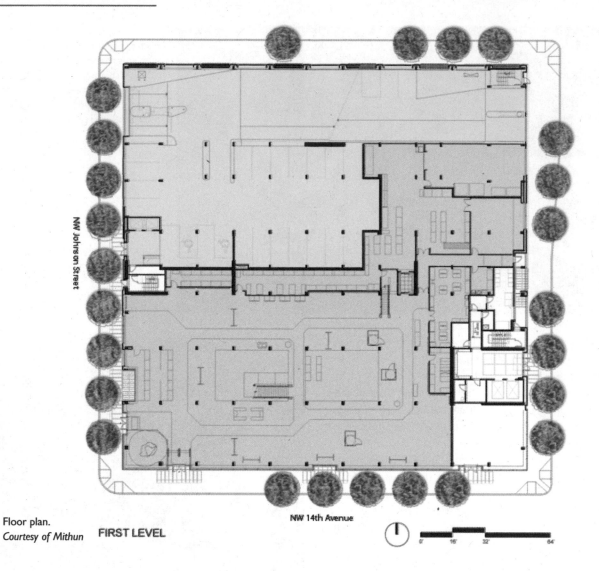

NW Johnson Street

NW 14th Avenue

Floor plan.
*Courtesy of Mithun* **FIRST LEVEL**

0'    16'    32'    64'

program. However, the program was not ready for release at the time of store development, so REI chose instead to participate in LEED-CI, with the intention to aid in the development of the LEED for Retail program. With strong support from senior management, the retail design and construction team was given clear direction to commence with the project. Perhaps the biggest challenge, according to those involved, was communicating goals and allowing the appropriate documentation time for all parties involved with the development of a new store.

Overall, however, the REI Portland project had a significant influence on the retail business, and REI intends to use the lessons learned at this store to develop standards for the development of future stores—some sustainable choices researched for the Portland store have already become standard in new store design. "The LEED-CI process required REI to cast our decision-making net further across the company, including our consultants and outside vendors, as we educated ourselves on the various LEED strategies," Laura Rose, head of retail for REI, has commented. "It truly took a 'village' effort."

# Herman Miller BG Building: Continuing the Commitment

One of the initial founding members of the U.S. Green Building Council, commercial furniture manufacturer Herman Miller, has a long-standing involvement in the sustainable design movement. In fact, its Greenhouse manufacturing plant in Zeeland, Michigan, designed in the early 1990s by William McDonough, was one of the first buildings validated by the U.S. EPA to have shown demonstrable financial improvements as the result of its green building strategies. This groundbreaking research directly linked increases in productivity and energy savings to environmentally sensitive and sensible building strategies, sounding the trumpet that green buildings made good business sense.

The company's efforts have earned it recognition from the Michigan Business and Professional Association as one of west Michigan's "Best and Brightest Companies to Work For." In 2005, *Business Ethics* magazine ranked Herman Miller (for the fifth year in a row) among its "100 Best Corporate Citizens"—one of only twenty-nine companies to earn a place on the list every year since it began in 2000.

Herman Miller's commitment to green building facilities can be traced back to company founder D. J. De Pree, who (per the company's website) directed fifty years ago that "all employees should be able to look out from a window from no more than 75 feet." He also declared "any new properties the company developed would dedicate 50 percent or more to green space to promote a healthy environment." The company is still following De Pree's mandate today, as it has gone on to build or renovate seven buildings that have achieved LEED certification.

These efforts include the renovation of the Herman Miller BG Main Site, a 30,000-square-foot, two-story office building located on the company's campus in Zeeland, which was LEED-CI certified in the rating system's pilot process.

## Adhering to Principles

Tapping the green building knowledge of practitioners at The Chicago firm The Environments Group, the redesign and refurbishment of the BG Main Site required the cre-

The BG Building connects the manufacturing facility to one of the corporate office buildings, housing support facilities used by both entities. This view of the BG building shows the work environment created on the second floor and highly collaborative spaces on the first floor designed for interaction between the corporate and manufacturing groups. *Photography: Steve Hall © 2004 Hedrich Blessing*

ative blending of two distinct work groups within the building: the engineering and security groups, who safeguard the company's assets and trade secrets, as well as the highly trafficked home of the corporate health center, human resources/payroll office, and credit union. In assigning the task, Herman Miller charged The Environments Group to strictly adhere to its published philosophy—principles that call for openness, egalitarianism, interaction, care and leadership for the environment, and sustainable building, as well as instilling stewardship toward the community. As to be expected, another major prerequisite was the imaginative use of Herman Miller's furniture lines within the building's design.

The building's dual function provided an interesting space-planning challenge for the designers, who sought a

The first floor consists of the corporate health center, human resources/payroll office, and credit union. This view shows the reception area supporting these groups. The artwork was specifically commissioned for this location and inspired graphics used throughout the space. Herman Miller products have been used in conjunction with millwork to create a custom seating area. *Photography: Steve Hall © 2004 Hedrich Blessing*

In the main corridor, demountable partitions were designed to slide open when the credit union is in operation. Classic Eames chairs are used throughout in collaborative spaces and business center kiosks. *Photography: Steve Hall © 2004 Hedrich Blessing*

way to render public areas accessible and welcoming while maintaining security and confidentiality in other areas. This was particularly problematic in a building where a busy employee services center sits below engineering and security groups that require high degrees of privacy. After observing and interviewing the diverse population of building employees about their work processes and business needs, The Environments Group team designed a flexible, inventive solution that embodies the client's high standards for design, humanity, community, and the environment.

Specific project goals included:

- Achieve marketing and cost objectives while satisfying the varied needs and tastes of multiple departments, teams, and individuals.
- Minimize perceived cultural distinctions between production workers, office workers, and credit union customers to support an egalitarian culture.
- Help occupants and visitors find their way around the meandering campus.
- Earn LEED certification for the building's environmental performance, a complicated task given the age of the building and the extensive building envelope investments required.

To accomplish the tasks at hand, The Environments Group product selection was driven by the work process, in which the teams' needs overrode personal preference. Additionally, the design team sought to balance the needs of users and facility managers through flexible design and standards that are inexpensive to reconfigure and easy to maintain.

## Collaboration and Creativity

Herman Miller products were utilized to create zones that support collaboration as well as independent creativity and varying degrees of privacy. For example, engineers can retreat to private spaces to discuss manufacturer drawings, while the credit union utilizes a movable wall to provide heightened security for customers making financial transactions.

The Environments Group also repurposed an adjacent former loading dock into a functional workspace, taking advantage of the building's industrial past—especially a 22-foot ceiling and expansive windows that flood the

This collaborative area along a major corridor on the second floor overlooks a large conference room on the first floor. *Photography: Steve Hall ©2004 Hedrich Blessing*

Built architectural elements are at a minimum in the workplace design, with systems furniture panels separating the work areas from the public corridors. Here you see one of the fixed elements, a permanent meeting area, in an otherwise flexible floor plan. Informal collaboration areas utilize Herman Miller seating and tables. *Photography: Steve Hall © 2004 Hedrich Blessing*

room with filtered natural light. Herman Miller has gathered data from its many green buildings to show that huge increases in productivity result from the introduction of daylight into workspaces. The project also integrated thermal comfort control and monitoring, again reflecting its concern for employee health and well-being.

Special attention was also paid to the signage used for wayfinding and as a means to identify the people and functions in each space. Most of the open office systems furniture was refurbished and used as architectural elements and assemblies, thereby reducing first-cost expenses as well as providing the potential for reuse to solve future needs.

The project team also paid close attention to balancing first costs versus life cycle or long-term costs. Substantial investments were made in energy-efficient lighting and electrical systems, as well as a new HVAC system, all of which served to generate a wise return on investment. In fact, a substantial portion of the credits received for its LEED-CI certification were earned in the Energy and Atmosphere section for optimal energy performance of lighting, HVAC and equipment, and appliances, as follows:

■ *Lighting.* The energy performance for connected lighting power density is 33.5 percent under ASHRAE 90.1 minimum compliance.

The two-story conference room utilizes the George Nelson bubble lamps in honor of the building's original designers. The twenty-year-old structure was upgraded with a new roof, an improved fire protection system, and more efficient lighting. *Photography: Steve Hall © 2004 Hedrich Blessing*

■ *HVAC.* The HVAC system performance is 38 percent under ASHRAE 90.1 minimum compliance.
■ *Recycled content.* BG exceeded the base requirement of credit MRc 4.1 by 100 percent.
■ *Local/regional materials.* BG exceeded the base requirement of credit MRc 5.1 by 100 percent.

Angled reveals inspired by the vast lines of the mysterious Nazca Plateau in Peru are applied to accent walls. Clusters of soy candles illuminate the alcove. © *Eric Laignel*

Nusta Spa is also designed as an environmental respite where patrons will enjoy high standards of clean air and thermal comfort surrounded by materials provided by manufacturers at the forefront of the sustainability movement. The spa is the first in the world to be certified by the U.S. Green Building Council's LEED program and, in March 2005, received a LEED-CI Gold rating. Participation in the program influenced decision making throughout the process.

The design for Nusta (the Quechua word for royalty) draws its inspiration from the ancient Inca culture of Peru, with sight, sound, smell, and touch integrated in a refined manner. Soy candles and an indoor waterfall provide a soothing atmosphere, and the interplay of diverse materials—limestone, bamboo, and salvaged rustic oak, among others—offer visual pleasure.

A limestone wall in the reception area recalls the construction of the Inca city of Machu Picchu. © *Eric Laignel*

# Nusta Spa: Defining Green Tranquility

There simply couldn't be a better way to spend the day than at the Nusta Spa in Washington, D.C. It is a sophisticated and innovative urban day spa where patrons can expect the highest quality in treatments and products, combined with exceptional client service. The intention is to give customers the feeling of being completely removed from the hustle and bustle of urban stress.

## Where to Start

Environmental responsibility began with the selection of the designers. Envision Design is among the top green architectural firms in the nation and is arguably the leader in sustainable interiors. Principal Ken Wilson broached the subject of a green spa with his client, owner and president Elizabeth Snowdon, who immediately and enthusiastically signed on to the concept. The process began with a "green plan" outlining and itemizing all the environmental goals at the beginning of the project.

The first decision—location—set an example for the choices to come. The spa is located in a dense urban district near public transportation, in a space previously occupied by a deli and financial institution. Office equipment and furniture were donated to local nonprofit organizations, while food service equipment from the restaurant went to local charities. "It was our goal," said Wilson, "to salvage, recycle, and donate as much as possible to prevent the waste from ending up in a landfill. Through diligent sorting and organization we managed to divert and recycle half of the construction waste."

> *"Nusta Spa's vision is to treat our guests, our staff, and our environment with the greatest respect and care."*
>
> —Elizabeth Snowdon, owner and president, Nusta Spa

Energy use, thermal comfort, and air quality received equal care and attention. An HVAC system separate from the rest of the building, with state-of-the-art mechanical equipment that exceeds current standards for energy efficiency, will be continuously and professionally monitored to ensure peak operation. Energy needs for lighting have been dramatically reduced though the use of natural daylighting, fluorescent lamps, LED lighting, and occupancy sensors. Nusta Spa has also entered into an agreement to purchase a two-year 100 percent green power contract from renewable sources such as solar, water, and wind.

A thermally comfortable environment supports the well-being of the spa staff and clients. Specific controls in the treatment rooms accommodate personal preferences for temperature and airflow. Low-VOC materials were used,

Each treatment room is designed for individual customization. Patrons can select the temperature, select music, and even control the color of the room through a hidden LED lighting system that washes a sheer curtain wall. © *Eric Laignel*

and a specialized air filtration system removes three times as many particulates from the air than would a normal filter. In addition, $CO_2$ sensors continually monitor air quality and increase fresh air intake based on occupancy levels.

## Educated Material Choices

Several factors guided the selection of materials for the spa. The use of bamboo with its short harvest cycle, for example, contributes to both the project's aesthetic and environmental goals. The carpet used throughout, specifically designed by the designers, raises the bar for green floor coverings. Composed of more than 50 percent recy-

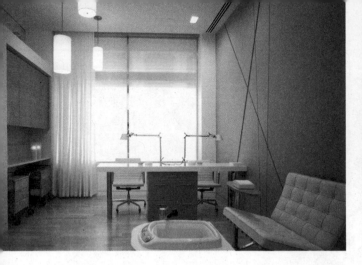

Classic furniture in the manicure/pedicure room and through-out the spa was chosen to support the manufacturer's environmental commitment. © *Eric Laignel*

The casework is produced locally and is made from wood procured from ecofriendly forests. The substrates have a very high recycled content. © *Eric Laignel*

The aesthetic and environmental message of Nusta Spa are reflected in their packaging and marketing materials, created by Envision Design. © *Envision Design, PLLC*

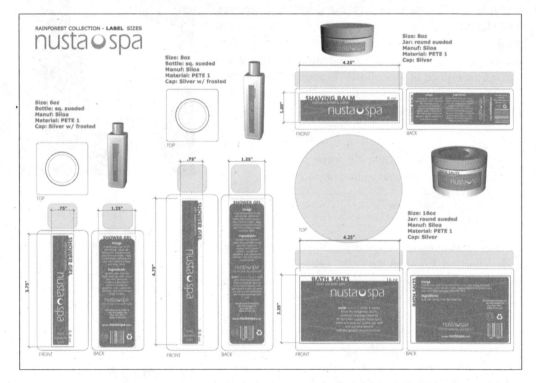

cled content and rapidly renewable resources, it is locally produced in neighboring Virginia. Instead of using virgin solid wood for the base, a wood-like material composed of annually renewable wheat straw fiber was specified. The ceiling tile used in the support spaces was salvaged during the demolition of another renovation project.

Partitions in the spa are finished with a painted drywall that has an interesting and sustainable composition. Panels are made from a sandwich of synthetic gypsum enveloped in 100 percent postconsumer recycled paper. The synthetic gypsum is actually benign residue reclaimed from the interior of smokestacks. Wood in the project, from doors to the hardwood flooring, comes from well-managed sources certified by the Forest Stewardship Council.

Concerted efforts were made to avoid the use of any toxic materials. For example, back-of-the-house support areas, typically finished with vinyl flooring, received linoleum flooring and a rubber base, each made with natural raw materials. The designers also went to great lengths to research, find, and install ecofriendly paints, adhesives, and sealants that emit few or no VOCs, thus reducing the quantity of these harmful contaminants in the air. They also specified fluorescent lamps with the lowest mercury levels on the market.

Environmental responsibility guided the choice of products and paper goods. The architect designed all graphic and printed materials in a sustainable manner using postconsumer, chlorine-free paper with soy and vegetable inks. Print materials include business cards, letterhead, envelopes, note pads, shopping bags, spa service menus, an environmental commitment brochure, and other promotional materials.

The client and designer's vision for Nusta Spa was to marry a sophisticated design concept with the highest standards of sustainability to demonstrate that being green no longer means having to do without. The choice to design a spa using high-performance healthy materials is only logical—a spa should be a healthy environment.

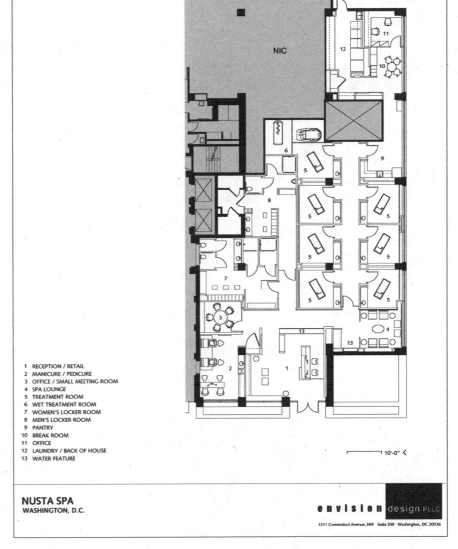

1   RECEPTION / RETAIL
2   MANICURE / PEDICURE
3   OFFICE / SMALL MEETING ROOM
4   SPA LOUNGE
5   TREATMENT ROOM
6   WET TREATMENT ROOM
7   WOMEN'S LOCKER ROOM
8   MEN'S LOCKER ROOM
9   PANTRY
10  BREAK ROOM
11  OFFICE
12  LAUNDRY / BACK OF HOUSE
13  WATER FEATURE

10'-0"

**NUSTA SPA**
WASHINGTON, D.C.

**envision** design PLLC
1211 Connecticut Avenue, NW   Suite 250   Washington, DC 20036

Floor plan. © *Envision Design, PLLC*

# Sauer–Danfoss: An American Building with European Sensibilities

Visitors to the Sauer-Danfoss North American headquarters in Lincolnshire, Illinois, are immediately struck by the firm's high-tech image, which begins in the reception area and is carried throughout the space. *Photography courtesy of OWP/P.* *Photographer: Chris Barrett © Hedrich Blessing*

As one of the world's largest manufacturers of mobile hydraulics, Sauer-Danfoss places a priority on environmental concerns. For its new North American headquarters in Lincolnshire, Illinois, the company sought a high-tech, modern, crisp image in a space that encourages employee satisfaction and productivity, and they chose OWP/P, a Chicago-based firm providing architecture, MEP/FP, structural engineering, and interior design services, to help them accomplish those objectives.

Based on corporate traditions and environmental sensitivities established in its offices in Denmark and Germany, Sauer-Danfoss desired daylight and unobstructed visual access to the outdoors. In selecting a building, the company placed equal priority on functional considerations, such as access to the airport, and on matters that affect the work environment, including higher-than-average ceilings and large windows.

During an extensive interview conducted with OWP/P project designers, they explained the difficulty in finding an appropriate site for the client. Sauer-Danfoss, they said, "didn't want to go into a typical spec office building that had eight-foot or nine-foot ceilings. Because half of the executives were European and the other half were from the U.S., they really wanted to be somewhere that was unconventional in order to keep their European character."

What this case study illustrates, says Mark Hirons, design principal in OWP/P's corporate/commercial group, is that site selection is crucial to the success of any project incorporating sustainable design principles. "So far we haven't emphasized enough the importance of the selection of a building," he noted. "While the amount of interior glass can be created, the access to light is a function of the building architecture and location. Security, net-to-gross, 24/7 power, image—these have always been part of building selection criteria. Now, as tenants and their designers seek sustainable goals, additional criteria are needed: orientation, glazing, operability of windows, power efficiency, controls."

In the end, the building chosen for the Sauer-Danfoss project—originally developed for a dot-com company—had deep space and tall ceilings, with angles that projected what the designers described as "an interesting, quirky geometry, almost like a quarter of a circle." Another attractive feature: the building's 12-foot floor-to-ceiling windows opened onto balconies.

In fact, it was the building's odd aesthetic that served as the starting point for the space planning and programming. Open, low workstations and work areas are located near the window wall adjacent to private glass-fronted offices, so daylight reaches all occupied areas within the office. Full-height windows throughout the headquarters allow every employee to connect visually with the outdoors and help reinforce the company's interactive work environment. They also foster the company's desired sense of community, not only throughout the entire office but also within working units. The executives who occupy perimeter offices wanted to provide views to all in order to facilitate interaction with their assistants. "They also want-

ed to share the sunlight with the open office," stated the design team members.

Floating white ceiling planes work in concert with translucent end panels on each of the workstations as part of an integrated design approach that throws daylight deep into the floorplate. Members of the OWP/P project design team described light penetration as one of their biggest challenges. Because the building is long and curved, one end of the floorplate is 90 feet deep, while the other end is half that. "Creating the central space was difficult because we wanted to make sure that light was coming in from both ends." In the end, though, a dynamic space was designed, despite the fact that columns also fell in odd

The building chosen for the Sauer-Danfoss offices featured an interesting geometry, one the designers described as "interesting" and "quirky," almost like a quarter circle. *Photography courtesy of OWP/P. Photographer: Chris Barrett © Hedrich Blessing*

Designers were able to penetrate daylight deep into the floorplate through the use of floating white ceiling planes that work in concert with translucent end panels on each of the workstations. *Photography courtesy of OWP/P. Photographer: Chris Barrett © Hedrich Blessing*

places. "We couldn't move them, so we decided to let them become part of the plan's unique geometry."

Additionally, the team was able to couple an effective daylight strategy with efficient, well-placed fluorescent lighting fixtures to ensure minimal energy use and glare.

## Crisp and Clean

The interior finishes and furniture standards for this office space promote environmentally sensitive products, from workstation panels composed of recycled soda bottles to office furniture manufactured with virtually VOC-free processes. The furniture systems make extensive use of recycled content—between 20 and 30 percent of the steel and 70 to 100 percent of the aluminum.

The furnishings and finishes chosen deliver an aesthetic that suits the Sauer-Danfoss culture well. In an interview with the managing director of this office, he said the firm sought an open feeling, one that appeals to the Danish preference for very light and airy spaces—"minimalist but not stark," as he described it, adding that the designers "hit it right on."

When Sauer-Danfoss was in the planning stages for its new location, he added, many people internally were questioning why the North American office was relocating to a place that projected a Taj Mahal-like image. "A few weeks ago, we had 150 of our leaders from all around the world here for a conference and we brought them to the office," he noted. "They said, 'Hmmm. It's clean, it's crisp, it's the right image.'"

Interestingly—and perhaps understandably, considering the company's insight and appreciation of sustainable development—since relocating to this facility Sauer-Danfoss has moved into the Fortune 1000 on the strength of revenues that increased 25 percent over 2003 figures.

Sauer-Danfoss is pleased that the office not only projects the desired image but also satisfies the company's desired sense of community. *Photography courtesy of OWP/P. Photographer: Chris Barrett © Hedrich Blessing*

The main lobby is a guest's first glimpse of Boulder Associates' commitment to sustainability. The custom designed signage utilizes the same rapidly renewable materials found throughout the rest of the office space. © *LaCasse Photography*

# Boulder Associates: Well Worth the Wait

It took four years of site research, some progressive thinking, and the innovative use of materials, but today Boulder Associates has a healthy and inspiring office space that serves as a sort of living laboratory, bringing sustainable concepts to life for clients, consultants, and staff. It was, in fact, the firm's growing commitment to responsible practices that was the driving force behind the programming for the office's design, making possible an environment that is water- and energy-efficient, has superb indoor air quality, and is punctuated with careful attention to materials usage and respectful of its historical heritage. The completed project was the first in the nation to receive LEED-CI Version 2.0 Certification, garnering a Gold rating for its environment- and employee-friendly offices.

The firm's new office is located on Pearl Street in downtown Boulder, Colorado, a dramatic departure from its previous home for the past twenty-two years in a remote, suburban location. The firm devoted four years to finding the right space in the downtown area, evaluating available

space by its ability to meet space demands, its proximity to a wide array of services and cultural opportunities, and the ability for staff members to walk to work or have access to public transportation. The firm eventually found a prime site: 13,000 square feet embedded in Boulder's city center, located on the third floor of the historic Citizens' National Bank Building, which served as a dance hall and jazz club over the years (frequented by such well-known performers as Glenn Miller). The office now houses approximately fifty architects, interior designers, and support staff, specializing in the healthcare and senior living sector. It is a shining example of the creative combination of old and new—at $60 per square foot for tenant improvements, the space effectively blends functional efficiency with a high degree of visual interest.

## Mindful of Materials

Working within the historical framework, the designers created a unique aesthetic that highlights the beauty of both new and existing materials. Being mindful that reuse is key

275

to sustainability, existing materials were reused wherever possible:

- The original tin ceiling and a 100-year-old brick demising wall were left intact to become organizing features that provide glimpses of the structure's history.
- Lumber, insulation, ceiling tiles, and grid were salvaged and incorporated into the new construction.
- Existing materials that did not become part of the design were salvaged for use by others, and include sinks, vanities, doors, glass, and light fixtures.
- Participation in Armstrong's closed-loop ceiling tile recycling program and Interface's carpet reclamation program ensured that dated carpet and ceiling tile went back into the manufacturing process for recycling.

Once the existing materials had been assessed and incorporated, Boulder Associates sought out materials salvaged from other structures to include in the design. Wood reclaimed from barrels formerly used to brine pickles was retooled to become a wood-slat ceiling, while brick of the same vintage as the structure was located to patch the existing demising wall. Additionally, a surprising 42 percent of furnishings in the new office were reused or refurbished items.

Products and materials made from rapidly renewable materials and those that remain biodegradable in their manufactured state were also top priorities. The firm estimates that nearly 10 percent of construction materials and

products purchased for the space were made from raw materials that can be harvested in one growing season. Wheatboard, sunflower board, linoleum flooring, and cork bulletin boards are on display, while cotton insulation made from scraps of the blue jean industry is visible through one carefully placed "truth window." Ceiling panels, door cores, and window-wall framing members called laminated strand lumber (LSL) are made from fast-growing trees such as aspen. Finally, fabric for tackable panels on the systems furniture is biodegradable, as are the aspen ceiling panels.

When materials could not be reused or did not fit under the rapidly renewable category, Boulder Associates paid close attention to products containing recycled content, respecting the third leg of the reduce-reuse-recycle triad of sustainability. The result is that nearly 39 percent of construction materials and furniture are composed of either postconsumer or postindustrial recycled waste, and 40 percent were manufactured within a 500-mile radius.

## Making the Most of Space

Careful selection of materials combined with thoughtful space planning helped to ensure the best use of the available space. Enclosed offices were positioned and outfitted with transom glass so as not to obstruct daylight and views from adjacent interior studio spaces. The main conference area (or "Biscuit Oven," as it is fondly referred to) was designed to accommodate large or small teams through the use of overhead garage-style doors with glass window inserts that divide the area and mobile furnishings for maximum flexibility. It was especially important to the firm's staff members that the conference room be able to facilitate the design charrette process—a goal achieved with full-height glass marker boards and galvanized steel magnet boards that provide pin-up space without requiring tape or damaging tacks.

Adhering to the precept that reuse is an important part of sustainable design, Boulder Associates selected Interface carpet to ensure that when replaced it could be reclaimed and go back to the manufacturing process for recycling. © LaCasse Photography

The staff lounge benefits from southern exposure and access to an exterior patio. In any season, employees can be found sharing conversations over lunch. Reclaimed pickle-finish wood was retooled to become a wood-slat ceiling in a reference to the building's historic heritage.
© LaCasse Photography

## Strategic Daylighting

To provide the maximum amount of daylight into the space, the firm used clerestory monitors in the middle of the main space as well as in the west studio space. Clerestory monitors—an alternative to horizontal skylights—required the roof to be "popped up," with glass on the north and south sides, said Dave Nelson, of David Nelson Associates, the lighting consultant on the project. "This is a better way to make use of daylight because we can control solar gain and direct glare by using the proper profile of the monitor, and size the overhang and the glass appropriately," he noted. Special attention to the design of the clerestory windows was paid to ensure approval by the city—because of the building's historic status and the architectural guidelines imposed due to its location on the mall, no changes in rooflines could be visible. "We calculated the amount of daylight coming into the space, and even though we couldn't get a 2 percent daylight factor—enough to meet the LEED credit—it was still the right thing to do because it provides a significant amount of light and a wonderful change in the space. It made a huge difference in the project from a daylighting perspective," Nelson said.

Light shelves were also used for the southern exposure, manufactured from a translucent material called polygal, a polycarbonate material that is often used for conference walls and for clerestory glass or sidelight glazing. Polygal has a 20 percent transmittance, and Nelson said the firm debated using a material with a lower transmittance level; however, it proved effective due to the high ceilings and resulted in better light distribution.

Light monitors, skylights, and reflective ceiling finishes help to distribute daylight throughout interior studio spaces, contributing positively to staff morale. Sunflower board provides oversized layout space at custom-designed casework islands. Note the interesting use of the rolling garage door as an entrance to this studio.
© LaCasse Photography

277

Occupancy sensors were also employed, as were daylight sensors. All circulation spaces are operated by timers to turn off after hours. The mercury content of all lamps was also examined. The firm chose T-5 HO for the linear lamps because of the high ceiling heights; in open areas where the ceiling reflectance wasn't extraordinarily high (around 70 percent), the lamps were used to indirectly uplight the ceiling. Additionally, 26-watt compact fluorescent lamps are used in the large industrial-looking pendants, with custom CFL sconces placed on the walls. The firm chose low-voltage 35-watt MR-16 lamps for wallwashing where art was placed.

Nelson said that one of the most interesting challenges was in appropriately lighting Boulder Associates' conference room. The firm wanted to have a direct/indirect pendant luminaire in the room, but when the rolling garage door dividers were up (and thus covering the ceiling), there wasn't anywhere to hang the pendant. An innovative mounting system using aircraft cable was devised to allow the luminaire to hang from the wall. A perforated shield on the luminaire prevented glare that might have reflected off the garage door glass.

## Responsibility Throughout

A forward-thinking landlord and existing building features also offered many sustainable opportunities to help Boulder Associates achieve its programmed goals. Ample windows, individual utility meters, an exterior recycling collection area, and shower rooms for bicycle commuters all played an important part in the project's success. Energy efficiency goals were achieved through the daylighting strategies mentioned earlier, as well as PVC-free foil-backed shades that minimize unwanted heat gain and Energy Star–rated appliances and electronics that account for 92 percent of the more than 100 pieces of equipment.

Responsible water management is critical to the environmental health of Colorado. Boulder Associates' water consumption was reduced by 43 percent through the installation of dual-flush toilets, waterless urinals, and low-flow showerheads in the restrooms and shower rooms. Additionally, micro-hydro-powered turbines charge the batteries of the sensor lavatory faucets, significantly extending the life of the batteries while minimizing water use.

Indoor air quality was protected by specifying low-emitting materials, minimizing contaminants during construction, and flushing the space with high volumes of fresh air prior to occupancy. To reduce greenhouse gas emissions, the office contracted with Renewable Choice Energy to provide 100 percent of its electrical power from renewable wind energy, and purchased its carpet through Interface's Cool Carpet Option. Participation in these two programs will offset over 148 tons of $CO_2$ and 320 pounds of nitrogen oxides.

In the end, the finished project was well worth the time and effort expended: the Boulder Associates office effectively blends functional efficiency with a high degree of visual interest and an impressive array of environmental achievements. The North Chapter of the AIA and the ASID agree: the project won a Merit Award in 2005 from the AIA chapter, and ASID's eighth annual Interior Design Award for Sustainability in 2006.

Waterless urinals and micro-hydro-powered faucets save water in style, while weekly fresh flower arrangements add a nice finishing touch. © *LaCasse Photography*

# Encore! The Gordon and Betty Moore Foundation

Programming for the new Washington, D.C., offices of the Moore Foundation called for a live/work-like approach that included different types of meeting space, workspace for eight, a pantry, and a library. Old solid timber joists were left to enhance the natural beauty of the setting. *Photography by Richard Greenhouse*

Designing for a nonprofit with a sensitivity to environmental issues always comes with a unique set of criteria, as Gensler learned when, in 2001, its San Francisco office was selected as the interior architect to renovate the historic Presidio for the new headquarter office of the Gordon and Betty Moore Foundation. The foundation occupied its new facilities in early 2002. A few months later, Gensler's Washington, D.C., office was given the opportunity for an encore: support the relocation of the foundation's satellite office in the D.C. area.

The Moore Foundation is a nonprofit organization that promotes environmental conservation. Its Washington office specifically sponsors initiatives to safeguard the ecological function and biodiversity of the Amazon basin watershed. The workplace needed to be a sustainable space that echoed the pro-environmental mission and values of the organization.

As it did in San Francisco, the foundation once again selected from existing building stock—this time a 3,000-square-foot suite on the third floor of a 100-year-old, low-rise commercial office building. An old Packard showroom in a previous life, the building is located north of Dupont Circle, which is one of the most vibrant neighborhoods in northwest Washington. This building fit in with the foundation's overall goal to be a vital part of the community that it occupies.

## The Objectives

The Washington, D.C., office of Gensler worked closely with the San Francisco office to re-create the successful initia-

In keeping with the goal to use as many reclaimed materials as possible, the pivot doors were saved and preserved from a recently demolished Victorian home in the neighborhood. *Photography by Richard Greenhouse*

tives carried out in the Presidio headquarters project. The layout of the D.C. office reflects the openness created in San Francisco. Workstation standards were adopted, and the same material selection criteria were utilized.

Because the Washington office of the Moore Foundation supports projects in Central and South America, providing office space for jet-setting program officers and touchdown stations for visiting San Francisco staff was an important element in space planning. Programming also called for different types of meeting spaces, individual workspace for eight staff members, a pantry with a movable island, an informal library, and a "chill zone" made up of a large window seat and a shag rug.

In all phases of planning, the objective was to approach every aspect from a sustainable design approach. Specifically, the client set three primary goals for the project:

- Create a sustainable space that is a visible reminder of what the Moore Foundation is about.
- Develop a simple, ecofriendly design strategy that doesn't bring an abundance of new construction materials onto the site (including the reuse of an existing building).

- Make a workplace that doesn't look or feel like one, blurring the lines between commercial and residential.

Other design elements include an open floor plan, abundant access to natural light, and the use of salvaged, recycled, and environmentally friendly materials throughout the space. Even the furniture strategy made use of abandoned and unclaimed furniture.

## The Solution

The design direction yielded a workplace for the Moore Foundation that is an extension of who it is as an organization and who staff members are as individuals. Existing conditions of the space served as inspiration for the design. With a masonry perimeter, steel beams, and wood flooring, the building is very atypical for the Washington, D.C., market. Gensler chose to bring out the natural characteristics of the space, recognizing the beauty in this raw, loft-like setting. As a result, the design team used reclaimed materials to create much of the new architecture within the space.

- Several dozen ceiling beams were removed from the loft space to create shelving in the team area and library as well as the main library table.
- Parlor doors from a recently demolished Victorian home in the neighborhood were preserved and used as pivot doors into the library.
- Windows from an old warehouse building in Washington were combined to create the clerestory glazing in the library.
- Reconstituted wood veneers were used for new millwork items in the pantry.
- Glass shards from recycled bottles were set into an epoxy base to form the pantry counters.
- Existing hardwood floors were refinished in one part of the building that used to be a dance studio.
- Some of the original brick construction was left exposed and old solid timber joists were left bare.
- Copper was salvaged to create a partial enclosure around a conference room.

With a masonry perimeter, steel beams, and wood flooring, the building is very atypical for the Washington, D.C., market. In the kitchen area, glass shards from recycled bottles were set into an epoxy base to form the pantry counters. *Photography by Richard Greenhouse*

An environmentally sensitive design strategy also governed the selection of new materials for the space. In fact, each material has some kind of environmental story: recycled tires make up the flooring that covers part of the space; wool carpet was chosen because of its performance, comfort, and ecofriendly content; durable, terrazzo-like countertops in the pantry are made from colorful recycled glass; ceramic tiles in the restrooms and shower are also made from recycled glass; cork covers a wall in the map room; bamboo blinds cover the large windows and provide light control; and hemp curtains enclose the interior conference room. Ecofriendly adhesives, paints, and coatings were used in all aspects of the construction.

All of these efforts resulted in 90 percent of materials coming from within 500 miles of the project site.

Thirty percent of the furniture budget comes from furniture that was purchased from salvage sources—mainly abandoned and unclaimed furniture bought from local warehouses. The new custom workstations that were built for the client used ecofriendly materials.

The wood used for the shelving in the team area and library, as well as the main library table, came from removing and cutting several dozen ceiling beams from the building's loft space. *Photography by Richard Greenhouse*

The mechanical design includes strategies for dealing with the single-pane historical windows, the placement of heating devices and ceiling fans, and personal controls for temperature and humidity. Workstations provide for individual lighting control for both daylighting and task lighting.

The project was completed in twelve weeks, resulting in an on-time, on-budget delivery to the Moore Foundation. The design team was also able to stay within the fee parameters despite the large amount of time necessary to research the sustainable materials. But most of all, the staff at the Moore Foundation received exactly what they ordered: a unique place where staff members can work, rest, innovate, and inspire.

This intimate space with window seats and a shag rug provides a respite from the day's activities, allowing Moore Foundation employees a place to rest and rejuvenate. *Photography by Richard Greenhouse*

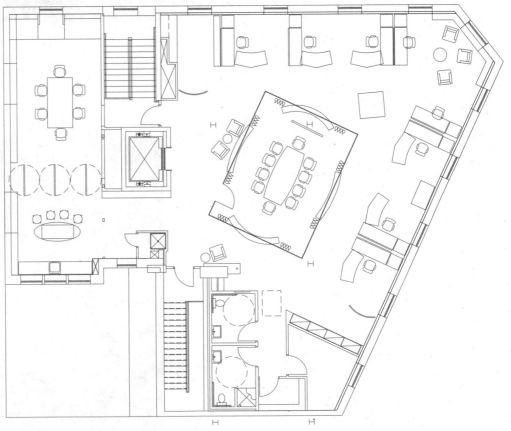

Floor plan. *Courtesy of Gensler*

# NOTES

## CHAPTER 1

1. Philip Sutton, "Sustainability: Woolly, Feel-good & Unachievable? Or a Goal for Practical Action?" June 2000, Green Innovations, Inc., www.green-innovations.asn.au.
2. Ibid.
3. United Nations Conference on Environment and Development, 1992, www.un.org.
4. United Nations Economic and Social Commission for Asia and the Pacific, "Integrating Economic and Environmental Policies: The Case of Pacific Island Countries," 2005.
5. Sandra Mendler, "HOK Reexamines Future for Sustainable Design," *Design Intelligence,* August 15, 2002.
6. Earth Day Network, www.earthday.net.
7. William McDonough, "Design, Ecology, Ethics and the Making of Things," Centennial Sermon, Cathedral of St. John the Divine, New York, February 7, 1993.
8. William A. McDonough, *The Hannover Principles: Design for Sustainability,* prepared for EXPO 2000, Hannover, Germany, 1992.
9. Mendler, "HOK Reexamines Future for Sustainable Design."
10. Nadav Malin and Jim Newman, "Greening Your Firm: Building Sustainable Design Capabilities," *Environmental Building News,* May 2004.
11. David Nelson, "Meeting Maximum Potential: The Sustainable Design Charrette," *Environmental Design + Construction,* September/October 2000.
12. Nadav Malin, "Building Commissioning: The Key to Buildings That Work," *Environmental Building News,* February 2000.

## CHAPTER 2

1. Elizabeth Kolbert, "The Climate of Man," *The New Yorker,* May 2, 2005.
2. Ibid.
3. Juliet Elperin, "World Temperatures Keep Rising With a Hot 2005," *The Washington Post,* October 13, 2005, p. A7.
4. "Time to Connect the Dots" (editorial), *New York Times,* September 28, 2005. Reprinted with permission.
5. Eileen Claussen, "Tackling Climate Change: 5 Keys to Success," presentation at the Fourth Annual Dartmouth Student Science Congress, May 2, 2003.
6. S. Pult del Pino and P. Bhatia, *Working 9 to 5 on Climate Change: An Office Guide,* 2002. World Resources Institute, www.safeclimate.net.

7. James Howard Kunstler, "Home From Nowhere," *Atlantic Monthly,* September 1996.
8. www.newurbanism.org.
9. www.cnu.org.
10. Laura Hager, "The There There," *North Bay Bohemian,* April 22–27, 2004.
11. Paul Simon, *Tapped Out: The Coming World Crisis in Water and What We Can Do About It,* 1998. Welcome Rain Publishers.
12. Jan Eliasson and Susan Blumenthal, "Dying for a Drink of Water," *Washington Post,* September 20, 2005.
13. www.cleanair.org.
14. www.pprc.org.
15. Bette K. Fishbein, "EPR: What Does It Mean? Where Is It Headed?," *P2: Pollution Prevention Review,* pp. 43–55, Volume 8, No. 4 © 1998 John Wiley & Sons, Inc.
16. www.productpolicy.org.
17. Garth T. Hickle and David Stitzhal, "Apportioning the Responsibilities for Product Stewardship: A Case for a New Federal Role," *Environmental Quality Management,* Vol. 12, Issue 3, Spring 2003, p. 2.
18. www.productstewardship.net.
19. David Malin Roodman and Nicholas Lenssen, "A Building Revolution: How Ecology and Health Concerns Are Transforming Construction," Worldwatch Paper #124, March 1995, Worldwatch Institute.
20. Sebastian Moffatt and Peter Russell, "Assessing the Adaptability of Buildings," Annex 31, Energy-Related Environmental Impact of Buildings, November 2001.
21. William J. Fisk, "Health and Productivity Gains from Better Indoor Environments and Their Relationship with Building Energy Efficiency," *Annual Review of Energy and the Environment* 25 (2000): 537–66.
22. Ibid.
23. Ibid.
24. www.oaklandnet.com.
25. Cited in Corey Griffin, "An Introduction to Biophilia and the Built Environment," Rocky Mountain Institute, www.rmi.org/sitepages/pid1079.php.
26. Cited in "Natural Selections: Past as Prologue?" *Material Matters* (The Hardwood Council/The American Hardwood Information Center), October 2004, www.hardwood.org/pdf/articles/072105040954White_paper_9.20.04.pdf.
27. E. O. Wilson, *Biophilia.* Cambridge, MA: Harvard University Press, 1984.

28. S. R. Kellert, *Building for Life: Designing and Understanding the Human-Nature Connection.* Washington, DC: Island Press, 2005.

29. J. Heerwagen and L. Zagreus, "The Human Factors of Sustainable Building Design: Post-occupancy Evaluation of the Philip Merrill Environmental Center," 2005, University of California, Berkeley, Center for the Built Environment; www.cbe.org.

30. J. Heerwagen and G. Orians, "Humans, Habitats and Aesthetics," in S. R. Kellert and E. O. Wilson, eds., *The Biophilia Hypothesis.* Washington, D.C.: Island Press, 1993.

## CHAPTER 3

1. www.boma.org.

2. www.realtor.org.

3. Charles Lockwood, "Raising the Bar: Town Centers are Outperforming Traditional Suburban Real Estate Products," *Urban Land,* February 2003.

4. Robert Lang, "Office Sprawl: The Evolving Geography of Business," Brookings Institution, Washington, D.C., October 2000.

5. The CBRE team included Patrick Marr, Sherry Cushman, Sally Wilson, and Chau Leung.

6. Alex Wilson, "All About Toilets," *Environmental Building News,* January 2004.

7. www.cuwcc.org.

8. Alex Wilson, "Electric Lighting: Focus on Lamp Technologies," *Environmental Building News,* June 2002.

9. www.lrc.rpi.edu.

10. Ibid.

11. Alex Wilson, "Lighting Controls: Beyond the Toggle Switch," *Environmental Building News,* June 2003.

12. *Advanced Lighting Guidelines,* 2003 edition, p. 76.

13. Ibid, p. 77.

14. Ibid, p. 81.

15. www.energystar.gov.

16. "Creating a High Performance Workspace," *Tenant Improvement Guide,* www.green-rated.org.

17. www.energystar.gov.

## CHAPTER 4

1. Amory B. Lovins, "Your Choices," summer 2005 Patagonia catalog, www.patagonia.com.

2. U.K. Building Research Establishment, www.bre.co.uk.

3. Cradle to Cradle Design Protocol: Glossary of Key Concepts, www.mbdc.com.

4. Alex Wilson, "Flame Retardants Under Fire," *Environmental Building News,* June 2004.

5. www.nike.com.

6. International Organization of Standardization (ISO), Reference Number 14040: 1997.

7. U.S. EPA and Science Applications International Corp., "LCAccess–LCA 101," 2001.

8. Ibid.

9. Sheila L. Bosch, "Resilient Flooring: A Comparison of Vinyl, Linoleum and Cork," Georgia Tech Research Institute, fall 1999, http://maven.gtri.gatech.edu/sfi/resources/techreports.html.

10. Helena Moussatche and Jennifer Languell, "Flooring Materials: Life-cycle Costing For Educational Facilities," *Facilities,* October 2001.

## CHAPTER 5

1. www.arb.ca.gov.

2. U.S. EPA, *Indoor Air Quality and Work Environment Study,* volume IV. Research Triangle Park, NC: 1991.

3. J. Home Winter, "Sick Home: Indoor Air Pollution Is Definitely Something to Sneeze At," *Rocky Mountain News,* July 11, 2000, p. 3D.

4. Asthma Statistics, Media Resources: Media Kit, American Academy of Allergy, Asthma and Immunology. Milwaukee, WI, 2005, www.aaai.org.

5. American Lung Association Fact Sheet, "Asthma in Adults," American Lung Association, New York, March 2003.

6. W. J. Fisk, "Estimates of Potential Nationwide Productivity and Health Benefits from Better Indoor Environments: An Update," chapter 4 in *Indoor Air Quality Handbook,* eds. J. D. Spengler, J. M. Samet, and J. F. McCarthy (New York: McGraw-Hill, 2000).

7. www.greenguard.org.

8. "Mold: Cause, Effect and Response—A Study of Wallcovering Products," Wallcoverings Association, Chicago, 2003.

9. www.epa.gov/iaq.

10. Lawrence Berkeley National Laboratory, http://eetd.lbl.gov.

11. "Heating, Ventilation and Air-Conditioning (HVAC) Systems in Offices and Schools," www.arias.org, 2001.

12. Alex Wilson, "Air Filtration in Buildings," *Environmental Building News,* October 2003.

13. Camfil Farr, 2006, www.filterair.info.

14. Marilyn S. Black, "The Impact of Construction and Furnishing Materials on Indoor Environmental Quality," Air Quality Sciences.

15. www.buildinggreen.com.

16. Rochelle Sharpe, "Mold Getting a Costly Hold on Homes," *USA Today,* June 19, 2002.

17. "What Office Tenants Want: 1999 BOMA/ULI Office Tenant Survey Report," Building Owners and Managers Association and Urban Land Institute, www.boma.org or www.uli.org.

18. "Underfloor Air Distribution (UFAD) Technology Overview," Center for the Built Environment, University of California at Berkeley, 2000.

19. "Sound Solutions: Increasing Office Productivity Through Integrated Acoustic Planning and Noise Reduction Strategies," American Society of Interior Designers, 1996.

20. "Sound Solutions: Increasing Office Productivity Through Integrated Acoustic Planning and Noise Reduction Strategies," American Society of Interior Designers, 2005.

21. "The Sound of the Effective Workplace," Armstrong World Industries, 1997.
22. "Sound Solutions," 2005.
23. CRI Technical Bulletin, "Acoustical Characteristics of Carpet," Carpet and Rug Institute, 2000.
24. www.daylighting.org.
25. *Advanced Lighting Guideline,* New Buildings Institute, 2003, p. 84 (4-10).
26. Heschong Mahone Group, "Windows and Offices: A Study of Office Worker Performance and the Indoor Environment," report prepared for the California Energy Commission, 2003, p. vii.
27. Ibid, p. 43.
28. www.iwfa.com.
29. *Advanced Lighting Guideline,* 2003, p. 52 (3-14).
30. http://oikos.com.
31. Heschong Mahone Group, "Windows and Offices," p. 8.
32. Ibid., p. vii.
33. Penny Bonda, "Environmental Defense: Pure and Simple," *Interiors & Sources,* May 2002.

## CHAPTER 6

1. Penny Bonda, "Eco-Design Matters," *Interiors & Sources,* October 2003.
2. Nadav Malin, "BEES 3.0 LCA Software Makes a Quantum Leap," *Environmental Building News,* December 2002.
3. MBDC Cradle to Cradle Certification Program.
4. Bonda, "Eco-Design Matters."
5. Nadav Malin, "Getting from Design to Construction: Writing Specifications for Green Projects," *Environmental Building News,* July/August 2002.
6. Penny Bonda, "Creating Sustainable Interiors," © 2005 NCIDQ.
7. Ibid.

## CHAPTER 7

1. Social Investment Forum, www.socialinvest.org.
2. Mark Thomsen, "The Data Game," *green@work,* March/April 2004.
3. Social Investment Research Analysts Network, www.siran.org.
4. Turner Green Building Survey, September 15, 2004, Turner Construction, www.turnerconstruction.com.
5. *Green Building SmartMarket Report,* 2006 Green Building Issue, www.smartmarket.construction.com.
6. Rocky Mountain Institute, www.rmi.org.
7. U.S. Green Building Council, www.usgbc.org.
8. Turner Green Building Survey.
9. "Green City Buildings: Applying the LEED Rating System," June 2000, prepared by Xenergy Inc. and SERA Architects for the Portland Energy Office, Portland, Oregon, www.sustainableportland.org.
10. "Examining the Cost of Green," October 2004, Davis Langdon and Seah International, www.davislangdon.com.

11. Ibid.
12. Ibid.
13. DPR Construction, www.dprinc.com.
14. Gregory Kats, "Are Green Buildings Cost Effective?" *green@work,* May/June 2004.
15. Ibid.
16. *Green Building SmartMarket Report,* 2006 Green Building Issue.
17. International Facility Management Association (IFMA), www.ifma.org.
18. World Health Organization, www.who.int.
19. "What Office Tenants Want: 1999 BOMA/ULI Office Tenant Survey Report," Building Owners and Managers Association and Urban Land Institute, www.boma.org or www.uli.org.
20. *The Kiplinger Letter: Forecasts for Management Decisions,* October 17, 2003.
21. Vivian Loftness, "e-BIDS: Linking Energy to Productivity and Health," Energy 2005, Long Beach, California, August 2005.
22. "High Performance Building Delivers Results," Sustainable Demand Project, City of Seattle, December 2000.
23. Lawrence Berkeley National Laboratory, www.lbl.gov.
24. Jonathan Finer, "Red-Letter Day for a 'Green' Building," *Washington Post,* April 24, 2004.
25. *Benefits Guide: A Design Professional's Guide to High Performance Building Benefits,* New Buildings Institute, 2004, www.newbuildings.org.
26. "Hidden Value: Recognizing the Asset Value of High-Performance Building," prepared by the Institute for Market Transformation for the New York State Energy Research and Development Authority, www.nyserda.org.
27. Chris Corps and Ross Davies, "Green Value: Bringing Real Business Benefits," *RICS Business,* November/December 2005, www.rics.org.
28. "Green Value: Relating the Market Value of a Real Estate Asset to Its Green Features and Related Performance," Royal Institution of Chartered Surveyors, www.rics.org.
29. U.S. Environmental Protection Agency, www.epa.gov.
30. Robin Pogrebin, "High-Rises That Have Low Impact on Nature," *New York Times,* February 2, 2006.
31. Tax Incentives Assistance Project, www.energytaxincentives.org.
32. "New York's Green Building Tax Credit," Natural Resources Defense Council, www.nrdc.org.
33. "Bank of America and the Durst Organization Break Ground on the Bank of America Tower at One Bryant Park in New York City," Durst Organization news release, August 2, 2004, www.durst.org.
34. "Sierra Club Statement on Wal-Mart's New Environmental Initiatives," Sierra Club, www.sierraclub.org.

# GLOSSARY

**Abatement**
Reducing the degree or intensity of, or eliminating, pollution. (EPA)

**Acetone**
A colorless, volatile, extremely flammable liquid ketone, $CH_3COCH_3$, widely used as an organic solvent.

**Acrylics**
A family of plastics used for fibers, rigid sheets, and paints.

**Acute exposure**
A single exposure to a toxic substance which may result in severe biological harm or death. Acute exposures are usually characterized as lasting longer than a day, as compared to longer, continuing exposure over a period of time. (EPA)

**Acute toxicity**
The ability of a substance to cause severe biological harm or death soon after a single exposure or dose. Also, any poisonous effect resulting from a single short-term exposure to a toxic substance. (EPA)

**Adsorption**
Removal of a pollutant from air or water by collecting the pollutant on the surface of a solid material. (EPA)

**Advanced treatment**
A level of wastewater treatment more stringent than secondary treatment; requires an 85 percent reduction in conventional pollutant concentration or a significant reduction in nonconventional pollutants. Sometimes called tertiary treatment. (EPA)

**Airborne particulates**
Total suspended particulate matter found in the atmosphere as solid particles or liquid droplets. Chemical composition of particulates varies widely, depending on location and time of year. Sources of airborne particulates include dust, emissions from industrial processes, combustion products from the burning of wood and coal, combustion products associated with motor vehicle or non-road engine exhausts, and reactions to gases in the atmosphere. (EPA)

**Air pollution**
The presence of contaminants or pollutant substances in the air that interfere with human health or welfare or produce other harmful environmental effects. (EPA)

**Air quality standards**
The level of pollutants prescribed by regulations that are not to be exceeded during a given time in a defined area. (EPA)

**Ambient lighting**
General illumination throughout a space.

**Ambient temperature**
Temperature of the surrounding air or other medium. (EPA)

**American National Standards Institute (ANSI)**
A premier source for timely, relevant, actionable information on national, regional, international standards and conformity assessment issues.

**American Society for Testing and Materials (ASTM)**
A standards development organization that serves as an open forum for the development of international standards.

**Antimony**
A toxic chemical used in metal coating that has been identified by the U.S. EPA as a persistent, bioaccumulative pollutant.

**Asbestos**
A mineral fiber that can pollute air or water and cause cancer or asbestosis when inhaled. The EPA has banned or severely restricted its use in manufacturing and construction. (EPA)

**Asbestos abatement**
Procedures to control fiber release from asbestos-containing materials in a building or to remove them entirely, including removal, encapsulation, repair, enclosure, encasement, and operations and maintenance programs. (EPA)

**ASHRAE**
American Society of Heating, Refrigerating and Air-Conditioning Engineers (ASHRAE) is an international membership organization founded to advance the arts and sciences of heating, ventilation, air-conditioning, and refrigeration and related human factors to serve the evolving needs of the public.

**ASHRAE Standard 55**
Thermal Environmental Conditions for Human Occupancy. Specifies the combinations of indoor thermal environmental factors and personal factors that produce acceptable thermal conditions.

**ASHRAE Standard 62**
Ventilation for Acceptable Indoor Air Quality. Details two methods for compliance: Ventilation Rate Procedure and the Indoor Air Quality Procedure. Rapidly becoming the standard of care for building ventilation and indoor air quality.

**ASHRAE Standard 90.1**
Energy Standard for Buildings Except Low-Rise Residential Buildings. Specifies minimum energy requirements.

**Attainment area**
An area considered to have air quality as good as or better than the national ambient air quality standards as defined in the Clean Air Act. An area may be an attainment area for one pollutant and a non-attainment area for others. (EPA)

**Bake-out**
A process used to remove VOCs from a building by elevating the temperature in the fully furnished and ventilated building prior to human occupancy.

**Benzene**
A clear, colorless, highly refractive flammable liquid derived from petroleum and used in or to manufacture a wide variety of chemical products, including DDT, insecticides, and motor fuels. Also called *benzine*.

**Bio-based**
Materials derived from natural renewable resources such as corn, rice, or beets.

**Biodegradable**
Capable of decomposing under natural conditions. (EPA)

**Biological nutrient**
A biological material posing no immediate or eventual hazard to living systems that can be used for human purposes and can safely return to the environment to feed environmental processes. (MBDC)

**Biomass**
A plant material, such as trees, grasses, and crops, which can be converted to heat energy to produce electricity.

**Biomimicry**
A new science that studies nature's models and then imitates or takes inspiration from these designs and processes to solve human problems.

**Biophilia**
A concept defined by Harvard biologist E. O. Wilson, who coined the term, as "the connections that human beings subconsciously seek with the rest of life."

**Blackwater**
Water that contains animal, human, or food waste. (EPA)

**Brominated flame retardant (BFR)**
A flame retardant chemical used for its effectiveness in stopping or slowing combustion, especially in polymer-based materials such as polyurethane foam cushioning, carpet cushion, and textile coatings. Also known as halogenated.

**Brownfield**
Abandoned, idled, or underused industrial and commercial facilities/sites where expansion or redevelopment is complicated by real or perceived environmental contamination. They can be in urban, suburban, or rural areas. EPA's brownfield initiative helps communities mitigate potential health risks and restore the economic vitality of such areas or properties. (EPA)

**Building density**
The floor area of the building divided by the total area of the site (square feet per acre). (USGBC)

**Building envelope**
The exterior surface of a building's construction—the walls, windows, roof, and floor. Also called a building shell. (EPA)

**Building-integrated photovoltaics (BIPV)**
Solar panels that have been integrated into the design of the building or structure. (ASID)

**Building-related illness (BRI)**
Diagnosable illness whose cause and symptoms can be directly attributed to a specific pollutant source within a building. (EPA)

**By-product**
Material, other than the principal product, generated as a consequence of an industrial process or as a breakdown product in a living system. (EPA)

**Carbon dioxide**
A colorless, odorless, incombustible gas formed during respiration, combustion, and organic decomposition and used in inert atmospheres, fire extinguishers, and aerosols.

**Carbon monoxide**
A colorless, odorless, poisonous gas produced by incomplete fossil fuel combustion. (EPA)

**Carcinogen**
Any substance that can cause or aggravate cancers. (EPA)

**Carpet America Recovery Effort (CARE)**
A voluntary initiative of the carpet industry and government to prevent carpet from burdening landfills, CARE focuses on developing carpet reclamation and recycling methods. (ASID)

**Certified wood**
Wood-based materials used in building construction that are supplied from sources that comply with sustainable forestry practices, protecting trees, wildlife habitat, streams, and soil as determined by the Forest Stewardship Council (FSC).

**Chain of custody**
A document that tracks the movement of a product from the point of harvest or extraction to the end user.

**Chlorofluorocarbons (CFCs)**
A family of inert, nontoxic, and easily liquefied chemicals used in refrigeration, air-conditioning, packaging, and insulation, or as solvents and aerosol propellants. Because CFCs are not destroyed in the lower atmosphere they drift into the upper atmosphere, where their chlorine components destroy ozone. (EPA)

**Chronic effect**
An adverse effect on human or animal whereby symptoms recur frequently or develop slowly over a long period of time. (EPA)

**Chronic exposure**
Multiple exposures occurring over an extended period of time or over a significant fraction of an animal's or human's lifetime—usually seven years to a lifetime. (EPA)

**Chronic toxicity**
The capacity of a substance to cause long-term poisonous health effects in humans, animals, fish, and other organisms. (EPA)

**Clean Air Act 1972**
Groundbreaking legislation administered by the EPA that mandates specific measures to protect the air quality and respiratory health of U.S. inhabitants.

**Closed-loop recycling**
Recovered materials are reused to manufacture new products containing 100 percent recycled sources.

**Commissioning (Cx)**
The start-up phase for a new or remodeled building, which includes testing and fine-tuning the HVAC and other systems to ensure proper functioning and adherence to design criteria. A building industry service for evaluating the performance of building systems.

**Compact fluorescent lamp (CFL)**
Small fluorescent lamps used as more efficient alternatives to incandescent lighting. (EPA)

**Composite wood**
A product consisting of wood or plant particles or fibers bonded together by a synthetic resin or binder. (USGBC)

**Compostable**
The ability of a material or product to be used as compost. Refers to any organic substance which can be returned to the soil and biodegrade without any harmful effects. (MBDC)

**Composting toilet**
A dry plumbing fixture that contains and treats human waste via microbiological processes. (USGBC)

**Connected lighting power (CLP)**
The power, in watts, connected to the building electrical service.

**Conservation**
Preserving and renewing, when possible, human and natural resources. The use, protection, and improvement of natural resources according to principles that will ensure their highest economic or social benefits. (EPA)

**Construction and demolition waste**
Waste building materials, dredging materials, tree stumps, and rubble resulting from construction, remodeling, repair, and demolition of homes, commercial buildings, and other structures and pavements. May contain lead, asbestos, or other hazardous substances. (EPA)

**Construction waste management plan (CWMP)**
A plan that diverts construction debris from landfills through the processes of recycling, salvaging, and reusing.

**Corporate social responsibility (CSR)**
Operating a business in a manner that meets or exceeds the ethical, legal, commercial, and public expectations that society has of business. (Business for Social Responsibility)

**Cradle to cradle**
A concept introduced by architect William McDonough and chemist Michael Braungart that prescribes that at the end of a product's useful life the product will decompose entirely with no negative environmental impact.

**Cradle-to-grave or manifest system**
A procedure in which hazardous materials are identified and followed as they are produced, treated, transported, and disposed of by a series of permanent, linkable, descriptive documents (e.g., manifests). (EPA)

**Daylighting**
Natural daylight introduced into interior spaces and controlled specifically to reduce levels of electric lighting, minimize glare, and optimize lighting quality.

**Daylight factor**
The ratio of interior illuminance at a given point on a given plane to the exterior illuminance under known overcast sky conditions. (USGBC)

**Daylight-responsive lighting controls**
Photosensors used in conjunction with other switching and dimming devices that control the amount of electric lighting in relationship to the amount and quality of natural daylight.

**Dematerialization**
The concept of eliminating materials from products while maintaining the same or better performance. Companies dematerialize by substituting intelligence and creativity for materials, by restructuring their products, or by resizing the product.

**Design for adaptability**
A design process that refers to the capacity of buildings to accommodate substantial change, thus making them less vulnerable to becoming poorly utilized, prematurely obsolete, and unable to accommodate new and more efficient technologies.

**Design for deconstruction**
A design practice focusing on the ease of disassembling elements and components for reuse and recycling when a building is wholly or partially deconstructed or demolished. By carefully disassembling a building, components and equipment may be able to be reused in a closed-loop materials cycle rather than entering the waste stream.

**Design for disassembly**
Designing a product to be dismantled for easier maintenance, repair, recovery, and reuse of components and materials.

**Design for the Environment (DfE)**
The process of incorporating life cycle analysis into the product development process to meet market demands for greener products, as well as a company's own internal corporate social responsibility standards.

**Downcycling**
Recycling a material in such a way that much of its inherent value is lost.

**Eco-effectiveness**
A strategy proposed by MBDC for designing human industry that is safe, profitable, and regenerative, producing economic, ecological, and social value. (MBDC)

**Eco-efficiency**
A strategy that calls for minimizing harm to natural systems by reducing the amount of waste and pollution generated by human activities. (MBDC)

**Ecological/environmental sustainability**
Maintenance of ecosystem components and functions for future generations. (EPA)

**Ecological impact**
The effect that a human-caused or natural activity has on living organisms and their nonliving environment. (EPA)

**Ecological indicator**
A characteristic of an ecosystem that is related to, or derived from, a measure of biotic or abiotic variable, that can provide quantitative information on ecological structure and function. An indicator can contribute to a measure of integrity and sustainability. (EPA)

**Ecosphere**
The "biobubble" that contains life on earth, in surface waters, and in the air. (EPA)

**Ecosystem**
The interacting system of a biological community and its nonliving environmental surroundings. (EPA)

**Electromagnetic sensitivity (EMS)**
The physical reaction from exposures to electrical devices and frequencies that can be generated from office equipment and other sources, as well as from noise and vibration.

**Embodied energy**
The sum of all energy used to grow, extract, and manufacture a product, including the amount of energy needed to transport it to the job site and complete the installation.

**Encapsulation**
The treatment of asbestos-containing material with a liquid that covers the surface with a protective coating or embeds the fibers in an adhesive matrix to prevent their release into the air. (EPA)

**Endocrine disruptors**
Chemicals thought to be dangerous to human hormone systems and fetal development because they mimic the hormones that control bodily functions; considered especially hazardous to fetuses and children.

**Energy-efficient**
Products and systems that use less energy to perform as well or better than standard products.

**Energy management system**
A control system capable of monitoring environmental and system loads and adjusting HVAC operations accordingly in order to conserve energy while maintaining comfort. (EPA)

**Energy Policy Act of 1992 (EPAct)**
Addresses energy and water use in buildings.

**Energy Star rating**
The designation given by the EPA and the U.S. Department of Energy (DOE) to appliances and products that exceed federal energy efficiency standards. This label helps consumers identify products that will save energy and money.

**Environmental Protection Agency (EPA)**
Established in 1970 to consolidate the federal government's environmental regulatory activities under the jurisdiction of a single agency, the mission of the EPA is to protect human health and to safeguard the natural environment. The EPA ensures that federal environmental laws are enforced fairly and effectively. (EPA)

**Environmental sustainability**
Long-term maintenance of ecosystem components and functions for future generations. (EPA)

**Environmental tobacco smoke (ETS)**
Mixture of smoke from the burning end of a cigarette, pipe, or cigar and smoke exhaled by the smoker. (EPA)

**Environmentally friendly**
A term that refers to the degree to which a product may harm the environment, including the biosphere, soil, water, and air. (ASID)

**Extended producer responsibility**
A term coined early in the 1990s by Thomas Lindhqvist to describe a policy that extends the responsibility of producers for the environmental impacts of their products to the entire product life cycle, and especially for their take-back, recycling, and disposal.

**Flush-out**
The operation of mechanical systems for a minimum of two weeks using 100 percent outside air at the end of construction and prior to building occupancy to ensure safe indoor air quality.

**Formaldehyde**
A colorless, pungent, and irritating gas used chiefly as a disinfectant and preservative and in synthesizing other compounds such as resins. (EPA)

**Fossil fuels**
Fuel derived from ancient organic remains, e.g., peat, coal, crude oil, and natural gas. (EPA)

**Genetic modification**
Human-designed changes in a plant or animal.

**Graywater**
Domestic wastewater composed of washwater from kitchen, bathroom, and laundry sinks, tubs, and washers. (EPA)

**Green-e Renewable Electricity Certificate Program**
A voluntary certification and verification program for green electricity programs. (USGBC)

**Greenfields**
Land not previously developed beyond agriculture or forestry use.

**Greenhouse gas emissions**
Emissions into the atmosphere of gases that affect the temperature and climate of the earth's surface. The leading greenhouse gases emitted due to human activity are carbon dioxide, methane, and nitrous oxide.

**Green power**
Electricity generated from renewable energy sources.

**Halogen**
An incandesent lamp with a quartz bulb and gas filling that includes a halogen element, producing a brilliant light from a compact unit.

**Harvested rainwater**
Rainwater captured and used for indoor needs, irrigation, or both.

**Hazardous waste**
By-products of society that can pose a substantial or potential hazard to human health or the environment when improperly managed. Possesses at least one of four characteristics (ignitability, corrosivity, reactivity, or toxicity), or appears on special EPA lists. (EPA)

**High-intensity discharge**
A generic term for mercury vapor, metal halide, and high-pressure sodium lamps and fixtures. (EPA)

**High-performance green building**
Buildings that include design features that conserve water and energy; use space, materials, and resources efficiently; minimize construction waste; and create healthy indoor environments.

**Hydrochlorofluorocarbon (HCFC)**
A fluorocarbon that is replacing chlorofluorocarbon as a refrigerant and propellant in aerosol cans; considered to be somewhat less destructive to the atmosphere.

**Impact assessment**
The process of assessing the human and ecological effects of energy, water, and material usage and the environmental releases identified in the inventory analysis. (EPA)

**IESNA**
Illuminating Engineering Society of North America, the recognized technical authority in the lighting design industry; has established guidelines to ensure proper lighting design.

**Indoor air pollution**
Chemical, physical, or biological contaminants in indoor air. (EPA)

**Indoor air quality (IAQ)**
The supply and introduction of adequate air for ventilation and control of airborne contaminants, acceptable temperatures, and relative humidity.

**Indoor environmental quality (IEQ)**
The evaluation of five primary elements—lighting, sound, thermal conditions, air pollutants, and surface pollutants—to provide an environment that is physically and psychologically healthy for its occupants.

**Integrated design team**
The team of all individuals involved in a project from very early in the design process, including the design professionals, the owner's representatives, and the general contractor and subcontractors.

**Life cycle assessment (LCA)**
The comprehensive examination of a product's environmental and economic effects throughout its lifetime, including raw material extraction, transportation, manufacturing, use, and disposal.

**Life cycle cost**
The amortized annual cost of a product that includes first costs as well as installation, operating, maintenance, and disposal costs over the product's lifetime.

**Life cycle cost analysis (LCCA)**
The examination of a product's economics, including owning, operating, maintaining, and disposing of a product over a period of time.

**Life cycle inventory**
The process of quantifying energy and raw material requirements, atmospheric emissions, waterborne emissions, solid wastes, and other releases for the entire life cycle of a product, process, or activity. (EPA)

**Light-emitting diode (LED)**
A long-lasting illumination technology that requires very little power. (EPA)

**Lighting power density (LPD)**
The maximum lighting power, per unit area, of a building classification of space function. (USGBC)

**Luminaire**
A complete lighting unit consisting of a lamp or lamps together with the housing designed to distribute the light, position and protect the lamps, and connect the lamps to the power supply. (USGBC)

**Material Safety Data Sheet (MSDS)**
A compilation of information required under the OSHA Communication Standard on the identity of hazardous chemicals, health and physical hazards, exposure limits, and precautions. (EPA)

**Mechanical ventilation**
Ventilation provided by mechanically powered equipment, such as motor-driven fans and blowers. (USGBC)

**Multiple chemical sensitivity (MCS)**
An acute physical sensitivity to various types of chemicals; the range and severity of reactions are as varied as the potential triggering agents.

**National Institute of Occupational Safety and Health (NIOSH)**
An agency of the Centers for Disease Control of the Department of Health and Human Services. NIOSH is the research arm of OSHA.

**Natural ventilation**
Ventilation provided by thermal, wind, or diffusion effects through doors, windows, or other intentional openings in buildings. (USGBC)

**New urbanism**
A movement pioneered by architect Peter Calthorpe that opposes suburban sprawl, advocating instead for the reintroduction of the concept of community in urban planning. Its mission statement calls for "the restoration of existing urban centers and towns within coherent metropolitan regions, the reconfiguration of sprawling suburbs into communities of real neighborhoods and diverse districts, the conservation of natural environments, and the preservation of our built legacy."

**Nonrenewable**
Of or relating to an energy source, such as oil or natural gas, or a natural resource, such as a metallic ore, that is not replaceable after it has been used.

**Non-water urinal**
A dry plumbing fixture that uses advanced hydraulic design and a buoyant fluid instead of water to maintain sanitary conditions. (USGBC)

**Occupational Safety and Health Administration (OSHA)**
A branch of the U.S. Department of Labor responsible for establishing and enforcing safety and health standards in the workplace.

**Off-gassing**
A process of evaporation or chemical decomposition through which vapors are released from materials.

**Ozone layer**
The protective layer in the atmosphere, about 15 miles above the ground, that absorbs some of the sun's ultraviolet rays, thereby reducing the amount of potentially harmful radiation that reaches the earth's surface. (EPA)

**Persistent bioaccumulative toxin (PBT)**
Substances that build up in the food chain and do not break down easily.

**Photovoltaic (PV)**
Capable of producing a voltage when exposed to radiant energy, especially light.

**Phthalates**
An endocrine disruptor found in many personal care products, medical supplies, toys, and other soft vinyl products. In the buildings industry they are commonly found in flooring, wall-covering, upholstery, and shower curtains as the additive that gives these products their flexibility.

**Plasticizers**
Any of various substances added to plastics or other materials to make or keep them soft or pliable.

**Plug load**
Refers to all equipment that is plugged into the electrical system, such as task lights, computers, printers, and refrigerators.

**Pollutant**
Generally, any substance introduced into the environment that adversely affects the usefulness of a resource or the health of humans, animals, or ecosystems. (EPA)

**Pollution**
Generally, the presence of a substance in the environment that, because of its chemical composition or quantity, prevents the functioning of natural processes and produces undesirable environmental and health effects. (EPA)

**Postconsumer materials/waste**
Recovered materials that are diverted from municipal solid waste for the purposes of collection, recycling, and disposition. (EPA)

**Postconsumer recycling**
Use of materials generated from resident and consumer waste for new or similar purposes, e.g., converting wastepaper from offices into corrugated boxes or newsprint. (EPA)

**Potable water**
Water that meets drinking water quality standards and is approved for human consumption by the state or local authorities having jurisdiction.

**Preconsumer materials/waste**
Materials generated in manufacturing and converting processes, such as manufacturing scraps and trimmings and cuttings. Includes print overruns, overissue publications, and obsolete inventories. (EPA) (Previously referred to as "postindustrial" by LEED.)

**Product as service**
The concept of product leasing whereby a consumer leases a product in order to utilize the service it provides. For example, consumers usually don't want to own the plastics and glass in a television set; rather, they want the service—viewing of TV programs—that the television set provides.

**Rainwater harvesting**
The practice of collecting, storing, and using precipitation from a catchment area such as a roof.

**Rapidly renewable**
Materials that are not depleted when used. These materials are typically harvested from fast-growing sources and do not require unnecessary chemical support. Examples include bamboo, flax, wheat, wool, and certain types of wood.

**Rated power**
Maximum amount of power a single piece of equipment can draw under any circumstance. Rated power is often at least two times greater than the actual power used by a single piece of equipment.

**Reclamation**
The practice of taking back used products when consumers are finished with them in an effort to acquire low-cost feedstock for manufacturing or remanufacturing parts for reuse.

**Recyclability**
The ability of a product or material to be recovered or otherwise diverted from the solid waste stream for the purpose of recycling.

**Recycled/recovered materials**
Waste materials and by-products that have been recovered or diverted from solid waste. Recycled/recovered materials do not include materials and by-products generated from and commonly reused within an original manufacturing process.

**Recycle/reuse**
Minimizing waste generation by recovering and reprocessing usable products that might otherwise become waste. (EPA)

**Refurbished materials**
Materials that have been restored to serve in place of a new item. The refurbishing typically includes replacement of worn and nonfunctioning parts, and possibly refinishing. (USGBC)

**Remanufacturing**
A recycling concept by which an existing product can have its useful life extended through a secondary manufacturing or refurbishing process, such as remanufactured systems furniture. (ASID)

**Renewable energy**
Alternative energy derived from sources that do not use up natural resources or harm the environment. Examples are solar, hydroelectric, or wind energy.

**Resource efficiency**
A practice in which the primary consideration of material use begins with the concept of "reduce-reuse-recycle-repair" (stated in descending order of priority).

**Sick building syndrome (SBS)**
Building whose occupants experience acute health and/or comfort effects that appear to be linked to time spent therein, but where no specific illness or cause can be identified. Complaints may be localized in a particular room or zone, or may spread throughout the building. (EPA)

**Sink**
Place in the environment where a compound or material collects. (EPA)

**Smart growth**
Managing the growth of a community in such a way that land is developed according to ecological tenets that call for minimizing dependence on auto transportation, reducing air pollution, and making infrastructure investments more efficient.

**Socially responsible investing (SRI)**
An investment philosophy that considers both social and environmental impacts alongside economic considerations.

**Sprawl**
Unplanned development of open land that typically results in loss of rural areas.

**Stakeholders**
All parties that might be affected by a company's policies and operations, including shareholders, employees, customers, suppliers, business partners, and surrounding communities.

**Sustainability**
A resource or system that "meets the needs of the present without compromising the ability of future generations to meet their own needs." (Brundtland Commission, 1983)

**Sustainable yield forestry**
Sustainable yield forestry dictates planting the same number of trees cut down.

**Systems furniture**
Defined as either a panel-based workstation consisting of modular interconnecting panels, hang-on components, and drawer/filing components or a freestanding grouping of furniture items and their components that have been designed to work in concert. (USGBC)

**Technical nutrient**
MBDC's term, modeled on natural systems, for the processes of human industry that maintain and perpetually reuse valuable synthetic and mineral materials in closed loops. (MBDC)

**Thermal comfort**
The appropriate combination of temperature combined with airflow and humidity that allows one to be comfortable within the confines of a building.

**Third-party certification**
An independent, objective assessment of an organization's practices or chain of custody system by an auditor who is independent of the party undergoing assessment.

**Tipping fees**
The fees charged to dump construction and demolition waste at landfills and waste transfer stations.

**Transect planning**

Town planning that places the highest densities at town centers and progressively less dense building toward the edges. It seeks to preserve natural space by maintaining appropriate land uses for each sector.

**Trichloroethylene**

A stable, low-boiling-point colorless liquid, toxic if inhaled. Used as a solvent or metal degreasing agent, and in other industrial applications. (EPA)

**Triple bottom line**

A term coined by John Elkington that calls for measurement of corporate performance along three interlinked lines: profits, environmental sustainability, and social responsibility.

**TVOCs**

The total VOC level in air; used as an indicator of whether or not elevated VOCs exist in a building. (Aerias)

**Urea formaldehyde**

A combination of urea and formaldehyde that is used in some glues and may emit formaldehyde at room temperature. (USGBC)

**Urethanes**

A family of plastics (polyurethanes) used for varnish coatings, foamed insulations, highly durable paints, and rubber goods.

**Ventilation**

The process of supplying air or removing air from a space for the purpose of controlling air contaminant levels, humidity, or temperature within the space. (USGBC)

**Vision glazing**

That portion of exterior windows above 2 feet 6 inches and below 7 feet 6 inches that permits a view to the outside. (USGBC)

**Volatile**

Any substance that evaporates readily. (EPA)

**Volatile organic compound (VOC)**

A highly evaporative, carbon-based chemical substance that produces noxious fumes; found in many paints, caulks, stains, and adhesives.

**Waste = food**

A principle of natural systems that MBDC proposes will eliminate the concept of waste. In this design strategy, all materials are viewed as continuously valuable, circulating in closed loops of production, use, and recycling. (MBDC)

**Waste reduction**

Using source reduction, recycling, or composting to prevent or reduce waste generation. (EPA)

**Waste stream**

The total flow of solid waste from homes, businesses, institutions, and manufacturing that is recycled, burned, or disposed of in landfills; also, segments thereof, such as the residential waste stream or the recyclable waste stream. (EPA)

**Wastewater**

The spent or used water from a home, community, farm, or industry that contains dissolved or suspended matter. (EPA)

**Xeriscape**

Landscapes that are based on sound horticultural practices and incorporate native plant species that are adapted to local climate conditions. (USGBC)

**Xylene**

Found in paints, varnishes, lacquers, and solvents; observed to off-gas.

## LEED Terminology

**LEED (Leadership in Energy and Environmental Design) Green Building Rating System**

A voluntary, consensus-based, market-driven building rating system based on existing proven technology. The LEED Green Building Rating System represents the U.S. Green Building Council's effort to provide a national standard for what constitutes a "green building." Through its use as a design guideline and third-party certification tool, LEED aims to improve occupant well-being, building environmental performance, and building economic returns using established and innovative practices, standards, and technologies.

**Application Guide (AG)**

A document that adapts the LEED rating criteria for use in specific market segments. Currently under development: application guides for campus, healthcare, laboratories, retail, schools, and volume build. Also referred to as "market sector guides."

**Category**

LEED Green Building Rating System component. Each LEED prerequisite and credit falls within one of five core categories —Sustainable Sites, Water Efficiency, Energy and Atmosphere, Materials and Resources, Indoor Environment, Quality—plus bonus credits for Design and Process Innovation.

**Credit**

LEED Green Building Rating System component. Compliance is optional, and meeting credit criteria results in the earning of points toward certification.

**Credit Interpretation Ruling (CIR)**

Used by design team members questioning or experiencing difficulties in the application of a LEED prerequisite or credit to a project.

**Energy and Atmosphere (EA)**

LEED Rating System category. Prerequisites and credits in this category focus on optimizing energy efficiency and performance, reducing ozone depletion, and encouraging the use of renewable energy.

### Indoor Environmental Quality (IEQ)

LEED Rating System category. Prerequisites and credits in this category focus on the strategies and systems that result in a healthy indoor environment for building occupants.

### Intent

LEED Green Building Rating System component. Identifies the primary goal of each prerequisite or credit.

### Innovation and Design Process (ID)

LEED Rating System category. Credits in this category recognize projects for innovative building features and sustainable building knowledge.

### LEED Reference Guide

The LEED Reference Guides are supporting documents to the LEED Green Building Rating Systems, intended to assist project teams understand LEED criteria and the benefits of compliance with the criteria.

### LEED-CI

LEED for Commercial Interiors. One of the six LEED Green Building Rating Systems. LEED for Commercial Interiors addresses the design and construction of tenant space fit-outs.

### LEED-CS

LEED for Core and Shell. One of the six LEED Green Building Rating Systems. LEED for Core and Shell focuses on buildings being developed where the developer is responsible for the core and shell of the structure and has no responsibility for the design and decisions concerning the interior space fit-outs.

### LEED-EB

LEED for Existing Buildings. One of the six LEED Green Building Rating Systems. LEED for Existing Buildings establishes a set of performance standards for the sustainable upgrades and operation of existing buildings.

### LEED-H

LEED for Homes. One of the six LEED Green Building Rating Systems. LEED for Homes addresses single-family homes, both detached and attached, and multifamily residential buildings with up to three stories developed on a single lot.

### LEED-NC

LEED for New Construction. One of the six LEED Green Building Rating Systems. LEED for New Construction focuses on the design and construction process for new construction and major reconstruction of buildings.

### LEED-ND

LEED for Neighborhood Developments. One of the six LEED Green Building Rating Systems. LEED for Neighborhood Developments addresses the design and location of new, multi-lot residential, commercial, or mixed-use developments.

### LEED Steering Committee (LSC)

Oversight committee of the USGBC responsible for direction and decisions for the LEED program.

### Materials and Resources (MR)

LEED Green Building Rating System category. Prerequisites and credits in this category focus on reducing material use, using materials with less environmental impact, and waste management.

### Performance/Intent-Equivalent Alternative Compliant Path (PIEACP)

A strategy of incorporating technical, up-to-date refinements to LEED.

### Points

Compliance with each LEED credit earns one or more points toward certification. Compliance with prerequisites is required and does not earn points.

### Prerequisites

LEED Green Building Rating System component. Compliance is mandatory for achieving certification but does not count toward the accumulation of points.

### Requirements

LEED Green Building Rating System component. Specifies the criteria to satisfy the prerequisites or credit and identifies the total number of points available.

### Submittals

LEED Green Building Rating System component. Specifies the documentation required for LEED certification.

### Sustainable Sites (SS)

LEED Rating System category. Prerequisites and credits in this category focus on location issues such as land use and protections to eliminate and/or minimize the impact of the building on the environment.

### Technical Advisory Group (TAG)

Subcommittees that consist of industry experts who assist in developing credit interpretations and technical improvements to the LEED system.

### Technical and Scientific Advisory Committee (TSAC)

The Technical and Scientific Advisory Committee is a standing LEED committee representing a diversity of building community perspectives and technical areas of competency. The Technical and Scientific Advisory Committee provides support for each of the LEED products and advice on topics as assigned by the LEED Steering Committee and the USGBC Board of Directors.

### Technologies and Strategies

LEED Green Building Rating System component that suggests products or systems that can be used to achieve the credit requirements and methods or assemblies that facilitate compliance.

### Water Efficiency (WE)

LEED Green Building Rating System category. Prerequisites and credits in this category focus on the reduction of potable water used by buildings and tenant spaces.

# RESOURCES

## PRINT RESOURCES

Anderson, Ray. *Mid-Course Correction: Toward a Sustainable Enterprise*. White River Junction, VT: Chelsea Green Publishing Co., 1999.

Barnett, Dianna Lopez, and William Browning. *A Primer on Sustainable Building*. Rocky Mountain Institute. 1995.

Benyus, Janine. *Biomimicry: Innovation Inspired by Nature*. New York: William Morrow & Co., 1997.

Brown, Lester R. *Eco-Economy: Building an Economy for the Earth*. New York: W. W. Norton & Co., 2001.

Browner, Michael, and Warren Leon. *The Consumer's Guide to Effective Environmental Choices*. New York: Three Rivers Press, 1999.

Browning, William, and Joseph Romm. *Greening the Building and the Bottom Line*. Rocky Mountain Institute, 1994.

Carson, Rachel. *Silent Spring*. New York: Houghton Mifflin Co., 1962.

Gore, Al. *An Inconvenient Truth*. Rodale Books, 2006.

Gottfried, David. *Greed to Green*. Berkeley: WorldBuild Publishing, 2004.

Hawken, Paul. *The Ecology of Commerce*. New York: Harper Collins, 1993.

Hawken, Paul, Amory Lovins, and Hunter Lovins. *Natural Capitalism*. Boston: Back Bay Books, 1999.

Kellert, Stephen R., and Edward O. Wilson. *The Biophilia Hypothesis*. Island Press, 1993.

McDonough, William. "A Centennial Sermon: Design, Ecology, Ethics and the Making of Things." The Cathedral of St. John The Divine, New York, February 7, 1993.

———. *The Hannover Principles: Design for Sustainability*. Prepared for EXPO 2000, Hannover, Germany. William McDonough Architects, 1992.

McDonough, William, and Michael Braungart. *Cradle to Cradle: Remaking the Way We Make Things*. New York: North Point Press, 2002.

McGraw-Hill Construction. *Green Building Smart Market Report*. In conjunction with the U.S. Green Building Council. 2005.

Mendler, Sandra, William Odell, and Mary Ann Lazarus. *The HOK Guidebook to Sustainable Design*. Hoboken, NJ: John Wiley & Sons, 2005.

National Audubon Society and Croxton Collaborative Architects. *Audubon House: Building the Environmentally Responsible, Energy-Efficient Office*. New York: John Wiley & Sons, 1994.

Nattress, Brian, and Mary Altomare. *The Natural Step for Business: Wealth, Ecology and the Evolutionary Corporation*. New Society Publishers, 1999.

Pilatowicz, Grazyna. *Eco-Interiors: A Guide to Environmentally Conscious Interior Design*. New York: John Wiley & Sons, 1995.

Quinn, Daniel. *Ishmael*. New York: Bantam, 1992.

Romm, Joseph. *Cool Companies*. Island Press, 1999.

Ryan, John C., and Alan Thein Durning. *Stuff: The Secret Lives of Everyday Things*. Seattle: Northwest Environment Watch, 1997.

Speth, Gus. *Red Sky at Morning: America and the Crisis of the Global Environment*. New Haven: Yale University Press, 2004.

Spiegel, Ross, and Dru Meadows. *Green Building Materials*. New York: John Wiley & Sons, 2006.

Wilson, Alex, ed. *GreenSpec Directory*. BuildingGreen Inc., 2006.

Wilson, Alex, and the Rocky Mountain Institute Staff. *Green Development: Integrating Ecology and Real Estate*. New York: John Wiley & Sons, 1997.

Wilson, Edward O. *The Future of Life*. New York: Alfred A. Knopf, 2002.

Yudelson, Jerry. *The Insider's Guide to Marketing Green Buildings*. Portland, OR: Green Building Marketing, 2004.

## INTERNET RESOURCES

### Air Quality

Aerias *www.aerias.org*
Clean Air/Cool Planet *www.cleanair-coolplanet.org*
Clean Air Council *www.cleanair.org*

### Building

Alliance for Sustainable Built Environments
*www.greenerfacilities.org*
Carnegie Mellon University Center for Building
Performance and Diagnostics *www.arc.cmu.edu/cbpd*

Center for the Built Environment *www.cbe.berkeley.edu*
Davis Langdon and Seah International
  *www.davislangdon.com*
DOE High-Performance Buildings Database
  *www.eere.energy.gov/buildings/database*
Energy and Environmental Building Association
  *www.eeba.org*
Global Green USA *www.globalgreen.org*
Green Building Alliance *www.gbapgh.org*
Green Building Initiative *www.thegbi.org*
Healthy Building Network *www.healthybuilding.net*
Minnesota Sustainable Building Guidelines
  *www.msbg.umn.edu*
National Institute of Building Sciences *www.nibs.org*
Natural Resources Defense Council's BuildingGreen
  *www.nrdc.org/buildinggreen*
New Buildings Institute *www.newbuildings.org*
OIKOS *www.oikos.com*
Pennsylvania Governor's Green Government Council
  *www.gggc.state.pa.us*
Rocky Mountain Institute *www.rmi.org*
U.S. General Services Administration *www.gsa.gov*
U.S. Green Building Council (USGBC) *www.usgbc.org*
Whole Building Design Guidelines *www.wbdg.org*

## Business Practices

Aspen Institute's Business and Society Program
  *www.aspeninstitute.org*
BELL: Business-Environment Learning and Leadership
  *http://bell.wri.org*
Beyond Grey Pinstripes *www.beyondgreypinstripes.org*
Business for Social Responsibility (BSR) *www.bsr.org*
Center for Environmental Leadership in Business
  *www.celb.org*
Coalition for Environmentally Responsible Economies
  (CERES) *www.ceres.org*
Environmental Business Association of New York State
  *www.eba-nys.org*
Environmental Careers Organization *www.eco.org*
Facility Reporting Project *www.facilityreporting.org*
Global Reporting Initiative *www.globalreporting.org*
International Institute for Sustainable Development
  *www.iisd.org*
Izaak Walton League of America *http://iwla.org*
National Environmental Education and Training
  Foundation *www.neetf.org*
Net Impact *www.netimpact.org*
Rocky Mountain Institute *www.rmi.org*
Safe Climate for Business *www.safeclimate.net*
Schwab Foundation for Social Entrepreneurship
  *www.schwabfound.org*
Second Nature *www.secondnature.org*

Southface Energy Institute *www.southface.org*
Suppliers Partnership for the Environment
  *www.supplierspartnership.org*
U.S. General Services Administration *www.gsa.gov*
World Business Council for Sustainable Development
  *www.wbcsd.org*
World Resources Institute *www.wri.org*

## Certifications and Standards

American National Standards Institute (ANSI)
  *www.ansi.org*
American Society for Testing and Materials (ASTM)
  *www.astm.org*
Building for Environmental and Economic Sustainability
  (BEES) *www.bfrl.nist.gov/oae/software/bees.html*
Building and Institute Furniture Manufacturers
  Association (BIFMA) *www.bifma.org*
Carpet and Rug Institute *www.carpet-rug.org*
Collaborative for High Performance Schools (CHPS)
  *www.chps.net*
Energy Star *www.energystar.gov*
FloorScore *www.rfci.com*
Forest Stewardship Council *www.fscus.org*
GreenBlue *www.greenblue.org*
Green Globes *www.greenglobes.com*
Greenguard Environmental Institute *www.greenguard.org*
Green Guide for Health Care *www.gghc.org*
Green Seal *www.greenseal.org*
Institute for Market Transformation
  *www.mts.sustainableproducts.org*
Leadership in Energy and Environmental Design (LEED)
  *www.usgbc.org/LEED*
McDonough Braungart Design Chemistry
  *www.mbdc.com*
Scientific Certification Systems *www.scscertified.com*
Sustainable Forestry Initiative *www.aboutsfi.org*

## Climate Change

Center for Energy and Climate Solutions (CECS)
  *www.cool-companies.org*
Chicago Climate Exchange *www.chicagoclimatex.com*
Climate Action Network *www.climatenetwork.org*
Climate Neutral Network *www.climateneutral.com*
GHG Protocol Initiative *www.ghgprotocol.org*
Pew Center on Global Climate Change
  *www.pewclimate.org*
Safe Climate for Business *www.safeclimate.net*

## Conservation

Audubon International *www.audubonintl.org*
Conservation International *www.conservation.org*

Environmental Defense *www.environmentaldefense.org*
National Wildlife Federation *www.nwf.org*
The Nature Conservancy *www.nature.org*
Sierra Club *www.sierraclub.org*
World Conservation Union *http://iucn.org*
World Wildlife Fund *www.wwf.org*

## Design

Big Green Discussion Group *www.biggreen.org*
Build It Green *www.builditgreen.org*
Carnegie Mellon Green Design Initiative
    *www.ce.cmu.edu/GreenDesign*
Center for the Built Environment *www.cbe.berkeley.edu*
Centre for Sustainable Design *www.cfsd.org.uk*
Healthcare Without Harm *www.noharm.org*
Illuminating Engineering Society of North America
    *www.iesna.org*
Minnesota Sustainable Design Guide
    *www.sustainabledesignguide.umn.edu*
National Lighting Product Information Program
    *www.lrc.rpi.edu*
Natural Resources Defense Council's BuildingGreen
    *www.nrdc.org/buildinggreen*
New Buildings Institute *www.newbuildings.org*
Oakland Sustainable Design Guide
    *www.oaklandpw.com/page46.aspx*
OIKOS *www.oikos.com*
Whole Building Design Guide *www.wbdg.org*

## Education and Training

Council for Interior Design Accreditation
    *www.accredit-id.org*
LEED (Leadership in Energy and Environmental Design)
    *www.usgbc.org/leed*
National Environmental Education and Training
    Foundation *www.neetf.org*
North America Association for Environmental Education
    *http://eelink.net*

## Energy

Alliance to Save Energy *www.ase.org*
American Solar Energy Society *www.ases.org*
American Wind Energy Association *www.awea.org*
California Climate Action Registry *www.climateregistry.org*
Center for Energy and Climate Solutions (CECS)
    *www.cool-companies.org*
Center for Resource Solutions *www.green-e.org*
Clean Energy Group *www.cleanegroup.org*
Energy and Environmental Building Association
    *www.eeba.org*
Energy Foundation *www.ef.org*
Energy Information Administration *www.eia.doe.gov*

Energy Star Program *www.energystar.gov*
Green-e Renewable Electricity Certification Program
    *www.green-e.org*
Lawrence Berkeley National Laboratory *www.lbl.gov*
National Renewable Energy Laboratory *www.nrel.gov*
Northwest Energy Efficiency Alliance *www.nwalliance.org*
Rocky Mountain Institute *www.rmi.org*
Southface Energy Institute *www.southface.org*
Tax Incentives Assistance Project
    *www.energytaxincentives.org*
U.S. Department of Energy *www.ere.energy.gov*
U.S. Fuel Cell Council *www.usfcc.com*

## Environmental Law and Policy

Environmental Defense *www.environmentaldefense.org*
Environmental Law and Policy Center *www.elpc.org*
Natural Resources Defense Council (NRDC)
    *www.nrdc.org*
U.S. Environmental Protection Agency *www.epa.gov*

## Events

Earth Day Network *www.earthday.net*
EnvironDesign *www.environdesign.com*
Green Build *www.greenbuildexpo.org*
GreenWorld
    *www.iida-northernpacific.org/events/greenworld*

## Forest Products

American Forest Foundation *www.affoundation.org*
American Forests *www.americanforests.org*
Center for International Forestry Research
    *www.cifor.cgiar.org*
Conservatree *www.conservatree.org*
Forest Stewardship Council *www.fscus.org*
Friends of the Earth *www.foe.org*
Global Forest Watch *www.globalforestwatch.org*
Rainforest Action Network *www.ran.org*
Rainforest Alliance *www.rainforest-alliance.org*
Sustainable Forestry Initiative *www.aboutsfi.org*
Tropical Forest Foundation
    *www.tropicalforestfoudation.org*

## General Information

Center for a Livable Future *www.jhsph.edu/environment*
Center for a New American Dream *www.newdream.org*
EcoIQ *www.ecoiq.com*
Greenpeace *www.greenpeace.org*
OIKOS *www.oikos.com*
U.S. Environmental Protection Agency *www.epa.gov*

## Global Trends and Statistics

Earth Trends *www.earthtrends.org*

Natural Resources Defense Council (NRDC)
www.nrdc.org
World Resources Institute www.wri.org
The Worldwatch Institute www.worldwatch.org

### Green Roofs

Greening Gotham www.greeninggotham.org
Green Roofs www.greenroofs.com
Green Roofs Initiative
www.earthpledge.org/GreenRoofs.html

### Indoor Air Quality

Air Quality Sciences, Inc. www.aqs.com
Center for the Built Environment www.cbe.berkeley.edu
New Buildings Institute www.newbuildings.org

### Life Cycle Analysis

Athena Sustainable Materials Institute www.athenasmi.ca
International Design Center of the Environment
www.idce.org
International Society for Industrial Ecology www.is4ie.org
Lawrence Berkeley National Laboratory www.lbl.gov
Whole Building Design Guide Life Cycle Tools
www.wbdg.org

### Lighting and Daylighting

Daylighting Collaborative www.daylighting.org
Heschong Mahone Group, Inc. www.h-m-g.com
Illuminating Engineering Society of North America
(IESNA) www.iesna.org
National Lighting Product Information Program
www.lrc.rpi.edu
Whole Building Design Guide www.wbdg.org

### Materials and Resources

American Society for Testing and Materials (ASTM)
www.astm.org
Greenguard Environmental Institute www.greenguard.org
Green Seal www.greenseal.org
GreenSpec www.greenspec.com
Healthy Building Network www.healthybuilding.net
McGraw Hill Construction Network for Products
www.products.construction.com
OIKOS www.oikos.com
Tectonic Studio www.bluebolt.com
Used Building Materials Exchange www.build.recycle.net

### Municipal Initiatives and Regulations

Acton, Massachusetts http://doc.acton-ma.gov
Alameda County, California www.acgov.org
Albuquerque, New Mexico www.cabq.gov
Arlington, Massachusetts www.town.arlington.ma.us
Arlington, Virginia www.arlingtonva.us
Atlanta, Georgia www.atlantaga.gov
Austin, Texas www.ci.austin.tx.us
Berkeley, California www.ci.berkeley.ca.us
Boulder, Colorado www.ci.boulder.co.us
Bowie, Maryland www.cityofbowie.org
Calabasas, California www.cityofcalabasas.com
Calgary, Alberta, Canada www.calgary.ca
Chicago, Illinois http://egov.cityofchicago.org
Cook County, Illinois www.co.cook.il.us
Cranford, New Jersey www.cranford.com
Dallas, Texas www.dallascityhall.com
Eugene, Oregon www.eugene-or.gov
Frisco, Texas www.ci.frisco.tx.us
Gainesville, Florida www.cityofgainesville.org/gov
Grand Rapids, Michigan www.grand-rapids.mi.us
Houston, Texas www.houstontx.gov
Issaquah, Washington www.ci.issaquah.wa.us
Kansas City, Missouri www.kcmo.org
King County, Washington http://dnr.metrokc.gov
Long Beach, California www.ci.long-beach.ca.us
Los Angeles, California www.ci.la.ca.us
New York, New York www.nyc.gov
Normal, Illinois www.normal.org
Oakland, California www.oaklandnet.com
Pasadena, California www.cityofpasadena.net
Phoenix, Arizona www.ci-phoenix.az.us
Pleasanton, California www.ci.pleasanton.ca.us
Portland, Oregon www.green-rated.org
Princeton, New Jersey www.princetonol.com
Sacramento, California www.cityofsacramento.org
Salt Lake City, Utah www.slcgreen.com
San Diego, California www.sandiego.gov
San Francisco, California www.sfgov.org
San Jose, California www.sanjoseca.gov
San Mateo County, California www.recycleworks.org
Santa Monica, California
http://greenbuildings.santa-monica.org
Sarasota County, Florida www.scgov.net
Scottsdale, Arizona www.scottsdaleaz.gov
Seattle, Washington www.cityofseattle.net
Suffolk County, New York www.co.suffolk.ny.us
Toronto, Ontario www.toronto.ca
Vancouver, British Columbia www.city.vancouver.bc.ca
Washington, D.C. www.dc.gov

### News Portals

Corporate Social Responsibility Newswire Service
www.csrwire.com
EnviroLink Network www.envirolink.org
Environmental News Network www.enn.com
GreenBiz www.greenbiz.com
Green@Work Today www.greenatworktoday.com

Sustainable Business Insider
*www.sustainablebusiness.com*
Sustainable Development Communication Network
*http://sdgateway.net*

## Organics

Organic Farming Research Foundation *www.ofrf.org*
Organic Trade Association *www.ota.com*

## Periodicals

*Environmental Building News* www.buildinggreen.com
*Environmental Design & Construction* www.edcmag.com
*green@work* www.greenatworkmag.com
*GreenSource* www.construction.com/greensource
*Interior Design: The Green Zone*
*www.interiordesign.net/greenzone*
*Interiors & Sources* www.interiorsandsources.com

## Product Stewardship

Extended Producer Responsibility Working Group
*www.eprworkinggroup.org*
Northwest Product Stewardship Council
*www.productstewardship.net*
Product Policy Institute *www.productpolicy.org*

## Productivity

Heschong Mahone Group, Inc. *www.h-m-g.com*
New Buildings Institute *www.newbuildings.org*
Rocky Mountain Institute *www.rmi.org*

## Professional Organizations

American Institute of Architects (AIA) *www.aia.org*
American Society of Interior Designers (ASID)
*www.asid.org*
Building Owners and Managers Association (BOMA)
*www.boma.org*
International Facility Management Association (IFMA)
*www.ifma.org*
International Interior Design Association (IIDA)
*www.iida.org*
U.S. Green Building Council (USGBC) *www.usgbc.org*

## Recycling

Buy Recycled Business Alliance *www.brba.com.au*
Carpet America Recovery Effort (CARE)
*www.carpetrecovery.org*
Earth's 911 *www.earth911.org*
National Recycling Coalition *www.nrc-recycle.org*

The Remanufacturing Institute *www.reman.org*
Steel Recycling Institute *www.recycle-steel.org*
U.S. EPA WasteWise Program *www.epa.gov/wastewise*

## Socially Responsible Investing

Dow Jones Sustainability Index
*www.sustainability-index.com*
Social Investment Forum *www.socialinvest.org*
SRI World Group *www.socialfunds.com*

## State Government Initiatives and Regulations

Arizona *www.governor.state.az.us*
California *www.governor.ca.gov*
Colorado *www.colorado.gov*
Maine *www.maine.gov*
Maryland *www.maryland.gov*
Michigan *www.michigan.gov*
Minnesota Pollution Control Agency
*www.moea.state.mn.us*
New Jersey *www.state.nj.us*
New Mexico *www.governor.state.nm.us*
New York *www.dec.state.ny.us*
Nevada *www.leg.state.nv.us*
Oregon *www.energy.state.or.us*
Pennsylvania *www.state.pa.us*
Rhode Island *www.governor.state.ri.us*
Washington *http://access.wa.gov*
Wisconsin www.wisgov.state.wi.us

## Sustainable Development

Center for Sustainable Development in the Americas
*www.csdanet.org*
Smart Growth Network *www.smartgrowth.org*
United Nations Environment Programme *www.unep.org*
World Business Council on Sustainable Development
(WBCSD) *www.wbcsd.org*

## Urban Planning

Congress for the New Urbanism *www.cnu.org*
New Urbanism *www.newurbanism.org*
Smart Growth Network *www.smartgrowth.org*
Urban Land Institute *www.uli.org*

## Water

California Urban Water Conservation Council
*www.cuwcc.org*
Clean Water Network *www.cwn.org*
WaterWiser *www.waterwiser.org*

# INDEX

WILEY BOOKS ON
Sustainable Design

## Also from Wiley and the American Society of Interior Designers

SUSTAINABLE RESIDENTIAL INTERIORS
by Associates III

## Other Wiley Books on Sustainable Design

ALTERNATIVE CONSTRUCTION: CONTEMPORARY NATURAL BUILDING METHODS
by Lynne Elizabeth and Cassandra Adams

CITIES PEOPLE PLANET: LIVEABLE CITIES FOR A SUSTAINABLE WORLD
by Herbert Girardet

ECODESIGN: A MANUAL FOR ECOLOGICAL DESIGN
by Ken Yeang

GREEN BUILDING MATERIALS: A GUIDE TO PRODUCT SELECTION AND SPECIFICATION,
SECOND EDITION
by Ross Spiegel and Dru Meadows

THE HOK GUIDEBOOK TO SUSTAINABLE DESIGN, SECOND EDITION
by Sandra F. Mendler, AIA, William Odell, AIA, and Mary Ann Lazarus, AIA

SUSTAINABLE CONSTRUCTION: GREEN BUILDING DESIGN AND DELIVERY
by Charles J. Kibert

## Environmental Benefits Statement

This book is printed with soy-based inks on presses with VOC levels that are lower than the standard for the printing industry. The paper, Rolland Enviro 100, is manufactured by Cascades Fine Paper Group and is made from 100 percent postconsumer, de-inked fiber, without chlorine. According to the manufacturer, the following resources were saved by using Rolland Enviro 100 for this book:

| Mature trees | Waterborne waste not created | Water flow saved (in gallons) | Atmospheric emissions eliminated | Energy not consumed | Natural gas saved by using biogas |
|---|---|---|---|---|---|
| 225 | 103,500 lbs. | 153,000 | 21,470 lbs. | 259 million BTUs | 37,170 cubic feet |